The Practice of Dzogchen
in the Zhang-Zhung Tradition of Tibet

THE PRACTICE
OF DZOGCHEN IN THE
ZHANG-ZHUNG TRADITION
OF TIBET

Translations from the
Bonpo Dzogchen Practice Manual:
The *Gyalwa Chaktri* of Druchen Gyalwa Yungdrung,
and
The Seven-fold Cycle of the Clear Light

The Dark Retreat Practice from
The Zhang-zhung Nyan-gyud

Translated with Commentaries and Notes by
John Myrdhin Reynolds

VAJRA
BOOKS

Published & Distributed by
Vajra Books
Jyatha, Thamel, P.O. Box 21779, Kathmandu, Nepal
Tel.: 977-1-4220562, Fax: 977-1-4246536
e-mail: bidur_la@mos.com.np
www.vajrabooks.com.np

ISBN No. 978-9937-506-67-0

Printed in Nepal

Contents

Preface

The translations presented here all relate to the practice of Dzogchen according to the ancient Bonpo tradition of Tibet known as the Zhang-zhung Nyan-gyud, "the Oral Transmission from Zhang-zhung." In a previous volume, *The Oral Transmission from Zhang-zhung*, I have dealt with the history of the transmission of this lineage of Dzogchen teachings and practices from the remote land of Zhang-zhung, which once lay in what is now Western and Northern Tibet. As a written tradition, these teachings and practices are said to go back at least to the 8th century of our era, coming from the enlightened master Tapihritsa and transmitted to his disciple Gyerpung Nangzher Lodpo, who was given permission to write them down for the first time. This transmission represents a continuous and uninterrupted lineage from that early times to the present. However, the collection known as the Zhang-zhung Nyan-gyud is not set out specifically for practice. Nevertheless, we are fortunate to possess a practice manual or handbook (phyag-khrid) prepared by a 13th century master of the tradition who was also the abbot of Yeru Wensakha monastery (fd. 1072), namely Druchen Gyalwa Yungdrung (1242–1290). This manual, which is named after its author, opens with Book One dealing with the preliminary practices for Dzogchen, which I have translated elsewhere as the Appendix found in *The Oral Tradition from Zhang-zhung*. Included here in this volume are the translations of Book

Two dealing with the practices of Trekchod and Thodgal, and Book Three consisting of four supplementary texts dealing with the view, meditation, conduct, and fruit of Dzogchen. Also included in Part Two of this volume is a translation of the instructions for making a forty-nine day dark retreat according to the Zhang-zhung tradition, a text known as *The Seven-fold Cycle of the Clear Light*. Although included in the published Tibetan collection, this text was not composed by the above author. In this tradition from Zhang-zhung, the practice of vision, or what is called elsewhere Thodgal, is known here as Clear Light practice ('od-gsal). But in order to enter into the practice of vision, it is first necessary to become stable in the practice of the Natural State (gnas-lugs), or the state of contemplation (mnyam-bzhag), which characterised by the presence of Rigpa, or intrinsic awareness. Otherwise, one's practice will be no better than watching television and the practitioner remains in one's impure karmic vision.

It is with some trepidation that these translations are presented here for publication. One cannot successfully practice the advanced methods of Dzogchen known as the dark retreat, sky meditation, and sunlight practice without the guidance of an accomplished master of Dzogchen. After the initial practice of fixation of the mind on a visible object, or what is generally known as shamatha meditation (zhi-gnas), the practitioner must receive from the master a direct introduction (rig-pa ngo-sprod), where the Natural State of the Nature of Mind is pointed out in one's immediate experience here and now.

Nevertheless, Yongdzin Lopon Tenzin Namdak, and other Bonpo Lamas have been teaching their tradition for sometime to interested Western practitioners. Thus, there exists a real need for an English translation of the source texts. This is in accordance with the advice given in a vision by the goddess Sidpai Gyalmo, the special guardian to the Bonpo Dzochen tradition, to Lopon Sangye Tenzin (1928–1977) many years ago. The goddess warned that if the teachings and practices of Dzogchen were not made more widely available, the tradition would die out within a generation or two. It was Lopon Sangye Tenzin who was singularly responsible for reviving the teaching and practice of the

Zhang-zhung Nyan-gyud tradition at Menri monastery in Tibet, and later in India, whereas at the time the A-tri system of Dzogchen (A-khrid) was largely practiced. Of course, detailed explanations of the practices must be had from a qualified Lama.

These translations were done over a period of time under the guidance and instruction of Yongdzin Lopon Tenzin Namdak (LTN), beginning with the dark retreat text in 1989 during the Lopon's first visit to America. It is the translator's hope that these translations will prove useful to serious Western practitioners of the Bonpo Dzogchen tradition that comes from the ancient land of Zhang-zhung.

MU-TSUG SMAR-RO!

John Myrdhin Reynolds
Triten Norbutse Bonpo Monastery
Kathmandu, Nepal
November 2011.

Part ONE

The Practice Manual for the Zhang-zhung Nyan-gyud

Chapter One

Introduction

The Oral Tradition from Zhang-zhung

As will be explained in the introduction, part of which is also found
in a previous book, [1] the Gyalwa Chaktri represents a practice
manual for the Bonpo tradition of Dzogchen known as the Zhang-
zhung Nyan-gyud. This is one of the four principal transmissions of
Dzogchen within Bon, namely,

1. The *Zhang-zhung Nyan-gyud* (zhang-zung snyan-rgyud), or "the
   Oral Transmission from Zhang-zhung,"
2. The *A-tri* (A-khrid), or "the Guiding Explanation for the
   Primordial State," drawn from the *Gabpa Gukor* (gab-pa dgu
   skor), "the Nine Cycles of Secrets,"
3. The *Dzogchen Yangtse Longchen* (rdzogs-chen yang-rtse klong-
   chen), "The Great Perfection from the Highest Peak of the Great
   Vast Expanse," drawn from the *Dragpa Korsum* (bsgrags-pa skor
   gsum), "the Three Proclamations," and
4. The *Yetri Thasel* (ye-khri mtha'-sel), or "Removing Liminations
   from the Primordial State," and its commentary, the *Namkha
   Thrul-dzod* (nam-mkha' 'phrul mdzod), "the Magical Treasury of
   the Sky."

The latter three transmissions represent Termas, or hidden treasure texts, that were concealed at one time in the past during a time of persecution and were rediscovered in a later age. In the Nyingmapa tradition of Tibetan Buddhism, such rediscovered texts are of singular importance, most of them being attributed to Guru Padmasambhava who visited Tibet in the 8th century. It is said that the teachings found in these Terma texts were meant for later generations and these Nyingmapa Terma began to be rediscovered in the 11th century in Tibet and Bhutan. Two of the above Bonpo transmissions were also said to have been concealed in the 8th century by the masters Dranpa Namkha and Lishu Tagring respectively, who were contemporaries of Padmasambhava. The concealing of these texts was due to the persecution of Bon by the Central Tibetan government under king Trisong Detsan. However, the Zhang-zhung Nyan-gyud represents a a continuous transmission of an oral tradition (snyan-rgyud), also going back in its original written for to the 8th century of our era, coming from the country of Zhang-zhung, which lay in what is now Northern and Western Tibet. These texts are said to represent the teachings of the master Tapihritsa, who attained Buddha enlightenment in the 7th century in Northern Tibet, manifesting the Rainbow Body of the Great Transfer [2], and who transmitted the teachings to his disciple Gyerpung Nangzher Lodpo (gyer-spungs snang-bzher lod-po) in the next century. This master was also a contemporary of Padmasambhava and the Tibetan king Trisong Detsan. Thus, this transmissions represents what is called by the Nyingmapa tradition, Kama (bka'-ma), or a continuous transmission without interruption from the earliest times, and is, therefore, of singular importance for research into the question of the historical origins of Dzogchen. [3]

The texts in question are found in the two divisions of this tradition:

1. the Precepts Transmission (bka'-rgyud) and
2. the Experiential Transmission (nyams-rgyud).

The first collection is said to represent the Dzogchen precepts originally communicated by the master Tapihritsa to his disciple Gyerpung Nangzher Lodpo, whereas the second collection is said to be the teachings of the various masters in the lineage of transmission drawn from their own personal experiences in meditation.

However, these two collections are not in themselves arranged in a very systematic and progressive order, but deal with various different topics pertaining to the view of Dzogchen and its practice in meditation. In general, the Zhang-zhung Nyan-gyud may be classified as Dzogchen Upadesha, or Mangagide (man-ngag gi sde), in terms of the usual Nyingmapa classification. These Upadeshas, or secret oral instructions, are said to represent the very words of the enlightened master Tapihritsa delivered on a number of occasions to his disciple Nangzher Lodpo at the Darok lake in Northern Tibet. [4] Prior to Tapihritsa, the transmission of the Dzogchen precepts were said to be entirely oral. They directly originated from the Primordial Buddha Kuntu Zangpo himself, the Dharmakaya Buddha, and then were communicated to the Sambhogakaya Buddha, Shenlha Odkar, and from him to the Nirmanakaya Buddha, Tonpa Shenrab. [5] This process represents the Direct Mind-to-Mind Transmission of the Buddhas (rgyal-ba dgongs-rgyud) without recourse to any words. Then the transmission proceeded through a line of twenty-four masters, all of whom attained the Rainbow Body of Light [6] at the end of their lives. This process represented the Symbolic Transmission of the Vidyadharas (rig-'dzin brda-rgyud), because this entailed very few words and the transmission was mainly through signs and symbols. Finally, we have the Oral Transmission to Various Persons (gang-zag snyan-rgyud) when Tapihritsa communicated the Dzogchen Precepts to Nangzher Lodpo using many words. Moreover, he gave permission to Nangzher Lodpo to write down these precepts for the first time, in this case in the Zhang-zhung language on pieces of wood, paper at this time being largely unknown. In the next century the precepts where translated by Ponchen Tsanpo (dpon-chen btsan-po) into the Tibetan language for his two Tibetan disciples. [7] The lineages for the Precepts Transmission and the Experiential Transmission then split apart for a time, but then they were collected and recombined by Yangton Sherab Gyaltsan of Dolpo in the 11th century, who was largely responsible for the collection in its present form.

This Zhang-zhung tradition was preserved over the centuries at Yeru Wensakha monastery and thereafter at its successor, Tashi Menri monastery, in Tsang province in Central Tibet. [8] After the Bonpo Lamas fled Tibet following the completion of the Chinese Communist occupation in 1959, Lopon Tenzin Namdak re-established Menri monastery at Dolanji in Himachal Pradesh, India. Prior to this reestablishment, the A-tri system of Dzogchen practice was mainly taught and practiced at Menri. It was Lopon Sangye Tenzin (slob-dpon sangs-rgyas bstan-'dzin, 1928–1977) who was singularly responsible for reviving the teaching and practice of the Zhang-zhung Nyan-gyud. His principal disciple, Lopon Tenzin Namdak then began transmitting this tradition of Dzogchen to the West, in both Europe and America, beginning in in 1989. [9]

Druchen Gyalwa Yungdrung

Although the texts found in this Zhang-zhung Nyan-gyud collection are arranged into the four cycles of outer, inner, secret, and exceedingly secret corresponding to the view, the meditation, the conduct, and the fruit respectively, this arrangement is in fact not well suited to the actual practice of Dzogchen. This is because the texts in question deal with a variety of topics, more in terms of theoretical matters, rather than in terms of systematic practice. We must look elsewhere for that and fortunately there does exist a thirteenth century practice manual and commentary on the Dzogchen system of the Zhang-zhung Nyan-gyud. This latter collection is known as the *sNyan-rgyud rgyal-ba'i phyag-khrid* and was written by the illustrious Bonpo master belonging to the Dru family, Druchen Gyalwa Yungdrung. [10]

Druchen Gyalwa Yungdrung (Bru-chen rgyal-ba g.yung-drung) was born into the Dru clan at Yeru Wensakha (g.yas-ru'i dben-sa-kha) in Central Tibet in 1242. The Bonpo monastery bearing the same name, which was under the control and patronage of the Dru clan throughout its history, was founded by his ancestor, Druchen Yungdrung Lama (Bru-chen g.yung-drung bla-ma) in 1072. [11] It was destroyed in a devastating flood in the fourteenth century, whereafter it was rebuilt by Nyammed Sherab Gyaltsan (mNyam-med shes-rab rgyal-mtshan) and renamed Tashi Menri (bkra-shis sman-ri). Before its destruction, Yeru Wensakha became the greatest seat of Bonpo learning in Central Tibet, most of its abbots being drawn from the Dru family. According to family legend, the clan possessed this name because it originally came to Tsang province in Central Tibet from a country to the west known as Drusha (Bru-sha). Moreover, Yungdrung Lama's grandfather, Drusha Namkha Yungdrung (Bru-sha nam-mkha' g.yung-drung), [12] the patriarch of the clan, had been a disciple of the illustrious Shenchen Luga (gShen-chen klu-dga').

It was this Shenchen Luga who discovered in 1017 two large wooden boxes containing Bonpo texts, which had been buried near the ancestral seat of the Shen clan, of which he was a descendent. [13] It was principally this discovery that lead to the revival of Bon in Central Tibet in the eleventh century, this being similar in character to the revival of the Nyingmapas which occurred at the same time. In part, this renaissance was a reaction to the development of the Sarmapa, or New Tantra schools of Buddhism, that were inspired by the translation of Tantric texts recently brought out of India, many of them previously unknown in Tibet. [14] Shenchen Luga commissioned Namkha Yungdrung, together with the latter's son, to copy and record the philosophical texts (mtshan-nyid) that he had recovered from this buried library of the Shen clan, which had reportedly been concealed in the eighth century at the time of the persecution of the Bonpos by the Central Tibetan government. This large collection of hidden treasure texts became widely known as the System of the Southern Treasures (lho gter lugs).

Prominent among these texts was that of the Bonpo cosmological work, the *Srid-pa'i mdzod-phug*, "the Source Treasury of Existence," which is extant as a root text in both Zhang-zhung and Tibetan versions. [15] The commentary to this root text, discovered at the same time, was by the eighth century Bonpo master Dranpa Namkha (Dran-pa nam-mkha'), also known to the Nyingmapa tradition, where he is made into a disciple of Padmasambhava. [16] Contained in this collection of rediscovered texts were also the *Khams-chen*, the large collection of the Bonpo redaction of the Prajnaparamita Sutras in sixteen volumes, and the *Gab-pa dgu skor*, also known as the *Sems phran sde bdun*, an important collection of Dzogchen texts closely related to the Zhang-zhung Nyan-gyud. Thus, it was recorded in the Bonpo histories that the Dru lineage became pre-eminant in the transmission of the Bonpo philosophical tradition. [17] Druchen Namkha Yungdrung himself wrote a commentary on the *Srid-pa'i mdzod-phug* and his son, Khyunggi Gyaltsan (Khyung gi rgyal-mtshan), also wrote a commentary that established the philosophical and exegetical tradition of this lineage. Both father and son had listened to Shenchen expound the philosophy and cosmology of the *Srid-pa'i mdzod-phug*, which represents a kind of Bonpo Abhidharma text. [18]

Possessing a brilliant intellect, even at a young age Druchen Gyalwa Yungdrung was expounding the philosophical and cosmological system of the *mTshan-nyid srid-pa'i mdzod-phug* to his listeners. Thereafter he took the vows of a monk, eventually becoming a fully ordained Drangsong, corresponding to the fully ordained Buddhist monk, [19] and he was given the name of Gyalwa Yungdrung. He received many transmissions and initiations in terms of the Bonpo Tantras, but he is said to have especially exerted himself in *gNas-lugs theg-chen*, "the Great Vehicle of the Natural State," that is to say, Dzogchen. Being widely renowned for both his scholarship and his pure conduct of life, he eventually obtained the abbacy [20] of his family monastery of Yeru Wensakha and it is said that he ceaselessly instructed his many students and disciples in the teachings of Yungdrung Bon.

According to the hagiography found in the *rNam-thar chen-mo*, there are five principal considerations with regard to this history of Druchen Gyalwa Yungdrung:

1. The history of his parents and how he obtained a pure human body,
2. How he met with his benevolent teachers who showed him great kindness,
3. How he resided at certain special places that served as his support during his lifetime,
4. How his virtuous qualities and his signs of realization that were ordinary manifested immediately in his present life, and
5. How his extraordinary understanding ultimately became manifest. [21]

"As for this disciple of the foregoing master (Chigchod Dadpa Sherab), [22] within the life story of Druchen Gyalwa Yungdrung there are five topics to be considered. First, there is the history of how he obtained a pure human body from his parents to be considered. His native region was Yeru Wensakha and his clan was called Dru. His father was named Druzha Sonam Gyaltsan (Bru-sha bsod-nams rgyal-mtshan) and among four brothers, he was the third son. [23]

"Furthermore, because he was a Nirmanakaya (from the very beginning) who had come into this world in order to benefit beings, from his earliest childhood he possessed the various virtuous qualities of purification. At eight years of age he explained to his listeners the meaning of the text of the *Srid-pa'i mdzod-phug*. Later, in the presence of his uncle Dulwa Rinpoche, he took the vows of a pure monk and the name of Gyalwa Yungdrung was bestowed upon him as his ordination name. Thereupon, in terms of his training and discipline, he acted consistently in accordance with real meaning of his monastic vows. [24]

"Elsewhere, it is said that he requested the initiations and the scriptural authorizations, together with the blessings, for the three sections of Bon, namely, the outer, the inner, and the secret, and thereby he purified his mind-stream (by practicing these teachings). In particular, he performed the commitments of his daily practice with one-pointed concentration and without distraction. [25]

"Moreover, according to the statements made by the Lama himself, 'In the beginning, having requested the training in the monastic vows which are to be guarded well, I guarded them without secrecy and without ostentatious display. Then, in between, having considered the kindness bestowed upon me by my masters in terms of hearing and reflecting upon their teachings, I thoroughly cut off all my doubts. And finally, I came to recognize correctly the face of the Natural State, even though I will not fully comprehend it in this present life nor in my next one– still all this represents the threefold kindness of my masters.'

"Elsewhere, from Yilton Namkha Sonam (dByil-ston nam-mkha' bsod-nams), the nephew of Yilton Khyunggodtsal (dByil-ston khyung-rgod rtsal), [26] from Lunggom Tashi Gyaltsan (Lung-sgom bkra-shis rgyal-mtshan) of the lineage of Lungton Lhanyan (Lung-ston lha-gnyan), [27] from Maton Drangsong (rMa-ston drang-srong) of the lineage of Maton Siddzin (rMa-ston srid-'dzin), [28] and so on, he requested the initiations, the scriptural authorizations, and the instructions, together with the blessings. [29]

"Then, at the time when Lama Togdan Dadpa Sherab was fifty-five years old he made a pilgrimage to all the monasteries, places of realization, and great holy places of the Bonpos found in Central Tibet. [30] And in particular, he went to meet the famous Dru Tsandan Dulwa (Bru tshan-ldan 'dul-ba), the uncle of Gyalwa Yungdrung, who was residing at Lhodrak (lho-brag). Coming into the presence of Tsandan Dulwa, the former requested such scriptural authorizations as the *rDzogs-pa chen-po A-khrid dmar byang*, the *Dri-med lhan-skyes dbang ye dbang chen-mo*, and so on. [31] And because there was some mention of the teachings on the *sZhang-zhung snyan-rgyud*, Tsandanpa himself said, "Indeed, you possess the complete scriptural authorizations for the *sNyan-rgyud*. [32] But now I am too old to ask for it. And if I should die soon, I would not have the opportunity to practice it. Therefore, please transmit this authorization (lung) to my nephew Gyalwa Yungdrung!"

"Second, because his karma had ripened and he possessed good fortune, he met with the kindness of his benevolent masters. Later, at the time when Lama Togdanpa (Dadpa Sherab) came from his pilgrimage journey to the Namtso lake and arrived at the monastery of Wensakha, Lama Gyalwa addressed him as follows: 'These instructions for the Oral Transmission from Zhang-zhung have never been concealed beneath the earth (as treasure texts). Their blessings have never declined nor disappeared. They are very special because they have been transmitted orally from one Mahasiddha to another without interruption. Just having heard the sound of their name and also seeing some words from some of the texts has produced great devotion within me. I made some inqueries regarding them to some Lopons who were said to have possessed these instructions. When I requested the scriptural authorization for these texts (dpe lung), I heard all of them speak of Yangalwa as the master holding the lineage for the descent of these teachings. [33] I sent a request with a messenger, together with some powerful medicine pills, to the monastic residence of Lama Yangalwa. Having considered the matter, he replied to me in a letter, writing, 'Now, there exists just a single essential explanation for the Experiential Transmission (nyams-rgyud dmar-khrid gcig). But we live in two distant places and so it is unlikely that we will meet personally. These instructions have not been previously set down in writing. And because they represent a singular transmission, there exist only the oral precepts from those previous Mahasiddhas. But even though that is the case, there is one of my disciples who has obtained the Experiential Transmission from me. You should try to meet him and look to him for this!' Also my uncle Tsandanpa had written to me and said, 'The Togdan is the one who has the scriptural transmission for the Oral Transmission (snyan-rgyud kyi lung). Therefore, you must request it from him! Now, let us discuss this question of the scriptural authority for the Oral Transmission.'

"There having occurred many such discussions regarding the Oral Transmission, finally the Togdan conferred the empowerment and the scriptural authority upon the three scholars, Lama Gyalwa and his two companions Lopon Mewon (sLob-dpon me-dbon) and Menyak

Ringdrak (Me-nyag ring-grags). When the ceremony was completed, Lama Gyalwa said to the master, 'Now, there exists the question of the existence of the Experiential Transmission that has in no way been contaminated by being set down in written words. Have you considered that?' But the Togdan replied, 'This is all of it. There is not even as much as a grain of sesame remaining. The authorization I have already given will have to do!' And he remained adamant in this.

"However, Lama Gyalwa cited once more the history contained in the letter from Lama Dansapa [34] which clearly indicated that what the three scholars had received was not sufficient, and that there existed a further Experiential Transmission. He should consider transmitting that also. To this the Togdan replied, "Well then, if you have such a fervent desire, according to the system of these teachings, now we must make examinations of your name, your conduct, your body marks, as well as your dreams. Although there are many examinations to be made, for a man such as yourself, it will not be necessary to examine all of them. But let us at least propitiate the non-human spirits [35] and then tomorrow we will make an examination of our dreams.

'That night, among the experiences of the master, he dreamed that he saw a beautiful valley that resembled the mountain of Yartse Hauri (ya-rtse ha'u ri) and this valley appeared to be filled with various different flowers and fruit trees. Moreover, there were innumerable beautiful young girls, aged fifteen and sixteen, adorned with jewel ornaments, who came forward carrying fruits and kusha grass on their backs. And as they came, the entire region of Wensakha monastery became filled with fruits and kusha grass. Where there were no fruits, they freely scattered them about. In the direction south of Wensakha also, there were the trunks of many fruit trees that bore bright blossoms. In the middle of all that, there was a spring gushing forth that resembled that spring at Damkhari. At the head of that spring, three Bonpo priests had gathered. They had prepared many extensive offerings and they were engaged in invoking the gods (lha gsol). This was how he described his dream.

"Then again Lama Gyalwa dreamed that he found himself on the road. Then, in a valley filled with flowers and fruit trees, there was the facade of a high castle. At that site he blew a conch shell, raised a silken banner, and scattered many flowers into every direction. [36]

"Third, as for the special places of practice that served as his supports anywhere during his lifetime, he principally engaged in the practice of meditation at such places of realization (grub gnas) as the rock at Yeru Kharna (g.yas-ru mkhar-sna'i brag) and at Ragong Yonpo (Ra-gong yon-po), and elsewhere. Moreover, the Lama himself said, "Due to the compassion created by my fervent devotion to those earlier Mahasiddhas, there came forth within me a confident belief and definitive decision (regarding the Natural State), which cut off the extremes that are conceptual elaborations." [37]

"Furthermore, there arose from within the interior of his mind the bliss of pristine awareness without thoughts and he cut off the stream of distinguishing characteristics associated with subject and object. [38] And because of that, there arose for him without interruption the Clear Light, which is the spontaneously perfected Base (in terms of Thodgal visions). The distinctive characteristics of the three: the sounds, the lights, and the rays, were liberated into their own original condition on the Path. And as the Fruit, at the ultimate stage (in the development of vision) the Trikaya became visibly manifest to him. [39] Thereby the Great Bliss remained in its own original condition of the Dharmakaya and he came to behold the face of his own meditation deity, the Yidam Tsochok (gtso-mchog), whereupon the Generation Process and the Perfection Process, all emanating and reabsorbing, were liberated into their own original condition. In consequence, immeasurable numbers of liberations of experience and understanding were born in his mind. [40]

"Moreover, the treatises composed by him, born of the above understanding, and after having condensed them into the outer, the inner, and the secret classes, were as follows: [41]

1. *Lag-len pod chung* (outer, inner, and secret rituals),
2. *gZungs 'dus* (dharani-mantras),
3. *rDzogs-chen snyan-rgyud kyi lag-len dmar-khrid* (essential explanations regarding the practice manual for the Zhang-zhung Nyan-gyud),
4. *dBal-gsas khrig-ma lag khrid* (the practice manual for the deity Walse),
5. *rTsa rlung gi gdams-pa* (instructions on Tsalung practice),
6. *Drang-don snod bcud kyi yig-sna* (assorted texts on the universe and its inhabitants according to Relative Truth),

7. *Dong sprugs zlas lung* (mantra recitations for stirring up the depths of Samsara),
8. *Zhal gdams mgur 'bum* (songs of spiritual instruction),
9. *gSol-'debs* (various invocations and prayers),
   (And in particular)
10. *A-khrid kyi gzhung rgyab skor* (the cycle of the principal and ancillary texts of the A-khrid system of Dzogchen practice) [42] whereby he arranged innummerable disciples on the Path of spiritual instruction and liberation.

"Fourth, his virtuous qualities and the signs of his realization that were ordinary manifested during his lifetime. According to the prophecy found in the *gNad byang drug-cu rtsa gcig-pa*: of Chyangphak: [43] 'There will come forth in the future one called Drusha Tsun (Brusha btsun) who will be an emanation of (the ancient sage) Nangwa Dogchan (sNang-ba mdog-can). There will be fourteen Bodhisattvas who are lineage-holders (in his lineage of transmission) and he will come to guide living beings. Gyalwa Yungdrung will come as the emanation of the Sugatas, those noble ones who are the makers of medicines, for the sake of benefiting living beings. Those who merely touch his lotus-like feet will become arrayed on the path to freedom from the five aggregates of rebirth and the doors to liberation for some three hundred-thousand beings will be opened.' [44]

"Fifth, his extraordinary understanding became manifest. All of his experiences and signs (nyams rtags) in meditation practice were very auspicious and even the non-human spirits could not bind him with their disturbances. Having requested his two companions to depart from the room first, Lama Gyalwa, in the presence of his own master (Chigchod Dadpa Sherab), requested to receive the oral instructions, together with the permissions for the practices (zhal-gdams rjes-gnang). Moreover, Lama Gyalwa agreed to preserve the Single Transmission (gcig brgyud) and not to dispense the teachings either for wealth or for fame. There arose within him a confident belief and a definitive decision (yid-ches thag-chod) regarding the Natural State without reverting to either hopes or fears. All of his conceptual elaborations in the form of doubts, as well as his hopes and fears regarding the cycles of instructions (gdams skor) were removed for him like cutting through a spider's web. And he obtained all of the words and the meanings (tshig don) from the transmissions. Up until his own time, this teaching of the Zhang-zhung Nyan-gyud had not spread very much, but during the lifetime of Lama Gyalwa, the teaching spread widely like the rays of the sun and became well known.

"Finally, as for the life-span of his physical body, having attained fourty-nine years, he displayed the method of passing beyond sorrow. He is said to have died at his monastery of Yeru Wensakha. His principal disciples were his younger brother Dru Namkha Odzer (Bru Nam-mkha' 'od-zer) and his nephew Druton Sonam Gyaltsan (Bru-ston bsod-nams rgyal-mtshan)." [45]

Contents of the Practice Manual: *rGyal-ba phyag-khrid*

Among his many literary works cited above is a noted commentary on the practice of the *A-khrid* system of Dzogchen, entitled the *Thun-mtshams bco-lnga-pa man-ngag khrid kyi rim-pa lag-len thun-mtshams dang bcas-pa.* [46] And in addition, he composed the practice manual and commentary on the *Zhang-zhung snyan-rgyud* that we have here, namely, the *sNyan-rgyud rgyal-ba'i phyag-khrid.* I am aware of two published versions of this text:

1. A litho edition in the *dbu-med* script published in India, no date; and
2. The reprint of a xylograph edition published in a volume entitled *sNyan rgyud nam-mkha' 'phrul mdzod drang nges skor* and *Zhang-zhung snyan-rgyud skor*, Tibetan Bonpo Monastic Centre, New Delhi 1972, ff. 539–726.

Within this collection composed by Gyalwa Yungdrung, we find three classes of texts:

(1) The preliminary practices (sngon-'gro),
(2) The principle practices (dngos-gzhi), and
(3) The ancilliary texts or branches (yan-lag). These latter texts are four in number and deal with the view (lta-ba), the meditation (sgom-pa), the conduct (spyod-pa), and the fruit ('bras-bu), respectively.

The texts included in the *rGyal-ba'i phyag-khrid* collection are as follows:

0. *Zhang-zhung snyan-rgyud kyi lo-rgyus rnam-thar dang bcas-pa*, "The History of the Oral Transmission from Zhang-zhung, together with the Hagiographies," (ff. 539–589). This history is found in the xylograph reprint, but not in the *dbu-med* manuscript. It is a different text than the one similarly titled found in the collection that is the basis for the present study. [47]

1. *sNgon-'gro rim-pa rnams*, "the Stages of the Preliminary Practices" (ff.1–22), including an invocation of Tapihritsa, *sNgon 'gro gsol-'debs*, "the Invocation for the Preliminary Practices" (ff.23–28). In the xylograph reprint the text is called *Bon-spyod dgu-rim*, "the Nine Stages for the Conduct of Bon" (ff. 591–607). This text contains the explanations by Druchen for the preliminary practices (sngon-'gro) and it is divided into nine distinct practices:

(1) The Conferring of Empowerments (dbang-bskur),
(2) The Meditation on the Impermanence of Life (tshe mi rtag-pa),
(3) The Confession of Sins (sdig-pa bshag-pa),
(4) The Producing the Bodhichitta (sems bskyed),
(5) The Going to Refuge (skyabs 'gro),
(6) The Offering of the Mandala (mandal 'bul)
(7) The Reciting of Mantras for Purification (sngags kyi bzlas-pa),
(8) The Cutting off of Attachments (gcod), and
(9) The Praying to receive the Guru's Blessings (gsol-'debs) which is the Guru Yoga (bla-ma'i rnal-'byor) proper. [48]

2. *Zab-mo gnad kyi gdams-pa dngos-gzhi*, "The Instructions concerning the Profound Essential Points for the Principal Practices" (ff.29–76), and in the xylograph reprint *Khrid rim lag-len*, "The Manual for the Stages of the Explanation" (ff.609–638). This text represents the principle practice, including both Trekchod (khregs-chod) and Thodgal (thod-rgal), but with the emphasis on the latter. The Thodgal practice for the development of vision (snang-ba) is divided into dark retreat practice (mun-mtshams), space or sky practice (nam-mkha'), and sunlight practice (nyi 'od) which represents Thodgal as such. Complete instructions for these practices are provided by Druchen. [49]

3. *gZhi rang ngo-sprad-pa gcer-mthong lta-ba'i khrid*, "The Explanation of the View, being a Direct Introduction to one's own Base through Seeing Nakedly", abbreviated as *lTa-khrid* (ff. 77–100; ff. 639–655). Here begins the section consisting of four texts or commentaries known as auxiliaries or branches (yan-lag). They are also composed by Druchen. The first provides the explanation of the view (lta-khrid) of Dzogchen.

4. *Lam nyams su len-pa'i 'od-gsal sgom-pa'i khrid*, "The Explanation of the Meditation regarding the Clear Light Practice on the Path," abbreviated a *sGom-khrid* (ff.101–124; 657–673). The text provides the explanation of the meditation practice (sgom-khrid) in relation to Dzogchen, focusing on Clear Light vision practice, or Thodgal.

5. *rKyen lam du slong-ba rtsal sbyong spyod-pa'i khrid*, "The Explanation of the Conduct concerning the Forceful Purifications employed on the Path in accordance with Secondary Conditions," abbreviated as *sPyod-khrid* (ff.125–156; ff.675–697). The text provides explanations for the activities that are practiced along the path (spyod-khrid) from the standpoint of Dzogchen, including forceful purifications (rtsal sbyong).

6. *'Bras-bu rang sa bzung-ba sku gsum dmar thag-bcad-pa'i khrid*, "The Explanation that is Clear and Definitive Decision regarding the Trikaya apprehended as one's own Original Condition which constitutes the Fruit," abbreviated as *Thag-bcad-pa'i khrid* or *Thag gcod-pa'i khrid* (ff.157–176; ff.699–713). The explanation for clearly and definitively deciding upon (dmar thag-bcad-pa'i khrid) the Fruit which is the Trikaya as realized through the practice of vision. [50]

7. *'Od-gsal gyi dmigs-pa dang gags sel*, "Visualizations for the Clear Light Practice and the Removing of Obstacles," abbreviated as *dmigs-rim*, "The Stages of Visualization" (ff. 177–204). A text dealing with the visualizations (dmigs-pa) used in practice and various methods for removing obstacles to practice (gags sel). This text is not found in the xylograph reprint.

8. *'Od-gsal bdun skor* (ff. 295–222) or *gCig-rgyud 'od-gsal bdun skor* (ff.715–726). This text, "the Seven-fold Cycle of the Clear Light", gives intructions for making a forty-nine day retreat in total darkness (mun-mtshams) according to the Zhang-zhung Nyan-gyud tradition. Both this and the preceding text appear to be later additions to the collection and not to have been written by Druchen. [51] Then there follows some additional material (mkhas-pa.... zhal gdams) in the manuscript (ff. 223–228).

Here are presented translations of the principal practices text (dngos-gzhi) and of the four supplementary texts providing the guiding instructions (khrid) to the view, the meditation, the conduct, and the fruit respectively. As said previously, the preliminary practices text (sngon-'gro) is translated elsewhere, [52] and the instructions for the dark retreat will be vound in Part Two of this volume.

Chapter Two

Outlines of the Contents of the Texts

The Preliminary Practices

In the reprint of the xylograph edition used for the translations here, [1] the collection opens with a history or series of hagiographies of the masters of the lineage of transmission. However, this text is not by the author of the principal text. [2] It is followed by the first text in the Gyalwa Chaktri, dealing with the preliminary practices, or Ngondro, for this tradition, namely, "The Nine Stages of the Preliminary Practice." [3] Ideally, each of these preliminary practices are to be performed one hundred thousand times ('bum dgu). This text was composed by our author Druchen Gyalwa Yungdrung and represents the instructions for practicing the Ngondro, whereas the actual recitations for this are found in a separate text, the "The Exposition of the Words." [4] The translation of these two texts may be found elsewhere. [5]

The Principal Practices

The text of the nine preliminary practices, designated by the author as Book One, is followed by the text of the principal practices (dngos-gzhi), designated as Book Two, which is translated below and is entitled *Khrid rim lag-len*, "the manual for the stages of the explanations," or more fully in the earlier litho edition, *Zab-mo gnad kyi gdams-*

pa dngos-gzhi, "the instructions concerning the profound essential points for the principal practices." The principal practices consist both of Trekchod (khregs-chod) and Thodgal (thod-rgal), but with the emphasis on the latter, representing vision practice. In the Tibetan text, these classical Nyingmapa terms do not occur, but are variously designated Kadak (ka-dag), "primordial purity," and Odsal ('od-gsal), "clear light practice," respectively. Herein the practice of Dzogchen is expounded in terms of four principal practices, namely,

1. Fixation of the mind (sems 'dzin) on the white Tibetan letter A, and this meditation practice serves to discover and develop the state of contemplation, or Trekchod. The practice consists of shamatha meditation with a visible object (dmigs-bcas).
2. The dark retreat (mun-mtshams) links the practice of contemplation with that of Clear Light, or vision practice as such. It consists of shamatha meditation without an object (dmigs-med) because the practitioner is in total darkness.
3. Clear Light ('od-gsal), or vision practice, is of two types according to the support for the visions. First, there is sky meditation (nam-mkha' ar-gtad), where the practitioner gazes into the clear, open, empty sky while being in the state of contemplation.
4. Second, there is vision practice with sunlight, or Thodgal as such.

The text of the principal practices are followed by four branches or supplementary texts (yan-lag) further expanding on the view, the meditation, the conduct and the fruit.

The text opens with the salutation to the Primordial Buddha Kuntu Zangpo, who is the manifest inherent awareness being the all-pervading supreme guide for every sentient being. Then there are three sections:

1. There is the practice of fixating the mind (sems zin-pa),
2. Abiding in mindfulness while the path (dran-pa gnas-pa), and
3. The making of this inherent awareness clear (rang-rig gsal-bar bya).

Section I, Fixation: In terms of practicing fixation of mind, or shamatha meditation, one assumes the five point meditation position and gazes at the object in the space in front of oneself, conventionally the white Tibetan letter A painted on a dark background card mounted on a stick and surrounded by a rainbow circle, the colors of which represent the five elements. At first one focuses intently and acutely on this object and then relaxes attention while yet remaining present. If distracting thoughts arise, one focuses again with intensity, like aiming an arrow at a target. In the beginning, one engages in short periods of fixation, but progressively are lengthens the sessions. The duration can be measured by burning an incense stick. Then, when a discursive thought arises, one looks back and searches for where the thought arises, where it stays, and where it goes when it dissolves. One asks oneself, what does one find? This is the beginner's practice, that is, looking back to the source of thoughts. When one becomes proficient in meditation practice, this is no longer necessary. The signs of success in fixation (zin rtogs) will arise., including the experiences of pleasurable sensations, clarity, and non-discursiveness (bde gsal mi rtog-pa'i nyams gsum).

Section II, Dark Retreat: In order to stabilize one's mindful awareness, one makes a meditation retreat in total darkness (mun-mtshams) in a special cave, room, or dark retreat house (mun-khang). One may begin with shorter term retreats, however, the convention is a full forty-nine day dark retreat, this being the symbolic duration of the Bardo experience after death. One may perform four or six sessions of practice a day, beginning with the purification exercises, entailing visualizations and pranayama breathing. These exercises are performed only at the beginning of the session; they are changed each week and they are communicated by the Lama guiding the retreat on the outside. [6] However, during the principal practice in the dark retreat, one does nothing special, but simply remains in the state of contemplation, or Trekchod. One has already discovered this state while engaging in fixation practice and the Lama has pointed it out to the practitioner, when successful, like pointing out some mysterious, unidentified, extraterrestrial object. While in the dark retreat, one does not engage in visualization, mantra recitation or chanting, or yoga exercises, other than assuming the five point body position. The whole point in this sensory deprivation experience is to totally relax, a radical relaxation of one's body, energy, and mind. Physical, verbal, and mental activities only serve to stir up the functional mind (yid), giving rise to distracting thoughts and emotions. The whole point of contemplation is not thinking about something, but to find oneself in a space that is beyond the mind and the thought process, but where one is totally and globally aware.

At first one does practice fixation, but only on a point in empty space in front of oneself. This is only an empty location; nothing is visualized there. But fixation, entailing attention and concentration, represents a function of mind or mental activity (yid-byed) requiring effort and mental energy. Therefore, one always relaxes this attention, nevertheless, while remaining present and aware. This condition provides the space and opportunity for the inherent energy (rang rtsal) of the mind to manifest as visions in the total darkness. It is natural for them to arise, but one does not think about them, judge them, or follow after them. They are merely like reflections appearing in a mirror. Being alone in total darkness, these visions do not arise from anything outside of oneself. In this way, one comes to realize that they are self-manifestations (rang-snang) of the inherent energy of the mind. Moreover, they give evidence of the survival of consciousness after death in the Bardo. [7] The practitioner may also develop clairvoyant sight, seeing through walls, even seeming to illuminate the interior of the dark retreat house.

Section IIIA, Sky Meditation: These visions (snang-ba) that arise in total darkness, as well as sky practice, are not visualizations (dmigs-pa), which are something created by the activities of the functional mind (yid). Rather, they arise spontaneously without conscious intervention or manipulation. They arise from the deeper Nature of Mind and represent the hidden propensities of mind. At first they are predominately impure karmic visions (ma dag las snang), arising from one's memories and past karma, but when these initial layers of the energy of negative emotions, or kleshas, and of conceptual thoughts are exhausted, there is the space and the opportunity for pure visions (dag snang) to arise spontaneously, first as bindus or thigleys, tiny points of light in space, initially white and black, but later in colors. These then come to form awareness-chains (rig-pa'i lu-gu-rgyud), and as they develop, these thigleys not only form chains, but other geometric patters, lattice works, cross-hitching, and so on. Moreover, partial forms, such as the heads and torsos of Buddha figures may appear inside the thigleys. Eventually these visions evolve into those of fully developed mandalas. Therefore the texts speak of four or five stages in the develop of vision (snang-ba bzhi). Whereas the previous practice of fixation, with or without a visible object, was equated with shamatha meditation (zhi-gnas), attaining a state of calm, according to the Dzogchen viewpoint, the practice of vision, whether with the empty sky or with sunlight as the support, is equated with vipashyana meditation, or higher insight (lhag-mthong). In the text here, the latter is known as Clear Light practice.

Again, in this section, the body position is considered, as well as the gaze of the eyes and the condition of the mind. In conventional Tantric visualization practice, one generally does so with the eyes closed because it is easier to visualize in this way. The practitioner can eliminated one's impure karmic vision simply by closing the eyes and then engage in visualization. Thereby one simulates pure vision and creates a virtual reality occupied with ideal forms (sku) and ideal symmetrical sacred space (dkyil-'khor). Here the Dzogchen practitioner does not visualize anything, which would be an activity of mind, but as with the dark retreat, simply gazes fixedly into the empty space of the sky. For sky meditation practice, one selects a site where one will not be distracted or disturbed by others or by circumstances. One sits with one's back to the sun in the morning and gazes into the empty sky in the west. In the late afternoon, again with one's back to the sun, one gazes into the empty sky in the east. One enters and remains for the entire session in Trekchod, or the state of contemplation, and simply allows the visions to spontaneously manifest just as they did in the dark retreat as thingleys, chains, and so. But unless the practitioner is in contemplation, the state of pure presence and awareness without thoughts, which is beyond the operations of mind and the producing of thoughts, one's vision practice, whether in the dark retreat or with the empty sky, will be no better than watching cinema show.

In this context, three different gazes are described:

1. The gaze of the Chakravartin, or wheel-turning monarch, which is straight ahead,
2. The gaze of the dignified lion, which is upward, and
3. The gaze of the Bodhisattva Sangwa Dupa, which is downward.

It is best not to do vision practice at midday because the sunlight may be too intense. The practice may be enhanced by doing some gentle kumbhaka, or holding of the breath. This sky meditation practice is in many ways similar to the practice of Longde, or space meditation, found in the Nyingmapa system, whereas fixation is similar to their Semde practice. Through this practice, one comes to separate impurities (negative emotions and discursive thoughts) from the purity of Rigpa. The inherent radiance of Rigpa, or pure awareness, manifests as Clear Light.

This Clear Light of Rigpa abides in the hollow space inside the physical heart (tsita). From there, it overflows spontaneously through the hollow translucent Kati channel as its pathway, this channel connecting the heart to the eyeballs. In the brain it divides into two hollow tubes which terminate in the two eyeballs. The five clear lights, having the colors of a peacock's feather, shine out through the eyes and manifest in the space in front of oneself. Thus, the texts speak of four or six Lamps (sgron-ma drug), the term "lamp" meaning a source of light. Because one radically relaxes the elements of one's body, certain secret signs are produced. The relaxing of the earth element gives rise to the vision of smoke, that of the water element to the vision of a mirage, that of the fire element to the vision of fire-flies, that of the air element to the vision of daybreak, and that of the space element to the vision of the radiance of sunrise. These same secret signs also appear to the dying individual during the disintegration process (thim-rim) of the elements of one's body and energy. [8]

Section IIIB, Sunlight Practice: Finally, the practice of vision with sunlight, usually known elsewhere as Thodgal, is considered. The site of practice should have a clear open view to the east where the sun rises and to the west where it will set. One practices in the early morning when the sun is just rising above the horizon, or when it is setting. One never looks directly at the orb of the sun, but below, or to the side, with eyes half closed. Otherwise, one will injure the eyes. One should sit in the shade, or else wear a broad-brimmed hat in order to protect oneself from the bright sunlight. Sunlight, the empty sky, and total darkness serve as the supports (rten) for the spontaneously arising of the Thodgal visions, but they in themselves are not the cause of these visions, which come from within. In terms of sunlight practice, the support is the rays of the sun.

With regard to the practice, there are five postures:

1. The posture of the dignified lion, sitting like a dog on his haunches,
2. The posture of the reclining elephant, lying down on one's belly,
3. The posture of the crouching ascetic, crouching like an old man,

4. The posture of the waddling goose, and
5. The posture of the crystal antelope, the most difficult of all.

Of these five postures, the easiest is that of the crouching Rishi, or ascetic, and for this one may also use a meditation belt (sgom-thag), holding the knees against the chest and supporting the chin on the palms of the hands. There are also five associated gazes:

1. The gaze of the Dharmakaya, looking upward,
2. The gaze of the Sambhogakaya, looking straight ahead,
3. The gaze of the Nirmanakaya, looking downward,
4. The gaze of Skilful Means, looking to the right, and
5. The gaze of Discriminating Wisdom, looking to the left.

In this way, with postures and gazes, the practitioner unites the three Lamps:

1. The Lamp of Existence: that is, the rays from the sun, moon, candle flame, and so on,
2. The Lamp of the Senses, that is, the eyes, and
3. The Lamp of Rigpa, that is to say, intrinsic awareness.

As was the case with the dark retreat and sky meditation, during a session of practice, the practitioner should remain in the state of contemplation, that is, in the Natural State of the Nature of Mind (sems-nyid gnas-lugs). Otherwise, little benefit will come from vision practice and one will simply remain in Samsara and impure karmic vision. In general, it is easiest for visions to develop in total darkness, but they are most clear and radiant in sunlight. The visions develop through the five stages detailed in the text. As an alternative practice, one can cover one's head with a blue cloth and gaze into the rays of the sun. Nevertheless, one should never engage in practice at midday when the sun its at its strongest. As suggested earlier, various signs and visions may arise indicating the release of the energies of the five elements.

Instructions are given regarding the disposition of the various psychic channels (rtsa) in the human body. These channels are not anatomical structures in the body that may be revealed in a post-mortem autopsy. Rather, they represent the pathways in a living being through which the vital winds, or energies (rlung), move. Therefore, descriptions of the channels may vary in detains in different practice texts. The vital winds move according where they are visualized to move. It is the same with the descriptions of the chakras. The phenomenon of inner psychic heat, or Tummo (gtum-mo), which is referred to here, is similar to Kundalini, well known in its Hindu form in the West.

Also sleep yoga and dream yoga are briefly described, which enables the practitioner in retreat to practice twenty-four hours a day. By means of practicing sleep yoga one may come to recognize the Clear Light when one falls asleep at night, where falling asleep corresponds to the process of dying. In summery, falling asleep corresponds to the Chikhai Bardo, the Bardo of the Dying Process, the manifestation of the Clear Light corresponds to the Bon-nyid Odsal Bardo, the Bardo of the Clear Light of Reality, and the dream state corresponds to the Sidpai Bardo, the Bardo of Existence, that is, the rebirth process. The individual experiences the Clear Light every night at the precise moment when one falls asleep and the mind disintegrates, all of its operations being temporarily suspended. The same process occurs at the time of dying. With the onset of the dream state, the mind re-manifests from the state of dissolution in the Kunzhi and starts to operate again. The dream state itself represents a mental process. The purpose of sleep yoga is to recognize the Clear Light experience when one falls asleep and before the onset of dreaming, whereas the purpose of dream yoga to experience lucid dreams, that is, to recognize and be aware that one is dreaming without waking up. By becoming aware in one's dreams, the practitioner is able to modify them and even to do meditation practices. When falling asleep, the practitioner focuses one's attention on the heart chakra in terms of sleep practice and on one's throat chakra in terms of dream practice. Thus, one is able to integrate sleep and dream with Clear Light practice. [9]

Brief English Outline of the Topics in the Principal Practices Text

BOOK TWO
PART ONE: Fixating the Mind
A. The Position of the Body
B. The Position of the Gaze

C. Training in the Fixating of the Mind
PART TWO: The Practice for the Dark Retreat
A. The Meditation Practice
  A1. The Essential Point of the Body
  A2. The Essential Point of Speech
  A3. The Essential Point of the Mind
B. Training in the Practice of the Dark Retreat
C. The Arising of Visions in the Darkness
PART THREE: The Practices for the Empty Sky and for Sunlight
A. The Practice in General in terms of Higher Insight
  A1. Controlling the Body, the Gaze, and the Mind.
  A2. Observing the Practice
  A3. The Arising of Visions in Space
B. The Practice of Vision with the Sky and with the Sunlight
  B1. Sky Practice
    B1.1. The Places for Practice
    B1.2. The Times for Practice
    B1.3. The Method of Practice
    B1.4. The Arising of Phenomena
  B2. The Practice with Sunlight
    B2.1. The Places of Practice
    B2.2. The Times for Practice
    B2.3. The Methods of Practice
      B2.3a. The Positions of the Body
        B2.3a.1. The Position of the Dignified Lion
        B2.3a.2. The Position of the Reclining Elephant
        B2.3a.3. The Position of the Crouching Ascetic
        B2.3a.4. The Position of the Waddling Goose
        B2.3a.5. The Position of the Crystal Antelope
      B2.3b. The Five Gazes
      B2.3c. Training in the Practice
    B2.4. The Arising of Visions
IIIC. Special Methods for Developing the Vision Practice
  C1. Visions and the Appropriate Gazes
  C2. Purification of the Vital Winds and the Mind
    C2.1. How the Psychic Channels Abide
    C2.2. Why it is Necessary to Purify the Psychic Channels
    C2.3. The Methods of Purification
      C2.3a. Gentle Breathing

Detailed English and Tibetan Outline of the Contents of the Principal Practices Text

BOOK TWO

Here is contained the Practice Manual for the Stages of the Explanation (of the Principal Practices) of the Oral Transmission from Zhang-zhung [Zhang-zhung snyan-rgyud kyi khrid rim lag-len bzhugs-so].

Second, with regard to the stages of the principal practices (dngos-gzhi) that bring about the ripening and the liberation of one's stream of consciousness in between (the Base and the Fruit, that is to say, as the Path), there are three parts [gnyis-pa bar du rgyud smin zhing grol-bar byed-pa dngos-gzhi'i rim-pa la gsum ste]:

1. In the beginning (of the path), when one has not (previously) fixated the mind, one now fixates the mind [thog-mar sems ma zin-pa zin-par byed-pa],

2. In the middle (of the path), when mindfulness is not abiding (and stable), one employs (various methods) to bring about its abiding (thereby stabilizing it) [bar du dran-pa mi gnas-pa gnas-par byed-pa], and

3. And finally (toward the conclusion of the path), when Self-Awareness is not yet clear, one employs (various methods) in order to make it clear [tha-ma rang-rig mi gsal-ba gsal-bar bya-ba].

PART ONE: Fixating the Mind [sems 'dzin gyi khrid]

With respect to this, there exist three considerations:

A. The essential point of the body [lus kyi gnad],
B. The essential point of the gaze [lta-stangs kyi gnad], and
C. The essential point of the training (of the mind) [bslab-bya'i gnad].

A. The Position of the Body

With reference to the first consideration, the five mudras, or positions, are as follows:

1. One assumes a cross-legged sitting position in order to control the vital winds and psychic channels which are below [smad kyi rtsa rlung sdom phyir skyil-khrung bca'],

2. One keeps the spine straight in order to control the bones of the spine and the internal organs [rus tshigs khrol bu sdom phyir tshigs-pa bsrang],

3. One assumes the samadhi-mudra or gesture of equipoise, (with the hands) in order to control the essential point of the samskaras (the emotions and impulses) ['du-byed gnad du gcun phyir mnyam-bzhag bya],

4. One bends the neck (a little) in order to subdue the exertion of speaking and talking [smra brjod rtsol-ba gzhoms phyir mgrin-pa dgug], and

5. And one gazes fixedly (straight ahead) in order to discard and renounce (the dichotomy of) subject and object [gzung 'dzin gcud la bor phyir lta-stangs gzir].

B. The Position of the Gaze
C. Training in the the Fixating of the Mind

PART TWO:. The Practice for the Dark Retreat

Second, in terms of making mindfulness abide stably when it has not yet abided stably [dran-pa mi gnas-pa gnas-par bya-ba la]: Then, in terms of the method of practice [nyams su blang tshul la gsum ste], there are three considerations:

A. Practicing meditation in whatever way [ji ltar sgom-pa dang],

B. The training in that [de'i bslab bya dang], and

C. The modes for the arising (of visions in the total darkness) to the mind-stream (of the individual in retreat) [rgyud la 'char tshul-lo].

A. The Meditation Practice

Thus, there are three further considerations:

1. Having bound and controlled the activities of the body, one relaxes without engaging in any actions [lus kyi bya-ba bsdam nas byar med du glod-pa],

2. Having bound and controlled the activities of the speech of the voice, one relaxes without speaking or expressing oneself [ngag gi smra-ba bsdam nas brjod med du glod-pa], and

3. Having bound and controlled the memories and thoughts in the mind, one relaxes, transcending all thinking and thereby one produces a samadhi, or state of contemplation, that is devoid of thoughts [sems kyi dran-pa bsam bsdam nas bsam 'das su glod-pas/ mi rtog-pa'i ting-'dzin skye-ba'o].

A1. The Essential Point of the Body [lus gnad]

A2. The Essential Point of Speech [ngag gnad]

A3. The Essential Point of the Mind [sems gnad]

B. Training in the Practice of the Dark Retreat

With respect to the second consideration, how one should train in that [bslab bya].

C. The Arising of Visions in the Darkness

PART THREE: The Practices for the Empty Sky and for Sunlight

Third, within the instructions for making clear what is not yet clear [gsum-pa mi gsal-ba gsal-bar byed-pa'i gdams-pa la gsum ste], there are three major considerations:

A. The practices in general [spyir nyams su blang-ba],

B. The practices in detail [bye-brag tu nyams su blang-ba], and

C. Development by way of the instructions on the essential points [gnad kyi gdams-pas bogs 'don-pa'o].

A. The Practice in General in terms of Higher Insight

With respect to the first major consideration: With regard to that (Upadesha), there are three further considerations:

1. Controlling (the body, the gaze, and the mind) by way of the five essential point, [gnad lnga'i sgo nas gcun-pa],
2. Observing (the practice) by means of the secondary conditions on the path of method [thabs lam gyi rkyen gyis btsa'-ba], and
3. The modes for the arising (of visions) that depend upon the mind-stream [rgyud la bsten-pa'i 'char tshul].

A1. Controling the Body, the Gaze, and the Mind

With regard to the first consideration, the place for the meditation practice is very important. [sgom-pa'i gnas shin tu gnad che ste].

A2. Observing the Practice

With respect to the second consideration, there exists also the full measure of the session of practice [thun tshad].

A3. The Arising of Visions in Space

With respect to the third consideration, the modes for the arising (of visions) that depend upon the mind-stream [rgyud la bsten-pa'i 'char tshul].

B. The Practice of Vision with the Sky and with the Sunlight

Second, with reference to the practices in detail, there are two divisions [bye-brag tu nyams su blang-ba la gnyis te], namely,

1. Purification practice in terms of the contemplation of the sky that is clear and visible (that is, sky practice) [snang gsal nam-mkha'i ting-nge 'dzin la sbyang-ba] and
2. Purification practice in terms of the contemplation of the lamp that represents inherent clear luminosity (that is, Thodgal) [rang gsal sgron-ma'i ting-nge 'dzin la sbyang-ba].

B1. Sky Practice

Within the first division, there are four considerations:

1. Practicing in any place [gnas gang du nyams su blang-ba],
2. Practicing on the occasions that are the times [dus nam gyi tshe nyams su blang-ba],
3. Practicing by whatever methods [tshul ji-ltar nyams su blang-ba], and
4. The modes for the arising of the Clear Light as experiences and as visions [nyams snang 'od-gsal gyi 'cher tshul].

B1.1. The Places for Practice

With reference to the first consideration, there are the places of practice [gnas],

B1.2. The Times for Practice

Second, there are the times for practicing [dus],

B1.3. The Method of Practice

Third, there is the method of meditation [sgom tshul], and

B1.4. The Arising of Phenomena

Fourth, there are the modes of the arising (of visions) ['char tshul].

B2. The Practice with Sunlight

Second, within the practice of contemplation of the lamp of inherent clarity [rang gsal sgron-ma'i ting-nge 'dzin nyams su blang-ba la bzhi ste], there are four considerations, namely,

1. The places where to practice [gnas gang du nyams su blang-ba],
2. The times for the occasions of practicing [dus nam gyi tshe nyans su blang-ba],
3. Practicing in terms of whatever methods [tshul ji-ltar nyams su blang-ba], and
4. Because one has practiced in that way, there are the modes for the arising of the virtuous qualities [de ltar nyams su blangs-pas yon-tan 'char tshul-lo].

B2.1. The Places of Practice

First, the places of practice [gnas]

B2.2. The Times for Practice

Second, the time for practice [dus]

B2.3. The Methods of Practice

Third, as for the methods, with regard to that (method of practice), there exist three further considerations:

B2.3a. The Positions of the Body

First, with regard to the essential points of the body [lus gnad], there are the assuming of the five essential points (or positions) of the body that will suddenly produce the Clear Light (that is to say, the Thodgal visions). [dang-po lus gnad la 'od-gsal glo-bur bskyed-pa'i/ lus gnad lnga bca' ste]. With reference to that, there are five (postures for the practice), namely,

1. The posture of the dignified lion [seng-ge 'gying stabs],
2. The method of the reclining elephant [glang-po-che'i brkyang thabs],
3. The method of the crouching ascetic (shramana) [dge-sbyor gi tsog-pu tshul]
4. The method of the waddling goose [ngang-mo'i zur 'gros], and
5. The method of the crystal antelope climbing a rock [shel gyi rwa-pho brag la 'dzeg-pa'i tshul].

B2.3a.1. The Position of the Dignified Lion [sen-ge'i 'gying stabs tshul]

B2.3a.2. The Position of the Reclining Elephant [glang-po-che'i brkyang thabs tshul]

B2.3a.3. The Position of the Crouching Ascetic [dge-sbyor gyi tsog-pu tshul]

B2.3a.4. The Position of the Waddling Goose [ngang-mo'i zur 'gros tshul]

B2.3a.5. The Position of the Crystal Antelope [shel gyi rwa-pho brag la 'dzeg-pa'i tshul]

B2.3b. The Five Gazes

1. The Gaze of the Dharmakaya [bon-sku lta-stangs],
2. The Gaze of the Sambhogakaya [rdzogs-sku'i lta-stangs],
3. The Gaze of the Nirmanakaya [sprul-sku'i lta-stangs],
4. The Gaze of Skilful Means [thabs kyi lta-stangs] , and
5. The Gaze of Discriminating Wisdom [shes-rab kyi lta-stangs].

B2.3c. Training in the Practice

With respect to the third further consideration, this training represents the essential point of the mind [gsum-pa la gcun-pa sems kyi gnad la].

B2.4. The Arising of Visions

Third, with regard to the mode of arising (of the visions) [gsum-pa 'char tshul la]:

IIIC. Special Methods for Developing the Vision Practice [bogs 'don-pa]

Third, in terms of development by way of the instructions on the special essential points [gsum-pa khyad-par gnad kyi gdams-pas bogs 'don-pa la gsum te], there are three considerations, namely,

1. Development by means of the essential points for the Path of Method [thabs lam gnad gyis bogs 'don-pa],
2. Development by means of the purification of the vital winds and the mind [rlung sems kyi sbyong-bas bogs 'don-pa], and
3. Development by means of the instructions concerning the visions at night [mtshan snang gi gdams-pas bogs 'don-pa].

C1. Visions and the Appropriate Gazes

C2. Purification of the Vital Winds and the Mind

Second, in terms of the yoga of (the vital winds and) the mind, there exist three considerations [gnyis-pa sems kyi sbyor-ba la gsum ste], namely,

1. The disposition or mode of abiding for the psychic channels, the vital winds, and the bindus [rtsa rlung thig-le'i gnas tshul],
2. The reasons why it is necessary to purify them [de la sbyang dgos-pa'i rgyu-mtshan], and
3. The methods for purifying them in whatever way [ji ltar sbyong-ba'i tshul-lo]

C2.3. The Methods of Purification

Third, with respect to the methods of purification, there exist three (kinds of breathing), [gsum-pa sbyong-tshul la gsum ste]:

1. Purification in terms of gentle breathing ['jam rlung la sbyang-ba],
2. Control in terms of rough breathing [rtsub rlung la gcun-pa], and
3. Stabilization in terms of natural breathing [rang rlung la brtan-par bya].

C2.3a. Gentle Breathing
Within the first consideration (gentle breathing), there are three aspects:

1. The essential point of the body [lus gnad],
2. The essential point of the functional mind [yid gnad], and
3. The essential point of the breathing [rlung gnad].

C2.3b. Rough Breathing
With regard to the second (the rough breating), there are two considerations:

1. Meditating in whatever manner [ci ltar bsgom-pa] and
2. The modes for the arising of experiences [nyams-myong 'char tshul]

C3. Sleep and Dream Practice
Third, in terms of the instructions for the visions in the night time, there exist three considerations, [gsum-pa mtshan snang gi gdams la gsum ste]:

1. The integrating of sleep with the Clear Light ['od-gsal gnyid dang bsre-ba],
2. The modes for the arising of both the defects and the virtuous qualities from that [de yi skyon yon 'char tshul], and
3. Apprehending the essential point which is fixating on the A [gnad zung A la gtad-pa'o]

Colophon

The Explanation of the View

The first of the four supplementary texts found in Book Three, "The Explanation of the View," represents a direct introduction (ngo-sprad-pa) to the individual's Base (gzhi) or Primordial State, which is the Nature of Mind (sems-nyid). In Dzogchen, a clear distinction is made between mind (sems), on the one hand, the ordinary thought process (blo), and the Nature of Mind, on the other hand, which is beyond the thought process, yet the matrix for it. "Seeing nakedly" (gcer mthong) means that one's awareness (rig-pa) is unobscured by perceptions, discursive thoughts, and conceptions. However, the individual is not unconscious, but totally and globally aware, being in the condition of the mirror. Here there are three sections or divisions:

1. The direct introduction to the Primordial Base, the Nature of Mind, where this is pointed out to the practitioner by the Lama,
2. The direct introduction by way of certain special activities, and
3. The extensive explanation regarding liberation and delusion.

The first section directly introduces one to the three aspects of the Nature of Mind, as well as their unity, namely,

1. The Mother (ma), which is the Kunzhi (kun-gzhi), "the basis of everything,"
2. The Son (bu), which is Rigpa, or intrinsic awareness,
3. The Energy (rtsal), which is the pure potentiality for all possible manifestations, and
4. Their unity or inseparability (dbyer-med).

The Mother Kunzhi, characterized as the basis of everything, is the Essence (ngo-bo), that is to say, the state of Shunyata, and this is equated with the Dharmakaya. This Kunzhi is distinguished from and should not be confused with the Kunzhi Namshe (kun-gzhi rnam-shes, Skt. alaya-vijnana), which is a type of consciousness. Consciousness (rnam-shes) represents awareness (rig-pa) when it is mixed up with and limited by mind, or mental processes. The Kunzhi is beyond mind and consciousness, but provides the space and matrix for their manifestation. In the text, the Mother is characterized by eight possible designations. The Son Rigpa, is characterized as luminous clarity (gsal-ba), and as being the Nature (rang-bzhin). This is equated with the Sambhogakaya. These two, the Mother and Son, are not separate entities or emanations; they have been inseparable from the very beginning (ye nas dbyer-med), like the two sides of the same coin. They are only distinguished for purposes of human understanding. The Kunzhi may be compared to the open and unobstructed dimension of the sky and Rigpa may be compared to the face of the sun appearing in the sky and which illuminates that space. Thus, whereas Kunzhi is compared to space, Rigpa is compared to light. This Rigpa, or intrinsic awareness, is fundamental to existence itself and is not something derived from anything other than itself. Their inseparability represents the potential energy (rtsal) of this illuminated space to give birth to all possible forms and manifestations. This potential energy becomes visible as sounds, lights, and rays (sgra 'od zer gsum). Sounds means subtle vibrations, lights means the pure lights in five colors, and rays means visible forms.

At the moment of true death, on the occasion when even the mind and all its processes and functions have disintegrated and dissolved into the empty space of the Nature of Mind, the Namshe, or deceased consciousness, awakens to discover itself as simply being empty space without limits or borders. But because Kunzhi and Rigpa have been inseparable from the very beginning, the Clear Light of Rigpa, which is intrinsic awareness, inevitably arises in this clear, open space that is the Nature of Mind. With the dawning of this Clear light of Reality, being the light of the Dharmakaya itself, there arises simultaneously, because of residual karma, a very subtle mind. The Clear Light manifests to this subtle mind as these sounds, lights, and rays. If the awareness of this very subtle mind recognizes the Clear Light as its own face reflected in the mirror of space, it liberates instantly and realizes the Dharmakaya. This occasion is the moment known as the Boundary (so-mthsams) between death and the onset of the Bardo experience, and, therefore, it provides the maximum opportunity for liberating oneself from Samsara and realizing Buddha enlightenment. But if this very subtle mind does not recognize the phenomena of the sounds, lights, and rays as self-manifestations (rang-snang) of the inherent energy of one's Nature of Mind, it comes to erroneously believe that these phenomena are objects external to itself. Thereby it falls into the fundamental existential ignorance of the duality of subject and object (lhan-skyes ma rig-pa) and consequently the delusions of Samsara arise once again. Perceiving them as external objects, subsequently there arises the secondary ignorance which conceptualizes everything (kun-brtags ma rig-pa).

This Energy is equated with the Nirmanakaya. From being potential energy, it becomes kinetic as visibly manifest phenomena (rol-pa). Initially the primal cognitions of awareness (rig-pa'i ye-shes) arise spontaneously and unceasingly because they represent the inherent potential energy (rang rtsal) of the Nature of Mind. These phenomena are self-manifestations (rang-snang) and they do not appear due to the activity of another (gzhan-snang), to something outside of itself, such as a prior cause or a creator. They are, therefore, radiant and translucent (mdangs), unobscured and uncovered by discursive thoughts and by conceptions. Thus, they are seen nakedly. Thereupon the visions of the Bardo unfold. At the moment of the Boundary following death and the disintegration of the mind, there extend from this single source, the Primordial Base, which is the Nature of Mind, two diverse evolutionary pathways, Samsara and Nirvana, traversed by two types of beings, Buddhas, or enlightened beings, who are liberated, and ordinary sentient beings, who are deluded and bound, and thus still caught up in the rounds of Samsara. Enlightened beings on the side of pure vision behold visions of divine forms and mandalas, whereas deluded sentient beings, on the side of impure karmic vision, behold the six destinies of rebirth. The Mother, the Son, and the Energy are equated with the Trikaya of the Base inherent in evry sentient being, but unrecognized.

Following the death of the material body and the separating of consciousness from it, the Namshe persists as a unit, a combination of psychic energy (rlung) and mental consciousness (sems). Its primal cognitions experience the sounds, lights, and rays. These primal cognitions are present prior to the mind, or thought processes, coming into operation. The individual has a single Nature of Mind and a single Rigpa, even though the Kunzhi, the side of emptiness, is all-pervading like space itself. Individuals are like points of light within this infinite space. For the individual, there is a single Rigpa, but a plurality of Yeshes, or primal cognitions. Thus, whereas Rigpa is compared to the face of the sun visible in the sky, the Yeshes are compared to the rays of the sun that illuminate the surface of the earth. Western books in English usually translate *ye-shes* as "wisdom." But this is confusing because wisdom as such is a higher intellectual process that is dualistic in its operations. Wisdom (shes-rab) distinguishs between true and false, real and unreal, moral and immoral, good and bad, beautiful and ugly, and so on. However, Yeshe is non-dual awareness, present before the mind and the process of perception comes into operation. This follows also from the usage of the term in Sanskrit Buddhist texts, where *ye-shes* translates Sanskrit *jnana*, which is cognate with Greek *gnosis*.

The text refers to the inseparability of these three aspects of the Nature of Mind, namely, the Mother, the Son, and the Energy (ma bu rtsal gsum dbyer-med). There is a difference between Yermed (dbyer-med), "inseparability," as used in Dzogchen texts and Zungjuk (zung-'jug), "unification" in Tantra texts. Unification implies that two different things are brought together and merged into one, whereas inseparable means that they have never been separate. Tsal, or potential energy, gives rise to apparitional displays (cho-'phrul), which in modern terms might be though of as holograms, but which involve all five senses and not just visible light. The Namshe finds itself inside this global holographic structure, much like being inside a video game as an actual participant, and not outside looking at a two-dimensional screen. This game is programmed by karma.

In the next section, Rigpa is called "the king who is knowing awareness" (shes rig gi rgyal-po). The term "king" means the most important member of any group. The masses of thoughts that arise are compared to winds and the negative emotions to waves on the ocean which are stirred up by these winds. Delusion comes about because one follows after thoughts and perceptions, taking them to be ultimately real, and not looking back to their source. The delusion system ('khrul-lugs) is the individual's constructed reality, which constitutes Samsara. Samsara, the round of existence, is not just the cycle of death and rebirth, which has continued from time without beginning, but it also refers to the way the individual's mind works. The six aggregates of consciousness (tshogs drug) refer to the five sense consciousnesses, plus mental consciousness. The functional mind (yid, Skt. manas) is like a computer running its many programs day and night. In addition to this,, there is an awareness present which is aware of this running of many programs. This is called mental consciousness (yid-shes). Consciousness (rnam-.shes) represents a limiting of Rigpa because it now becomes caught up in time and the running of these various programs and processes by the functional mind. The five poisons are the five defilements, or negative emotions, of anger, desire, confusion, pride, and jealousy. This term Timuk (gti-mug, Skt. moha) is often translated as "ignorance," but this does not represent a lack of knowledge, but rather, it is an emotion, therefore, "confusion." The six aggregates of consciousness are compared to rainbows spanning the sky. They arise from the dimension of the sky and later fade and dissolve again into the sky. In the same way, consciousness arises from Sunyata and dissolves again into Shunyata. However, this is not the end of the story because Kunzhi and Rigpa are inseparable. The Nimanakaya is compared here to the rainbow; it is visible, but insubstantial.

As explained in the thrid section, coming face to face with the Clear Light after death, that is to say, with the radiant light of one's own intrinsic awareness, there are two possibilities, namely, proceeding into liberation (grol tshul) or falling again into delusion ('khrul tshul). Liberation occurs when the Clear Light is recognized and understood and delusion occurs when it is not recognized and not understood . This non-recognition is due an existential ignorance, inherent in the dualistic mode of existence of the individual, and is said to be co-emergent (lhan-skyes) because it arises simultaneously with the advent of the Clear Light. At the very beginning, the primordial Buddha Kuntu Zangpo recognized the Clear Light as the light of his own awareness, and, therefore, he never fell into ignorance and the delusions of Samsara. Indeed, he is the Primordial Buddha because he never experienced Samsara. But the rest of the infinite masses of sentient beings did not recognize the Clear Light, and so, lifetime after lifetime, they fell again into rebirth in Samsara. This Samsara was not created by anyone at any one point in time. It simply goes round and round like a wheel turning. No point on its circumference or rim can be taken as the absolute beginning for creation. Samsara never had a beginning. It was not created by the Primordial Buddha Kuntu Zangpo, nor by some god. Rather, Samsara is perpetually and continuously generated by the collective karma of all the sentient beings inhabiting it. Thus, they are all participants in the process of creating the world.

Instead of remaining on the side of pure awareness and being like the mirror simply reflecting whatever appears before it, the ordinary sentient being follows after the reflections on the object side. Therefore, one does not live in the nature of the mirror, but lives in the reflections. Thus, the visions unfold and evolve. From being originally pure clear lights of five colors, they progressively grow duller and more dense, until they become the five great elements which comprise our material universe. These Samsaric visions increasingly appear solid, substantial, and real, whereas actually they are just space and light. The clear white light becomes the space element, the clear green light becomes the air element, the clear red light becomes the fire element, the clear blue light becomes the water element, and the clear yellow light becomes the earth element. Beginning with these five great elements, there evolve the five skandhas, the five organs of the body, the five bodily cavities, the five sense faculties, the five paths, the five realms, the five poisons, and so on. This process of unfolding represents the evolution of delusion.

Eventually, in terms of cosmology, there appear the three realms or worlds:

1. The Arupadhatu, the formless higher mental realms,
2. The Rupadhatu, the higher mental planes with subtle forms, and
3. The Kamadhatu, the lower worlds where sentient beings are ruler by their sensual desires.

The Arupadhatu is created by a subtle confusion, the Rupadhatu by the aggressive anger of the intellect, and the Kamadhatu by addiction to sensual desires. Within the latter, the six destinies of rebirth ('gro drug), or six realms (rigs drug), are generated, namely,

1. The realm of the Devas or gods by an excess of all five poisons,
2. The realm of the Asuras, or anti-gods, by an excess of pride,
3. The human realm by an excess of jealousy,
4. The animal realm by an excess of confusion,
5. The realm of the Pretas, or hungry ghosts, by an excess of desire, and
6. The realm of the hells by an excess of anger.

Note that the correspondences here are little different than found in the Buddhist system.

Encountering the Clear Light, when one understands, that represents the process of liberation (rtogs te grol tshul). Kuntu Zangpo understood and so he was liberated at the very beginning, even though he had done nothing to accumulate good karma. Rigpa arose like the sun at dawn; he recognized its face and became the sun.

Thus, when this occurs, it is said that the Son returns to the lap of his Mother. Practicing contemplation during one's lifetime, one may realize the Son Clear Light, but following death, one encounters the Mother Clear Light Thus, the Son returns to his Mother, his own original condition. With the spontaneous unfolding and evolution of the visions of Nirvana, the five vast spaces (klong lnga) arise and in them there spontaneously appear the five Dhyani Buddhas and their mandalas and realms. This represents pure vision as against impure karmic vision and represents the way enlightened beings see things. This is the evolution of Nirvana in terms of vision.

Outline of the Explanation of the View

BOOK THREE

Here is contained "The Guiding Explanation of the View through Seeing Nakedly, which represents the Direct Introduction to one's own Primordial Base" [gzhi rang ngo-sprad-pa gcer-mthong lta-ba'i khrid].

In detail:

I.   Relying upon the Essence and the Nature of the the primordial Base, one is introduced thereby directly to it [gzhi'i rang-bzhin ngo-bo la brten nas ngo-sprad-pa],

II. Relying upon certain special activities, one is further introduced to it [byed las khyad-par la brten nas ngo-sprad-pa], and

III. There is the extensive explanation regarding (the origins of) Liberation and of Delusion respectively [grol 'khrul rgyas-par bshad-pa]

In detail:

I.   Relying upon the Essence and the Nature of the the primordial Base, one is introduced thereby directly to it [gzhi'i rang-bzhin ngo-bo la brten nas ngo-sprad-pa]

A.   The direct introduction to the Mother [ma'i ngo-sprad-pa]

B.   The direct introduction to the Son [bu'i ngo-sprad-pa]

   1. The Natural State of the Son [bu'i gnas-lugs]

   2. The direct introduction to that [de la ngo-sprad-pa]

C.   The direct introduction to the Energy or Potentiality [rtsal gyi ngo-sprad-pa]

   1. The Natural State of Energy [rtsal gyi gnas-lugs]

2. The direct introduction to it [de la ngo-sprad-pa]

D. The direct introduction to the unity and inseparability of all three, namely, the Mother, the Son, and the Energy [ma bu rtsal gsum dbyer-med zung-'brel du ngo-sprad-pa]

    1. The Natural State [gnas-lugs]

    2. The direct introduction to it [de'i ngo-sprad-pa]

II. Relying upon certain special activities, one is further introduced to it [byed las khyad-par la brten nas ngo-sprad-pa]

A. The direct introduction through thoughts and memories that are like clouds in the sky [bsam dran nam-mkha'i sprin ltar ngo-sprad-pa]

    1. The teaching on the Natural State [gnas-lugs bstan-pa]

    2. The direct introduction to it. [de la ngo-sprad-pa]

B. The direct introduction through the masses of thoughts that are like gentle breezes in the atmosphere [rtog tshogs bar-snang gi ser-bu ltar ngo-sprad-pa]

C. The direct introduction through the emotional defilements that are like the waves on the sea [nyon-mongs mtsho dang rba-rlabs ltar ngo-sprad-pa]

D. The direct introduction through the six aggregates (of consciousness) that are like the rainbows spanning the sky [tshogs drug mkha' yangs gzha'-tshon ltar ngo-sprad-pa]

III. There is the extensive explanation regarding (the origins of) Liberation and of Delusion respectively [grol 'khrul rgyas-par bshad-pa]

A. The method of delusion where one does not understand [ma rtogs 'khrul tshul]

    1. The co-emergent or spontaneously-born ignorance [lhan-skyes ma rig-pa]

    2. The ignorance which conceptualizes everything [kun brtags kyi ma rig-pa]

B. The method of liberation where one does understand [rtogs de grol tshul]

    1. The method of liberation in whatever fashion at the very beginning [dang-po ci ltar grol tshul]

    2. The extensive direct introduction to the system of liberation [grol-lugs rgyas-par bshad-pa]

The Explanation of the Meditation Practice

The second supplementary text deals with the meditation practice of the Clear Light, and again there are three principal sections:

1. Methods for continuing in the progressive stages of the path,
2. Cleansing the impurities of mind, and
3. Experiences in meditation.

In terms of the first topic, one reflects on the fear of death and future rebirth and one carries the presence of the Lama, or spiritual guide, always on one's head. One enters into a solitary retreat in a suitable place, such as a remote hermitage where one will not be disturbed by outside circumstances. Nevertheless, it will be necessary to have the visits of a good spiritual friend, the Lama, and possibly also an attendant. Then there are instructions regarding the vital winds and mind, and also instructions regarding the characteristics of visions.

Then, the arising of obstacles (bgegs) during the retreat are considered. External obstacles are represented by worldly attachments and by the activities of non-human spirits. These latter are overcome by ritual and magical practices. Internal obstacles are chiefly represented by sickness and other ills. These may be mitigated or overcome by breathing exercises, physical exercises, visualizations, and medicines. Finally, secret obstacles consist of certain experiences in meditation. These arise from deviations from the proper view of Dzogchen. Then there are also defects to meditation practice, principally drowsiness, dullness, and agitation. Finally, there are various forms of conduct to be avoided.

Then, while in retreat, there will most likely come the arising of Clear Light visions, that is, Thodgal visions. As explained previously, as against visualizations that are deliberately created by the mind and external visions arising to the senses, these visions are spontaneous and arise as self-manifestations (rang-snang) from the inherent energy of one's Nature of Mind. These visions develop in five stages:

1. The visions increase (snang-ba 'phel-ba), where one sees thigleys and awareness chains,

2. The visions multiply (snang-ba mched-pa), where one sees thigleys in five colors, threads and patterns, and partial images inside the thigleys,

3. The visions develop further (snang-ba rgyas-pa), where one sees visions in all directions and the complete divine forms of Buddhas,

4. The visions become completed (snang-ba rdzogs-pa), where one sees complete mandalas and Pure Buddha realms everywhere, and

5. The final visions (snang-ba mthar-thug-pa), where, at this final stage, the energy producing the visions becomes exhausted and they dissolve back into their source, the Clear Light, which is the Dharmakaya itself.

Thereupon, from the state of the Dharmakaya, because the elements of the polluted material body become liberated into their pure unpolluted states, pure visions continue to arise. One attains the Rainbow Body of Light ('ja'-lus), appearing as the Sambhogakaya with its thirty-two marks and eighty characteristics. One's inner reality becomes the Peaceful and Wrathful Deities (zhi khro lha rnams), specifically, the hosts of one hundred and eight Prosperity Deities (rgyas-pa'i lha tshogs), the hosts of forty-five Peaceful Deities (zhi-ba'i lha tshogs), and the hosts of eighty-six Wrathful Deities (khro-bo'i lha tshogs).

Next, the text relates Thodgal vision practice to the five Paths of the Sutra system:

1. The Path of Accumulation corresponds to the Ngondro, or preliminary practices,

2. The Path of Unification corresponds to the practice of contemplation, or Trekchod,

3. The Path of Vision corresponds to Clear Light practice (Thodgal),

4. The Path of Meditation Development corresponds to the developing of visions, and

5. The Path of Ultimate Attainment corresponds to the Fruit of the Rainbow Body.

Moreover with regard to Dzogchen practice, three levels of practitioner are distinguished:

1. The superior practitioner who understands instantly (gcig-car-ba),
2. The intermediate practitioner (thod-rgal-ba) who needs a direct introduction from the master and needs also to practice, and
3. The gradualist practitioner (rim-gyis-pa) who must be taught in a progressive and sequential manner.

Outline of the Explanation of the Meditation Practice

The Progressive Stages of the Explanation of the Meditation Practice for the Clear Light, which represents the Practice of the Path [lam nyams su len-pa 'od-gsal sgom-pa'i khrid rim bzhugs-so]:

I. Practicing the methods of the meditation involving the means for continuing in the progressive stages of the path [bsgom tshul lam gyi rim-pa brkyang thabs],

II. Practicing meditation where there exists the system for removing the impurities of mind [bsgom-byed blo yi dri-ma bsal-lugs], and

III. Experiences due to meditation practice and the manner in which the Clear Light (Thodgal visions) arise [bsgom-pas nyams dang 'od-gsal 'char tshul].

In detail:

I. Practicing the methods of the meditation involving the means for continuing in the progressive stages of the path [bsgom tshul lam gyi rim-pa brkyang thabs]:

When one actually discovers the real meaning of Rigpa or intrinsic awareness, which is the great Clear Light without obscurations [lar thabs-lam dang khrid tshul dang bogs 'don lam-khyer ngo-sprod las sogs mang du gsungs kyang/ gal-che shos kho-rang la thug-pas/ rig-pa sgrib-med 'od-gsal chen-po'i don la], where this meaning is condensed in one-pointed terms, there exist two procedures to be considered:

1. The instructions on the essential points of the vital winds and the mind [rlung sems gnad kyi gdams-pa] and
2. The encountering, on certain occasions, of the visions having characteristics [mtshan snang skabs sbyar du sprad-pa].

When at all times and under all conditions, one remains continuously in that state of contemplation (the Natural State) and meditates uninterruptedly [de nyid la rkyang ded byed cing bar-chad med-par sgom-pa], there exist four principal considerations:

1. Continuing to meditate in accordance with the method (described in the text) [tshul dang mthun-par bskyangs shing bsgom-pas],
2. The manner in which external appearances or visions arise [phyi'i snang-ba 'char tshul],
3. The manner in which internal experiences are produced and how one engages with all of them [nang gi nyams-myong skye tshul thams-cad 'jug-pa], and
4. Their increasing and developing more and more like the face of the waxing moon [zla-ba yar gyi ngo bzhin je 'phel je rgyas la 'byung].

II. Practicing meditation where there exists the system for removing the impurities of mind [bsgom byed blo yi dri-ma bsal-lugs].

With respect to performing the practices in terms of the real meaning of the Mahayana, the Greater Vehicle, this (real meaning) being the Natural State [gnas-lugs theg-chen gyi don nyams su len-par byed-pa la], there may originate three kinds of obstacles:

A. Externally, there may arise obstructions due to human beings and to non-human spirits [phyi mi dang mi ma yin-pa'i bar-chad].
B. Internally, there may arise obstructions such as sicknesses due to imbalances in the humors (within the physical body) [nang 'du-ba nad kyi bar-chad].
C. Secretly, there may arise obstructions that are experiences in meditation [gsang-ba bsgom-pa nyams kyi bar-chad]:
   (1) Obstructions to the View [lta-ba la bar-chad],
   (2) Obstructions to the Meditation [bsgom-pa la bar-chad], and
   (3) Obstructions to the Conduct [spyod-pa la bar-chad].

III. Experiences due to meditation practice and the manner in which the Clear Light (Thodgal visions) arise [bsgom-pas nyams dang 'od-gsal 'char tshul]:

A. The manner in which the visions that arise originate [shar-ba'i snang-ba 'byung tshul]:

  (1) The manner in which external visions come to be seen [phyi'i snang-ba mthong tshul] and

  (2) The manner in which internal experiences are produced [nang gi nyams-myong bskyed tshul].

B. The manner in which these visions increase (and develop) when they become familiar [de la goms-pa'i snang-ba 'phel tshul]:

  (1) The manner in which the visions increase [snang-ba 'phel-ba'i tshul]:

  a. The manner in which external visions are seen to increase [phyi'i snang-ba mthong tshul] and

  b. The manner in which internal experiences are produced [nang gi nyams-myong bskyed tshul].

  (2) The manner in the visions progressively multiply [snang-ba mched-pa]:

  a. The manner in which external visions progressively multiply [phyi'i snang-ba mched tshul] and

  b. The manner in which internal experiences are produced [nang gi nyams-myong bskyed tshul]

  (3) The manner in which the visions develop further [snang-ba rgyas-pa'i tshul]:

  a. The manner in which external visions develop further [phyi'i snang-ba rgyas tshul] and

  b. The manner in which internal experiences are produced [nang gi nyams-myong bskyed tshul].

  (4) The manner in which the visions arise as complete and perfect [snang-ba rdzogs-pa'i tshul]:

  a. The manner in which external visions arise as complete [phyi'i snang-ba rdzogs tshul] and

  b. The manner in which internal experiences are produced [nang gi nyams-myong bskyed tshul].

  (5) The manner in which the final visions arise [snang-ba mthar thug-pa'i 'char tshul]:

  a. The manner in which the final visions arise [phyi'i snang-ba mthar thug-pa'i 'char tshul] and

  b. The manner in which the internal experiences are produced [nang gi nyams-myong bskyed tshul].

C. Uniting the Development of Visions with the Progressive Stages of the Path [de dag gi lam gyi rim-pa dang sbyar-ba], there are
(1) One who realizes instantly [gcig-car-ba]
(2) One who practices non-gradually [thod-rgal-ba] and
(3) One who practices gradually [rim-gyis-pa].

The Explanation of the Conduct

The third supplementary text is concerned with conduct in terms of the forceful purification of the secondary conditions encountered along the path of practice. Again, there are three principal divisions or sections:

1. Purifying during one's lifetime,
2. Purifying during the dying process, and
3. Purifying at the time of the Bardo experience after death.

Purifying (sbyong-ba) means the process of purifying one's negative emotions, or kleshas, and of one's wrong ideas regarding the nature of reality. Forceful purification (rtsal sbyong) means doing so in a deliberate and energetic manner. This process of purification allows one's inner enlightened nature to manifest and shine through.

In terms of the first section, while one is yet alive, the performing of religious rituals in between meditation sessions, should be integrated with the state of contemplation. In the Tantric practice of sadhana, the process of transformation, a distinction is made between the state of even contemplation (mnyam-bzhag), realized upon dissolving the visualization into emptiness, and the period of subsequent realization (rjes thob) when the practitoner returns to mundane, ordinary reality and engages in various activities, whether these be religious rituals, or otherwise. In the context of Dzogchen, this sharp distinction tends to be obliterated and one carries Rigpa, or the state of contemplation, into all mundane actions. Thus, one becomes totally and globally aware in whatever one is doing. At first this will be religious rituals, such as reciting of mantras and prayers, but eventually Rigpa is carried into all worldly activities, even negative ones. Consequently, the practitioner's behavior becomes spontaneous, without any planning, calculation, forethought, or premeditation.

Such spontaneous activities of body, speech, and mind are called Jyar-med (byar-med), meaning "non-action," and this may be compared with the Taoist notion of wu wei. Such spontaneous behavior or activity is sometimes called "crazy wisdom" (ye-shes 'chol-ba). To outsiders it may appear that the practitioner has lost one's mind and gone completely mad. It is true that when one is in contemplation, or the Natural State, one's actions of body, speech, and mind leave no karmic traces behind, just like a bird flying through the sky leaves no traces. However, this is only true when one is in Rigpa, or the Natural State. If one thinks one is in the Natural State, one is most definitely not, because one is thinking and being in a state of mind. Therefore, one's actions will continue to generate karmic results. The danger in Dzogchen practice is that inferior practitioners can delude themselves that they are in the Natural State and then think they can do whatever they like without karmic consequences. This is the thinking of the Rudra demon and only serves to fuel ego-inflation. Therefore, the advice given here to the Dzogchen practitioner is to continue with engaging in conventional religious practices (dge-sbyor).

In terms of the six sense consciousnesses, one becomes like a mirror simply reflecting appearances, which are understood to be mere illusions. All sounds are like echoes. All tastes, scents, and textures are the same, whether a pile of gold or a pile of faeces. Even though the hosts of thoughts may continue to arise in one's mind-stream, they would be like snowflakes falling on the surface of a lake, or like frost melting in the morning sunlight. One avoids all judgments regarding thoughts being good or bad; they simple represent the energy of the mind. One's conduct and behavior may be compared to that of a dog or a pig, where nothing is pure or filthy. All sensations have the same taste (ro-snyoms). One's behavior is self-arising, utterly spontaneous and without inhibitions and premeditations, like that of a small child. Diversity has but a single taste (ro-gcig) and one becomes victorious (rgyal-ba) because the distinction between doer and deed vanishes and one is without any partialities. These instructions refer to conduct while the advanced practitioner is alive, then the process of dying and the Bardo experience after death are considered.

When one is dying and approaching the Boundary between this present life and the experience of the Bardo, there occurs the progressive disintegration and reabsorption of the elements that complise one's body and physical existence. The process of the disintegration of the elements ('jig-tshul) during dying occurs in five stages:

1. The earth element deteriorates in the spleen, one cannot perceive touch sensations with the body, one cannot lift the left arm, and secretions flow freely from the orifices.
2. The water element deteriorates in the kidneys, one cannot hear with the ears, one cannot lift the left leg, and one is not aware to hold the urine.
3. The fire element deteriorates in the liver, one cannot discern tastes with the tongue, one cannot lift the right arm, and blood flows freely from the nose.
4. The air element deteriorates in the lungs, one cannot perceive smells with the nose, one cannot lift the right leg, and one is not aware to retain the faeces.
5. The space element deteriorates in the physical heart, one cannot discern forms with the eyes, one cannot lift up the head, and semen escapes from the sex organ.

The simultaneous process of the reabsorbing of the elements (sdud-tshul) when dying also occurs in five stages:

1. The earth element is reabsorbed into the water element and the chakra of the earth element in the navel disintegrates. As signs of loosing its power: bodily strength is lost and the body feels heavy, like it is sinking into the earth. Appearances arise as yellow lights.
2. The water element is reabsorbed into the fire element and the chakra of the water element in the secret place disintegrates. As signs of loosing its power: the body looses its color, the mouth and nose become very dry. Appearances arise as blue lights.
3. The fire element is reabsorbed into the air element and the chakra of the air element in the heart disintegrates. As signs of loosing its power: the body looses its heat and the tongue turns back. Appearances arise as red lights.
4. The air element is reabsorbed into the space element and the chakra of the air element in the throat disintegrates. As signs of loosing its power: the breathing becomes laborious and one

panics and seeks to hold on to something. Appearances arise as green lights.

5. The space element is reabsorbed into the consciousness element, and this is, in turn, reabsorbed into the Kunzhi, and the chakra of the space element in the crown disintegrates. As signs of loosing its power: sight grows dim and things start to become dark, one cannot blink the eyes and they turn upward, and all breathing eventually ceases. Appearances arise as white lights.

These signs of this process of disintegration and re-absorption are outer, inner, and secret. The outer signs may be observed by those present, such as the doctors and nurses, whereas the inner and secret signs may only be observed by the dying person.

According to the Tantra system, the Namshe, or consciousness, exits the body by way of any number of orifices. In Phowa practice, "the transference of consciousness," these orifices are sealed with visualizations, so that the Namshe exits through the aperture at the crown of the head, the gateway of Brahma. Brief instructions are give here in the text for the practice of Phowa in the Tantric style. During one's lifetime, one engages in the Phowa practice until the signs of success appear. Then it is no longer necessary to continue doing the practice because one knows how to do it. The actual Phowa, or projection of consciousness out of the physical body, is only done at the time of death when the breathing is about to cease. For this reason, the practitioner should be acquainted with the signs of the approach of death. Generally, in a Dzogchen practice manual like this one, the Phowa and the Bardo instructions are given after the complete instructions for performing the principal practices. This is just in case the practitioner does not attain liberation and enlightenment by the time one dies. One has recourse to the Phowa practice to insure a fortunate rebirth among the Devas or among humans.

There is also reference to a special explanation of consciousness exiting the body in the case of a Thodgal practitioner. Even though the Rigpa pervades the entire living body, it is said to be concentrated in the hollow space within the physical heart, the Tsita. At death, it overflows through the translucent Kati channel connecting the heart with the eyes. It then exits the eyes, the right eye with the male and the left eye with the female.

The last section provides instructions regarding the Bardo experience following death and before rebirth in a new embodiment. In the Bonpo system, following the Bardo of the process of dying, the Chikhai Bardo, three Bardos are experienced, namely,

1. The Bardo of the Base that Abides (the state of Shunyata),
2. The Bardo of the Clear Light of Reality, and
3. The Bardo of the Rebirth Process.

In the Nyingmapa system, as elaborated in the so-called Tibetan Book of the Dead, the *Bar-do thos grol,* this Bardo of the Base, the experience of the state of Shunyata, is incorporated in the Chikhai Bardo, before the dawning of the Clear Light.

At the time of death, when the mind disintegrates and dissolves into the vast empty space of the Nature of Mind, the deceased finds oneself in a vast space without limits or boundaries, that is to say, the infinite space of the state of Shunyata. One may remain in this state of Shunyata for three to seven days. However, the yogi, because one has experienced this state in meditation practice previously, recognizes it and often remains in for seven days. Because it did not liberate, the Son Clear Light dissolves into the Mother Clear Light, which is the Kunzhi, and falls unconscious.

Here the exiting of the Namshe from the material body is described in terms of the Thodgal practitioner. From the Tsita, the hollow space in the heart where the Rigpa normally resides, it overflows via the Kati channel, which divided in two in the brain, and comes to the lamp of the eyes. With males it is expelled from the right eyeball and with females from the left eyeball due to the polarity of energies in male and female bodies. It temporarily lodges in the spot between the eyebrows on the forehead, the site of the so-called third eye, in the urna (mdzod-spu), classically being a circle of hair between the eyebrows in the middle of the forehead, one of the particular marks of a Buddha, from which he sends out rays of light. The urna then fades. After exiting the body, the Namshe awakens to find itself in the Bardo, and creates for itself a mind-made body (yid-lus). Due to memories and past karma, this subtle body perfectly resembles the body one had when one died, including the very clothes one was wearing. The Namshe in this subtle body remains in the vicinity of its dead body for three and a half days, for which reason Tibetans do not dispose of the corpse until the fourth day. This Bardo is known as the Bardo of the Clear Light of Reality (Bon-nyid 'od-gsal gyi bar-do) and within it visions arise, beginning with the sounds, lights, and rays. In the Nyingmapa tradition this experience is known as the Bardo of Reality (chos-nyid bar-do).

At first the visions that arise, representing impure karmic visions, are the scenes surrounding one's corpse and the life one has just left behind. But gradually one becomes distracted and wanders off into the landscapes of the mind. At first these visions are personal in nature, like the dreams occurring to the individual every night, but gradually they become more collective, although culturally conditioned, and from time to the time the visions of the Peaceful and Wrathful Deities arise to the individual, being somewhat similar to those described in the famous Tibetan Book of the Dead. But these deities will not appear as precisely described, unless one has done the Zhithro (Zhi-khro) meditations while still alive. At this time one is advised to regard all these visions as self-manifestations and as illusions created by one's own mind. One is told to recollect one's Lama and recall his instructions.

The next section deals with the Bardo of Rebirth (srid-pa'i bar-do). The term *srid-pa* (Skt. bhava) means in general "existence," but also coming into existence, therefore, in this context "rebirth." Again because of memories and karma, the deceased in a subtle body may frequent scenes from one's previous life. In one's mind-made body, one can move about instantly with the speed and power of thought. However, it cannot re-enter its previous body. It can, however, see Bardo beings of the same class, but such encounters are fleeting. One can even become a ghost (gshin) haunting its old residence and become irritated when the family does not provide a place at the table for it at meal times. Such restless ghosts, or poltergeists, need to be subdued and exorcised by a Lama with a Dur ceremony.

At this time one should become aware that one is in the Bardo and wandering about aimlessly like in a dreams. One should remember the instructions of the Lama and engage in the Yidam, or meditation deity practice, one has learned. Depending on the wealth and resources of the family of the deceased, the Lamas will conduct puja ceremonies from time time during seven weeks, the symbolic duration of the Bardo experience. These ceremonies are accompanied by the reading aloud of *Bar-do thos-grol* texts, "liberation through hearing while in the Bardo," describing to the deceased consciousness what one is experiencing and giving instructions for remedial practices. It is believed that from time to time, the deceased consciousness can see and hear these rituals. But generally, the Namshe of the deceased is driven relentlessly onward through strange and bizarre landscapes by the winds of karma, as if being caught in a great storm, and one begins assuming the type of body one will have in one's future rebirth. One also comes possess the five clairvoyant powers and the six recollections.

Finally, the process of liberation (grol-tshul) from Samsara is contrasted with the process of entering again into the delusions of Samsara ('khrul-tshul) by following, not the Clear Light, but the pathways of dull lights leading to rebirth in the six destinies of rebirth.

Outline for the Explanation of the Conduct:

Here is contained the Guiding Explanation of the Conduct for the Forceful Purification of the Secondary Conditions that arise along the Path [rkyen lam du slong-ba rtsal sbyong spyod-pa'i khrid bzhugs-so].

I.   Forceful purification (in meditation practice) during this present lifetime [tshe 'dir rtsal sbyong-ba],

II. Forceful purification during the process of dying ['chi-khar rtsal sbyong-ba], and

III. Forceful purification at the time of the Bardo. [bar-dor rtsal sbyong-ba].

In detail,

I.   Forceful purification (in meditation practice) during this present lifetime [tshe 'dir rtsal sbyong-ba]:

A.   Carrying on along the path of the three gates [sgo gsum lam du khyer-ba],

B.   Carrying on along the path of the six consciousness aggregates [tshogs drug lam du khyer-ba],

C.   Carrying on along the path of the masses of thoughts [rtog tshogs lam du khyer-ba], and

D.   Carrying on along the path of diversity [sna-tshogs lam du khyer-ba]:

     (1) The private conduct [gsang-ba'i spyod];

(2) The conduct consisting of ascetic practices that are secret [gsang-ba brtul-shugs kyi spyod-pa]; and

(3) Conduct that is completely victorious and without partialities [phyogs-med rgyal.ba'i spyod-pa].

II. Forceful purification during the process of dying ['chi-khar rtsal sbyong-ba]:

A. The practice relating to the disintegration of the elements and their being reabsorbed ['byung-ba 'jig dang bstun la nyams su blangs-pa],

B. The practice relating to their ingathering and being reabsorbed, [bsdus-pa dang bstun la nyams su blangs-pa],

C. Expounding the instructions of the special essential point. [khyad-par gnad kyi gdams-pa gdab-pa]

III. Forceful purification at the time of the Bardo. [bar-dor rtsal sbyong-ba]:

A. The Bardo of the Base that abides [gnas-pa gzhi'i bar-do]

B. The Bardo of the Clear Light of Reality [bon-nyid 'od-gsal gyi bar-do]:

(1) The recognition of it [ngos bzung-ba] and

(2) The Cutting off of this Bardo [bar-do bcad-pa]

C. The Bardo of Rebirth, which is empty [stong-pa srid-pa'i bar-do]:

(1) The manner in which it arises at the beginning [dang-po 'char tshul],

(2) The method for cutting it off [bcad tshul], and

(3) Then, the methods of liberation [grol tshul]:

(3)a. The method of liberation for the practitioner of superior capacity [rab gyi grol tshul],

(3)b. The method of liberation for the practitioner of intermediate capacity ['bring-po'i grol tshul],

(3)c. The method of liberation for the practitioner of inferior capacity [tha-ma'i grol tshul].

(4) The method of delusion for some individuals ['khrul tshul].

The Explanation of the Fruit

The fourth supplemental text deals with the question of the Fruit or final result of the practices of the Path, that is to say, the realization of the Trikaya, or Three Bodies of the Buddha. Again, there are three sections:

1. The direct introduction by way of linking together examples with the real meaning,
2. The direct introduction to Energy being self-manifested, and
3. The direct introduction to the Trikaya as being the Fruit.

In the first section, six examples are given to illustrate the qualities of the Nature of Mind with their various meanings being explained, namely, the butter lamp, the lotus, the sun, the mirror, the crystal ball, and the empty sky. Some of these objects would be held up or pointed out by the Lama during the direct introduction. Here the direct introduction is considered in terms of the example (dpe), the actual meaning (don), and what is indicated (rtags). Sometimes this process is known as a Rigpai Tsalwang (rig-pa'i rtsal dbang), "the empowerment which directly introduces the energy of awareness."

According to the second section, the energy (rtsal), of the Nature of Mind being spontaneous and self-arising, there are various self-manifestations of this. It may be illustrated by way of four examples: the water, the crystal, the sun, and the butter lamp. Moreover, one is directly introduced by way of the inherent lights (rang 'od) emanating from the Nature of Mind, which has its own inner light of awareness. Thodgal visions may be illustrated by rainbows, reflected images in a mirror, and reflections on water. As an exercise, one is advised to press gently on the closed lids of the eyeballs with one's fingers. One will see lights that do not originate from outside. The second exercise entails holding the breath and the third exercise is the practice of sky meditation as described above.

As for the direct introduction by way of inherent sounds (rang sgra), as an exercise, one goes into a cave or a steep ravine and shouts loudly. Thus, one hears the echoes. In the second exercise, one plays cymbals loudly for a few moments, then dropping them, one puts one's fingers in one's ears and hears sounds that do not come from outside. As a third exercise, one puts a conch shell to one's ear and hears the distant sounds of the winds and the sea.

The third section is concerned with the direct introduction to the Trikaya. The Dzogchen tradition distinguishes among three meanings to the term Trikaya. The first is the Trikaya of the Base, which is inherent in every sentient being, but which goes unrecognized because in each lifetime in Samsara, it is covered up by obscurations that are both emotional and intellectual. This Base Trikaya consists of the Essence (otherwise known as the Mother Kunzhi and the state of Shunyata), which is the Dharmakaya, the Nature, (otherwise known as the Son Rigpa or luminous clarity), which is the Sambhogakaya, and Energy, the visible manifestations of which are unceasing, which is the Nirmanakaya. This Base Trikaya is the potential for Buddhahood latent within each sentient being, but at this time is it not manifest. With the Trikaya of the Path, gradually by way of purification practices, the Trikaya is revealed within one's immediate experience in life, like the clear blue sky and the face of the sun being revealed when the clouds part. The Trikaya of the Fruit is the attainment of the manifest enlightenment of a Buddha.

The Dharmakaya is inherent in the core of every sentient being like a spark of celestial light, but it has gone unrecognized for countless lifetimes in Samsara. Moreover, according to the special teaching of Thodgal, this divine spark of light, which is Rigpa, or intrinsic awareness, is principally located in the hollow space in the heart (tsita) as an immeasurable celestial palace that abides in the highest plane of existence, Akanishtha. At the time of death, when awareness is freed from the limiting restraints of the material body, its inherent energy manifests as sounds, lights, and rays, Whereupon everything found in Samsara and Nirvana derives from this single source, which is the Sambhogakaya. However, because of ignorance and delusion, and because one does not recognize these visions as self-manifestations, the five lights evolve into the physical elements and into the destinies of rebirth.

In the heart while one is alive, the Dharmakaya abides in its own form as light, but in the practice of Thodgal, the inherent energy of Rigpa overflows and moves along the pathway of the translucent Kati channel that links the heart and the eyeballs. This is the Sambhogakaya. Arriving at the doorway of the eyes, this light projects visible appearances into the space in front of the eyes. These phenomena represent the Nirmanakaya, appearing as various Kulas, or families of divine forms, in mandala patterns. This process occurs not only in Thodgasl vision practice, but also after death in what is known as the Bardo of the Clear Light of Reality.

According to the traditions of the Bonpo Books of the Dead (zhi khro skor), the five Dhyani Buddhas (de-gshegs lnga), or the Lords of the Five Families (rgyal-ba rigs lnga), arise successively to the consciousness of the deceased on the first five days of the experience of the Bardo of the Clear Light of Reality.

On the first day, from the clear yellow light arising in the eastern direction, appears the Buddha Salwa Rangjyung (gsal-ba rang-byung), the Deity of the Body , whose body colour is yellow and who is seated on the elephant throne, holding the swastika scepter (chags-shing). He is the progenitor of the Swastika Family and his pure dimension is the Swastika Realm . He embodies the Mirror-like Gnosis (me-long ye-shes) and thereby he purifies the negative defiling emotion of confusion. By his power of great intelligence (ye-shes chen-po), he closes the door to rebirth in the animal world. He confers empowerment in the vast expanse of the earth element and his consort is the earth goddess, Sayi Lhamo (yum sa yi lha-mo). He governs the internal organ of the spleen. He and his consort abide in the navel chakra as the two yellow syllables OM KHAM on a yellow lotus of four petals. His wrathful aspect is Yungdrung Throsay (g.yung-drung khro-gsas).

On the second day, from the clear green light arising in the northern direction, appears the Buddha Gewa Garchyug (dge-ba gar-phyug), the Deity of Quality, whose body colour is green and who is seated on the horse throne, holding the wheel ('khor-lo). He is the progenitor of the Chakra Family and his pure dimension is the Chakra Realm. He embodies the Gnosis of Sameness (mnyam-nyid ye-shes) and thereby he purifies the negative defiling emotion of pride. By his power, he closes the door to rebirth in the Asura world. He confers empowerment in the vast expanse of the air element and his consort is the air goddess, Lunggi Lhamo (yum rlung gi lha-mo). He governs the internal organ of the lungs. He and his consort abide in the throat chakra as the two green syllables DZA YAM on a green wheel of four spokes. His wrathful aspect is Throwo Ngamsay (khro-bo rngam-gsas).

On the third day, from the red light arising in the western direction (nub phyogs), appears the Buddha Jyedrag Ngomed (bye-brag dngos-med), the Deity of Speech (gsung gi lha), whose body colour is red and who is seated on the dragon throne ('brug gi khri), holding the lotus (padma). He is the progenitor of the Padma Family (pad-ma'i rigs) and his pure dimension is the Padma Realm (pad-ma zhing-khams). He embodies the Gnosis of Discrimination (sor-rtog ye-shes) and thereby he purifies the negative defiling emotion (klesha) of desire ('dod-chags). By his power, he closes the door to rebirth in the Preta world (yi-dwags). He confers empowerment in the vast expanse of the fire element ('byung me'i klong) and his consort is the fire goddess, Meyi Lhamo (yum me yi lha-mo). He governs the internal organ of the liver. He and his consort abide in the heart chakra as the two red syllables OM RAM on a red lotus of four petals. His wrathful aspect is Throwo Walsay.

On the fourth day, from the clear blue light arising in the southern direction, appears the Buddha Gawa Dondrub (dga'-ba don-drub), the Deity of Action, whose body colour is blue and who is seated on the garuda throne, holding the precious jewel (rin-chen). He is the progenitor of the Ratna Family and his pure dimension is the Ratna Realm. He embodies the Gnosis that is All-Accomplishing (bya-drub ye-shes) and thereby he purifies the negative defiling emotion of jealousy. By his power, he closes the door to rebirth in the human world among the Tirthikas. He confers empowerment in the vast expanse of the water element and his consort is the water goddess, Chuyi Lhamo (yum chu yi lha-mo). He governs the internal organ of the kidneys. He and his consort abide in the secret place (genitals) as the two blue syllables HUM MAM on a blue lotus of three petals.

On the fifth day, from the clear white light arising in the central direction, appears the Buddha Kunnang Khyabpa (kun-snang khyab-pa), the Deity of Mind, whose body colour is white and who is seated on the lion throne, holding the auspicious knot (dpal gyi be'u), or in some texts a wheel. He is the progenitor of the Tathagata Family and his pure dimension is the Tathagata Realm. He embodies the Gnosis of Emptiness (stong-nyid ye-shes) and thereby he purifies the negative defiling emotion of anger. By his power of great love (byams-pa chen-po), he closes the door to rebirth in the hot and cold hells. He confers empowerment in the vast expanse of the space element and his consort is the space goddess Namkhai Lhamo (yum nam-mkha'i lha-mo). He governs the internal organ of the heart. He and his consort abide in the crown chakra as the two dark blue syllables E A on a white lotus of four petals. His wrathful aspect is Throgyal Tsochog Khagying (khro-rgyal gtso-mchog mkha'-'gying).

These divine figures represent the inner aspect (nang ltar) where the Five Dhyani Buddhas signify the five skandhas, the Five Gnoses or Wisdoms, and so. The five outer aspects (phyi ltar) are Godse (rgod-gsas), Garse (gar-gsas), Seje (gsas-rje), Namse (gnam-gsas), and (shen-lha). Finally, there appears the secret aspect (gsang-ba ltar), namely the wrathful deities Trose (khro-gsas), Ngamse (rngam-gsas), Walse (dbal-gsas), Tumse (gtum-gsas) and Tsochok (gtso-mchog). These groups represent different aspects of the same deities. There also appear the mandalas of the eight male Bodhisattvas (ye-gshen brgyad) and the eight female Bodhisattvas ye-sangs brgyad) who represnt the eight aggregates of consciosness and the eight objects of consciousness.

There also appear the six Dulshen ('dul gshen drug) are the six sages, emanations of Tonpa Shenrab, who appear in the six realms, or destinies of rebirth, to counteract the respective causes for rebirth in these realms and to lead beings to liberation. Sangwa Ngagring (gsang-ba ngang-ring) purifies anger and liberates beings from the hot and cold hells. Mucho Demdruk (mu-cho ldem-drug) who purifies desire and liberates beings from the Preta realm. In some lists, these two are reversed. Tisang Rangzhi (ti-sangs rang-zhi) purifies confusion and liberates beings from animal existence. Sangwa Dupa (gsang-ba 'dus-pa) purifies jealousy and liberates beings from human rebirth among the Tirthikas, or non-religious nations. Chegyal Parti (che-rgyal par-ri) purifies pride and liberates beings from rebirth in the Asura realm. And finally, Yeshen Tsugphud (ye-gshen gtsug-phud) purifies sloth and all the passions together and liberates beings from rebirth in the Deva realms. These six correspond to the six Munis in the Buddhist system.

This makes a total of forty-five Peaceful Deities and eighty-six Wrathful Deities. In addition there is an outer aspect consisting of one hundred and eight Prosperity Deities. In total, they all represent an interlaced network of illusions (sgyu-'phrul drwa-ba) and their iconography is drawn from the Tantra known as the *Khro-bo dbang-chen*. Thus, these *Zhi-khro lha tshogs*, or hosts of Peaceful and Wrathful Deities, are similar to the Nyingmapa system found in the Guhyagarbha Tantra. The yab-yum images represent the unity of skilful means and discriminating wisdom, as well as clarity and emptiness.

It is a single non-dual self-originated primordial awareness (rang-byung ye-shes) that gives rise to the five primal cognitions, that of Shunyata (stong-nyid ye-shes), equality (mnyam-nyid ye-shes), all-accomplishing (bya-grub ye-shes), discriminating (sor-rtog ye-shes), and mirror like (me-long ltar ye-shes). This single primordial awareness represents the Ultimate Truth and the Knowledge of Quality and the five primal cognitions represent the Relative Truth and the Knowledge of Quantity, and in tern, they give birth to eighty-four thousand primal cognitions, which is how enlightened beings know things.

Having attained enlightenment, then the individual engages in enlightened activities in order to liberate sentient beings from their suffering in Samsara, and these represent skilful means, great compassion, and omniscience. One employs many different methods in order to subdue sentient beings who are difficult to subdue, and thereby lead them on to the path to liberation and enlightenment. These methods are in accordance with the intelligence, temperament, and level of development of each sentient being.

Finally, there are considered what are the qualities of the disciple and to whom to grant the precepts of Dzogchen. Also considered are the non-virtuous qualities of those individuals to whom one should not grant the teachings.

Outline to the Translation of the Explanation of the Fruit

Here is contained the Guiding Explanation for coming to an intensely Clear and Definitive Decision regarding the Trikaya, where one remains in one's own Original Condition, which represents the Fruit.

['bras-bu rang sa bzung-ba sku-gsum dmar thag-bcad-pa'i khrid bzhugs-so]

I.   The direct introduction where the example and the real meaning are linked together, [dpe don 'brel-ba'i ngo-sprod],
II. The direct introduction to Energy as being self-manifestation [rang-snang rtsal gyi ngo-sprod-pa], and
III. The direct introduction to the Trikaya that represents the Fruit ['bras-bu sku-gsum gyi ngo-sprod-pa].

In detail:

I. The direct introduction where the example and the real meaning are linked together, [dpe don 'brel-ba'i ngo-sprod], by way of the six examples, namely, the butter lamp, the lotus, the sun, the mirror, the crystal ball, and the sky [dpe drug: mar-me pad-ma nyi-ma me-long shel-sgong nam-mkha']:

A. The meaning of the example is illustrated by means of the lamp of illustrative examples [mtshon dpe'i sgron-mas dpe'i don mtshon-pa], and

B. One is directly introduced to the sign, or indication, by means of the lamp of the sign indicating primal awareness (ye-shes), [ye-shes rtags kyi sgron-mas rtags thog tu ngo-sprad-pa]

C. Whereupon these two (the Natural State and primal awareness) should be linked together and unified [gnyis zung 'brel du bya].

II. The direct introduction to Energy as being self-manifestation [rang-snang rtsal gyi ngo-sprod-pa]:

A. The direct introduction (to visions) as being self-arising [rang shar du ngo-sprad-pa]

B. The direct introduction (to visions) being self-manifestations [rang-snang dun go-sprad-pa]

  B1. The direct introduction where the lights are like the inherent lights of the rainbow ['od rang 'od gzha'-tshon ltar ngo-sprad-pa]

  B2. The direct introduction where the rays (or images) are like the inherent rays that are the reflected images (in the mirror) [zer rang zer gzugs-brnyan ltar ngo-sprad-pa]: The method for directly introducing both the lights and the rays at the same time ['od dang zer dus gcig la ngo-sprad tshul]:

  a. Externally, in terms of the Lamp of Existence, one presses against (the neck) and presses down (on the eyeballs) [phyi srid-pa'i sgron-ma brtod la mnan-pa],

  b. Internally, in terms of the Lamp of the Sense Faculties (that is, the eyes), one gazes fixedly into space [nang dbang-po'i sgron-ma ar la gtad-pa], and

  c. Secretly, in terms of the Lamp of Awareness, one lets it abide and leaves alone everything (the visions that arise) and thereby one is directly introduced [rig-pa'i sgron-ma gnas la bor-ba ngo-sprad-pa].

B3. The direct introduction where the sounds are like the inherent sounds of the echoes [sgra rang sgrar brag-cha ltar ngo-sprad-pa]:

a. Externally, one is directly introduced to the self-returning of the empty sounds [phyi stong sgra rang log la ngo-sprad-pa],

b. Internally, one is directly introduced to the secondary conditions that are due to other (extrinsic causes) by way of symbolic methods [nang brda thabs gzhan rkyen la ngo-sprad-pa], and

c. Secretly, one is directly introduced to inherent sounds as self-awareness. [gsang-ba rang-rig rang sgra la ngo-sprad-pa].

III. The direct introduction to the Trikaya that represents the Fruit ['bras-bu sku-gsum gyi ngo-sprod-pa]:

A. The direct introduction to Buddhahood in its own form [sangs-rgyas rang chas su ngo-sprad-pa]

B. The manner of the arising of the divine forms and of primal awareness [lha sku ye-shes kyi 'char tshul]

B1. The manner in which the Bodies or divine forms arise [sku yi 'char tshul]

a. The base for their arising ['char gzhi] and

b. The manner in which they arise ['char tshul].

B2. The method for knowing them by means of primal cognitions [ye-shes kyi(s) mkhyen tshul].

B3. The method for accomplishing deeds by means of enlightened activities [phrin-las kyi(s) mdzad tshul]:

a. The actuality itself [dngos] and

b. The method for accomplishing it [mdzad tshul].

C. The additional teaching on the methods for establishing a suitable arrangement [btang bzhag gi tshul bstan-pa/ btang bzhag zur gyis bstan-pa]:

The successive stages for establishing a suitable arrangement for the granting of permission and the issuing of the the commandments– [btang-bzhag rjes-gnang bka' rgya'i rim-pa]

C1. The granting of permission [rjes su gnang-ba] and

C2. The issuing of the command [bka' rgya gdab-pa].

Chapter Three

The Principal Practice:
dngos-gzhi

Here is contained "The Practice Manual for the Stages of the Explanation (of the Principal Practices) of the Oral Transmission from Zhang-zhung" (Zhang-zhung snyan-rgyud kyi khrid rim lag-len bzhugs-so).

Homage to Kuntu Zangpo who, becoming manifest as Self-Awareness, is the all-pervading and all-encompassing Guide to living beings! [1]

VOLUME TWO

Second, with regard to the stages of the principal practices (dngos-gzhi) that bring about the ripening and the liberation of one's stream of consciousness in between (the Base and the Fruit, that is to say, as the Path), there are three parts:

1. In the beginning (of the path), when one has not (previously) fixated the mind, one now fixates the mind,
2. In the middle (of the path), when mindfulness is not abiding (or stable), one employs (various methods) to bring about its abiding (thereby stabilizing it), and

3. And finally (toward the conclusion of the path), when Self-Awareness is not clear, one employs (various methods) in order to make it clear. [2]

PART ONE: Fixating the Mind

With respect to the first part, it says according to the *sGron-ma*, "As for the thought which is to be remembered, one should fixate on the light." [3]

And again, as it says in the *mThing-shog*, "There exists the clear explanation of Samsara as being a mansion of light." [4]

Because it is stated thus, then with respect to this, there exist three considerations:

1. The essential point of the body,
2. The essential point of the gaze, and
3. The essential point of the training. [5]

A. The Position of the Body

With reference to the first consideration, it is said, "The prana is controlled by means of the five mudras of the body." (These five mudras, or positions, are as follows:)

1. One assumes a cross-legged sitting position in order to control the vital winds and psychic channels which are below;
2. One keeps the spine straight in order to control the bones of the spine and the internal organs;
3. One assumes the samadhi-mudra, or gesture of equipoise, (with the hands) in order to control the essential point of the samskaras (the emotions and impulses);
4. One bends the neck (a little) in order to subdue the exertion of speaking and talking;
5. And one gazes fixedly (straight ahead) in order to discard and renounce (the dichotomy of) subject and object. [6]

Furthermore, the left hand is placed on top and the right hand is suppressed below and the thumbs press down on the fleshly parts of the palm just below the ring finger. This is the essential point (in order to close the klesha-nadi, or channel of impurities that runs through that spot). At that time, one tames the confusion (of the mind) by systematically controlling the parts of the body, such as the four channels and the four muscle ridges of the body. [7]

B. The Position of the Gaze

With respect to the second consideration, at a location in the space in front of oneself, neither too close nor too distant, surrounded appropriately by a circle of light (of the rainbow colors of the elements), the Rigpa, or intrinsic awareness, is harmonized (or integrated) with the eyes (as the white Tibetan letter A). One does not look upwards nor downwards, nor to the right nor to the left, but one focuses only on this shape in front. One focuses intently like making a small hole, or like inserting a thread into the eye of the needle, or like shooting an arrow at a target. One remains present without making any changes (in the position of) the body, without making any efforts to speak with the voice, and without any thinking about the past or speculating about the future with one's mind. In a natural manner, in its own terms, one fixates one-pointedly (on the white letter A) strongly, intensely, clearly, and lucidly. [8]

C. Training in the Fixating of the Mind

With regard to the third consideration, whatever may occur at that time, such as water in the mouth (saliva) or water in the nose (mucus), one should just let it by itself. One should control the body and the mind and not neglect these essential points. [9]

As for the full measure of the meditation session (thun tshad): With respect to the previous session, one should light an incense stick (and observe the time it takes) to recite the mantra (sa le 'od) some two hundred times. Then in the next session, let it burn for an additional time such as some three hundred recitations, and so on. [10]

Again, in the morning and in the afternoon, one looks at the Buddhas and sentient beings, the good and the bad, existence and non-existence, and because one meditates that everything in this cycle (of Samsara and Nirvana) is (just mind), one sits looking at it (the mind) in order to see what it is like and to recognize its characteristics, that is to say, what are its causes and conditions, its essence, its shape and form, its color, and so on. Again and again one trains in looking (at the mind in this way). [11]

Again, one sits searching at the beginning for the location where (a thought) originates, in the middle for the location where it abides, and, at the end, the location where it goes. [12]

Again, do they (thoughts) originate outside (the body) or is their cause inside the body? One sits there searching (for the mind and thoughts) from the big toes (of the feet) to the crown of the head, moving from the lower extremities of the soles of the feet upward (though the body). One should thoroughly examine whatever is faulty or virtuous. By being (mindful) and well aware, one cuts off the root (of the negative emotions). [13]

And similarly, when one has an experience, whereupon the memories that cause movement having occurred in a state of quiescence and rest, the individual of superior capacity, who is totally without grasping, becomes like a tortoise put into a wide bowl. He becomes intrepid and not afraid of anything. For the individual of intermediate capacity, it is like drawing water through an iron tube where everything is clearly distinct and unmoving without distractions. Whereas for the individual of inferior capacity, it is like a bee sucking nectar from a fruit flower. Thus, there comes forth only a small change in one's disposition. These individuals settle into a quiescent (and relaxed) state and the signs of (success in) fixation practice become complete. This occurs without characteristics and one remains (continuing) in meditation. [14]

Moreover, with regard to that, if the signs of fixation are not complete, one should fixate Rigpa, or intrinsic awareness, on the sky, focusing it intensely in front of oneself. And it is also explained that it is proper to utter any neutral sounds, such as HUM and HRI. [15]

Then also, in terms of the inner difficulties, because one exerts oneself (strenuously) in activities that are fatiguing, there exist explanations of how to induce fatigue deliberately with certain exercises and how to cure fatigue that are in agreement with this. [16]

Furthermore, as the support of the visualization, one may fixate on such objects as a mirror or the ushnisha (the protuberance on the crown of the head) of a divine form. In this way, there will come forth, as there did previously, the signs of fixation (zin rtags), the signs for the greater part (of the phenomena of) fire and wind. Following that, they will go into cessation and then there will come other signs of fixation, for the greater part those of water and wind. Thereafter, these phenomena will become as friends (and helpers for one's practice).

However, if the previous explanation does not strike one, it is easy to explain this auspicious conjunction of events (rten 'brel) by symbolic means. But in terms of various different kinds of indifference, it is difficult to counter them by bad habits. [17]

However, if one has a master who possesses the nectar (of enlightened awareness), it will not be possible that one does not arrive there. Because one forcefully fixates on the King who is Self-Awareness, the armies of memories and the contents of consciousness will only occur in a discontinuous fashion and these hosts of thoughts, accompanied by the wild dogs of delusion, will be obstructed. [18]

According to the *sPyi rgyud*, it is said, "By forcefully fixating on the king, the armies (of thoughts) and the wild dogs of the kleshas, or negative emotions, will be fettered and tamed." [19] Again, according to the *Lung drug*, "In terms of the armies of characteristics, if one fixates the mind, discursive thoughts will become more and more pacified and it produces a primal awareness (or gnosis) that is more and more clear."[20] So it says.

This represents the guiding instructions for fixating the mind in terms of characteristics (that is, in terms of fixating on visible objects and on visualizations, in particular, on the white Tibetan letter A). [21]

PART TWO: The Practice for the Dark Retreat

Second, in terms of making mindfulness abide with stability when it has not yet abided with stability: The site for meditation practice (sgom-pa'i gnas) should be some place that possesses the nature of total darkness, such as an excavation in the ground, a cave in the rocks, or a thatched hut. Moreover, the roof should be high and the interior spacious. The surfaces (of the walls) should be well made and the outside holes for light are sealed. Because the doorway to this spacious interior is constructed in three staggered stages, the interior is completely cut off (from any outside sources of light). One can thus remain there, sitting comfortably, without any interference from openings for the appearing of visible light (penetrating from outside). [22]

Then, in terms of the method of practice, there are three considerations:

1. Practicing meditation in whatever way,
2. The training in that, and
3. The modes for the arising (of visions in the total darkness) to the mind-stream (of the individual in retreat) [23]

A. The Meditation Practice

First, according to the *gZer-bu*, it is said, "One renounces all activities that are distracting by means of the three bindings, whereupon the mind settles into a relaxed quiescence by way of the three relaxations." Thus, there are three further considerations:

1. Having bound or controlled the activities of the body, one relaxes without engaging in any actions,
2. Having bound or controlled the activities of the speech of the voice, one relaxes without speaking or expressing oneself, and
3. Having bound or controlled the memories and thoughts in the mind, one relaxes, transcending all thinking and thereby one produces a samadhi or state of contemplation that is devoid of thoughts. [24]

A1. The Essential Point of the Body

With reference to the first consideration (that of the body), it is said (that at the beginning when entering into the dark retreat, one should think as follows:) "We have taken on a physical body whenever it was possible, from all previous lifetimes until the present. But all of these courses of conduct (in our past lifetimes), committing all actions both pure and impure, whatever was possible, has been without any purpose (up until now). And in the making all of these efforts, we have only come to suffering. And because of delusion and circulating in Samsara, our awareness has been like a blind man. Our actions of body have continued to commit the three non-virtues (of killing, stealing, and raping). Or we fall into neutral activities like just living, engaging in commerce, hanging out in the market, just running around, pursuing fancy clothes and manufactured articles, and so on. Or else, we postpone matters, striving after virtuous actions, such as making prostrations and circumambulations, mudras and yantra movements, and so on. Yet, at sometime or another, relaxing without any activity whatsoever, we come to establish ourselves in the cure for this weariness (which is Samsara). But if we do not do like that, we disturb our psychic channels with various kinds of activities (even though they be virtuous actions). And because of that, the vital winds are disturbed. And because of that, the mind becomes disturbed and consequently we do not remain in the producing of a samadhi or contemplation that is without thoughts. But because we relax in this way the psychic channels are tamed, the vital winds are controlled, and Awareness having settled into its own original condition, thereupon a condition of no thought occurs and this is the essential point." [25]

"Then, with reference to the special essential point of the body, one binds and controls the vital energies of the body by means of the five mudras." That is to say, the legs are crossed (while sitting), the hands are held in equipoise position, or samadhi-mudra, the spinal column is held straight, the neck is bent just a little, and the eyes gaze straight ahead. [26]

A2. The Essential Point of Speech

With respect to the second consideration (that of speech), it is said, "From our previous lifetimes until the present, these masses of expressions by means of speech, all of these expressions whatever they may be in essence, whether good, bad, or indifferent, were without any purpose and the making of exertions only serves to bring about the cause of (further) suffering. (Therefore) from today forward, impurities such as the four non-virtues of speech (namely, lying slandering, speaking harshly, and gossiping maliciously), or just neutral (verbal) activities such as gossiping idly, telling jokes, laughing, story telling, shouting, and so on, are renounced. [27] And even virtuous actions such as reciting mantras, the reading aloud of the scriptures, singing and chanting – all of these (virtuous activities) are renounced as well (in the dark retreat). We shall relax (totally) without expressions whatsoever, like a man who is completely dumb, and settle down into curing (and alleviating) our fatigue."

Because one simply remains like that, without even moving the breath to produce words and expressions, one does not shake (or vibrate) the psychic channels. The mind being left undisturbed, one is able to produce a samadhi or contemplation that is devoid of thoughts. [28]

A3. The Essential Point of the Mind

With respect to the third consideration (that of the mind), it is said, "From all our previous lifetimes until the present, however many thoughts and memories were thought by the functional mind – all of these thoughts were without purpose and the engaging in efforts (based on them) has only led to further suffering. Because we circulate in the delusions of Samsara, therefore, from today onwards we should renounce engaging in the three non-virtues of mind (covetous thoughts, malicious thoughts, and wrong views) and the five poisons, as well as neutral states of mind, and, of course, the fixations done previously, the making of divisions (among things), all analyzing, discrimination, reflecting, and thinking that represent natural processes, even though these may be good (and positive) thoughts, such as meditating on deities, emanating and re-absorbing letters and syllables, engaging in samadhi or contemplation with characteristics (or visualizations), and so on – all of these (mental activities) only postpone the matter. Rather, each of these (mental activities), without any desires or wants, any hopes or expectations, any fears or anxieties, or any yearning or longing, should be relaxed into the vast expanse of the Basis of Everything (the Kunzhi, or state of Shunyata), which transcends (all further) thoughts, cognitions, and memories, and then settles into alleviating (or curing) all fatigue (incurred from Samsaric or cyclical existence." [29]

When one proceeds in that way, there will be no more movements of the functional mind (who is like a man) riding on the horse of the vital winds along the pathways of the psychic channels. And consequently, there will not be brought about any obstructions to the producing of a samadhi that is without thoughts. Therefore, without changing or modifying anything directly in terms of its original condition without lying down and restlessly turning to the left and the right, suddenly and without reason, one finds oneself in a sparkling and lucid state that is without any foundation and free of any root. [30]

One does not pursue those traces which are past nor go to meet in front that which is the future. Within the vast expanse of the totally all-pervading and all-embracing Kunzhi, the Rigpa, being without any movement or agitation, without any dress or artifice, fresh in its own original condition without any root (free of any source), simply remains in its own system of existence. [31]

B. Training in the Practice of the Dark Retreat

With respect to the second consideration (how one is to train in that), at the time of being a beginner, if one makes long sessions (of meditation practice), there may come (problems, such as) drowsiness, agitation, and dullness. [32] But if they (the sessions of practice) are too short, then experiences and understanding will not be produced.

From each cycle or series of the burning of a lighted incense stick, on each day, one lengthens the time with incremental additions and in between the meditation sessions, one may move to and fro in terms of the essential points of compassion and devotion. But one should not eat foods that are impure, nor foods which are unbalanced in their elements, such as garlic, onions, spices (sngo rngad), and so on. In general, one should balance one's food and clothing (according to local conditions). One should not stay in the sun nor by a fire. One should not move between the outdoors and the indoors. Because one's primal cognitions (ye-shes) may become obscured, at the times between any two (sessions of practice), one should take a little rest. And one should not remain (in the dark retreat) without access to a wise and learned master who is skilled in the methods that are essential (for the practice). If there should come forth any laziness or indifference, one should enumerate to oneself one's sins and faults and make entreaties again and again with fervor and with diligence (to the Gurus and the Yidams). One should cultivate an eagerness for purity and do not become timid (or faint-hearted) in the face of obscurations. [33]

C. The Arising of Visions in the Darkness

With respect to the third consideration, in the beginning there will be produced a shamatha, or abiding in a calm state (zhi-gnas), by means of the action of mind. In the middle (period during the retreat), this shamatha will just arise naturally, and toward the end, one comes to realize stability in an ultimate shamatha. [34]

According to this (text), it is said, "Having dissolved the impurities into the vast expanse of space, the purity becomes visible as light. Having depleted the sheer abundance of thoughts in the mind, then Rigpa arises nakedly. Having cleared away the masses of clouds which are thoughts, primal awareness (or gnosis) becomes uncovered and without any obscurations." [35]

Having dissolved into the Kunzhi, the thoughts and memories occurring in the mind, these masses of thoughts caused by movements and which represent the impurities, thereupon purity arises as the light of self-originated primal awareness, like water being clear when the bottom has not been stirred up. Having been freed from the superfluous abundance of subject and object, which was like heavy clothing, the primal cognitions of intrinsic Awareness (rig-pa'i ye-shes) arise nakedly like a person who is entirely devoid of all clothing. Having cleared away all thoughts and memories of things both good and bad, these (mental phenomena) being like clouds (in the sky), because one has realized the inherent color of the Kunzhi, so to speak, it (Awareness or Rigpa) arises to the mind-stream like the purity of the sky itself. [36]

Or elsewhere, a pale light may be caused inside of the dark retreat house. Or everywhere inside and outside of that (house) may become clear and lucid (to one's clairvoyant sight) without any obscurations. Or there may arise a little bit some signs of the five elements which are below (one's line of sight). And because one's awareness is dispatched everywhere (in terms of the senses), there is produced in the mind-stream a samadhi, or state of contemplation, that is without discursive thoughts. [37]

This represents the guiding explanation for the shamatha practice that is without characteristics (that is to say, without some visible object for fixation). [38]

U-YA SMAR-RO!

PART THREE: The Practices for the Empty Sky and for Sunlight

Third, within the instructions for making clear what is not yet clear, there are three major considerations:

1. The practices in general,
2. The practices in detail, and
3. Development by way of the instructions on the essential points. [39]

A. The Practice in General in terms of Higher Insight

With respect to the first major consideration, it is said, "One moves upward the great ocean and fixates it at the limit of the darkness on the iron mountain. The mind which is mindful is held fixated in terms of the lights. The functional mind which moves is tamed in terms of the sounds. And the energy of Rigpa is purified in terms of the rays." So it is said. [40]

With regard to that (Upadesha), there are three further considerations:

1. Controlling (the body, the gaze, and the mind) by way of the five essential points,
2. Observing (the practice) by means of the secondary conditions on the path of method, and
3. The modes for the arising (of visions) that depend upon the mind-stream. [41]

A1. Controlling the Body, the Gaze, and the Mind

With regard to the first consideration, the place for the meditation practice is very important. [42] Even though the interior of total visibility (which is everyday life) is illuminated by the great fire (of the sun in the sky), still one is not able to make things very clear. However, inside the interior of total darkness (the dark retreat house), one is able to make everything clearly visible with just a small butter lamp. Because one essential point of this path of method is the site itself, the method is found to be very quick. Therefore, there is not even just a little hole for illumination in the total darkness. It is very important that such a place be very isolated and separate. If these (circumstances) do not come together, then one can cover the head and the eyes as much as one can, so that there will come about a darkness by way of the method of the hands (covering the eyes).

Moreover, the essential point of the body is very important. With respect to this present emanation (or rebirth as a human being), even though it has arms and legs, if one does not control them, there will come no clarity (in the visions). Therefore, one should control the body. (And for this) one must hold fast to the four muscles (of the arms and calves), as well as the four channels. One pulls firmly on the big toes of the two feet and holds fast the calves (of the legs) at the elbows.

The legs that are held fast are pressed with the thumbs of the hands. The two corners of the elbows are stretched straight and the shoulders are hunched. The tongue is joined to the palate and one takes care that the mouth is open. And one also takes care to gather the eyebrows and make a wrathful expression with the nose. The eyeballs are turned upward and the lids of the eyes are turned down. The ears are erect and the spinal column is held straight (and perpendicular). The neck is held tight and held strictly. The left foot is placed on top. And the stomach is pulled in and pressed against the spine.

Furthermore, the gaze is very important. Even though there may exist the pathways of the psychic channels for the Rigpa, if one does not control the gaze, the virtuous qualities will not arise into visible manifestation. Therefore, in terms of the Rigpa, in the very early morning, one gazes straight ahead and fixates on the atmosphere one full cubit above the crown of one's head. Gazing straight ahead represents the gaze of the Chakravartin, or wheel-turning monarch ('khor-lo bsgyur-ba'i lta-stangs). For a little time during the middle of the morning and at night, one fixates on the atmosphere some sixteen digits beyond the eyebrows. And this is the gaze of the dignified lion (seng-ge 'gying-pa'i lta-stangs). Then, at the time of midday, one should fixate just a little in front of the eyebrows. That represents the gaze of Sangwa Dupa. or Guhyasamaja (gsang-ba 'dus-pa'i lta-stangs).

And moreover, the essential point of the mind is very important. Because everything ultimately returns into that (the Natural State of the Nature of Mind), if one does not control the Rigpa, the virtuous qualities will not come forth. Therefore, at that time, one should not think of the past and similarly not speculate about the future. All memories which are adventitious and which suddenly originate are dispatched and cut off at the root. And with regard to awareness, one cultivates a firmness (and stability). One simply remains in a condition of presence without any foundation and is free of any root. [43]

In addition, the essential point of breathing is very important. Even though one has within oneself the Clear Light of Rigpa, or intrinsic Awareness, if that is not stimulated by the vital winds which may be either pure or impure, the signs of heat will not immediately arise. Therefore, at the time when one first settles into the session (of meditation practice), one should expel the poisons of the vital winds (as exhaled breath nine times). Then one should focus awareness on the prana-vayu, or vital energy, [44] and fixate it at such (locations) as the crown of the head or between the eyebrows. The breath that is controlled (by pranayama) remains moving internally and externally in a leisurely fashion through the two nostrils. At that particular time, the breath is moving, and at the time when the vital winds of the space element move, having controlled the essential points of the body and the gaze very much, when one meditates, there will be a change and a great development and a special vital wind will gather and move though the left nostril. Because this represents a very great development, one should perform the method of the hands for moving it through the left (nostril), such as during the daytime, adopting the essential points of breathing and the yantra movements and during the nighttime (the proper) sleeping position (that is to say, the position of the sleeping lion). The reason for this emphasizing the left side is that there exists a gateway for the channel of gnosis, or primal awareness (jnana-nadi), and the flow of the discursive thoughts embodying the kleshas, or emotional defilements, are cut off. [44]

A2. Observing the Practice

With respect to the second consideration, there exists also the full measure of the session of practice (thun tshad). At the beginning one should meditate for many enumerations in terms of short sessions. And progressively, on each day one should extend them by making (the sessions) longer. And finally one settles into being established in the calm state. At that point, the yoga of the dark retreat (mun-pa'i rnal-'byor) becomes very important to the individual. Any eating or other activity becomes integrated with contemplation. But because of the diminishing of the quality of gnosis, or primal awareness (ye-shes), at the time of midday one should relax a little bit (and cease the practice). Because one is dependent upon diligence in general, one should practice without laziness or indifference.

A3. The Arising of Visions in Space

With respect to the third consideration, because one has practiced in that way, one comes to separate the impurities from the purity of Rigpa (rig-pa'i dangs snyigs phyed). Here one adheres to the essential points of the vital winds and of the mind. Because one opens the gates of the channels, there exist the causes and the conditions for the purified fire (which is total or full) and this (fire within the body) is made to fly upwards (once ignited) by the winds. This represents the inherent radiance of Rigpa that abides as the Clear Light. There exists no method (to prevent) its arising afterwards. [46]

According to the *gNad drug*, it is said, "As for the Base, this abides in the middle of the Tsita, or physical heart, and overflows along the (kati) channel as its pathway, and arises at the lamp of the water (globe like eyeball) as its gateway. In the middle of the brain, in its conch shell casing (the skull), it is called the channel of *Tsang-ri pur-lang*. From its being but a single root (when it leaves the heart), it divides above into two peaks. This hollow tube for the gateway of Rigpa is like the open mouth of a flower where its fibers are the doors of the channels. From along the hollow tube of that channel, it arises as five lights like the eye in a peacock's feather." [47] So it is said.

And according to the *sGrom-ma*, it is said, "Within this dense darkness that possesses rays, one sees a celestial palace of light that is a clearly visible appearance." [48]

Even though there may exist many modes of arising, in the beginning the modes of arising appear to be external (to the practitioner). According to the *Lha-khrid*, it is said, "When the vital wind of the earth element is inserted into the central channel, it will appear like smoke. Accordingly, the vital wind of the water element like a mirage, the vital wind of the fire element like fire-flies or like sparks thrown out from a fire, the vital wind of the air element like daybreak, and the vital wind of the space element like the rising of the sun or like the radiance of the sky. These visions may arise in actuality or just as experiences. Internally, when the vital wind of the earth element is inserted (into the central channel) awareness becomes stable and firm. Accordingly, when the vital wind of the water element is inserted, the mind becomes happy, smooth, and flexible. When the vital wind of the fire element is inserted, it is clear and emanates a little. When the vital wind of the air element is inserted, one feels high, wild, and youthful. And when the vital wind of the space element is inserted one comes to fell spacious, radiant, and clear without any obscurations."

Elsewhere also, the exterior and the interior of the room (or house used for the dark retreat) may become clear without obscurations (that is to say, one can see in the dark and see the outdoors clairvoyantly). Also, the flesh and blood and channels of one's own body may become continuously clear (that is to say, one can see continuously inside one's own body as if translucent). There may also arise visions which seem that they can be explained as daytime visions. But with regard to them, one should (continue) to practice with a mind that is happy, cheerful, and confident, or without any timidity (or faint-heartedness) at their not arising.

This represents the guiding explanation of the Clear Light in terms of higher insight. [49]

U-YA SMAR-RO!

B. The Practice of Vision with the Sky and with the Sunlight

Second, with reference to the practices in detail, there are two divisions, namely,

1. Purification practice in terms of the contemplation of the sky that is clear and visible and
2. Purification practice in terms of the contemplation of the lamp that is inherent clear luminosity. [50]

B1. Sky Practice

Within the first division, there are four considerations:

1. Practicing in any place,
2. Practicing on the occasions that are the times,
3. Practicing by whatever methods, and
4. The modes for the arising of the Clear Light as experiences and as visions [51]

B1.1. The Places for Practice

With reference to the first consideration, as for the place of practice, it should be a place where one can gaze into the great (vast open) sky, such as from the peak of a high mountain or in the middle of a wide plain, or if one is lower down, even from the roof of a house or below the projection of the roof, and so on, will do. One should prop up one's body (comfortably) so that one can just look with ease. There should be wide open spaces in the directions above and in front. But, in particular, this should be so in terms of visible light. However, one's body and one's head engages in the method where the light of the sun does not directly fall on one (that is to say, one sits in the shade).

According to the *sNyan-rgyud lha-khrid*, it is said that, "In relation to the method of gazing, one may erect a half-house shelter or a canopy (to insure shade). One should stay in a healthy and pleasant place, or else, a high mountain. One should meditate in a place where one can see (clearly) the great vast expanse of the sky. One should gaze into the east in (the late afternoon) and the evening and into the distance at twilight." So it is said.

B1.2. The Times for Practice

Second, as for the times for practicing: When there have risen the sign (of success) for the yoga of the dark retreat above, it indicates that one has realized a little stability in contemplation or samadhi. [52] One meditates from the early morning when the sky is clear until the evening when it is still unshrouded in darkness. One should only forsake the meditation practice a little at midday.

According to the *Lha-khrid*, it is said, "At the beginning of the early morning, one gazes into the clear radiance of the sky that is without clouds or hail storms. And in the (late afternoon or) evening, one gazes into the east. And at twilight, one gazes far off into the distance.

Again, according to the *mThing-shog*, it is said, "In the early morning, one gazes into the direction of the powerful Nagas (the west) and in the evening (or afternoon) one gazes into the direction of the Gandharvas (the east)." [53]

B1.3. The Method of Practice

Third, with regard to the method of meditation (sgom tshul), it is said according to the *sGron-ma*, "The mirror of the mind is everywhere clear. So it is revealed in terms of clear visions when gazing into the sky." [54]

Because it said that, one should practice by way of the five essential points, namely, the essential points of the body in terms of the posture described above. [55]

As for the gazes which represent the essential points of the senses (lta-stangs dbang-po'i gnad), it is said according to the *Lha-khrid*, "One should gaze with the gaze of the dignified lion or with the gaze of Sangwa Dupa." [56]

Even though one may perform either of these two (gazes), one should practice the integrating of the three spaces (the external, the internal, and the secret). Because there is the space of the sky that exists externally, namely, the empty atmosphere, one should fixate on just that. The hollow tube of the (kati) channel is also empty. Because this represents the internal space of the senses, one should train oneself with regard to just that. Moreover, the Nature of Mind is empty. And because it represents the secret space of the meaning and the indication, one should produce firmness (or stability in contemplation) with regard to just that. [57]

Then, with regard to the essential point of the breathing, it is the holding (of the breath). According to the *mThing-shog*, it is said, "Forsaking them is the training with regard to the subject and object, whereas holding the breath is the essential point in terms of Rigpa." So it is said. [58]

With regard to that, one should engage in the practice of the three non-enterings The prana-vayu (the vital energy in the breath) should not enter from above. Because it represents the horse of the Rigpa, while focusing one's Rigpa, one should hold the breath. Because of the effort of pranayama, it does not enter into obstruction. The breathing is in equal parts and moves inside (inhalation) and outside (exhalation) in a leisurely fashion. Thereby, (breathing naturally) the secret wind does not enter into rigidity. Particularly, at the time when the vital winds of the air element are moving, one should tame and control (the breathing) very much. [59]

This with reference to the essential point of never being separated from the samaya commitment, according to the *gZer-bu'i rtsa 'grel*, it is said, "Without blinking the eyes, one should remain staring with open eyes at the object, thereby one will recognize the Kunzhi without thoughts." [60]

Consequently, one should perform the practice of the three immobilities. When the body is immobile, the psychic channels become immobile and so one does not then engage in actions, movements, or shaking (the body). When the channels are immobile and because the eyes are also immobile, one no longer engages in shifting or moving about. When the eyes are immobile, then the mind is immobile. Therefore, one should not squint, blink, or look from side to side. Thereafter, in terms of the essential point of Rigpa, one should just be aware of whatever arises before the eyes. [61]

Then, with regard to the essential points of the three relaxations (glod-pa gsum gyi gnad), it is said according to the *gZer-bu*, "Because it says to fixate the mind by means of the three methods of just letting things be (bzhag thabs gsum), one should engage in this practice of the method of just letting things be. Because it says that one should just be fresh without doing anything artificial (or contrived), one should free oneself from thoughts and memories that grasp at things. Because it says that one should settle naturally into one's total inherent condition, one should directly settle into the relaxation that represents the condition of existence of the Kunzhi. Because it says that one should settle down into a natural condition without modifications or adulterations, one should not revert to attempting to rectify things or put them in order (artificially). [62]

B1.4. The Arising of Phenomena

Fourth, with regard to the modes of arising ('char tshul) (of the visions), as it says in the *sGron-ma*, "In the (total) darkness one will see visions possessing light. One will see magical apparitions of networks of rays which are similar to cobwebs or threads." These (phenomena) represent the inherent radiance of one's own internal Rigpa or intrinsic awareness overflowing along the pathways of the psychic channels and arising into manifestation in the atmosphere (in front of oneself). As above, holding suspended the vital winds of the elements (produces visible) signs.

Elsewhere, there may appear white atmospheric phenomena, straight lines, [63] and zig-zag-like phenomena like lightening, or phenomena like a mirror of crystal, or like the wings of a bee, or like golden eyes, or like smoke, or like a mirage, or like a yak-hair blanket, or even becoming like the color of the sky. Or elsewhere, from the inherent radiance of the five gnoses, or modes of primal awareness, [64] there may arise various different forms such as rainbows, or glossy silk cloth being opened, or patterns of nets and half-nets, or chessboard patterns, or patterns of triangles, stupas, lotus flowers, and so on. Or (there may appear) the bindus of Rigpa (tiny luminous spheres of awareness) that have the color of crystal, being like scattered globules of quicksilver, or bindus (tiny rainbow spheres) arranged in pavilions of five lights surrounded five by five by perimeters of rainbow light, or like the threads of compassion that are rays, or like extended threads which are white or silver, or like chains of iron, or like chaotic ribs of parasols, or like combs scattered in the atmosphere, and so on. [65] In this way, there originate inconceivable modes for the arising for visions which are seen as these above.

By means of the instructions for the essential points of the Path of Means, in terms of primal awareness and bliss, the vital winds are gathered a little into the central channel. And because of the uniting of vital wind (or subtle energy) and mind, the gateways of the channels are opened just a little. And because of the strength of one's practice, the purity of Rigpa is separated from the impurities, thereby externally there commences the arising of visions of the Clear Light that represent higher insight and internally, having projected the Rigpa which is primordially pure in its nakedness, at this time experience and understanding come forth more and more clearly. Because there is produced in one's mind-stream simultaneously the entering into virtuous qualities both external and internal, it is very important that one produces diligence at that time. [66]

This represents the guiding explanation of the sky (practice) in terms of the Clear Light. [67]

U-YA SMAR-RO!

B2. The Practice with Sunlight

Second, within the practice of contemplation of the lamp of inherent clarity, there are four considerations, namely,

1. The places where to practice,
2. The times for the occasions of practicing,
3. Practicing in terms of whatever methods, and
4. Because one has practiced in that way, there are the modes for the arising of the virtuous qualities. [68]

B2.1. The Places of Practice

With regard to the first consideration, when one attains just a little stability with regard to these experiences in terms of the above, both in general and in detail (that is to say, the dark retreat and the sky practice), thereupon the signs of heat (or success in the practice) will arise in one's own mind-stream. Therefore, (at that time) one should practice in the boundary area between the shade and the sun, such as in a house that is open on one side which is built in a high place that is naturally isolated (and secluded), but where the rays of the sun (can clearly be seen) for long distance with a wide view. Or else, somewhere that there is shade, such as a rock over-hang, a large tree, or a cliff. [69]

B2.2. The Times for Practice

Second, the time (for practice) is properly the early morning just when the sun is rising (above the horizon). One can practice anywhere at that time when there is some shade and when (the sky) is not obscured by the wind or the clouds.

B2.3. The Methods of Practice

Third, as for the methods, according to the *sGron-ma* which refers precisely to that, it is said, "Mindfulness is the spear of the mind and one should fixate it (that is, aim it) at the shield of light that are these visions." [70]

Moreover, according to the Great Lama (Dranpa Namkha), "Those persons possessing the karma and the good fortune should cut off delusions in terms of the rays of the sun." [71]

Then, with regard to that (method of practice), there exist three further considerations:

B2.3a. The Positions of the Body

First, with regard to the essential points of the body (lus gnad), there are the assuming of the five essential points (or positions) of the body that will suddenly produce the Clear Light (that is to say, the Thodgal visions). With reference to that, there are five (postures for the practice), namely,

1. The method of the dignified lion,
2. The method of the reclining elephant,
3. The method of the crouching ascetic,
4. The method of the waddling goose, and
5. The method of the crystal antelope climbing a rock. [72]

B2.3a.1. *The Position of the Dignified Lion*

As for the first (of these positions): One assumes a position that is like a dog (sitting on his haunches). The two balls of the feet are planted firmly on the ground and one's weight is placed on the feet. The two arms are extended and perpendicular. They are placed inside the kneels and the palms of the hands are supported on the ground. The waist is straight and one sits in a crouching position. The lower wind is controlled a little and the arms are stretched out. [73]

In terms of its positive qualities, having suppressed the vital winds that cause the functional mind to move, (thereby producing discursive thoughts), the mouth of the channel of Bodhi, which is the central channel, is opened. Externally, the visions immediately arise and internally, the Dharmakaya, the pure contemplative state that transcends the thought process, arises. [74]

B2.3a.2. *The Position of the Reclining Elephant*

Second, lying down on one's belly, the weight is thrust upon the two elbows and the two balls of the feet. With the two hands one raises up without shaking and presses the knees to the chest. [75] The knees do not touch the ground.

As for its positive qualities, having suppressed the vital winds that cause movement, one obstructs desires that give rise to lust and attachment and extracts them from the root of existence, thereby increasing one's strength like an elephant. Externally the pure fields arise in their perfection (as complete) and internally developments are produced with regard to experiences and understanding. [76]

B2.3a.3. *The Position of the Crouching Ascetic*

Third, the soles of the feet are fixated on the ground and one sits in a crouching position. The two knees are gripped in the corners of the elbows and the two hands hold the middle parts of the arms. One controls the lower wind and the weight is bestowed on the feet. The neck is bent just a little.

As for its positive qualities, it increases the heat of fire which causes maturation. It pacifies both coarse and subtle discursive thoughts. Externally visions of the Nirmanakaya arise and internally special clear visions are produced in the mind-stream. [77]

B2.3a.4. The Position of the Waddling Goose

Fourth, as for the position of the waddling goose, one should plant one's right elbow on the ground, with the right cheek cradled in the (right) palm and one rests the left hand on the thigh and one presses the buttocks. The two legs are bent a little at the hollows of the knees, with the two calf muscles piled one on top of the other, and one gazes.

As for its positive qualities, having inserted the vital winds into the central channel, strange and marvelous phenomena are seen and the visions arise immediately. [78]

B2.3a.5. The Position of the Crystal Antelope

Fifth, sitting in a crouching position, one presses the knees to the chest. [79] The two hands pull from the outside to the inside of the knees and with the thumbs pull on the right and left ears. The spine is straight and the weight is bestowed on the feet.

As for its positive qualities, having obstructed the subject and object in terms of delight, this opens the doorways of the channels of gnosis, or primal awareness (ye-shes), on the right. Externally the masses of thoughts arise as primal cognitions and internally there arises a state of contemplation that is inherently clear and without grasping at anything. [80]

B2.3b. The Five Gazes

Second, with respect to the gazes, it is said that, "At the time of assuming the essential point of the body in the lion position, one gazes upward with the gaze of the Dharmakaya (bon-sku'i lta-stangs). Gazing upward through the eyebrows, a sense of presence is keenly felt." [81]

Similarly, at the time of assuming the second position (that of the reclining elephant), it is said that there exists the gaze of the Sambhogakaya (rdzogs-sku'i lta-stangs) which is intermediate. That is, one fixates in a staring fashion straight ahead without moving or shaking. [82]

At the time of assuming the third position (that of the crouching ascetic), one should perform the gaze of the Nirmanakaya (sprul-sku'i lta-stangs) which (looks) downward. The eye-lids are down (half closed) and one fixates downward.

At the time of assuming the fourth position (that of the waddling goose), one performs the gaze of Skilful Means (thabs kyi lta-stangs) to the right and one should look to the right out of the corners of the eyes.

And at the time of assuming the fifth position (that of the antelope), one performs the gaze of Discriminating Wisdom (shes-rab kyi lta-stangs) to the left. One looks to the left out of the corners of the two eyes.

B2.3c. Training in the Practice

With respect to the third further consideration, the training represents the essential point of the mind. Even though these gazes may be performed anywhere, one should engage in the practice of unifying the Three Lamps. Externally, the Lamp of Existence is tethered and held fast and it is fixated on (the light of the rays of) the sun, or the moon, and so on. Internally, the Lamp of the Senses is fixated on the space where Rigpa is in harmony with the eyes. Secretly, the Lamp of Rigpa is not loose, but controlled. One should not fall into laziness (and neglect), but remain scrupulous and firm (in terms of the practice). [83]

Furthermore, at that time, one should be aware of three important matters, namely,

1. The essential point of the body is indeed very important. Having kept under control the psychic channels and the vital winds, because it is necessary to produce suddenly a higher insight, without being irregular or defective, one should train oneself well in the essential points.

2. The gaze is also very important. Although hidden and concealed, (the visions) are certain to be projected into visibility and will come to exist in their full measure, where one does not fabricate any thoughts.

3. Moreover, the essential point of the mind is very important. Because everything comes to it (eventually), it is very important to integrate everything into it (the Natural State) in actuality. [84]

B2.4. The Arising of Visions

Third, with regard to the mode of arising (of the visions): Within the interior (of the heart), Rigpa, or intrinsic awareness, exists having the nature of the five lights and thereupon it overflows into the open hollow (tube) of the (kati) channel where it abides. But because, externally it encounters (in the outer world) the capacity for reflection (len-kha) of the mandala of the sun (in the sky), it arises visibly as the various visions of light, rays, and bindus (points of light). Furthermore, as it was shown above, because it encounters the capacity for reflection, which may be either external or internal, on these occasions those visions that arise previously are (especially) clear and pure, beautiful, sparkling, and clearly visible. Because these visions manifest, together with just a little moving and shaking, they come to arise so as to fill the entire sky and atmosphere. And with regard to them, without engaging in any exertions by way of thinking or analyzing them, as previously one practices (in relation to them) in a totally self-originated, self-arising, and self-liberating fashion. [85]

As for the positive qualities of this, it is said according to the *Lha-khrid* that "A state of contemplation or samadhi that is all-pervading and all-encompassing like the sky will be produced in one's mind-stream." [86]

And moreover, the *'Bum* (the Prajnaparamita Sutra) speaks of "A samadhi of light that is clear and bright and very quick," and "Having recognized (or apprehended that), one comes to obtain total release (which is liberation)." [87]

And elsewhere, according to the *Nyi-khrid*, "Because there exist methods for the development of both daytime visions and the nighttime visions such as above, at those times respectively and on those occasions one may perform the appropriate practices. However, if one relies upon them continuously (gazing at sunlight for too long a time), this may cause discomfort to one's health (in general) and to one's sense of sight (in particular). Therefore, one should know what to accept and what to reject (in terms of the amount and duration of practice). Afterwards, in terms of these three practices (above), by way of the method of adding one on top of them, all of them can be united in practice (and come to reinforce and help each other). [88]

But if one cannot endure the practice in terms of one's health and senses, then according to the *mThing-shog*, one may practice the vital instructions regarding the lustrous Chinese cloth. Here one employs the above method, but with one's head inside a curtain of blue cloth and then one gazes (at the light of the sun). [89]

This represented the guiding explanation for the daytime (practice) of the Lamp of inherent clear luminosity. [90]

U-YA SMAR-RO!

IIIC. Special Methods for Developing the Vision Practice

Third, in terms of development by way of the instructions on the special essential points, there are three considerations, namely,

1. Development by means of the essential points for the Path of Method,
2. Development by means of the purification of the vital winds and the mind, and
3. Development by means of the instructions concerning the visions at night. [91]

C1. Visions and the Appropriate Gazes

First, with respect to the visions, there may arise lights and rays and bindus and (at first) and at first their color will be white for the most part. When there arise (in one's visions) many crescent moon shapes, it is because one is holding (and suspending) the vital winds of the space element. (At that time) the gaze of the Dharmakaya, where one looks upward (as much as possible), will be the most important. [92]

When, for the greater part, there arise oblong (and rectangular) shapes and (the predominant) color is red, it is because is holding (suspended) the vital winds of the fire element. (At that time) the gaze of the Nirmanakaya, where one looks downward, will be the most important. [93]

When, for the greater part, there arise square shapes and the (predominant) color is yellow, it is because one is holding (suspended) the vital winds of the earth element. (At that time) the gaze of Means will be the most important. [94]

When, for the greater part, there are round shapes and green is the (predominant) color, it is because one is holding (suspended) the vital winds of the air element. (At that time) the gaze of Wisdom will be the most important. [95]

When, for the greater part, there are triangular shapes and azure colors (are predominant), it is because one is holding (suspended) the vital winds of the water element. (At that time) the gaze of the Sambhogakaya, where one gazes straight ahead (in the middle), will be the most important. [96]

When all the lights and the rays and the bindus originate in equal proportion, when the five colors are perfected and the five shapes are also complete, then (it is a sign) all of the five vital winds and the five elements have come under control in terms of the essential points (of the practice). [97] (At such a time) any of these three: the gaze of the dignified lion, the gaze of the Chakravartin, or wheel-turning monarch, and the gaze of Sangwa Dupa, may become the most important.

These gazes represent the essential points for the Path of Means which is taught here, together with the modes of arising (for the visions) externally. Because there is the assuming of these positions in general with respect to all the practices for the daytime visions and the nighttime visions, one should know them thoroughly. [98]

C2. Purification of the Vital Winds and the Mind

Second, in terms of the yoga of (the vital winds and) the mind, there exist three considerations, namely,

1. The disposition or mode of abiding for the psychic channels, the vital winds, and the bindus,
2. The reasons why it is necessary to purify them, and
3. The methods for purifying them in whatever way [99]

C2.1. How the Psychic Channels Abide

With respect to the first consideration, there is the hollow tube opening of the central channel at the heart (she-thun) by means of the vital wind (of Udana) that pulls (or draws) upward. It enters at the mouth of the gateway of Brahma and this represents the veritable pathway to Nirvana. And by means of the Apana wind, (the central channel) is opened downward. it enters into the secret place and this represents the Pathway to Samsara. [100]

From the large mouth of the right-side white channel at the spine, it moves upward to the right of the central channel at the spine, it moves upward to the right of the central channel. [101] From the brain to the right nostril, it comes out of that gateway. This represents pathway of fault (or defect) because of the rough breathing of ignorance and the kleshas or emotional defilements that move there. From the juncture (at the spine) of the left-side red channel, it moves from the left of the central channel and it comes out the left nostril as its gateway. This represents the Path of the Virtuous Qualities because the vital winds of bliss and the primal cognitions of Rigpa that move there. From (these three channels), they separate into some eighty-four thousand lesser branch (channels) and in turn into twigs and leaves. And all of them serve as the support for the mind and the body. However, if one condenses all of them, they are principally these three (channels). [102]

And with regard to the breathing, even though there are many kinds of breathing, if one condenses them, on the right side there are the movements of the rough breathing (rtsub rlung) of the kleshas or emotional defilements, and on the left side there is the movement of the pleasurable or blissful breathing of gnosis, or primal awareness. And (thirdly), there are the inherent winds of Rigpa which move in the central channel. With regard to that, one should hold inside oneself the blissful winds of gnosis and expel outside the rough winds of the kleshas. Just this holding represents the essential point of the inherent winds of Rig-pa. [103]

Even though there exist many bindus, they may be condensed into two (principal kinds of energy droplets), namely, the pure bindus of Awareness and the impure bindus of semen. Furthermore, having relied upon these impure bindus, one should enter into the essential point in terms of the pure bindus. [104]

C2.2. Why it is Necessary to Purify the Psychic Channels

As for the second consideration, one should endeavor to insert the blissful winds of gnosis into the central channel, which is the king among all the channels. When one adheres to this essential point of the bindus of Rigpa which are pure in themselves, externally there will come visions that can be seen with clarity and internally there will originate from that all of the energies of experience and understanding. And when one forcefully purifies the pathways of Rigpa, there will come no deviations from these pathways of Rigpa. So it is said.

Again, according to the *sGron-ma*, it is said, "Kunzhi and Rigpa have remained as the essence which have abided from the very beginning and they have abided in the center of the Tsita (or the physical heart). This (Rigpa) has arisen in a self-arisen manner within the central channel which is the pathway. [105]

"Moreover, the Kunzhi, which is like the sky, pervades everywhere in general, but having be come obscured by the masses of clouds that represent delusions, there exists clarity no longer. However, with regard to the pathway of the central channel, being in itself like the sky without clouds, it abides there as total directly penetrating primal awareness or gnosis." [106] So it says.

C2.3. The Methods of Purification

Third, with respect to the methods of purification, there exist three (kinds of breathing), namely,

1. Purification in terms of gentle breathing,
2. Control in terms of rough breathing, and
3. Stabilization in terms of natural breathing. [107]

C2.3a. Gentle Breathing

Within the first consideration (gentle breathing), there are three aspects, namely,

1. The essential point of the body,
2. The essential point of the functional mind, and
3. The essential point of the breathing. [108]

C2.3a.1. The Essential Point of the Body

In terms of the first (essential point), as for the times (for practice), such times as the early morning, the evening twilight, and daybreak (are appropriate). (However) there is no reason to meditate when one is drowsy or feeling dull at midday, nor (when tired or asleep) in the middle of the night. So said the great Lama. [109]

As for the place (of practice), one should stabilize and greatly develop (the presence of) Rigpa while (practicing) in the dark retreat house. [110]

Then, in terms of the methods, it says according to the *gZer-bu*, "It is said that the essential point of the body is to control it and one should assume the position possessing the five mudras (as described) above. And one should keep (the position) tightly according to the rule and not loosely." [111] In this way one should proceed to the essential point.

C2.3a.2. *The Essential Point of the Functional Mind*

With regard to the second, from inside the interior (of the body), the white right channel, the left red channel, and the central channel (all meet) at the secret place, whereat the right and the left channels enter into the central channel and become a single central tube. At the crown of the head, the azure-colored central channel is like a cut-off hollow tube of bamboo, whereas the right and the left channels are similar to an entwining lasso and its knots.

And in terms of that, there are produced (by visualization) three (chakras that are above, in between, and below known as) the *Pu-she-li* chakras. Moreover, in terms of each of these (chakras), they separate (and divide) into 4 x 4 petals which themselves have channels (originating from them). From these channels at their edges, they divide into the eighty-four thousand lesser channels. which are above, below, and in between. These have the aspect of fine threads (or cobwebs) on trees. And one's own physical body generates them as a network of channels.

C2.3a.3. The Essential Point of the Breathing

Then, with regard to the breathing, it is said according to the *gZer-bu*, "Because it says that one should hold (and reign in) the horse of the breath, by checking the side of the non-movement of the breath through the nostrils, (one finds where) the breath is blocked. Then by performing the yantra exercise of the Chinese lady weaving silk and exhaling the breath strongly, and because one does this a few times, (the breathing) will become equalized (through both nostrils). Then one should inhale and exhale together nine times equally.

Then, according to the *mThing-shog*, it is said, "The antidote to discursive thoughts is found in carrying out the essential explanation of the three letters or syllables that are recollected, where one moves the breath outside and inside." [112]

Furthermore, the OM on the left side, the A on the right side, and the HUM in the center (channel) emanate and return (rays of light) in harmonization with the breathing. Moreover, one should think that the HUM abides, the OM enters, and the A expels. [113] One just keeps breathing normally without forcing the breathing or holding it. By that means, the pathways of the channels are purified, the gateways of the channels are opened, the knots in the channels are liberated, and so it is necessary to cleanse the hollow tubes of the channels.

C2.3b. Rough Breathing

With regard to the second (the rough breathing), there are two considerations:

1. Meditating in whatever manner and
2. The modes for the arising of experiences. [114]

C2.3b.1. The Method of Psychic Heat

With regard to the first consideration, the psychic channels and the essential points of the body are as they were above. At the juncture of the three channels, there is a green (letter) YAM. On top of that, at about four finger widths, is a dark red (letter) RAM. Then, straight in front of the heart is Self-Awareness having the nature of the (syllable) A. It unfolds effulgently with the five lights and being clearly visible as just (the size) of the egg of the lark, one meditates that it radiates brilliantly and dazzlingly. [115]

Then one holds the breath. From the channels on the right and the left, because it is invoked by the YAM syllable, the vital winds of primal awareness (or the prana-vayu of gnosis) rises up (in the central channel) and because this blows upon the RAM syllable, the latter blazes up fiercely like a copper needle held in the fire. It is hot like the touch of fire. There exists this capacity of being blown by the winds because these two (wind and fire) come together. Thereby the closed mouth of the central channel is suddenly opened without any independence (or self-power). And the tongues of flame, rising higher and higher as bindus ascend to the aperture of Brahma Here the white letter HAM is visible with its head turned downward. (Due to the proximity of the flames from below) from this letter HAM, there drip bindus like drops of melted human fat. Thereupon one meditates that everywhere, at the heart center and below the navel, together with the lesser channels below, becomes filled with these bindus of vital energy and subtle mind (that have the quality of ecstatic bliss). [116]

Then, at the time of inhaling the breath, the white and red HUM syllables having entered into the right and the left nostrils respectively, (descend through the two side channels and) become united together like feet at the secret place. One should think that, because of the strength of that (action), all of the bindus are collected together and pressed into the central channel. One utters the long HUM syllable nine (or many) times.

Then, the hands and the head are planted on the ground and by the power of uttering many short HUM syllables forcefully, one pulls them up to the crown of the head and they swim there. One turns the head and shakes the upper part of the body, together with many soundings of PHAT!

From the Mahasukha Chakra at the crown of the head, one should think that they (these bindus) become scattered into all of the lesser channels (of the bode). One should maintain well the essential points of the body, hold the gaze of the dignified lion, and fixate Awareness (rig-pa). On this occasion, in terms of the breathing, one uniting face to face (the upper air and the lower air), one diminishes and augments, fills and holds. One should know well these essential points of the breathing (or pranayama).

C2.3b.2. The Arising of Experiences

With regard to the second consideration, with each cycle of the yoga of breathing which is like that (the practice of psychic heat), one meditates for each cycle of the visualization on the Clear Light. Externally, because one meditates in that way, the modes for the arising of visions will be high as was the case above. [117] And also many that are rougher or coarser than that may come to increase. They will fill everywhere in the sky, in the atmosphere, and in the land. They will arise excessively, being both brilliant and radiant, as various forms and shapes, projecting a little in the sense-fields, being beautiful, attractive, bright, and clear, whether as rays of lights or bindus or images or threads. Internally, in terms of the experiences in the channels, one may be made to think that there are pains in the channels such as soil or large stones. And there may also come pains in the joints, as well as shaking and moving (involuntarily), and so on.

With regard to experiences of the vital winds: The mind may feel very light and unstable and there may come odd sensations of itching or one may feel restless and ungrounded. With regard to the experiences of the bindus: One's body may feel flexible and experience pleasurable sensations and when touched, it will tickle. The bindus may be experienced to descend, drop down, become concentrated, drawn up again, and scattered (diffused into the lesser channels). All (of these methods) will be made known later. With regard to the experiences of mind: One opens a little the mouth of the central channel and one comes to control the essential points of the vital winds and the mind. Because the bindus are drawn up again into the upper part (of the body, experiences) will arise distinctly and possess a clarity (like clairvoyance), but without becoming recognizable individually.

These phenomena, both external and internal, are not able to be covered over or obscured. While in the state of Rigpa, they abide without distractions and without any grasping at bliss or emptiness. All thoughts of whether they are good or bad are straightforwardly cut off at the root by their inherent power. One is alertly relaxed, free of all effort, and undistracted, but one is able to fixate on this continuous creative process (of the arising of these phenomena). Without grasping at anything, they come forth as clear and empty, joyous and blissful. So it is expounded in the *A-gsal*.

And according to the *gZer-bu*, it is said, "There is no deviation (nor mistake) on this path because one has purified (and cleansed) the channels in terms of Awareness."

This represented the guiding explanation for the development in terms of vital wind and mind. [118]

U-YA SMAR-RO!

C3. Sleep and Dream Practice

Third, in terms of the instructions for the visions in the night time, there exist three considerations, namely,

1. The integrating of sleep with the Clear Light,
2. The modes for the arising of both the defects and the virtuous qualities from that, and
3. Apprehending the essential point which is fixating on the A. [119]

C3.1. Integrating Sleep with the Clear Light

With regard to the first (among these considerations, that is to say, the integrating of sleep with the Clear Light), it is said according to the *sNyan-rgyud chen-mo*, "With reference to the Bardo of the Dream State, the instruction is that the inter-weaving together of the karmic traces is like the central current of a river." [120]

Because it is expounded (in that way), with regard to practice (lag-len), on top of a comfortable seat and a thick cushion, one assumes the position of the sleeping lion (seng-ge'i nyal stabs), where the right side of the body is laid below and with the thumb, index, middle, and ring fingers, one obstructs the openings (of the various orifices) and thereby one obstructs (and closes) the doors for the vital winds and the gateways of the channels of the kleshas, or emotional defilements, on the right side. [121]

Then one should think happily that one's seat (or mattress is supported on) a lion, an elephant, a horse, a dragon, and a garuda, and that one's pillow is the sun and the moon. Then one expels the poisons with the three exhaustions of the inner breathing. The Rigpa that resides inside the central channel is clearly visible as a ball of threads of light just about the size of a peacock's egg (located in) the navel of the throat center (ag-sho 'khor-lo). One should not emanate the masses of thoughts that think about the past or which speculate upon the future. One should close the eyes. [122]

Then, with regard to that, because one falls asleep without disturbances, for the individual of superior capacity, all of the delusory visions (or manifestations) of the dream state will arise as Clear Light (visions). [123] Furthermore, when going to sleep, one will retain the nectar of memory (or mindfulness and thereby recognize the dream to be a dream) and one will never become separated from pious practices (dge-sbyor) (by sleep or unconsciousness). Because they meditate as above, these above practitioners will uninterruptedly see visions of the Clear light. All of them, becoming aware of their own dreams (as being dreams), will cut off the current of all their ordinary (dreams) instantly and pious activities will come to increase more at night (in their dreams) than during the daytime. At night, these pious activities will come forth increasingly. But even by day, the profit from this becomes greater and greater. Also, at that time, without deciding from memory, it is very important to practice with diligence. Finally, on occasion after occasion, when one is dreaming, one comes to recognize them as being dreams. Practice will come forth (spontaneously) just as a memory. Because one purifies oneself, and having gone into increasing this more and more, one will come in the end to recognize them very well. At that time, one should make the effort (as described).

C3.2. Recognizing Dreams as Dreams

Second, in general, there exist a number of causes for not recognizing dreams (as dreams), [124] namely, (1) not having devotion (flourishing) within one's mind-stream, (2) or not producing within oneself a certain and sure knowledge with regard to the instructions. (3) By means of diligence (alone), one may not be capable of striving for it. (4) The mind-stream may be stirred up with discursive thoughts. As for these four, because they represent faults or defects of the mind, they should be renounced.

Then again, (1) the elements (of the body) may not be balanced because of eating certain foods. (2) Or one may feel very tired from engaging in strenuous labor (or other physical activities to excess). (3) Or again, sexual desires and lustful thoughts with regard to males and females. (4) Or the strength of the elements (of the body) have become old (and weak). In terms of these four: Because there exist such defects of the body, one should stay (quietly in bed) and on occasion after occasion at the beginning, one should fixate (the mind) only a little. And at the time when for the most part, one is not fixating, one gradually falls into sleep. And at the time when one has not directly awakened, one trains with the essential points of the body and with the previous visualization. One causes these masses of thoughts not to go elsewhere, (but to dissolve) and so one falls asleep. One may do this at such times as the evening, the very early morning, and even in the daytime. Consequently, all visions (or appearances) in the present, even though they manifest, they will appear only as dreams. Even though they may seem to exist, they will be dreams. Even though they may exist, one thinks the thought that they are only dreams without real activities such as being karmic traces and so on.

Then in the middle, (sometimes) there is grasping at memories. On those occasions when (dreams) arise as half as many and are not remembered, one should fixate on any that do. And with regard to that, one should remember the practice. It is very important to become habitual in this and act with diligence.

Finally, at the time of integrating sleep with the Clear Light, because there may come forth experiences and other psychic phenomena (or apparitions) from non-human spirits, their modes of arising as visions that are seen, originate in whatever ways, but one should become familiar with them as self-manifestations that are like illusions. Therefore, one's thoughts should not be allowed to become delighted, cheerful, nor conceited.

At the end, one's dreams will become dissolved into the vast expanse of space and one's awareness will attain independence (and its own power) and the memories that cause movements (of thought) will cease to lead one anywhere. [123] By merely thinking that every thing is located higher or lower, or is good or bad, any visions (or dreams) like that are (immediately) transformed. Because (these visions or dreams) are indeed pure self-manifestations, one is able now to transform them at any time, anywhere into anything. They come to arise into manifestation according to these transformations. Even the delusory visions (or appearances experienced in) the Bardo can be interrupted (and transformed) in this way. Eventually all appearances go into reverse, even the flesh reverts and the hair reverts, and one is no longer afraid of the Bardo of Dying or of rebirth. At that time, others also, all diverse visions, become forcefully purified in terms of the condition of dreaming. By carrying on along this path, one dispatches them directly. One integrates defeat and victory, laziness and strenuous conduct. Thereafter it will be easy to transform karmic traces by means of the Awareness in dreams. [126] At that time, whatever one does in terms of pious activities there will be (produced clairvoyant powers) nine times more than at present and they will develop greatly.

C3.3. Fixating on the White A

With regard to the third, even though one practices in whatever manner, if one does not recognize them (dreams), but falls asleep contentedly like above, in terms of fixation on the visualization. [127] one should control a little the *'Phar-rtsa* channels of enjoyment (on the sides of the neck), and having obstructed the visions (or appearances) of one's own mind-stream (by pressing on these channels for too long), one will feel strange and because there exists the danger of not remembering, awareness should be controlled very much. And then one relaxes the channels just a little. Even though one does not awaken directly, one purifies in that way. If one controls for a long time the *'Phar-rtsa* (the two channels at the sides of the neck), one must grasp the full measure (and not press them for too long), because there exists the danger of the consciousness transmigrating (involuntarily and one dies). Therefore, it is impossible that one will not come to recognize one's dreams.

This has been the guiding explanation for the integrating of sleep with the Clear Light. [128]

U-YA SMAR-RO!

Colophon

Like that, the nectar of the Mind, the Upadesha which is the innermost essence of the Oral Tradition, the ultimate instructions on the essential points of the profound Meaning, the handbook for the principal practices has been felicitously arranged herein. [129] May this come forth as a benefit for all suitable vessels (disciples) and mature their mind-streams and bring them (eventually) to liberation! The instructions for the principal practices is hereby completed.

Gya Gya U-YA AG-THAM!

Chapter Four

The Explanation
of the View: *lTa-khrid*

Here is contained "The Guiding Explanation of the View through Seeing Nakedly, which represents the Direct Introduction to one's own Primordial Base" (gzhi rang ngo-sprad-pa gcer-mthong lta-ba'i khrid).

Homage to Kuntu Zangpo, the all-pervading and all-encompassing Guide of Beings who is (in reality) one's own intrinsic Self-Awareness become visibly manifest. [1]

As for Book Three: [2] Having come to understand one's own mind-stream and this understanding having become manifest (in one's practice of contemplation and of vision), there then exist four supplementary branches (or ancillary texts of the teaching) for continuing in this state, [3] namely,

1.   The Explanation of the View through Seeing Nakedly that represents the direct introduction to one's own Base, or Primordial State (gzhi rang ngo-sprad-pa gcer-mthong lta-ba'i khrid);

2.   The Explanation of the Meditation on the Clear Light that represents the practice of the Path (lam nyams su len-pa 'od-gsal bsgom-pa'i khrid);

3. The Explanation of the Activity or Conduct consisting of the forceful purifications that purify the secondary conditions encountered along the Path (rkyen lam du byangs-pa rtsal sbyong spyod-pa'i khrid); and

4. The Explanation of the Fruit where one clearly and definitively decides upon the Trikaya, which remains in its own original condition ('bras-bu rang sa bzung-ba sku-gsum dmar thag-bcad-pa'i khrid).

The Explanation of the View

As for the first (of these four supplementary texts, namely, "The Explanation of the View where one Sees Everything Nakedly," this representing the direct introduction to one's own Base or Primordial State), there are three parts:

I.   Relying upon the Essence and the Nature of the the Primordial Base, one is introduced thereby directly to it (gzhi'i rang-bzhin ngo-bo la brten nas ngo-sprad-pa);

II. Relying upon certain special activities, one is further introduced to it (byed las khyad-par la brten nas ngo-sprad-pa); and finally,

III. There is the extensive explanation regarding (the origins of) Liberation and of Delusion respectively (grol 'khrul rgyas-par bshad-pa).

I. Direct Introduction to the Primordial Base

Within this first part, there are four sections that need to be considered:

A. The direct introduction to the Mother (ma'i ngo-sprad-pa),

B. The direct introduction to the Son (bu'i ngo-sprad-pa),

C. The direct introduction to the Energy or Potentiality (rtsal gyi ngo-sprad-pa), and

D. The direct introduction to the unity and inseparability of all three, namely, the Mother, the Son, and the Energy (ma bu rtsal gsum dbyer-med zung-'brel du ngo-sprad-pa).

A. Direct Introduction to the Mother

Now, with respect to the first section (the direct introduction to the Mother), the Mother is, in fact, the Kunzhi, "the basis of everything," which represents the Natural State of the real disposition of things, (that is to say, the state of emptiness, or Shunyata). [4] Indeed, it is the base and the root (or source) of everything in both Samsara and Nirvana. And therefore, it is the First Great Ancestor of all the Buddhas, as well as of all sentient beings. But if one were to try to illustrate it in words, any name or designation would be appropriate. However, if one would try to distill the actual meaning in words, this would not be found to exist anywhere.

As for the first of these (eight possible) designations: Its essence is without any obscurations whatsoever. Furthermore, one may say that it is self-luminous or inherently clear, empty, and without a source. It is naked and without clothes; from the very beginning it was not attired in any delusions or any obscurations or any passions. Therefore, it may be called the Great Primordial Purity (ka-dag chen-po) (that is to say, the state of total primordial purity). [5]

Because it is not been obscured by anything whatsoever, it is colorless and unchanging. It is completely pure and everywhere it is directly penetrating. It is not produced from a primary cause, nor is it modified or changed by any secondary causes. It cannot be realized or created by any kind of effort. And because it does not fall into any limitations or extremes as represented by conceptual elaborations, it may be called the Great Self-Origination (rang-byung chen-po) (that is to say, it is totally self-created, self-manifested, and self-originated).

Because everything that is known to living beings in both Samsara and Nirvana is complete and perfect just as it is in that (Natural State), [6] one may say that at this present moment, nothing has been karmically ripened and nothing will be liberated (because there is nothing to be ripened nor to be liberated). And because this situation is not something understandable (in terms of conceptions by way of the rational intellect), this may be called the Great Spontaneous Perfection (lhun-grub chen-po) (that is to say, all things are totally and spontaneously perfected in themselves just as they are when they come into visible manifestation). [7]

In terms of recognizing (the Mother), it may be said that it does not display any particular form, or shape, or color, or size as its defining characteristic. Because nothing is asserted anywhere regarding its essence, it may be called the Great Transcendence of Limitations (mtha' bral chen-po) (that is to say, it is totally beyond all conceptual limitations and extremes).

Indeed, it falls neither on the side of Samsara nor on the side of Nirvana, and it cannot be divided into parts. From Kuntu Zangpo, who is the highest among all beings, downward to the smallest most insignificant insect, it does not increase nor does it decrease. In these terms, it is neither more subtle nor more gross, neither more dense nor more ethereal. Yet, because it encompasses everything and everyone, it may be called the Great All-Pervasiveness (kun khyab chen-po) (that is to say, it totally pervades everything).

Everything originates from that state, has its existence in it, and dissolves back again into it. Even though, within that state (that is, the Natural State), all things arise as different kinds of apparitional displays, in itself it does not thereby become diminished nor filled up and congested. It does not become constructed in any way. And because nothing transcends nor goes beyond it anywhere, it may be called the Great Nature (bdag-nyid chen-po) (that is to say, the total state of being). [8]

With regard to that state, the conduct of the Buddhas does not proceed to what is called good nor does the conduct of Samsara proceed to what is called bad. Within it there exists no hope of ascending upwards (into the spirituality of Nirvana) nor fear of descending downwards (into the carnality of Samsara). Because it does not draw near to anything (as virtuous) nor does it reject anything as improper (and non-virtuous), it may be called the Great Universality (spyi-blugs chen-po) (that is to say, it is totally universal and all-inclusive).

Even though one cannot attach a specific name to it, because it does not go beyond this singular and unique meaning (which is emptiness), it is seen to have a single essence. Nevertheless, distinctive individual appearances come forth from it (unceasingly). Within this single Base there exist great multitudes of particular pleasures and sorrows. Even though diversity may arise everywhere, what is called just this (Natural State) does not reveal nor display itself openly anywhere, but rather, it remains concealed everywhere. It is not seen by anyone and it does not come forward to present itself, although it is always with us. Therefore, it goes mostly unrecognized. Because it encompasses and pervades everything, but nothing else encompasses it, it may be called the state totally that transcends Conception and Expression (blo 'das brjod med chen-po) (that is to say, it totally transcends the intellect and is totally inexpressible in words).

According to the *sGron-ma drug*, "The (individual) Nature of Mind originates from the Kunzhi, the basis of everything. Its Clear Light is empty, unfabricated, and unadulterated (by anything in Samsara). [9] Moreover, it is the Dharmakaya and the state of total primordial purity, being in no way tainted or defiled by anything whatsoever (belonging to Samsara) and is untouched by any conceptual limitations or extremes. Nevertheless, its Nature (rang-bzhin) is the Sambhogakaya which is spontaneously perfection. Indeed, it is completely perfect, entirely perfect, perfect in every way. [10] However, the Nirmanakaya is a neutral state (beyond virtue and defect) that is uncertain and unpredictable (in its manifestations). It may arise anywhere as an apparitional display without any partialities (or judgments). But it does not exist distinctly and individually (as something separate from the Natural State). [11] Yet it encompasses and pervades in their entirety both Samsara and Nirvana. It pervades and encompasses everything everywhere like the singular condition of the clear open sky. In the clear luminous sky which is without partialities (or limits), everything arises from this single great vast expanse of space. In the vast expanse of emptiness, there is neither broadness nor narrowness. In this single great dimension, everything abides (and has its existence). In this dimension which is the same everywhere, there is no higher or lower (in relation to anything else). And in those terms, it may be called the Bodhichitta, but with reference to the conventional meaning, it may be explained as being threefold." [12] When the text speaks in this way, the three referred to above represent the example, the meaning, and the indication. Thus there exist two sets.

Similarly, even though one may demonstrate it in words, there will occur in the mind-stream of the individual a condensing or distillation of the meaning whereby discursive consciousness and mere intellectual knowledge will become exhausted. [13] When one takes it (the Natural State) up into one's hand (to examine it concretely), one finds that its essential point consists of nothing whatsoever. Then in terms of practicing with a confident belief (in the Natural State), like before one establishes a regime of practice (lag-len) consisting of the three essential points (of the body, speech, and mind) and gazes with open eyes (cer-re lta-ba) into (the empty space of) the Kunzhi which abides cleanly as inherent clear luminosity and which is entirely devoid of discursive thoughts. And in terms of that, there will be a confident belief, a direct experience, and an intense definitive decision (regarding the Natural State without any doubts). The procedure of explanation that was demonstrated above is very well known and very prudent. [14]

The Nature of Mind, at just this immediate present moment, does not grasp at anything whatsoever and it is inherently luminous and clear like the purity of the sky. Indeed, it represents the self-appearance of the Trikaya and it is a primary cognition that is spontaneously perfected, self-aware, and inherently luminous. [15]

Again, according to the *gZer-bu*, "As for the King who is Awareness being luminously clear and self-originated, it is a non-apprehending primal awareness that transcends any colour, shape, or form. This inexpressible primal awareness or cognition is beyond names, words, and letters. This non-discursive primal awareness is beyond thoughts, analysis, and intellect. [16]

And according to the *dGongs-lugs*, "It simply exists and one gazes open-eyed into it (the empty space of the Natural State)." [17]

It is asked in the text, where does (Rigpa) now abide? Even though it is said that it pervades all of the physical body in general terms, in particular (Rigpa) resides inside of the hollow heart-nerve (she-thun rtsa 'dzin gyi nang) at the center of the reddish brown cornelian pervilion with projecting crystals that is the physical heart. At the center of a canopy-like pavilion of five (rainbow) lights, it abides in a state of total primordial purity that is unmixed with anything else (relating to Samsara). [18]

Again, according to the *sGron-ma drug*, "In the middle of the physical heart, which is free of all darkness and which is like the sun itself, one's own Awareness (Rigpa) abides as totally self-arising." [19]

Moreover, it is said, "It (Rigpa) abides like a butter lamp set inside of a vase. One does not see it (Rigpa or the flame of the lamp) from the outside because it is obscured by the physical body. But when Awareness separates itself from the corpse (at the time of death), it is explained that it will clearly come into view." [20] Thus it is said.

On this occasion (when the master reads aloud the text, the disciples) will be directly introduced to "the Cycle of the Base," (gzhi'i 'khor-lo'i ngo-sprad-pa). [26]

B. Direct Introduction to the Son

Second, with regard to the Son who represents the primal cognitions of Awareness (bu rig-pa'i ye-shes), there are two considerations:

1. The Natural State of the Son (bu'i gnas-lugs) and
2. The direct introduction to that (de la ngo-sprad-pa).

B1. The Natural State of the Son

In terms of this first consideration (the Natural State of the Son), within the Mother, the Kunzhi, which is like the vast (open, limitless) sky, the Son who is Awareness (bu rig-pa) arises as the inhabitant (of that vast dimension), being like the heart of the sun (rising high into the sky). The essence of this arising is that it is without any obscurations whatsoever. Moreover, its luminous clarity is naked and entirely cleansed of all obscurations. However, its nature is emptiness itself and it abides immaculately, having no root (or source in anything whatsoever). [22] Truly, (the Son) is a presence that is aware of the object and all of its aspects just as they are in reality. (This Son) is a sudden awareness arising as a naked primary cognition that is completely unattired in any thoughts, actions, movements, or efforts (that occur subsequently to it). At just that moment, there exists only a startled awareness without any memories (or thoughts) intervening. It is a startled awareness without fixation (or focusing on anything), being naked and devoid of discursive thoughts, and totally present without apprehending or grasping at anything whatsoever. [23] And that is called the primal cognitions of self-originated Awareness (rang-byung rig-pa'i ye-shes).

According to the *sGron-ma drug*, "As for the so-called primal cognitions of Awareness (rig-pa'i ye-shes), they are said to be like the sun in the vast expanse of the sky. In the same way, Rigpa or Awareness arises from the vast expanse of the Kunzhi (which is the Natural State). Its essence is clear luminosity and its nature is emptiness; and in terms of its aspect, this knowing awareness is without any discursive thoughts." [24]

B2. The Direct Introduction to the Natural State of the Son

As for the second (consideration, the direct introduction to the Natural State of the Son), the essential point of the body brings about the unification (and harmonizing) of the psychic energies and the mind. One then proceeds to separate the purity of Awareness from the impurities (of the discursive mind) by way of expelling the clear radiance of awareness (from the heart center via the central channel in the form of a tiny sphere of radiant light that exits from the top of the head). At the time when confident belief arises (within one's mind-stream due to this experience), one engages in gazing with wide-open eyes at this essence (which is empty space and clear luminosity). Thereby one is directly introduced to the Natural State. [25] Just this natural state of the primal cognition, which is Awareness itself, is Buddhahood in actuality. That awareness of the immediate present moment which is devoid of discursive thoughts is said to be clean and naked. And this primal cognition which is Awareness (rig-pa'i ye-shes) arises entirely without obscurations and is everywhere directly penetrating. [26]

According to the gZer-bu, "The six eyes of higher insight arise at the forehead (and so on). The primordial state, which sees everything nakedly, is entirely perfect (and complete with nothing lacking or needing development)." [27]

Again, according to the same text, "This miniature-sized gnosis, or primordial awareness, (found in the heart) is the unmanifest Dharmakaya. It is also known as the Awareness which is itself the essence (ngo-bo nyid gyi rig-pa). As for that primal cognition which is itself intrinsic Awareness, even though it does not arise from anywhere outside, neither does it arise from the inside. Rather, it simply arises from within itself by itself alone (rang la rang shar-ba)." [28]

So it was said according to the Prajnaparamita ('bum) and elsewhere; therefore, this represents the extensive direct introduction (rgyas-par ngo-sprad-pa). [29]

C. The Direct Introduction to Energy

With respect to the three total manifestations that represent the potentiality of energy, namely, the sounds, the lights and the rays, there also exist here two considerations:

1. The Natural State of Energy (rtsal gyi gnas-lugs) and
2. The direct introduction to it (de la ngo-sprad-pa). [30]

C1. The Natural State of Energy

With respect to the first consideration (the Natural State), from the potentiality of energy (rtsal) and the radiant translucency (mdangs) of the primary cognitions of Awareness that is like what (has been described above as the Son), there arise unceasingly (and without impediments) the sounds, the lights, and the rays as self-manifestations. This occurs because of the absence of any secondary causes represented by the "I", or sense of ego, which is active (as an agent or creator). [31] From this translucency on the side of the clear luminosity of Awareness, which is indeed without any obscurations or coverings (due to discursive thoughts or conceptual elaborations), these lights, which represent the inherent lights of Awareness, arise like rainbows. From the power (or potentiality) on the side of the emptiness of Awareness, which is totally without any root or source, these sounds, which represent the inherent sounds of Awareness, arise like echoes. [32] And from the energy (rtsal) that represents the non-dual essence of clarity and emptiness, the rays, which represent the inherent rays of Awareness, arise like the rays of the sun (at dawn).

Furthermore, (in terms of the unfolding of the visions in the Bardo), from this basis for arising (described above), where the inherent translucency (or radiance) of Awareness is linked and connected with the five primordial lights, all of the emanations of the unchanging Bodies (or divine forms) of the Buddhas arise (on the side of pure vision). But when these emanations arise (on the side of impure karmic vision), they are combined with the four kinds of beings (that is, the four kinds of rebirth for ordinary sentient beings). Similarly, from this same basis for arising, where Awareness becomes connected with the sounds, all the emanations of the Speech of the Buddhas arise (on the side of pure vision), whereas all the ordinary languages and voices of the speech of ordinary sentient beings arise (on the side of impure karmic vision). And with regard to this same basis of arising, where Awareness becomes connected with the rays, all the emanations of the primal awareness and knowledge of the Minds of the Buddhas arise (on the side of pure vision), whereas all the masses of thoughts and memories in the minds of ordinary sentient beings arise (on the side of impure karmic vision). Indeed, the Son, this primary cognition which is Awareness, is not created by anyone (because it arises spontaneously). Nevertheless, there exist the activities of the three total manifestations that arise as self-manifestations. [33]

According to the *sGron-ma drug*, "From that (Natural State which is Rigpa), there arise the three potencies that come into manifestations as visible appearances, namely, these three, the sounds, the lights, and the rays. The lights arise in the space of the sky that is totally clear. The sounds originate of themselves from the vast expanse of emptiness. And when (emptiness) is non-dual with Awareness, the rays come to emanate (as magical apparitions or holograms). Then they may be called visible objects (snang-ba'i yul)." [34]

And again, it is said, "Even though this Essence is primordially pure and immaculate, still it is the basis for both the defects of Samsara and the virtues of Nirvana ('khor 'das skyon yon). When the lights are linked and connected with Awareness, they become the basis for both the physical bodies (lus) (of ordinary deluded sentient beings in terms of impure karmic vision) and (the divine forms or) Bodies (sku) (of the enlightened Buddhas in terms of pure vision). When the sounds are linked and connected with Awareness, they become the basis for both the profane speech (ngag) (of ordinary deluded sentient beings) and for the (pure) Speech (gsung) (of the enlightened Buddhas as the teachings of the Dharma). And when the rays are linked and connected with Awareness, they become the basis for both the minds (yid) (of ordinary deluded sentient beings) and the Minds (thugs) (of the enlightened Buddhas)." So it was said. [35]

C2. The Direct Introduction to the Natural State of the Energy

From the second consideration (the direct introduction), by means of uniting the vayu, or the vital winds, and the chitta, or the mind, after separating the purity of Awareness from the impurity, [36] as previously one forces the essential points of the body, such as moving upward the ocean, and so on, and gazing with open eyes at the clarity between the brows without blinking and without distraction. One apprehands and listens to the continuous production of the inherent sounds of the mind, and one fixates uninterruptedly on the inherent rays of Awareness and the memories which are like the rays of the sun. By that belief one produces awareness and one is directly introduced. [37]

From that primal cognition which represents Awareness (rig-pa'i ye-shes), these three: the sounds, the lights, and the rays, arise as inherent translucency, or radiance (rang mdangs). From the very beginning they are not created by anyone nor are they realized by any cause, being without any distortions (or exaggerations), the states of the primal cognitions of Awareness arise as unobstructed (and unceasing) self-manifestations. [38]

According to the *sGron-ma drug*, "The mind which moves can be tamed by way of sounds. Moreover, the rays (or images), which are memories, can be purified. And as for the rays among the three (primal) energies, they also can be purified. Thereupon the Mandala of the Trikaya will arise by itself. [39]

"And again, as for the sounds, they represent the inherent sounds of awareness. These inherent sounds of emptiness have the manner of echos. As for the lights, they represent the inherent lights of awareness. These inherent lights of emptiness have the manner of the lights of the sun. As for the rays, they represent the inherent rays of Awareness. These inherent rays of emptiness have the manner of the rays of the sun. This is the Natural State of the real disposition of things from the very beginning." [40] So it is said.

This represents the extensive direct introduction.

D. The Unity and Inseparability of all Three

Fourth, with respect to the unity and the inseparability of the Mother, the Son, and the Energy (ma bu rtsal gsum dbyer-med zung-'brel du ngo-sprad-pa), there are two considerations:

1. The Natural State (gnas-lugs) and
2. The direct introduction to it (de'i ngo-sprad-pa).

D1. The Natural State

With respect to the first consideration (the Natural State), even though the three: the Mother, the Son, and the Energy, have revealed themselves to be like that everywhere, (in actual fact) their Essence represents the inseparability of the Mother and the Son from the very first in the individual mind-stream and the Nature represents their unity (or linkage together). There exists no distinction in terms of the characteristics between them. From the Mother Kunzhi, which is like the purity of the sky (that is, the Shunyata), [41] there arises the Son which is the primal cognition of Awareness, which is without obscurations and who is inherently clear (bu rig-pa'i ye-shes sgrib-med rang-gsal), like the heart of the sun. From that unity (of Mother and Son), the sounds, the lights, and the rays arise as apparitional displays like the rays of the sun. Furthermore, they are in their own forms without any preconditioning.

According to the *sGron-ma*, "The Base (gzhi), the heart-essence (snying-po), and the apparitional displays (cho-'phrul) are known as the Mother, the Son, and the Potentialty of Energy in the mind-stream of the individual. [42] As for the Natural State which is unconditioned, the Kunzhi is like the extent of the sky, the Rigpa is like the heart of the sun, and the Energy is like the rays of light of the sun."

D2. The Direct Introduction to Their Inseparability

With respect to the second consideration, [43] after one has practiced (being in contemplation, or the Natural State) rather tightly according to the rules (and not loosely) with respect to the threefold training: keeping the breath and the awareness concentrated, and after one has practiced (following that) the threefold relaxation, at that time when one looks at the state by means of the state itself, the Mother Kunzhi is emptiness. It is immaculate without a source (or root) and this is the Dharmakaya. The Son Awareness is inherent luminosity, totally naked, and exceedingly clear. This is the Sambhogakaya. The Energy (rtsal) is the apparitional display (of phenomena). It is self-originated and self-arising. This is the Nirmanakaya. These three: the Mother, the Son, and the Energy, abide in their inherent forms without separation as the total nature of the Trikaya from the very beginning. [44]

According to the *gZer-bu*, "The Kunzhi which is empty and clear like the vast expanse of the sky is the Dharmadhatu and the total primal awareness which is self-originated everywhere is the Dharmakaya." [45]

And again, "One's own Awareness in the vast expanse of the physical heart is the Dharmakaya. Its Nature in the pathway of the channels is the Sambhogakaya. And its self-arising at the gateways which are the lamps (of vision, the eyes) is the Nirmanakaya." [46]

According to the *sGron-ma*, "The great primordial purity is the Dharmakaya. It is untainted by anything whatsoever. It is untouched by limitations, and it rises like the sun in the sky devoid of clouds. The Mother and the Son arise on the path of the central channel in a manner that is inseparable." So it is said.

This represents the the extensive direct introduction.

II. Direct Introduction Through the Special Activities of the Base

Second, with respect to the direct introduction through the special activities of the Base (gzhi'i byed las khyad-par gyi ngo-sprod), there are four sections:

A. The direct introduction through thoughts and memories that are like clouds in the sky (bsam dran nam-mkha'i sprin ltar ngo-sprad-pa),

B. The direct introduction through the masses of thoughts that are like gentle breezes in the atmosphere (rtog tshogs bar-snang gi ser-bu ltar ngo-sprad-pa),

C. The direct introduction through the emotional defilements that are like the waves on the sea (nyon-mongs mtsho dang rba-rlabs ltar ngo-sprad-pa), and

D. The direct introduction through the six aggregates (of consciousness) that are like the rainbows spanning the sky (tshogs drug mkha' yangs gzha'-tshon ltar ngo-sprad-pa).

A. Direct Introduction Through Thoughts and Memories

In the first section, there ar two considerations:

1. The teaching on the Natural State (gnas-lugs bstan-pa) and
2. The direct introduction to it. (de la ngo-sprad-pa).

With respect to the first consideration (the Natural State), Awareness (rig-pa) is like the heart of the sun in the sky and the primal cognitions (ye-shes), which are thoughts and memories, are like the rays of the sun. In these terms, whatever is possible (as thoughts and memories) arises unceasingly. Furthermore, because the activity of the mind creates its own objects, in terms of thinking, the meaning of that object is remembered just as it is. And because that (conventional) meaning is experienced thereafter, it is called intelligence (rig-pa). [47]

According to the *sGron-ma*, "Even though the King who is knowing awareness (shes rig gi rgyal-po) is without thoughts, yet it is the base for the arising of various different thoughts and memories. For example, it is like the rays of light from the energy of the sun.

From the potency of Awareness, it arises as the thought process." [48] So it is said.

After one has forced awareness by means of the three essential points (of practice), one settles down into relaxation by way of relaxing. At that time, one gazess, staring with wide-open eyes (cer-re lta), [49] looking at thoughts such as the one who is forcing, the one who is relaxing, and the one who is settling down (that is to say, looking and searching for them as something concrete and real and not finding anything). At that time, when one apprehends and examines such memories, one will know them (and be aware of them as memories). But when one does not examine them, these memories that are not clear become uninterrupted and ordinary, (even overwhelming). And these two are called the knowing awareness that consists of thoughts and memories. There will exist masses of thoughts that may be good or bad, subtle or coarse. Nevertheless, all thoughts and actions of past thoughts and of future thoughts are created by mental processes, and that condition itself abides as the essence of self-originated primal awareness from the very beginning. [50]

According to the sGron-ma, "From the potential energy of awareness there arises as the thought process (rig-pa'i rtsal las blo du shar). The six aggregates and the six objects arise as energy. With respect to that, it is called the thought process that thinks. Because it remembers and is aware, it is called memory. Because its activity moves to its object, it is called mind." [51] So it is said.

B. The Direct Introduction Through the Masses of Thoughts

Second, with respect to these hosts of thoughts (rtog tshogs), from the state of Awareness which is without thoughts and which is like the (clear empty) sky, [52] when one produces thoughts of whatever kind, they come forth suddenly. Because, in the beginning, one examines the secondary causes that originated and are produced, it is free of a base and a root (or source). In the middle, because one examines their essence initially, they are without shape and color (that is, one sees that they have neither shape nor colour). At the end, they are purified into self-purification as the state of the Nature of Mind, destroyed into self-destruction, lost into self loss, and liberated into self-liberation. These empty movements become like gentle breezes in the atmosphere. And it arises as primal awareness which is self-originated and without thoughts. [53]

According to the *gZer-bu*, "Primal awareness without thoughts represents the Base, but the delusion-system ('khrul-lugs) is the following after the potentiality (or energy) of various different memories and thoughts. (Indeed, following after them represents delusion itself.) But looking at this as a fault is (itself) a deviation. Rather, the proper method is just relaxing into one's original condition. They are liberated at the end into the vast expanse. That is the non-dual understanding." [54] So it is said.

Or again, "(All) the various different thoughts and memories are exhausted into the space without thoughts. And whatever is created by the thought process (or actions of thought) is exhausted into the space that transcends the thought process. Sectarian philosophical tenets that grasp at one side (only) are exhausted into this space without partiality." [55] So it is said.

According to the *sGron-ma*, "One should just settle down into non-apprehending (and non-grasping) where there are no thoughts or memories!" [56] So it is said.

This represents the extensive introduction (rgyas-par ngo-sprad-pa).

C. The Direct Introduction to the Self-liberation of the Defilements

Second, with respect to the direct introduction to the self-liberation of the emotional defilements, or negative emotions (nyon-mongs-pa rang-grol du ngo-sprad-pa): From the state (that is, the Natural State) of the total Clear Light without thoughts, [57] one may create (and produce) deliberately such (defilements) as anger, and so on, and then looks directly at them arising on the path. (One sees that these emotional defilements) self-originate, self-arise, and self-liberate, becoming like the waves on the sea. Therefore, the passions are liberated into primal awareness, the poisons are purified into their own original condition, and the defects (skyon) arise now as virtuous qualities (yon-tan). And thus poison is called the nectar which arises on the path, (having no need any longer) to be renounced.

According to the *gZer-bu*, "Self-originated primal awareness is the Base, but if one follows after the energy (rtsal) of the poison of the passions, this represents the delusion-system. But looking at it (judging it) as a fault is also a deviation. Relaxing into its own original condition is the proper method. Liberation into the vast expanse is the path itself. And this non-duality represents understanding." [58] So it is said.

According to the *Lugs drug*, "If we realize the actual nature of the five poisons, then the activity of the five poisons represents the supreme conduct (or practice)." [59]

And according to the *Gab 'grel,* "In the state of the energy of anger, one will ultimately arrive at non-anger." [60] So it is said.

D. The Direct Introduction Through the Six Aggregates

Fourth, with respect to the direct introduction through the six aggregates (of consciousness) which are like the rainbows spanning the sky: From the state (that is, the Natural State) of the total Clear Light without thoughts, the six aggregates, once having arisen, move to the objects which are inherently pure in themselves. At that time, when (everything) is proceeding in the normal way with respect to the awareness of the one who acts, the six aggregates look with presence, [61] and they arise from the state that is unobstructed. From this basis which is without any source (or root), it (the phenomenon) arises in emptiness and is liberated again into emptiness, like the rainbow in the sky. [62] These various different manifestations of the six aggregates of consciousness, which arise through liberation, abide as the essence of the gnosis of one's own Awareness from the very beginning.

According to the *sGron-ma,* "From the primal cognitions of one's own Awareness, the energy (rtsal) arises as the six aggregates and the six objects of consciousness, thus creating the various activities of the body, speech, and mind. Because they arise as the Nirmanakayas, they abide in themselves as the realms of the Nirmanakaya. If one does not understand this, then they arise variously as the six realms of rebirth. [63]

According to the *gZer-bu,* "Because one comes to a thoroughly clear and definitive decision regarding Rigpa, delusions and obscurations (are understood to be) pure from the very beginning. And because one thoroughly clarifies and definitively decides with respect to the thought process, primal awareness arises as energy." [64] So it is said.

And according to the *Lugs drug,* "With respect to these phenomena or dharmas (bon), they are without any base or source (or root). Any that are let go (without interference from the mind), they manifest like this." [65] So it is said.

III. The Extensive Explanation of Liberation and Delusion

With respect to the extensive explanation of delusion and liberation from them (grol 'khrul rgyas-par bshad-pa), there are two sections:

A. The method of delusion where one does not understand (ma rtogs 'khrul tshul) and

B. The method of liberation where one does understand (rtogs de grol tshul).

A. The Method of Delusion

With respect to the first (the method of delusion), there are two considerations:

1. The co-emergent or spontaneously-born ignorance (lhan-skyes ma rig-pa) and

2. The ignorance which conceptualizes everything (kun brtags kyi ma rig-pa).

A1. Spontaneously Born Ignorance

With respect to the first (co-emergent, or spontaneously-born ignorance): Without their creating as much as a single hair-tip of sin, sentient beings have become deluded. At the beginning, when they became deluded in whatever manner, from the above Kunzhi, which is like the sky, there arises the primal cognitions of Awareness. With respect to that, there manifest memories that are moving and thoughts which are vibrating and one is ignorant (of the fact that) the appearances of the sounds, the lights, and the rays, which represent the inherent translucency (rang mdangs) of the Natural State are (in reality) self-manifestations. In this case, one is like the lion (gazing into the pool), who is deluded by his own reflected image, (thinking that it is another lion). [66] And because one behaves thereafter (in a deluded fashion), nevertheless, in an apparenttly normal and ordinary way, the three self-potencies arise before one as enemies. In this case, because the primal cognitions of Awareness become obscured, the situation is like the face of the sun in the sky being obscured by clouds, or a naked person donning clothes. This represents a veritable a wrapping up of the light of Rigpa in a net. [67] When there is only a little movement of grasping at a self, or "I", then the essence is just the very subtle part (that is, the essence which is just spontaneously born ignorance). As these above mentioned obscurations to the Kunzhi are very difficult to purify naturally (indeed, because they are very subtle), they represent ignorance and nothing other (than ignorance). Because the delusion and the Base exist simultaneously, this is called the spontaneously born, co-emergent ignorance.

According to the *sGron-ma*, "As for the reason that delusion exists for sentient beings in whatever fashion, (one may ask how do sentient beings become deluded?). At the time when the three visible objects arise manifestly, the memories and thoughts which are the actual objects of the awareness (and knowledge) of the thought process become darkened (and obscured). But not knowing these self-manifestations to be illusions, one sees these appearances as being due to other (extrinsic causes) and therefore one thinks that they are real. [68] This obscures the actual meaning of awareness, so that the thought process sees other things (as being due to extrinsic causes and as inherently existing). Not knowing Rigpa, one does not understand the actual meaning of the Kunzhi. As for that situation, this represents co-emergent spontaneously-born ignorance (lhan-cig skyes-pa'i ma rig-pa)." [69] So it is said.

A2. The Ignorance which Conceptualizes Everything

With respect to the second (kind of ignorance, that which conceptualizes everything): It is this original spontaneously-born ignorance that turns the primal cognitions of Awareness (rig-pa'i ye-shes) to the other side (that is to say, to the object side, whereby consciousness moves toward what appear to be actually existing external objects). Having caused these movements (of consciousness), the distractions only become greater. Because the sounds, the lights, and the rays, which are in themselves self-manifestations, come to be apprehended (and grasped at) in a coarse manner (thereby appearing to mental consciousness as solid, opaque, and real), [70] and possessing uncertainty (in terms of their manifestations), they thereupon arise as subject and object. And at that time, (because the individual does not know the Natural State), there will emanate the functional mind which moves, arising from the condition which does not recognize the knowing of objects. And because these (cognitions) are aroused (and stirred up) by the vital winds that move (g.yo-ba'i rlung), and because the three visible objects (of the sounds, the lights, and the rays) are disturbed like lassos of wind whipping the clouds about in the sky, the visible lights (of consciousness, at first subtle), become like a network (that is a snare and a trap). [71] Thereupon, the five lights, which are visible (and manifest), arise coarsely (and more grossly) as visible colours (or coloured lights). They arise in a five-fold manner, namely, as lights that are white, green, red, blue and yellow. [72] This process is called the ignorance which conceptualizes everything (kun brtags gyi ma rig-pa).

According to the *sGron-ma*, "The sense faculties thatare ignorant move to the objects of knowledge. They examine them discursively and appropriate the visible objects. Because they move to the objects of knowledge, they do not remain in their own original condition. Because they do not remain in their own original condition, they disturb the visible objects. Because the three visible objects are disturbed, there arise the five elements which represent the five causes. As for this (process), it represents the ignorance that conceptualizes everything." [73] So it is said.

With respect to the lights that are like that, there arise the five great elements. And with respect to that, there arise the five poisons that are the roots (sources) of the passions. From that arise one's own five elements. And with respect to that, they mature (and ripen) into the five skandhas which are fruitional. Thus originate the five internal organs which rely upon them (the elements). [74] With respect to that, there are created the five limbs which arise as potentiality of energy and there originate the five cavities (within the body), and so on. There are created five sense organs which are active with respect to that. There arise five sense consciousnesses which apprehend that. There are created five objects which are active with respect to that. There originate five activities which are secondary causes with respect to that. From that originate the five gateways to impure rebirth. With rspect to that, they ripen into the five diseases that afflict humans. And from entering into the five paths which are connected to that, the five realms which are created are ripened. One is tied to (and connected with) the five realms which arise with respect to that. Thus one should be introduced extensively to the cycle of interdependent origination which represents the mode (or method) of delusion. [75]

With respect to all of them, in the very beginning at the time when karma is not (manifest), but it only exists as latent propensities or karmic traces, (humanity collectively found itself) deluded (into rebirth) in the Arupadhatu, or Formless Realm. Then (in the course of time) it evolved into itself little by little, and at the time when there was produced great attachment and grasping, it was deluded (into rebirth) in the Rupadhatu, or Form Realm. Then (again in the course of time) at the time when it had evolved very extensively (becoming more and more gross and material) and in the usual and normal way (of potential human existence), it was deluded (into rebirth) in the Kamadhatu, or Desire Realm. In this way (the individuals belonging to the future humanity of this earth) transmigrated through the three realms of existence. Individuals took up embodiments within the six destinies of rebirth successively and so the individual transmigrates from one rebirth to the next one. [76]

According to the *sGron-ma*, "Since one sees (the world and other beings) by way of the power of the karmic traces of that (particular destiny of rebirth), discursive thoughts create, in terms of visible manifestation, a mind-body. Because of the power of the defilement of confusion, one becomes deluded (into being reborn) in the Arupadhatu, or Formless Realm. Because one sees everything by way of the power of these (particular) karmic traces from that (standpoint), there is created in visible manifestation the appearance of having a body of light. Because of the power of the defilemt of anger, one becomes deluded and transmigrates into the Rupadhatu, or Form Realm. Because one sees everything by way the great power of the karmic traces from that (particular standpoint), one becomes deluded, and in terms of visible manifestation, one is reborn into a material body of flesh and blood. Thus, by the power of defilement of desire, one becomes deluded and is reborn in the Kamadhatu, the Desire Realm." So it is said.

Similarly, the other emotional defilements or passions (grow and evolve) from that subtle condition, becoming more and more coarse, and one becomes (increasingly) deluded (by Samsara). [77]

At the beginning, one trains oneself slowly by degrees. And finally (one is guided to the point) where the explanation is given regarding the profound meaning (of the Natural State). (Having thus been introduced directly) thereafter one is liberated and finds oneself being without delusions. And because this single essential point at the very outset purifies (the mind-stream) with respect to Samsara, if one continues practicing, ultimately liberation is realized. All of them (those who attained liberation in the past) asserted just this single essential point. [78]

B. The Method of Liberation Through Understanding

Second, with respect to the method of liberation where one does understand (the Natural State) (rtogs te grol tshul), there are two sections:

1. The method of liberation in whatever fashion at the very beginning (dang-po ci ltar grol tshul), and
2. The extensive direct introduction to the system of liberation (grol-lugs rgyas-par bshad-pa).

B1. The Method of Liberation at the Beginning

With respect to the first (the method of liberation at the very beginning), when Kuntu Zangpo was liberated (from the very beginning) without doing so much as a hair-tip of virtue or merit (dge-ba), the three, namely, the sounds, the lights, and the rays, which represent inherent energy (rang rtsal), arose unobstructedly (and uninterruptedly) from the primal awareness of Rigpa, which is like the sun. Without his entering into the grasping or apprehending (of them) by way of the thought process, these three potencies were liberated as self-manifestations. [79]

Because one encounters the self-face of the Base and Rigpa (that is, because one meets one's own face which is the Base and Awareness) and the separation between the Mother and the Son (is overcome and the Son returns to the Mother), [80] one continues (and remains) here in the Kingdom of Kuntu Zangpo, which is the Nature of Mind. And since one continues in that, the contents of consciousness (sems 'byung), arise transcendently as primal cognitions without pollution. At that time, the virtuous qualities of the total Body, Speech, and Mind of Nirvana (arise naturally as pure visions, and all Nirmitas, or emanations of Compassion and Skilfull Means, which accomplish enlightened activities, arise naturally without looking to any effort or exertion.

According to the *sGron-ma*, "As for the conclusion that understands matters in whatever way, because the three visible objects (the sounds, the lights, and the rays) have arisen as energies (rtsal), by means of the consciousness associated with the thought process (blo'i shes-pa), as represented by memories and thoughts, one comes to see with a higher insight that these self-manifestations are really illusions. Because there are created secondary conditions which are one's own visible objects, a denuded Awareness arises nakedly. Now, the Kunzhi is without obscurations and one understands clearly. Because one understands, Rigpa remains in its own original condition and one does not follow after visible objects. At that time, one's own independence, or self-power (rang dbang), becomes manifest. The Nirmitas, or emanations of Nirvana, arise by way of that power without (the effort) to create or realize anything." [81] So it is said.

B2. The Extensive Explanation of the System of Liberation

Second, the primal cognitions of Awareness represent the inherent translucency (or self-luster) of becoming liberated into the essence of the Base. And from the potentiality of the capacity for pure vision arise the five inherent clear lights that manifest. From them arise the five spaces which originate and produce everything. From that arise the five vast expanses which are without substance (or a self). [82] From that arise the five Deities which are realized (created). From that arise the five Bodies which abide. From that originate the five Realms which manifest. From that arise the five bases which rely upon them. From that are created the five limbs which are mudras. From that arise the five treasures which originate everything. From that arise the five sense faculties which are unpolluted. From that arise the five primal cognitions which are without obscurations. From that arise the five primordial cognitions which are completely pure. From that arise the five objects which are completely pure. From that arise the five powers (or faculties) representing the matrix for the experience of "I". From that arise the five primal cognitions which are clear. From that arise the five fruits which are unsurpassed. From that arise the five perfect mandalas. From that arise the five realms which visibly manifest. This represents the method for understanding extensively the direct introduction to the cycle of interdependent origination. [83]

    Moreover, without looking at the practice of the path, those virtuous qualities, which understand and are aware of the real meaning of the Mother, the Son, and the Potentiality of Energy, were present from the very beginning. [84] and thus Kuntu Zangpo realized Buddhahood (without recourse to practicng the Path).

    According to the *sGron-ma*, "(In terms of Kuntu Zangpo), the two accumulations were never accumulated, but they originated solely from the power of understanding which was present from the very beginning." [85]

Now, because purifying oneself along the path is in agreement with the method generally, finally (the Fruit) becomes manifest [mthar mngon du gyur] by the power of effort and habitual practice. As for this Buddhahood, the path of liberation is Buddhahood itself. [86]

The Explanation of the View through seeing nakedly, which represents the direct introduction to one's own Base, (is hereby completed).

U-YA SMAR-RO

Virtue!

Chapter Five

The Explanation of the Meditation Practice: *sGom-khrid*

Here is contained "The Progressive Stages of the Guiding Explanation of the Meditation Practice for the Clear Light, which represents the Practice of the Path," (lam nyams su len-pa 'od-gsal sgom-pa'i khrid rim bzhugs-so).

Homage to Kuntu Zangpo, the all-pervading and all-encompassing Guide of Beings, who is one's own intrinsic self-awareness become manifest! [1]

As for the second (supplementary text): Within this guiding explanation of the meditation practice for the Clear Light, which represents the practice of the Path as such (lam nyams su blangs-pa 'od-gsal bsgom-pa'i 'od-gsal), [2] there are found three divisions, namely,

I.   Practicing the methods of the meditation involving the means for continuing in the progressive stages of the Path (bsgom tshul lam gyi rim-pa brkyang thabs),

II.   Practicing meditation where there exists the system for removing the impurities of mind (bsgom byed blo yi dri-ma bsal-lugs), and

III. Experiences due to meditation practice and the manner in which the Clear Light (visions) arise (bsgom-pas nyams dang 'od-gsal 'char tshul).

I. Methods of Meditation

With respect to the first division (that is, how to practice the method of the meditation) (bsgom tshul): Having given rise to a terror of death and rebirth from the depths (of one's heart) and being intent on the ultimate goal of enlightenment, one comes to guard one's faith and always carries one's Guru upon the crown of one's head. Having dismissed all worldly activities, the individual who possesses the capacity to remain continuously in the state of intrinsic awareness, or Rigpa, should obtain previously in their completeness the instructions which represent the essential guiding explanations, the practices, and the direct introduction (to the Natural State). [3]

Then, when one desires to continue, (one should retire to) some appropriate place (such as a retreat house) that is remote and which serves to increases virtues, or else, some other places that are high (in the mountains) and pure (in nature), such as an island in a lake, or a cave in a deep forest, or one on a glacial mountain, or among the rocks. In particular, it should especially be in a place that is pleasant and comfortable, where one can stay both day and night. And in such an agreeable place, one should not be without the helpful activities (and assistance) of an essential spiritual friend (that is to say, the presence and guidance of the Lama). One abandons all distractions until one has obtained stability (in the practice of contemplation). However, if one becomes tired (or exhausted) by the activities of practice, then one must take a break from the retreat. Nevertheless, one does not mix socially with others, or speak with them. One should make sure that one's food and clothing are adequate. One resolutely cuts all delusions represented by involvements with worldly entertainments and one accumulates efficiently those harmonious conditions that come together (that is, whatever is necessary to make the retreat).

Even though many things have been expounded (in the texts), such as the procedures for the means and the methods of explanation, as well as (the methods for) development, and carrying on along the path, together with the direct introduction (to the Natural State), what is most important here is that, by going into oneself, one actually discovers the real meaning of Rigpa, or intrinsic awareness, which is the great Clear Light without obscurations. [4]

When this meaning is condensed in one-pointed terms, there exist two procedures to be considered, namely,

1. The instructions on the essential points of the vital winds and the mind (rlung sems gnad kyi gdams-pa) and
2. The encountering, on certain occasions, of the characteristic visions (mtshan snang skabs sbyar du sprad-pa).

As for how to practice the method (len tshul): First, one obtains a thorough knowledge of the meditation practice by way of seeking out the essential Lama or master and obtaining from him a direct transmission of the profound instructions. Then, with a fierce determination, one proceeds to practice meditation diligently without neglecting this evenmindedness (in contemplation) for even a moment. One meditates for a long time, however long is necessary, whether days, months, or years, until the experiences (in terms of visions) arise in one's mind-stream. At all times and under all conditions, without being interrupted by anything, one remains continuously in that (state of contemplation) and meditates uninterruptedly. [5]

Here there exist four principal considerations:

1. Continuing to meditate in accordance with the method (described in the text) (tshul dang mthun-par bskyangs shing bsgom-pa),
2. The manner in which external appearances or visions arise (phyi'i snang-ba 'char tshul),
3. The manner in which internal experiences are produced and how one engages all of them (nang gi nyams-myong skye tshul thams-cad 'jug-pa), and
4. Their increasing and developing more and more like the face of the waxing moon (zla-ba yar gyi ngo bzhin je 'phel je rgyas la 'byung).

According to the *gZer-bu*, it is said, "In a hermitage located in a remote place possessing agreeable conditions, the individual who is terrified of death and rebirth (in Samsara) from the depths of one's heart, once having recognized the Kunzhi, the basis of everything, should clearly and definitively decide with suitable intensity upon what is Rigpa, or intrinsic awareness." [6]

And according to the *lDe-mig*, "When one does something that one wants to do, there will be no fatigue. But if not, then there are created all (manner of difficulties)." [7] So it is said.

II. Removing Obstructions to Meditation

Second, with respect to performing the practices in terms of the real meaning of the Mahayana, the Greater Vehicle, this (real meaning) being the Natural State, [8] there may originate three kinds of obstructions:

A. Externally, there may arise obstructions due to human beings and to non-human spirits (phyi mi dang mi ma yin-pa'i bar-chad),
B. Internally, there may arise obstructions such as sicknesses due to imbalances in the humors (within the physical body) (nang 'du-ba nad kyi bar-chad), and
C. Secretly, there may arise obstructions that are experiences in meditation (gsang-ba bsgom-pa nyams kyi bar-chad).

A. External Obstructions

With regard to the first of them (the external obstructions): As for attachments to the worldly life, such as affectionate thoughts (of attachment) towards one's near relatives, passionate attachments to wealth and country, all types of worldly entertainments, and so on, one should realize that these truly represent demons. (Therefore, when one is undertaking a retreat), one must forsake human society. To counteract these negative influences (which represent demons and evil spirits) (gdon), one has recourse to the performing of religious rituals (rim-gro), evocations of spirits (bka' bsgo), offering of obstacle tormas to them (gtor-ma sbyin), and throwing down one's physical body as food (phung-po gzan du bskyur), (that is, offering to them one's flesh and blood body (lus sbyin) as part of performing the Chod Rite).

B. Internal Obstructions

Second, with regard to sicknesses (nad), one may engage in yantra exercises, pranayama, and healing visualizations. [9] And one may endeavor to remove the obstructions by way of uttering sounds, and so on. However, when only minor ills arise, one does not need to take notice of them.

C. Secret Obstructions

Third, even though the obstacles represented by experiences in meditation are very many, [10] when one condenses them, they may be condensed into the three considerations of the view, the meditation, and the conduct (or action).

C1. Deviations from the View

With regard to the view, one should not slip into the five deviations, [11] which are as follows:

1. One may become completely attached to the citadel of the words, so that the real meaning becomes obstructed and one overflows at the mouth (with words) and goes astray thereby (tshig gi rdzong la la zhen/ don gyi 'gags la dred kha 'byams du song-ba).
2. Even though the intellect thinks that it understands (the view of Dzogchen), nevertheless, one loses, in general, the real meaning that arises from with its own characteristics (in terms of personal experience) (go blo yod kyang rang mtshan ma shor-ba'i don spyir shor-ba).
3. Failing to practice in the present, one loses (one's way) through desiring to put off (practice) until a later time (da lta nyams su mi len-par/ phyi dus 'debs-ap'i re 'dod du shor-ba).
4. One loses (one's way) through the intellect fabricating guesses without really knowing the actual system of existence (yin-lugs ma shes-pa'i 'ol-tshod bzos-pa'i blo byas su shor-ba).
5. Though looking into one direction, one has not yet truly decided and so one is attached to two (contradictory) points (spros mtha' ma chod-par phyogs gcig tu lta-ba rtse gnyis su zhen-pa).

C2. Defects to Meditation Practice

Then, with regard to the meditation (bsgom-pa), (there are also five points:)

1. There may exist manifest attachments to pleasurable sensations, the producing of connections of certainty with respect to clarity, and the grasping at the state of thoughtlessness as being supreme (bde-ba la mngon du zhen dang gsal-ba la nges-pa'i skyes-pa dang mi rtog-pa la mchog tu 'dzin-pa),

2. Without holding to mindfulness, meditation will lose its energy and sharpness (dran 'dzin med-pa gleng bsgom du song-ba),

3. Because drowsiness and dullness gather like clouds, clarity and lucidity depart (bying rmugs su 'thibs-pas gsal mdangs thon-pa),

4. Because there is agitation, floating about, and being scattered, one does not remain in a state of calm (rgod lding 'khor-bas gnas cha med-pa), and

5. Because (one's meditation) slips, gives way, and is not decisive, it is not productive of development ('dred 'dzur 'thab-pas bskyed bogs med).

Therefore, one should not proceed into these five deviations.

C3. Conduct to be Avoided

And with respect to the conduct (spyod-pa), (there are also five factors to be avoided:)

1. The conduct of telling fortunes and playing at being a Guru (zol zog tho-co'i spyod-pa),

2. The conduct of pretending to be spiritual for the sake of material gain (ched byas tshul chos kyi spyod-pa),

3. The conduct where one is lazy and indifferent (blang snyoms le-lo'i spyod-pa),

4. The conduct where one ties oneself up in (stubbornly) carrying out what one does not want to do (bsdug brtsir rang bcings kyi spyod-pa), and

5. The conduct of ordinary social behavior and wrong views (log lta tha-mal gyi spyod-pa).

Therefore, one should not proceed into these five deviations. As it is said in the *gSungs rabs* (the *Khams-chen,* or Prajnaparamita), [12] "When one enters on to the the path of those merchants who seek the precious wish-granting gem, because there exist many enemies who would cause them harm, all of these persons (joining the caravan) should don their armor."

III. Arising of the Clear Light Visions

Third, within (this topic, that is,) the experiences due to meditation and the manner in which the Clear Light (visions) arise (bsgom-pas nyams dang 'od-gsal 'char tshul), there are three subdivisions, namely,

A. The manner in which the visions that arise originate (shar-ba'i snang-ba 'byung tshul),
B. Then, the manner in which these visions increase (and develop) when they become familiar (de nas goms-pa'i snang-ba 'phel tshul), and
C. Uniting them with the progressive stages of the Path (de dag gi lam gyi rim-pa dang sbyar-ba).

A. How the Visions Originate

Within the first section, (the manner in which the Thodgal visions come forth), there exist two considerations. namely,

(1) The manner in which external visions come to be seen (phyi'i snang-ba mthong tshul) and
(2) The manner in which internal experiences are produced (nang gi nyams-myong bskyed tshul).

A1. How the External Visions come to be Seen

With respect to the first (how external visions come to be seen), it is said in the *sGron-ma,* "As for the teaching concerning the forceful method of purification (rtsal gyi sbyang thabs), the movements (of thoughts) are like a golden fish and the dark retreat house is like a net of light that holds them fast. The mirror of Awareness (rig-pa'i me-long) in which everything is clear reveals (the space) that is seen as the clear sky. Mindful (attention) is like the spear of the mind and fixation on the visions is like a shield of light. At that time, one sees the seeds of the Rupakaya, like a host of stars rising in the sky." [13]

Because one practices as described, at the beginning, the signs of the five elements arise as indicated above (in the Principal Practices text). [14] And elsewhere, it is said, "The lights and the rays (appear as if) one opens up a silk brocade cloth (in the bright sunlight). There exist uncountable and inconceivable (numbers of appearances) arising like rainbows, or like painted mandalas. (It is like looking at the sun through) a striped woolen shawl (phyar-ba), or through a felt blanket made of yak hair (re-lde). (The visions) arise and come to fill the sky and the atmosphere (before the practitioner) with familiar (visions) and (visions of) the countryside. And there is established the ground (or basis) for the (visible manifestations of) the realms. Inside of them, the seeds of the Rupakayas and the thigleys arise like scattered hosts of stars. [15]

According to the *gZer-bu*, it is said, "The five lights that manifest (provide) the base for (the appearing of) the realms and the mandalas. There will arise diverse Rupakaya forms, such as pavillions of thigleys, celestial palaces of the five kinds (of Buddha Families), and the divine forms of higher insight (these being visible manifestations of the Natural State)." [16] So it is said.

A2. How Internal Experiences are Produced

Then, with regard to the second consideration (how the internal experiences are produced): At that time, while one is practicing meditation, it is much like seeing the sun through the clouds (in the atmosphere). (At first) it appears faint and misty. Thus, one may still be afflicted and eaten by doubts. At the beginning of the first stage of meditation development, where one is meditating in discrete sessions (thun bsgom), (the vision of the Natural State) is like the first or second day of the waxing moon.

B. How Visions Evolve and Develop

Second, with respect to the manner in which visions evolve and develop when one has become familiar with them (de la goms-pa'i snang-ba 'phel tshul), there exist five progressive stages:

(1) The manner in which visions increase (snang-ba 'phel-ba'i tshul),
(2) The manner in which visions multiply (snang-ba mched-pa'i tshul),
(3) The manner in which visions develop further (snang-ba rgyas-pa'i tshul),
(4) The manner in which visions become completed (snang-ba rdzogs-pa'i tshul), and
(5) The manner in which visions finally culminate (snang-ba mthar thug-pa'i tshul).

B1. How Visions Increase

Within the first stage, the manner in which the visions increase (snang-ba 'phel-ba'i tshul), there are two considerations, namely,

a. The manner in which external visions are seen (to increase) (phyi'i snang-ba mthong tshul) and
b. The manner in which internal experiences are produced (nang gi nyams-myong bskyed tshul).

B1a. How the External Visions Increase

With respect to the first consideration, in terms of the external (visions), one practices one-pointedly as described above, and because of that, at sometime or another, there will arise various experiences of the visions increasing. (snang-ba 'phel-ba'i nyams sna 'char).

Innumerable visions of Clear Light (Thodgal visions) arise and inside of them, there will appear the thigleys of Awareness having the color of crystal and having just the size of a pea. More than that, they will grow larger. They may be single, or two linked together, or three linked together, or even many of them linked together. They may be linked both upwardly and transversely, and these (phenomena) are called the threads of compassion, which represent the Essence of Awareness (rig-pa'i thugs-rje'i nyag-thag). They are like yarn that is silver or white, or like threads. Various visions arise, such as thigleys in chains strung together, or single ones not strung together, but connected by threads, or single threads not connected with thigleys, and so on. [17]

However, because all of the five elements (in one's body) are not balanced or in equilibrium, [18] (initially) all of the colors are for the most part white, or each one of them is a single (colour), or else, because (the elements) may be in balance a bit, the five colors come forth complete in each of them (the thigleys). For the most part, single or multiple colors arise.

And in the middle of these thigleys, when one examines them, there may just appear aspects of divine forms; they abide there in each of them subtly without having the cause for being very clear. Furthermore, these lights and rays and thigleys never remain longer than a single moment and (these phenomena) are like a waterfall coming down from the steep face of the mountain. They may appear to move or to separate, to scatter, or to come together (chaotically), like quicksilver scatters and comes together (when dropped on the table). [19]

According to the *sGron-ma*, it is said, "Being familiar with these (phenomena) and becoming intimately acquainted with them, and because they (the thigleys) come together, there originate five special aspects of familiarity (here below delineated). At first, the visions will increase. One will see them (the thigleys) scattering or coming together like quicksilver." [20]

And according to the *gZer-bu*, "As for the rays of Awareness and the threads of compassion, at first they will manifest like a waterfall coming down from the steep face of the mountain." [21]

B1b. How the Internal Experiences are Produced

Second, with regard to internal (experiences being produced): At that time, experiences of one-pointed concentration arise (de'i dus su rtse gcig gi nyams 'char). A luminous awareness that does not move (from its own place) becomes very clear and pure, and this represents an experience of the calm state. [22] However, the meeting between the Mother, which is emptiness, and the Son, which is Awareness (rig-pa), is still rather shallow (and not profound).

Meditation practice (should commence) at the time of the day when the light (of the sky) is most clear. A special pleasurable sensation may be produced, but when it settles down, it may not be very clear. The developing of any single (session of) practice depends on the secondary conditions (of sunlight and space, and so on). Thus, the first progressive stage of meditating in discrete sessions (thun sgom) reaches its culmination, and this is said to be like third and fourth days of the waxing moon.

B2. How Visions Multiply

Second, (with regard to the manner in which the visions multiply (snang-ba mched-pa'i tshul), there are two considerations, namely,

a. The manner in which external visions multiply (phyi'i snang-ba mched tshul) and
b. The manner in which internal experiences are produced (nangi gi nyams-myong bsked tshul).

B2a. How External Visions Multiply

With respect to the first among these two considerations regarding the manner in which the visions multiply, (that is to say, how external visions continue to arise and multiply): The visions of the Clear Light (Thodgal visions) arise in all directions. And inside of them arise some thigleys of Awareness having the color of crystal. However, because the five elements are in balance and in equilibrium, for the most part each of these thigleys of the pavilions of the five lights possess rims (or auras) of the five-fold (colours). They appear clear and pure, bright and luminous. [23] Moreover, the threads also arise, some of them being white. Again, for the most part, the thigleys of the chains have diverse colors and are like (beads) on a single strand. Their rims have five-fold (colors). In their centers (may appear) various different forms that are appropriate, such as very subtle aspects of the Rupakayas in the form of letters and syllables, or else, stupas, and so on. In between and elsewhere there may be visible aspects, such as lights and rays and beautiful images. However, it is uncertain how these (phenomena) will arise or not arise. And even though they may have arisen previously, now they will be slower and more tame, being able to remain a little while longer.

As is is said, according to the *sGron-ma*, "Then the visions begin to multiply and one sees them directly, like seeing the moon or the sun shining in the sky, whereupon Rigpa, or intrinsic awareness, is seen as a pavilion of light." [24]

Again, according to the *gZer-bu*, "Second, it (the continuity of the visions) is like the flow of the current of a river."

At the time when these visions multiply, all of the rays and thigleys and lights and threads become slower and more tame; they are able to remain a moment longer. But the rays and threads appear quickly, in the manner of walking past on foot.

B2b. How Internal Experiences are Produced

Then, with respect to the second consideration (how internal experiences are produced):

The experiences of one-pointed concentration are still rather shallow and they arise as simply experiences of being free of conceptual elaborations (spros-bral gyi nyams su 'char). At that time, everything external and internal is released into total self-liberation. Furthermore, without going beyond this state of total inherent clarity that is unmoving, [25] just as is the case when the ocean is unmoved by the winds, these (experiences) arise free of all elaborations in terms of characteristics. For example, it is like the fifth and sixth day of the waxing moon.

At the time of meditation practice, these (experiences) increase very much. And even though one may not meditate, they will come forth on one occasion after another. And as for that, one has indeed arrived (at the second stage) (ngang sgom), that is, meditating in that state of the Nature of Mind. [26]

B3. How the Visions Develop Further

Third, (with regard to the manner in which the visions develop further (snang-ba rgyas tshul), there are again two considerations, namely,

a.   The manner in which external visions develop further (phyi'i snang-ba rgyas tshul) and
b.   The manner in which internal experiences are produced (nangi gi nyams-myong bskyed tshul).

B3a. How the External Visions Develop Further

With respect to the first of these two considerations regarding the manner in which (the external) visions increase and develop further (snang-ba rgyas tshul). Due to the vital winds having become obstructed, visions will arise in the mind-stream (of the practitioner). However, from the interior (of his heart), a little portion of the supreme Clear Light may visibly arise [27] and at present the impure visions due to (the activites) of (the elements) of fire, water, earth, and air having become obstructed in the mind-stream (of the practitioner), there will arise pure visions of the seeds of divine forms and even the visions of divine realms. Everywhere there arise various different visions in the cardinal and the intermediate directions, as well as above and below, in front and in back, which have the nature of Clear Light. There will arise various different thigleys of five-fold lights, such as those resembling a bamboo shield, or those (phenomena) seen in a felt blanket made of yak hair, or in the countryside, or those (phenomena) may be like very small mustard seeds. Moreover, each of them will divide themselves into five-fold thigley (patterns, that is to say, one in the center, four in the cardinal directions). And there may arise with respect to them both upward pointed spokes and vertical strands of light. [28] And these will adorn the the rims or circumference (of these thigleys). Outside of this, the rim is surrounded by lotuses, wheels, swastikas, and jewels, all of them of light, and so on. In the zone beyond that, there originate inconceivable numbers of visible objects, whether many or few, great or small, that entirely fill the field of vision (of the practitioner), [29] such as decorated and ornamented doors and windows that are very beautiful and complete. And in the middle arise aspects of divine forms (sku'i rnam-pa), either whole, or half, or just the head, as well as luminous seeds that are letters and syllables, together with lights, rays, and threads. Some of these visions that are like that abide even without moving or shaking, whereas some of them move about just a little bit.

As it says in the *gZer-bu*, "Third, they (the visions) become like a hawk (hovering nearly motionless in the sky) while searching for his food." [30].

And again, according to the *sGron-ma*, "Then visions come to proliferate and develop further [31] and one will actually see the Mandalas of the Sambhogakayas of the Five Families."

B3b. How the Internal Experiences are Produced

With respect to the second consideration (the producing of internal experiences): Having become free of the conceptual elaborations mentioned above and (allowing everything) to self-liberate, the side of the Natural State becomes deeper and more stable, (if one practices continuously), then after some time, one's intrinsic awareness (or Rigpa) will be without foundation (or base) and having suddenly gone into a singular (condition of) total primordial emptiness and which is devoid of any root (or source), consequently, everything that arises or originates in Samsara and Nirvana, whether external objects or internal consciousness, will come to have a single taste in terms of that (Natural State), and thus, that is called "the meditation where diversity comes to have a single taste." [32] (For example,) this is like the eighth and ninth day of the waxing moon.

Now one has gone just half way toward the Primordial State of Buddhahood. Having exhausted and overthrown "one's meditation in the state," one then proceeds into (the third) and final stage, which is "meditating in the vast expanse of space." [33]

B4. How the Visions become Completed and Perfected

Fourth, with regard to the manner in which the visions arise as complete and perfect (snang-ba rdzogs-pa'i 'char tshul), there are once more two considerations, namely,

a. The manner in which external visions are completed (phyi'i sang-ba rdzogs-pa'i tshul) and
b. The manner in which internal experiences are produced (nang gi nyams-myong bskyed tshul).

B4a. How the Visions become Completed

With respect to the first of these two considerations regarding the manner in which the visions arise in their completeness: The supreme Clear Light becomes visibly manifest, whereupon the divine forms and the divine realms of the Buddhas come to exist as spontaneously perfected in themselves (that is, in the Natural State). [34] They (de-nyid), that is to say, the visions arise without anything remaining hidden or concealed. Furthermore, these pure self-manifestations (rang-snang dag-pa) of the great celestial palaces and mandalas of the Shantika, Paushtika, and Raudra Deities (who are peaceful, prosperous, and ferocious respectively) are unmixed (or not merged) with each other. And individually they are clear and bright (in their manifestations). The walls, gateways, gate ornaments, together with altars, domes with garuda wings, parasols, and umbrellas, together with bird horns (as are seen on stupas, are all complete). And inside (the celestial palaces), with respect to the Shantika and Paushtika Deities, there are seats that are pure without defects, such having on them sun discs, moon discs, lotuses, swastikas, and so on. And with respect to the Vashya and Raudra Deities (who are enchanting and fierce respectively), they reside upon seats that are symbols of subjugation (thul-ba rtags gyi gdan), such as sitting upon the bodies of violent spirits (belonging to the eight classes), including Devas, Nagas, Gandharvas, the five wild animals, and so on. [35] And these principal deities, both inner and outer, belonging to the Five Families are surrounded by their respective retinues. Together with their messengers and servants that are emanations, there are immeasurable numbers of divine hosts of Shantika, Paushtika, Vashya, and Raudra Deities. Each of them remains on its own (appropriate) pure seat. All of their respective ornaments and attire, their marks and characteristics, as well as their body colors and hand-symbols are complete. As for their respective sizes, these transcend both large measures and small measures. They may be many or few, as the case may be, but they arise (before the practitioner) in inconceivable numbers.

In between them, there arise five by five everywhere, in abundance above and below, the thigleys of five-fold lights ('od lnga'i thig-le). In the middle of each of them, there will reside the perfect Five Families (that is, the five Dhyani Buddhas). Also, inside each thigley serving as a single base, there are divine realms in the four directions and in the center. These Five Families indeed reside therein, and also in the centers of the thigleys there abide the symbols of these Five Families. Furthermore, the deities, which are scattered about in these mandalas, reside on their own respective seats. Moreover, the deities manifest everywhere as Sambhogakayas, Nirmanakayas, and so on. The manner in which these pure visions arise is inconceivable. At that time, all of them, together with the thigleys and rays and threads and divine forms come forth and remain without moving or shaking.

According to the *sGron-ma*, "Then the visions become completed. One sees mandalas that are spontaneously perfected symbols. One sees visions that are divine realms of light. One sees magical apparitions without their moving or shaking." [36]

And also according to the *gZer-bu*, "Fourth, they (the visions) become like a tortoise put into a bowl (where he cannot move)." [37]

B4b. How Internal Experiences are Produced

With respect to the second (producing internal experiences): While engaging in the pious practice of allowing diversity to become of a single taste (du-ma ro-gcig gi dge-sbyor), confidence in one's experiences and understanding will grow just a little bit more. Gradually, everything where the mind exerts itself, including the meditator (the subject) and what is meditated upon (the object), having been liberated into the Nature of Mind, Awareness (rig-pa) will come to abide continuously in a state without distractions and even without meditation. And there will come forth nothing that will go beyond that. At that time, (because the practitioner is naturally and effortlessly in the Natural State), it will not be necessary to engage in meditation with the mind (or thought process). It will only be necessary to be just a little bit mindful of the state (that is, the Natural State). And that (condition) is called meditating without distractions and even without meditation itself. [38]

For example, this is like the thirteenth and the fourteenth days of the waxing moon. Now one has nearly reached the stage of Buddhahood. Moreover, this final stage, where one is meditating in the vast expanse of understanding, will most certainly arise within one's mind-stream, but on this occasion, it just does not become very visible (or well manifested). [39]

B5. How the Final Visions Arise

With respect to the manner in which the final visions arise (snang-ba mthar thug-pa'i 'char tshul), there are also two considerations, namely,

a. The manner in which the final visions arise (phyi'i snang-ba mthar thug-pa'i 'char tshul) and
b. The manner in which the internal experiences are produced (nang gi nyams-myong bskyed tshul).

B5a. How the External Visions Arise

With regard to the first of these two considerations, the manner in which the final visions arise (snang-ba mthar thug-pa'i 'char tshul): Even though all visible things with characteristics, which are elaborated in that way, now arise in the manner of pure self-manifestations, such as divine forms, lights, rays, thigleys, and divine realms, once having arisen in that way, (all of them) dissolve of themselves into the vast expanse of the Kunzhi, where there exist no conceptual elaborations, and there is only a single emptiness, without any root (or source).

Having collected them together, all of the characteristics of things that have been conceptually elaborated and fabricated by the efforts (of the mind) are ultimately liberated by way of releasing them (into the Natural State). Indeed, everything, all the visions of the gnosis, or primal awareness, of the divine forms, including sounds, lights, and rays, are gathered back into the Nature of Mind. [40] And one decides upon this definitively (discovering this is the ultimate and the final nature of everything).

According to the *sGron-ma*, "As for the rays, they represent the inherent rays of Awareness. They are empty images or forms in the same manner as reflections of the moon seen on the water. As for the sounds, they represent the inherent sounds of Awareness. They are empty inherent sounds in the same manner as echoes. As for the lights, they represent the inherent lights of Awareness. They are empty inherent forms in the same manner as as rainbows (seen in the sky)." [41]

And again, according to the *Lung drug*, "One sees the Sugatas as being as numerous as the grains of sand. (But these pleasant and beautiful visions) are like drinking honey in a dream. When one awakens there is nothing remaining on the object side. Nothing remains and nothing is seen (of them). They are empty and free of partialities." Or again, "They are like the dreams of a dumb man; it is difficult for him to describe them to others." [42]

And according to the *gZer-bu*, "Fifth, (these final visions) are similar to the space where the four elements have become exhausted (and have dissolved, disappearing into space)." [43] And again, "All of them, the manner in which visions arise, are described above and everything that arises as self-manifestations, such as sounds, lights, and rays, are dissolved back again into the vast expanse of the Kunzhi, in the same manner as the son is taken up again into his mother's lap. [44] They are annihilated into self-annihilation. They are liberated into self-liberation. They cease into self-cessation. They arise into self-arising and they ultimately arrive at a condition of exhaustion (where there are no more visions arising whatsoever). This repesents the manner in which the delusion process goes back into the single essential point (of the original condition of things, which is the Natural State). They arrive at their limit or end, which is liberation, and the source of origination." So it was expounded according to the *gZer-bu*.

B5b. How the Internal Experiences are Produced

With respect to the second consideration (the manner in which internal experiences are produced): Mindfulness (dran-pa) is without distractions and without meditation, but that state is just a little tied up (like a horse tethered by a rope to a stake). [45] But after some time, one should even cut through this tether of mindfulness, (whereas previously) one had tethered meditation to a stake in terms of whatever one does, one does not now go beyond that state where everything is free of effort. Thereupon, everything that arises, arises as gnosis (or primal awareness). Therefore, it does not matter in particular whether one meditates or does not meditate. It does not matter whether one is asleep or not. If one just lets everything be as it is, it will remain as such (bzhag na stod). But if one fixates (the attention) on it, it will go away (gtad na 'gro). But when it is needed, it will surely come. It is now under one's control and can be transformed by oneself. Thus, one's enemy becomes the same as one's son. Gold becomes the same as dross. There no longer exists any hope of progressing upward (on the path to Nirvana) nor falling downward again (into Samsara). Thus, it becomes manifest (as the final stage of meditation, namely,) meditation in the vast expanse of spontaneous understanding. For example, it is like the fifteenth day of the waxing moon. One has reached the end and the limits of familiarity (with visions) and they have become stable in one's original condition, which is Kuntu Zangpo. [46]

Furthermore, for example, if one examines the source of the deceit of a liar (confronting him with the truth), he becomes ashamed of himself. In the same way, if one examines the deceitful source (of these visions), which are the sounds, the lights, and the rays (that manifest to the practitioner), they will return directly back to the Nature of Mind. Thus, the source of delusions is cut off and one will realize the Fruit, which is Perfect Buddhahood. [47] One need not hope for any other more excellent (result).

Moreover, the visions that occur at the present moment become systematically (and globally) understood as actually being deities and celestial palaces. Therefore, all aspirations and desires revert (from worldly egotistical goals) and thereafter one (no longer) does evil things or violates morality. Because one has thoroughly cut off the source of delusion (by dissolving it) directly into the Base, thereafter no further delusions will arise. Rigpa becomes pure and immaculate, and with regard to the Essential State, it reaches its source or origin and (the manifestations of) energy are finished and completed. The energy departs and one discovers that nothing whatsoever is left behind. And because this (condition) becomes manifest, one finds that one does not move from that state which is the Dharmakaya. [48]

Then, from that state (the Dharmakaya), because the polluted material body has been liberated into an unpolluted state, [49] pure visions will arise to the disciple. For example, one's own body arises as a Sambhogakaya form, adorned with the (thirty-two) marks and the (eighty) characteristics and accompanied by the emanated arrays of the seats, the thrones, (the celestial palaces), and the divine realms.

Furthermore, from that same source of origination (byung khungs), the manner in which arise one's elements (dhatus), and one's sense fields (ayatanas), both root and branch, as well as one's eight consciousness aggregates, and the five gates of the senses, and so on, is as follows: [50]

1. In their outer aspect, they arise as the divine hosts of one hundred and eight Prosperity Deities, and so on, (phyi ltar rgyas-pa'i lha tshogs brgya dang rtsa brgyad las sogs),
2. In their inner aspect, they arise as the divine hosts of the forty-five Peaceful Deities, (nang ltar zhi-ba'i lha tshogs bzhi-bcu rtsa lnga), and
3. In their secret aspect, they arise as the divine hosts of the eighty-six Wrathful Deities (gsang-ba khro-bo'i lha tshogs brgyad-cu rtsa drug las sogs 'char-ba).
(These are all Sambhogakaya forms.)

Thus, with respect to the Sambhogakaya, having emanated (the figures of) the Guides (or the Nirmanakaya Buddhas of the six realms) throughout the different paths of methods in order to subdue (tame and convert) living beings everywhere, they accomplish the benefit of beings without negligence. There will come forth Nirmanakayas from that energy or state, [51] (naturally, spontaneously, and without effort). Thus, one does not have to pray that, at some future time, one will realize the Trikaya (because one has already realized full and perfect Buddhahood already).

It this is truly the case, then one does not need to strive arduously for many kalpas (in order to realize Buddhahood) by purifying one's karma and obscurations, as well as by generating the stages and the paths. (One understands that) the entire philosophical system of causality, which represents conventional truth, is false. And thus one can attain Buddhahood in this present lifetime by way of forceful methods in relation to the physical body. [52]

As it is said according to the *sGron-ma*, "The source of the falseness of appearances (or visions) is exhausted into the Nature of Mind. One comes to decide definitively that all the Rupakayas (that is, all visible forms) are indeed mind. Thereby one cuts off the source of delusion (at its root) and it is not possible for delusions (to arise again). The Trikaya becomes manifest at that present moment and one is no longer under the sway of the power of cause and effect, which represents the great lie. This represents the forceful method for attaining Buddhahood. [53]

Well then, when one attains the final visions and experiences in whatever manner as described in this instruction, then according to the *gZer-bu*, "One should take the measure of the intermediate pulse of the arteries, the count being not too long nor too short, and it must be interrupted. One hundred pulses are counted as a single unit. One will surely arrive at the limit of the full measure of familiarity with the visions in some eighteen thousand of these units."

The hundred-fold cycle of the intermediate measure of the breathing of the individual is made into one unit of measure of a meditation session of the Clear Light (that is, Thodgal practice). Therefore, the full measure of the sessions is eighteen hundred. Then, due to other secondary conditions, for one who possesses an intermediate capacity, if one practices continuously and uninterruptedly, the final visions will arise as described above in their perfection and completion. [54]

Elsewhere, individually, these five modes for the arising of visions may be introduced by the showing of individual pictures. [55]

C. Uniting the Development of Visions with the Progressive Stages of the Path

Third, with respect to uniting these (stages in the development of the visions) with the (usual) five stages of the Path (according to the Sutra system), it is much like the procedure with a chariot: one traverses the paths (and stages) in the same manner as did the holy Jinas (Buddhas) and Aryas (Arhats) of the past. [56]

Furthermore, at the beginning, one purifies one's sins and obscurations by means of the nine stages of the conduct of Bon, (that is, the Ngondro practices). [57] When one is in the process of amassing the two accumulations (of wisdom and merit), this is in agreement with the Path of Accumulation (tshogs lam). Then, as for the two instructions regarding what has characterisitcs and what does not have characterisitcs (that is to say, what is visible and invisible, or fixating the mind on an object and fixating without an object), clear visions with respect to the meaning of the Essence are produced, and because they are united to the meaning of the Natural State, this is in agreement with the Path of Unification (sbyor lam). [58]

Then, as for the instructions regarding the Clear Light (or Thodgal practice), both in general and in detail, because the primal cognitions of Awareness becomes displayed (and revealed) manifestly in whatever manner, this is in agreement with the Path of Vision (mthong lam). Then, as for the instructions regarding the development (of the visions), the real meaning of the Essential State (ngo-bo nyid) arises, and because that becomes familiar and one is intimately acquained with it, this is in agreement with the Path of Meditation Development (bsgom lam). [59] Then, having been directly introduced to rhe real meaning of Reality, one comes to understand it fully and this represents the final Path of the Ultimate Attainment (lam mthar phyin-pa).

Furthermore, "Having striven arduously on the path throughout various lifetimes for countless ages, one generates the essential point of the procedure of the method within a single lifetime and in a single instant, one comes to remain in one's own original condition. One comes to a completion without actually traversing the path (at length). Delusions come to be self-liberated without actually renouncing them. The Fruit manifests visibly as the spontaneously perfected Trikaya because the path has been completed in terms of its being the short path." [60] So it is said.

And again, "(The doctrine of) causality is a great and powerful falsehood and lie. Rather, this (teaching and practice of Dzogchen) is the most forceful method for attaining Buddhahood." [61] This was expounded according to the *sGron-ma*.

When one unites experiences and understanding at the time of meditating in sessions (thun bsgom), because one becomes familiar (and habitual) in terms of the method of the real meaning of the gnosis of Awareness, this is in agreement with the Path of Accumulation.

Because, at the time of meditating, the clear visions come forth, this is in agreement with the Path of Unification. Because there arises a beginning to meditating in the state and because one newly understands their inherent characterisitcs, this is in agreement with the Path of Vision. Furthermore, because one becomes familiar with the state and because it has finally come forth, this is in agreement with the Path of Meditation Development. Because it becomes a vast expanse of space, this represents the Fruit that is ultimately attained [62]

Furthermore, at the time when one obtains stability in meditation in the sessions (thun bsgom), (there will arise) the virtuous qualities of a mind that genuinely knows, as well as the virtuous qualities of pure speech. Accordingly, the view, and meditation, the conduct, and the activities will come to manifest very clearly. For a holy person in whom there are produced all of these experiences, there will come forth all the virtuous qualities that can arise. And accordingly, at the time of meditation in the state (ngang bsgom), all of these virtuous qualities that have arisen previously will become even greater and more exalted than before. And one will obtain the magical powers of the Bodhisattva, as well as clairvoyant knowledge, spiritual activities, and all the virtuous qualities of the view and the realization (of the practice), as well as the action and conduct. At the time of meditation in the vast expanse of space (klong bsgom), these (qualities) will become even more exalted than those cited above, and there will arise into visible manifestation within the mind-stream (of the practitioner) all possible virtuous qualities, such as the Body, Speech, Mind, Quality, and Activity of a completely perfect Buddha.

Furthermore, externally, the manner in which the visions arise are (exclusively) the seeing of the Clear Light (that is to say, Thodgal visions), and internally, there are in the manner of producing experiences that are the experiences of pious religious activities. And in between, there are all virtuous qualities, such as visions of clarity, which are magical apparitions, are gradually produced in the individual. Everything external and internal will arise gradually as (described) previously and they will enter into a single integration. [63]

From the very beginning, for the exceedingly superior individual who understands instantly (gcig-car-ba), there will arise the final visions (mthar thug gi snang-ba 'char) and the (final) stage of meditation as a vast expanse of space where there is full understanding (rtogs-pa'i klong bsgom). (However, such instantaneous realization is exceedingly rare.)

As for the individual who is a Thodgal practioner (thod-rgal-ba), because great precision in practice varies, (the visions) may become more diverse. Therefore, according to one's intellectual capacity, one should be given the instructions and the direct introduction (gdams-pa ngo-sprad) as is needed. Moreover, for the individual who realizes instantly (gcig-car-ba), the instructions as such may be taught immediately and directly, whereas for the gradualist practitioner (rim-gyis-pa), they should be taught progressively, step by step. In general, for the Thodgal practitioner (thod-rgal-ba), it is necessary to proceed with various different methods for the path. Furthermore, the instructions are bestowed in agreement with the attitude and intellectual capacity of the individual practitioner and this is of very great importance. [64]

The guiding explanation for the meditation practice of the Clear Light, which represents the actual practice of the Path (lam nyams su len-pa 'od-gsal bsgom-pa'i khrid) is hereby completed.

U-YA SMAR-RO!

SARVA MANGALAM!

Chapter Six

The Explanation of the Conduct: *sPyod-khrid*

Here is contained "The Guiding Explanation of the Conduct for the Forceful Purification of the Secondary Conditions that arise along the Path" (rkyen lam du slong-ba rtsal sbyong spyod-pa'i khrid bzhugs-so).

Homage to Kuntu Zangpo, the all-pervading and all-encompassing Guide for living beings (in Samsara), who becomes visibly manifest as one's own Self-Awareness! [1]

Part Three

As for the third (supplementary text): Within this guiding explanation concerning the forceful purification of the secondary conditions that arise along the path (of the principal practice), there are three divisions:

I. Forceful purification (in meditation practice) during this present lifetime,
    (tshe 'dir rtsal sbyong-ba)
II. Forceful purification during the process of dying, and
    ('chi-khar rtsal sbyong-ba)
III. Forceful purification at the time of the Bardo.
    (bar-dor rtsal sbyong-ba)

I. Forceful Purification during one's Lifetime

Within the first topic (forceful purification practiced during one's present lifetime), there are four subdivisions:

A. Carrying on along the path of the three gates,
    (sgo gsum lam du khyer-ba)
B. Carrying on along the path of the six consciousness aggregates,
    (tshogs drug lam du khyer-ba)
C. Carrying on along the path of the masses of thoughts, and
    (rtog tshogs lam du khyer-ba)
D. Carrying on along the path of diversity.
    (sna-tshogs lam du khyer-ba)

A. Continuing in Practice with the Three Gates

With regard to the first subdivision (continuing practices with the three gates of body, speech, and mind): Everything, whatever one is doing, whether pure or impure, one's course of action where one engages in the activities of the three gates (of body, speech, and mind, beginning) with actions in the condition of pious ritual practices (dge-sbyor) should be integrated (with the Natural State), whether in terms of an even state of contemplation or during the subsequent realization (mnyam rjes bsres). [2] (How does one begin to integrate? One should begin with) virtuous deeds possessing the characteristics of the body (or bodily activity), such as circumambulations, prostrations, making mudra gestures, performing yantra movements, and so on. [3] (If one is not disturbed or distracted by these actions, then one should proceed to engage in) impure actions, such as beating and striking, angry words, jumping and running, and so on. And then one should engage in neutral actions, such as eating, walking, sitting, dancing, drinking, working, and so on.

With respect to this engaging in all these different kinds of activities and conduct (spyod-pa) in whatever manner with one's physical body, (one should consider practitioners as having three levels of capacity, (namely, superior, intermediate, and inferior). For the individual of superior capacity (dbang-po rab), proceeding directly from one's view, one's activities in the external world are completely unobstructed (that is, uninhibited, spontaneous, and integrated in terms of the Natural State). As for the individual of intermediate capacity, (dbang-po 'bring-po), proceeding directly from one's meditation practice, one's course of action is without any grasping whatsoever and one's actions self-liberate (without leaving any traces). And as for the individual of inferior capacity (dbang-po tha-ma), one's attitude is to hold on firmly to mindfulness and to never be separated from that.

In the vast expanse of the total Clear Light, which is both empty and clear, from the state of the naked clear luminosity of the primal cognitions of self-awareness, one should engage in all actions energetically (and forcefully). [4]

So, according in the *gZer-bu rtsa 'grel*, it is said, "The various different actions of the body should arise forcefully (and spontaneously) without any (premeditated) deliberate action. [5] Accordingly, there are pure actions of speech, such as reciting (general) mantras and heart mantras (of Yidam meditation deities), reciting scriptures aloud, giving explanations or debating with others, singing hymns and chanting the liturgies, and so on, and impure actions (of speech), such as harsh words, telling lies and casting slanders, weeping and wailing, and so on, and even neutral actions (of speech), such as singing songs, bardic recitations, relating stories, making jokes, rehearsing plays, engaging in conversations and descriptions, and so on—all of these masses of verbal expressions, just as described above, (may be indulged in forcefully by these three kinds of individual practitioners). The individual of superior capacity proceeds directly in accordance with one's view, the individual of intermediate capacity, proceeds directly in accordance with one's meditation, and the individual of inferior capacity adheres to the calculations of mindfulness. [6]

"Within the vast expanse of the total Clear Light, which is empty and aware, from the state of the naked luminous clarity of self-originated awareness, one engages in activities continuously (and unobstructedly). The various different verbal expressions of speech are forceful and without deliberate premeditation.[7]

"Accordingly, pure (thoughts), such as devotion of mind, the Generation Process, samadhi and meditations, and so on, and impure thoughts, such as malicious thoughts, poisonous thoughts, wrong views, and so on, and even neutral thoughts regarding one's province (or homeland), one's wealth and cattle, one's tasks of farming and commerce, thinking beforehand and thinking afterwards, examining and analyzing, making calculations, and so on—in brief, the full measure of thinking with the mind (may also be considered in terms of these three kinds of practitioners). The individual of superior capacity proceeds directly according to one's view, the individual of intermediate capacity proceeds directly according to one's meditation, and the individual of inferior capacity adheres to everything with mindfulness (dran-pas bzung). From the state of naked luminous clarity of the gnosis of self-awareness, one engages in all activities continuously (and unobstructedly)." [8] So it was expounded at length.

Again, according to the *gZer-bu*, "All-pervading and all-encompassing without exterior or interior, the full measure of vision (or appearances) is the visible manifestation of Body, the full measure of sounds is the audible manifestation of Speech, and the full measure of mindfulness is the perceptable manifestation of Mind, the full measure of the elements is the visible manifestation of Quality, and the full measure of action is the visible manifestation of of enlightened Activity." [9]

Because this is said, in terms of the real meaning, all the activities of the three gates (of body, speech, and mind) are not envisioned or conceived to be deliberate actions (byed-par mi dmigs-pa) (which are premeditated). Rather, it is necessary that they arise naturally (and spontaneously) as continuous unobstructed Skilful Means from the state of wisdom and emptiness. [10]

According to the *gSal-byed*, "Whether going or sitting, eating or drinking, lying face downwards or face upwards when sleeping, whether one is in a state of even contemplation or subsequent realization, or in the dream state, or in the Bardo, if one does not know to connect with Rigpa continuously, it is similar to being made thirsty by a drought and having only a little water. Therefore, one will not be able (to access) the secondary conditions of both the view and the meditation."

Because this is said, by way of the activities of ascetic disciple (rtul shugs kyi spyod-pa), these actions of the three gates (of body, speech, and mind) are engaged in for their own sake with sincerity. Therefore, the beginner from the very first integrates well (one's actions) with pious religious practices (dge-sbyor). And in between, it will not be sufficient merely to integrate them, but it will be necessary that they not harm one's pious practices. And finally at the end, it will not be sufficient that they merely not harm (or injure) them, but it will be necessary that that they arise as helpers for one's pious practices.

B. Continuing in Practice with the Six Consciousness Aggregates

Second, with regard to carrying along the path with the six consciousness aggregates (tshogs drug gi lam khyer), it is said, "Any beautiful form arising as an object the eyes, accordingly, will not be beautified. Everything that may arise as an object of the eye consciousness, such as big or small, good or bad, short or long, and so on, (may be perceived). However, with regard to them, for the individual of superior capacity, they will self-arise and self-depart. For the individual of intermediate capacity, they will be seen nakedly and liberate nakedly. And for the individual of inferior capacity, there will be no hopes or fears, no accepting or rejecting, no obstructing or realizing, no thinking and analyzing. From the state of the total Clear Light which is emptiness itself, the forms which are seen are empty (forms) and totally free of any root (in reality or materiality). They arise in an uncertain fashion and are to be purified forcefully like illusions. [11]

According to the 'Bum, "As for visible forms, they are like illusions. Because they do not really exist anywhere, they are without any (real) action anywhere. The object of the senses is color, which represents clarity (or visiblity), but any color clearly visible anywhere is actually the dimension of the mind." [12] So it is said.

Accordingly, the word which is heard as the object (of hearing) by the ear, is the word which is not really heard (audibly). All the sounds that come forth from the language and signs of beings who are born, even the sounds of music, are empty sounds for individuals of superior, intermediate, and inferior capacities and they should be forcefully purified like echoes. The smells that are sensed as objects for the nose are smells that are not really sensed. All of these different kinds of scents, such as pure smells, impure smells, and smells that are united with subtle fragrances, are actually empty perceptions (tshor stong) for individuals of superior, intermediate, and superior capacities and they are to be forcefully purified. They should be forcefully purified into empty perceptions totally without traces. [13] Those tastes that arise as objects of sense for the tongue, such as tastes that are delicious or not delicious, good or bad, subtle or gross, and so on, for individuals of superior, intermediate, and inferior capacities. One practices again and again cutting off all the aspects of taste into being empty experiences (stimuli), being totally free of any root. [14] As for the sensations of touch which are the object of the body (sense), whether smooth or rough, hot or cold, light or heavy, good or bad, whatever may arise, for individuals of superior, intermediate, and inferior capacities, one should practice forcefully purifying them into empty sensations where they self-liberate without any grasping. [15]

According to the *sGron-ma*, "Due to the gnosis or primal awareness, which is self-awareness, the six energies having arisen as the six sense objects, their activities as various kinds of actions, indeed, arise to oneself as the Nirmanakaya." [16]

According to the exposition of Lachen Dranpa Namkha, [17] "One should not follow after the objects of the five senses. Even though one may follow after them, they should no be divided into aspects. Even though one may divide them, one should not grasp at a self. Even though one may grasp, one should not be attached to the karmic traces."

Because it was expounded thus, even for those with very little strength of practice, with regard to apprehending them, and so on, at the time of their conduct and view, there will be a recognition for the sake of knowing the looker and the actor. From the state of the naked clarity of the gnosis that is self-awareness, one should simply gaze continuously without exerting oneself in thinking and analyzing. Whereupon, in one's mind-stream, one integrates and does not loose it even for a moment. But it is not sufficient just to integrate, they should arise as friends (and helpers). Nevertheless, it is not sufficient just for them to arise, it is necessary that they be of the same even taste without any duality. [18]

C. Continuing in Practice with the Masses of Thoughts

Third, with regard to carrying on along the path in terms of the masses of thoughts (rtog tshogs lam du khyer-ba): Within the mind-stream of a single individual (gang-zag gi rgyud la), even though, on each day, it is said that there are the movements of eighty-four thousand masses of thoughts (rtog tshogs), because there is no action of the method of carrying on along the path, therefore, sudden memories (and thoughts), whether great or small, subtle or coarse, many or few, good or bad, are produced in whatever way. Thereupon, what should be renounced is not renounced. Because one exerts oneself in this, even though one practices, it is not realized and it is not brought under the power of that. For the individual of superior capacity, directly from his view, he vanquishes them like snowflakes falling on to a lake. For the individual of intermediate capacity, directly from his meditation practice, (the antidotes) swell up to vanguish them like (the frost melting when) being struck by the light of the sun (in the early morning). And for the individual of inferior capacity, in addition to taking hold of mindfulness (dran 'dzin), he follows them like he is giving advice to an angry person, and he practices non-action in the face of the kleshas, or emotional defilements. At that time, he looks directly into the essence of these masses of thoughts, [19] and thereby cuts off the root and the foundation of their proximate source. With regret, he expresses his shame, and afterwards, he is instructed not to produce them again.

According to the *gZer-bu*, "Self-originated primal awareness is the Base and the kleshas represent the five poisons. Following after them represents the system of delusion. However, looking at their defects also represents a deviation. Rather, the (proper) method is to relax them into their own original condition. The Path is liberating them into the the vast expanse of space, whereupon the Fruit becomes manifest as non-dual understanding." [20] So it is said.

D. Continuing in Practice with Diversity

Fourth, with regard to carrying on along the path with diversity (sna-tshogs lam du khyer-ba), (there are three considerations):

1. The private conduct (gsang-ba'i spyod),
2. The conduct consisting of ascetic practices that are secret (gsang-ba brtul-shugs kyi spyod-pa), and
3. Conduct that is completely victorious and without partialities (phyogs-med rgyal-ba'i spyod-pa).

D1. Conduct that is Private

From among these three, as for the first (the conduct that is private), this is much like being harmed by evil secondary causes (ngan rkyen gyis gnod-pa ltar), such as a lamp placed in a strong wind. At the time when one is a beginner, or one is an individual of inferior capacity, all the courses of action of one's body and speech should be made to conform to calculations by means of practice. At that time, one should renounce (and abandon) all disharmonious and mistaken secondary conditions and rely, on the contrary, on harmonious conditions such as one's friends and helpers. Indeed, the method (thabs) is the taking up of all manner of conduct of the Bodhisattvas, such as the ten Paramitas, and so on. [21]

According to the *'Bum*, "One should practice very much the profound conduct of the Bodhisattvas (sems-dpa' spyod-pa zab-mo)."

And according to the *Drang don*, "At the time when injury appears, one should rely upon the help of benefactors."

D2. Ascetic Conduct

As for the second (consideration), this is much like going to a friend (who is a helper), such as, for example, putting a large lamp in the wind (so that it grows even brighter). At the time when one may be an individual of intermediate capacity, or else, one is able to practice only a little on one's own, then one should carry on along the path in terms of development and forceful practice. This procedure is in agreement with the essential points of ascetic conduct. [22]

Because this conduct is like that of a dog or a pig to whom nothing is is either pure or filthy, so everything, whether pure or impure, sweet or not sweet, good or bad, proper or offensive, friend or enemy, now comes to have the same even taste (ro-snyoms), and one's conduct is without accepting or rejecting anything. Because this conduct is like behavior that is utterly without calculations (or premeditations), [23] one does not do anything with partiality or one-sidedness. One does not accept or reject anything. One does not make any calculations of profit and loss. One does not engage in any examination or analysis of anything. Indeed, this is conduct that is self-arising (and utterly spontaneous) and it is cut off entirely from (inhibitions and premeditations).

Because this conduct is like a little child who does not obstruct or create anything, one does not realize anything good or renounce anything as bad. One's conduct is free and open and one dispatches one's actions freely. Because one's conduct is thus without any inhibitions, it is like loose stones wildly rolling down (the mountain side). One follows freely in their face (when emotions arise) without doubts and without hopes and fears. One cuts off connections completely (with all plans, inhibitions, and premeditations). When one's actions are dispatched suddenly, this represents conduct that is without indecision (or hesitation). Because one's conduct is like that of the peacock (who can eat and ingest poison without harm to itself), one carries on along the path, even in the case of evil conditions. Even the spirit of scarcity will be summoned as prosperity; obstructions (and hindrances) will be accepted as siddhis. [24] Enemies and demons are cut off in terms of their very existence. Even the five poisons are transformed into medicines.

Because one's conduct is like a heroic man heavily burdened with antidotes (or weapons, so that no one can challenge him), one's conduct is without anguish or regret. One acts in a special way, such as, if one is frightened, one becomes more frightened, if one is dirty, one becomes more dirty, if one is hungry, one becomes more hungry, if one is cold, one becomes more cold, and so on. Thereby, one integrates everything and the conduct of the battle becomes victory and conquest.

According to the *Drang don*, "At the time of benefit by way of appearances, everything arises as friends (who are helpers)."

And according to the *Lung drug*, "The conduct of the five poisons is supreme among all conducts," and "If one is able to engage in total ascetic conduct, any such conduct is neither good nor bad. As for that, it is said that it is much praised as the vessel of Dzogchen. Such conduct is uninhibited (and unobstructed)." So it was expounded.

D3. Conduct that is Completely Victorious

At the time when one may be a superior practitioner, or when experiences and understanding (in one's practice) ultimately culminate, [25] in terms of one's conduct, diversity will come to have only a single taste (ro gcig), this being like a man finding himself on an island of gold (where he wants for nothing because everything is gold). Everything in no way goes beyond that. In that state, everything has an equal even taste (ro-snyoms). Because one understands that, everything becomes an illusory magical appearance (cho-'phrul). Consequently, the agent, or the doer of the action, and the action that is done are transcended in terms of everything. That represents the conduct that is completely victorious, being without any partialities what so ever (phyogs-med rnam-par rgyal-ba'i spyod-pa).

According to the *Lung drug*, "When one understands the "self" as the state of the Sugata itself, all of them (whatever actions one does) become the conduct of the Sugata. This cannot be measured by any measurement." [26] So it was expounded.

II. Forceful Purification during the Dying Process

Second, with regard to practicing forceful purification during one's process of dying ('chi-khar rtsal sbyong-ba), according to the *sGron-ma*, it is said, "At the time of dying, one will encounter the Boundary between happiness and sorrow. [27] Because of the great power of good and bad thoughts being projected (at this time), the instructions should be expounded without mistakes in terms of mixing them together in the vessel (of the disciple) according to one's capacity."

And according to the *gZer-bu*, "At the time when the body and the mind finally separate, (one finds oneself) at the Boundary between these two, happiness and sorrow, (that is to say, Nirvana and Samsara)." [28]

Here there are three subdivisions:

A. The practice relating to the disintegration of the elements and their being reabsorbed,
   ('byung-ba 'jig dang bstun la nyams su blangs-pa)
B. The practice relating to their ingathering and being reabsorbed, and
   (bsdus-pa dang bstun la nyams su blangs-pa), and
C. Expounding the instructions of the special essential point.
   (khyad-par gnad kyi gdams-pa gdab-pa)

A. The Disintegration of the Elements while Dying

With regard to the first (the disintegration of the elements during the process of dying), internally the earth element deteriorates in the spleen and externally one can no longer perceive touch sensations with one's body. [29] In terms of connections, one can no longer raise up one's left arm and in terms of the consequences, flowing according to their own system (that is, spontaneously), there will come forth polluted liquids (and secretions) from the doorways of the nine orifices (of the body).

At that time, the individual of superior capacity (dbang-po rab) is perfect (and complete in his singular knowledge (of the Natural State) (shes-bya cig rdzogs) and due to the vast expanse of one's view, even things of bad repute will arise for one as one's friends and helpers (at the time of dying).

For the individual of an intermediate capacity (dbang-po 'bring-po), there is no separation with regard to the state of the Essence (the Natural State). Because one does not move from this state of meditation, one is not harmed (or injured) by these (negative experiences at the time of dying).

And for the individual of an inferior capacity (dbang-po tha-ma), that is to say, those who have not yet entered into the gateway of the instructions, on that occasion (when one finds oneself dying), one should practice the recollection of death ('chi-ba rjes su dran-par bya), which is the first among the six recollections (rjes dran drug), and one understand the deterioration (and disintegration) of the elements (as they occur in one's body and in one's experience). [30] One should have no desire for anything (or any object), whether external or internal.

After that, one should practice the recollection of the Lama or Master (bla-ma rjes su dran-par bya). With intense and fervent devotion, one should meditate on him sitting on the crown of one's head. Then one should next practice the recollection of the Yidam or meditation deity. One should meditate on this Yidam as being one's own physical body, while performing the seva service and reciting aloud (the heart mantra of the Yidam). And one should not forget one's secret name (which one's Lama has given one during initiation). [31]

Then one should practice the recollection of the Bardo. The visible objects that arise in this way merely represent the uncertain appearances (and visions) of the Bardo and as such, one should think that they are like illusions. Then one should practice the recollection of the instructions. With regard to the real meaning here, which is free of any root (or source, that is, the Natural State), one remains unchanging in one's own self-awareness. [32]

Accordingly, in the same way, (internally) the water element deteriorates in the kidneys (mkhal-ma) and (externally) sounds can no longer be heard by the ears. One can no longer raise the left leg and one is no longer aware to hold the urine (dri-chu). Thereafter, the fire element deteriorates in the liver (mchin-pa) and one can no longer discern tastes with the tongue. One can no longer raise the right arm and blood comes forth freely from the nose. (Following that) the air element deteriorates in the lungs (glo-ba) and one can no longer perceive smells with the nose. One can no longer raise the right leg and one is no longer aware to retain their faeces. Finally, the space element deteriorates in the physical heart [tsi-ta] and one can no longer see (and discern) forms with the eyes. One cannot raise up the head and the semen (thig-le, bindu) escapes from the secret place (of the sex organ).

On each of these occasions, also, for both the superior and the intermediate individuals, it will be like the above (description). However, for the individual of inferior capacity, the instructions for the (above) five recollections (dran-pa lnga'i gdams-pa), as well as his own personal meditation practice, should be clearly explained to him by another (whether a Lama or a good friend). [33]

B. The Reabsorption of the Elements while Dying

As for the manner in which the elements are ingathered and reabsorbed (sdud tshul), it is said according to the *sGron-ma*, "The earth element is reabsorbed into the water element and thereby one loses the strength of the body. After this single element is exhausted, internally the chakra of the earth element, which is located at the level of the navel, having disintegrated, there will arise signs of its power being reabsorbed into the water element. Externally, the strength of the body will be lost. The body will come to feel heavy and one will think that one is sinking into the earth. [34] And in terms of self-manifestations, they will arise as yellow (in color), representing the radiance of the earth element (as it disintegrates and is reabsorbed). All appearances come forth (before the dying individual) as sparkling yellow lights. [35]

"Then the water element is reabsorbed into the fire element and so the luster (and complexion) of the body will become lost. The chakra of the water element, located in the secret place, having disintegrated, and because its power and capacities (nus-pa) are being reabsorbed into the the fire element, as signs of that (occurring), one's body will lose its color and luster, one's mouth and nose will become very dry, and in terms of appearances, they will come forth as blue lights.

"Then the fire element is reabsorbed into the air element, whereupon the body looses its heat. When this heat is reabsorbed, the tongue will turn back and all appearances thereby will come forth as red lights (for the dying person).

"Then the air element is reabsorbed into the space element. It is said that here there will be a drawing in of one's breath and then it escapes (one breathes with difficulty and laboriously). There will be panic and one will search for any place where one can hold on. One is no longer aware to hold the breath (within the body). In terms of appearances, they will all arise as green lights.

"Finally, the mind is reabsorbed into the Kunzhi, the basis of all. Thereupon, the breathing ceases (and is cut off) altogether, and the body and the mind will eventually come to separate. [36] The sight grows dim and everything starts to become dark. One is no longer aware to blink the eyes and they come to be averted upward (into the head). Thereupon, all appearances arise as white light." [37]

At that time, for both of those individuals possessing superior and intermediate capacities, coming from the states of their view and their meditation respectively, (they will experience matters) as described above. However, as for the individual of inferior capacity, in the future where the Lama or their relatives and friends (come to their bedside and reads aloud the instructions to them, they should say to the dying person as follows):

"Because there now are the signs that the earth element has been reabsorbed into the water element, you should remain in the state of the great Clear Light, which is your own immaculate intrinsic awareness. In terms of self-manifestations, there is a yellow light that will arise. This inherent radiance should be recognized as being like an illusion. The Ultimate Reality (Dharmata) is similar to this visible light and it will come forth again in the Bardo of the Clear Light. [38] One should become familiar with this manifestation!"

That should be clearly visualized by oneself and one ought to become thoroughly familiar with it accordingly. Also, with regard to those who follow later, they should see it clearly in a straight forward manner and become familiar with it.

Furthermore, for the most part, these elements are reabsorbed gradually. But in terms of a sudden terminal illness (or fatal accident), they may be reabsorbed instantly. Even at that time, the breathing may not be cut off immediately, but when it is cut off, there will occur a two-fold ingathering or reabsorption. At that time, all of the blood in the lesser channels (the veins and arteries) will be gathered into the principal vital channel (of the heart), known as the prana-nadi (srog rtsa), and thereby three rainfalls of blood will descend inside the heart. In terms of appearances (or visions), it will look like a rainfall of blood. It will be like oppressed by demons and evil spirits [39] and there will come forth many difficulties with holding things in memory.

at that time, the Dharmakaya will appear to overflow along the pathway of the central channel for Rigpa (known as the Kati channel), and it (Rigpa) will then be expelled (out of the body) through the gateways of the Lamp (of the eyes). For the male individual, it will be expelled through the right eye and for the female individual, it will be expelled through the left eye. [40]

C. Special Instructions for the Transference of Consciousness

With regard to the special (instructions): On the occasion when the outer breathing ceases (and is cut off), and the inner breathing has not been cut off (and continues), Rigpa will be like the rising of the sun in the (morning) sky devoid of clouds. With regard to that, one should expound aloud (to the dying person) these instructions pertaining to the special essential point as follows. [41]

"As for your body, it should be placed looking and facing to the east. It should be placed (in the meditation position possessing) the five attributes, or else, in the crouching position (of the Rishi), or even the method for lying down of the elephant. You should visualize (inside your body) the three channels as above. Then, in your heart center, your should visualize your own Nature of Mind as having the form of the white letter A, just about the size of the thumb, enveloped inside an extensive space of the five lights. Then you force your breath to fly upward as much as it can. By inserting (the winds) inside (the central channel), you can expell the impurities and thereby cleanse the pathway of the central channel and this purifies your karmic traces and obscurations (that conceal) your Rigpa. You should think that the aperture of Brahma becomes opened by this action.

"Then, because of repeating (this process with) the pure winds, by way of sounding HRIG!, (the white letter A) will rise higher and higher and through the process of doing this twenty-one times, it will rise to the aperture of Brahma. Moving up from below, it moves (to a point) a short distance (above the crown of the head) and you should think that the aperture of Brahma then closes (and is shut behind it), so that it cannot descend again into the physical body.

"Again, for twenty-one times, (sounding HRIG! as before), it (one's Rigpa in the form of the white A) is gathered upward into the extensive space of another white A that is located within a vast expanse of space and light (above your head). [42] The A itself is then reabsorbed into the heart center of the Guru, whereupon the Guru dissolves like the rainbow (fading into the sky), and you should think that you come to attain Buddhahood."

Now, in terms of this (forceful) purification practice (as preparation for dying), when sounding HIG! one shoots (one's consciousness in the form of the white A) upward (like an arrow), so that it passes out through the aperture of Brahma and [43] then the A descends again into one's heart center. With regard to that, when the Rigpa is clear, (it is a sign that) one is purified. The signs (of success in the practice) will surely come forth and one will not forget (how to do the actual transference of consciousness at the time of dying).

At the time of settling down again ('jog dus), it descends into the heart center and afterwards, one makes the dedication to enlightenment. As for this (special instruction for the transference of consciousness), it represents a forceful method by way of the essential point of the Path of Method (thabs lam) and thereby one will come to attain Buddhahood (thabs-lam gyi gnad kyis btsan thabs su sangs-rgyas-pa).

According to the *gZer-bu*, "(Figuratively speaking), Rigpa is the little Man of the Mind and memory (or mindfulness) is the horse of the functional mind upon which he is mounted. [44] Unobstructed wind shakes it with its wings and it traverses the pathway to enlightenment, which is the central channel. It arrives at the secret gate of bliss at the crown of the head, whereupon the king who is Rigpa arises nakedly. Thus, the abundance system of discursive thoughts and the thought process itself (in general) are cast aside. Self-originated gnosis comes to see one's own face and one awakens from the darkness of ignorance and delusion." [45]

Because of the virtuous qualities of that instruction (given above), in terms of the body, speech, and mind, (one seals) the nine orifices (bu-ga dgu) found along the pathway that produces (rebirth) in impure places. One cuts off the gateways for (ill-advised) transfers of consciousness (to other lower realms). When the heat departs (from the body), including the five senses, the six places, and the limbs, one will come to stir up the depths of the three worlds and the nine stages, and thereby one interrupts the pathways of the five poisons that are the negative emotions or kleshas. One dries up the great ocean of the Samsara of the six realms. One empties the doorways of the Samsara of the four kinds of birth. Thereupon, the Trikaya self-arises (spontaneously) and one always will help (to secure the benefit of other sentient beings). Therefore, one should prepare gradually for this.

Elsewhere, it is said that, "At that time, with regard to an individual of superior capacity, one's conscious awareness at that time becomes itself the spontaneously perfected Trikaya in its own original form as Buddhahood. Self-awareness becomes visibly manifest, arising to its full measure and the primal cognitions as well become visibly manifest in full measure, whereupon the Nature of Mind, having become manifest, simply exists. [46] The secondary conditions that represent the admonition (to the dying person) should be clearly enunciated (by the Lama or assistant) and because of this direct introduction, there is no doubt that one will come to see one's own face."

With regard to the individual of intermediate capacity, it is said that, "At that time, the self-manifestations arise to their full measure. Nevertheless, they are unreal like illusions. All of them have the nature of mind, and as for the Nature of mind itself, it is the totally root-free Rigpa of that time. Because one has been directly introduced to the Dharmakaya as abiding in its own original condition or form from the very beginning, there exists belief and a definitive decision regarding it. Therefore, there is no doubt that one will cut off (and shut) the doors to rebirth." [47]

With regard to the individual of inferior capacity, it is said, "Upwardly, one will enter into action with devotion and downwardly, one enters into meditation on love and compassion. In between one is directly introduced to non-attachment and desirelessness with respect to everything. Because of these Upadeshas, there is no doubt that one will obtain a palace of happiness (in terms of one's next rebirth)."

Elsewhere, the sounds, the lights, and the rays are (discussed) separately in detail. For the superior individual, they will self-arise and self-liberate. For the intermediate individual, they will be divine forms and primal cognitions of divine forms. And for the inferior individual, they are directly introduced as actually being self-sounds, self-lights, and self-rays (at the time when) the corpse and consciousnessness separate. [48]

Moreover, one should pray (at that time), such as going to Refuge and producing the Bodhichitta, as well as invoking one's Yidam. By way of such excellent thoughts at the time when one is dying, it is certain that one will be instantly reborn in a happy place (of a better rebirth). Because it has been expounded thus (in the scriptures), one will become cured like the wick of a butter lamp when the oil has become exhausted.

III. Forceful Purification in the Bardo

Third, with regard to forceful purification (at the time of) the Bardo (bar-dor rtsal sbyong-ba), there are three subdivisions:

A. The Bardo of the Base that abides,
    (gnas-pa gzhi'i bar-do)
B. The Bardo of the Clear Light of Reality
    (bon-nyid 'od-gsal gyi bar-do)
C. The Bardo of Rebirth, which is empty.
    (stong-pa srid-pa'i bar-do)

A. The Bardo of the Base that Abides

As for the first (the Bardo of the Base that abides), according to the *gZer-bu,* "All the discursive thoughts that represent apprehending and the apprehended (subject and object) are dissolved (and reabsorbed) into the vast expanse (of the Nature of Mind). At that time, intrinsic Awareness (rig-pa) abides nakedly and self-originated gnosis (or primal cognitions) are totally without obscurations and coverings." [49]

At the time of impurity when the body and the mind separate, [50] in terms of one phase (len gcig), one does not encounter or recognize any purity or impurity (that is to say, no visions arise at all). For all sentient beings, there will exist no particular great or small obscurations. With Kunzhi and Rigpa, it is like (the face of) the sun separating from the clouds. For one phase (len gcig), a pure inherent luminous clarity without obscurations, which is nude, unclothed, and directly penetrating, comes to abide nakedly. [51]

As for the manner of that, the King who is Awareness (lodged in) the Kunzhi, escapes (from the corpse of the body) through the right eye for males and through the left eye for females. And thereafter, for a moment, it abides at the urna. [52] As for the sign of that, at that time, especially with the face, the brightness and the radiance of the urna will deteriorate. At that time, because it becomes very difficult to remember things (or to be mindful), one should just strive to be mindful (dran tsam). And because of just that (singular) recognition, in an instant, the Son comes to encounter the Mother, and the three nets of the body, speech, and mind are rent assunder. And thereby one perfects the three energies of the Body, Speech, and Mind. [53] By way of condensing the two Lamps into one, thereby one will attain Buddhahood. This represents "the passageway of the hero" (dpa'-bo'i gseb lam).

Furthermore, one becomes liberated by way of meeting with the three essential points. At present, one becomes familiar with the real meaning of the direct introduction, and because one makes inqueries again and again, one should clearly visualize the process of dying again and again, and inserts questions well regarding karmic traces, [54] (becoming well acquainted with karmic traces). Because one encounters the three-fold Bardo of the Base that abides, one comes to attain Buddhahood.

According to the *gNad-drug*, "As for this, (phowa) represents the forceful method for attaining Buddhahood (sangs-rgyas btsan thabs), whereas karma and its consequences represent the great lie." So it was expounded (in the scripture).

At that time, mind is associated (or accompanies) the heat. [55] From any one of the orifices (bu-ga) located in the upper and lower parts of the physical body, it (the consciousness) may be expelled. But when the instructions for the transference of consciousness ('pho-ba dang gdams-ngag) have been explained, it will be expelled (consciously and deliberately) through the aperture of Brahma (at the crown of the head). And so, it will be impossible not to be reborn in a place of happiness (that is to say, a fortunate rebirth) (bde gnas).

As for the karmic traces lodged in the functional mind (yid kyi bag-chags), it (mental consciousness) will remain nearby in the vacinity of the dead physical body, having greater or lesser attachments to it, for some two or three days. Therefore, until that time, one should not do anything like cremating or disposing of the corpse (in burial). (One should postpone) the full measure of purification (such cremation or disposal of the corpse for three days, because) subtle experiences and and visions continue to come forth (to the consciousness of the deceased). If one asks what is the reason for these karmic traces (coming into visible manifestation), it is due to an excess of attachments (to one's former body and former life).

If one does not become liberated from that (condition), the Son who is Rigpa will dissolve into the vast expanse of the Mother who is the Kunzhi. Thoughts and memories will go into concealment (and occultation) within the folds of that (Kunzhi), and thereby the energies of the sounds, the lights, and the rays will be completely annihilated, and thus self-awareness will become enveloped within a net of light. In this state of the non-existence of anything, where thoughts, memories, appearances, and even clarity itself (are enveloped and concealed) within the thickness of the Kunzhi, the individual may remain abiding there for three days until the heat of the fourth day, or even for five or seven days. [56]

B. The Bardo of the Clear Light of Reality

With regard to the second (the Bardo of the Clear Light), there are two considerations:

(1)   The recognition of it (ngos bzung-ba) and
(2)   The Cutting off of this Bardo (bar-do bcad-pa).

B1. Recognizing the Bardo

With regard to the first consideration, it is said according to the *gZerbu*, "If one does not become liberated from that (the first Bardo), then there will arise two further Bardos."

Because that is stated (in the text), at the time when the body and the mind have just separated, if one does not liberate at the time of the Base that abides, then the individual will come to experience what is called the Bardo of the Clear Light of Reality, and awaken once more and the previous Rigpa will become clearly visible again like one is awakening from sleep. Due to secondary conditions, changes (in consciousness) will easily come forth. Then, visions of one's own form, that is, one's own (previous) body determined by karmic traces (and memories) will arise from the state of the Tsita of light as a miniature-sized primal awareness, and because of doing that, the Rigpa awakens. Because of the movement of thoughts and memories, the nets (or veils) of light that are visible manifestations (and visions) are rent asunder and torn open like the bringing forth of a butter lamp that had (previously been concealed) inside of a vase. Thereby the Clear Light of Awareness arises into visible manifestation. [57] Now the visions of fire, water, earth, and air having become obstructed, the manifestations of the sounds, the lights, and the rays arise (spontaneously) without being hidden or concealed anymore.

Furthermore, everything in the cardinal and the intermediate directions, including zenith and nadir, becomes bright and clear like a drawing made of rainbows having the nature of the five lights. The inherent sounds of Rigpa (rig-pa'i rang sgra) resound in the manner of roaring thunder that is self-originated and and discontinuous. They resound variously and roughly, whether being long or short, great or small, pleasant or unpleasant. The inherent rays of Rigpa (rig-pa'i rang zer), being like opening the face of a glossy silk cloth or a woolen blanket or the finger tip of the ray of sunlight, [58] arise everywhere in diverse fashion, whether fine or coarse, long or short, thin or thick.

According to the *gZer-bu*, it is said, "As for the lights, the realms are also without center or boundaries, like rainbows arising in the sky. As for the sounds, they are immaterial and resound in the vast expanse of space. The manner of these sounds is self-originated and discontinuous. As for the rays, they display (various different) magical apparitions in an uncertain fashion, similar to opening the face of a glossy silk cloth or a woolen blanket (in the bright sunlight)." [59] So it is expounded here.

"As for the length of time, they arise for five or seven days, and until seven days, the radiance arises gradually." [60] Because it is said that, accordingly on each day, they (the visions) arise successively as white light, green light, red light, blue light, and yellow light.

With regard to these (visions), for the individual of superior capacity, they are self-arising and self-liberating. For the individual of intermediate capacity, they arise as the Five Deities (lha lnga), the Five Bodies (sku lnga), and the Five Gnoses or Primal Cognitions (ye-shes lnga). [61] And with regard to the individual of inferior capacity, just as was the case above, one should become familiar with them as being self-manifestations that are like illusions.

B2. Cutting Off the Bardo

With regard to the second consideration (cutting off the Bardo experience): In terms of the instructions found here, for those who have a great strength of purification, the three manifestations (of the sounds, the lights, and the rays) will arise like the meeting with a man again that one has known very well previously. Afterwards, the advice (of the Lama) serving as a secondary condition should be clearly enunciated and one proceeds into a self-stopping or cutting off (of the Bardo experience). And here appearances (that is, the visions experienced in the Bardo) will become overthrown and exhausted. Even though the experiences that arise will just increase, they will arise there in their perfection (and completeness), but by applying practices for recognizing them, they will ultimately liberate. For the individual who has become familiar with them (the visions experienced in the Bardo) and knows them intimately, the divine forms and the mandalas are complete in their perfection. [62]

At that time, these will arise and one meets the three-fold visions with (six) clairvoyant powers and the (six) recollections. [63] And it is said that one will not accompany (and escort) these familiar self-manifestations.

As for those individuals of intermediate capacity in terms of purification (sbyangs-pa 'bring rnams), one will come to liberation by way of three essential points. In terms of the instruction for the Clear Light (practice) given previously, because of practicing to become familiar with them just a little and knowing them intimately, one will come to know (and recognize) them now (in the state of the Bardo). During the process of dying ('chi-khar), the real meaning regarding them was clearly articulated, and so there remains a proper memory (of the instructions). Then, when the Bardo of the Clear Light of Reality arises into manifestation, because of the essential points of meeting the three (the sounds, lights, and rays), it is impossible that one will not liberate (while in the Bardo).

According to the *gZer-bu*, "At that time, first one should recollect the Guru or the Master. Then one should recollect the Upadeshas and other instructions. The karmic traces that represent the secondary conditions having been awakened (into consciousness), then there will occur liberation. One will become liberated in the Bardo by way of secondary causes." So it is said.

As for the individual of inferior capacity, "Those who have attained little in the way of purification with regard to these instructions, they will not escape the self-arising of these three manifestations at this time. Because these self-manifestations of the sounds, the lights, and the rays arise like illusions, without producing any attachments or desires, or any fear or panic, one knows (and recognizes) these self-manifestations of divine forms and primal cognitions to be like illusions and one will become liberated without being deceived by them. [64]

Elsewhere, as for these manifestations of the sounds, the lights, and the rays, at that time, for the superior individual, they will arise as friends (and helpers), for the intermediate individual, they will remember the advice (of the Lama), which represents the secondary condition (for the bringing about of liberation), and also, for the inferior individual, by being simply aware of them as self-illuminations (of one's own mind), one will certainly become liberated. [65]

Again, according to the *gZer-bu*, "By way of these visions, one comes to see one's own face by oneself. Self-awareness meets itself, its own face, whereupon ignorance and delusion are awakened into their own original condition." [66] So it was said.

C. The Bardo of Rebirth

With regard to the Bardo of Rebirth (srid-pa'i bar-do), there are four considerations:

(1) The manner in which it arises at the beginning (dang-po 'char tshul),
(2) The method for cutting it off (bcad tshul),
(3) Then, the methods of liberation (grol tshul), and
(4) For some (individuals), there will be the method of delusion ('khrul tshul).

C1. The Manner in which this Bardo Arises

With regard to the first consideration, (the manner in which this Bardo arises), in terms of one who has become liberated above (in the Bardo of the Clear Light), there will arise the Bardo of Rebirth that will be entirely empty. At that time, the three manifestations of the sounds, the lights, and the rays, having ceased (their manifestations), Rigpa fades like a little chick who is unstable (and wobbly when it first emerges from the egg). And as the vital winds arise in in the heart, the consciousness wanders suddenly without any support. Because of past attachments which represent karmic traces, one proceeds to places that are connected with relatives (and friends), but one will not be recognized there. Even though one is exceedingly attached to food, wealth, one's possessions, and one's house, one finds that one has no power to act. Even though one is without any power or physical support, nevertheless, one is able to go unimpeded through the earth, stone, mountains, and rocks. Indeed, one can go anywhere by just thinking about it, (except re-entering into one's previous physical body). Moreover, one can know one's previous lives and even one's future rebirths, (and one can see clairvoyantly) distant places that are high or low, things that are external or internal, and so on, (that are normally hidden from view).

As for one's body, it appears as one's previous self-manifestation (that is, the body which one had in one's immediately previous life). Its form is due to karmic traces (and memories). Subsequently, there will arise three kinds (of feelings and experiences, that is to say, of one's past life, one's present life in the Bardo, and one's future life to come). Therefore, one roams about (in confusion, desperately searching) everywhere for the gateway to rebirth (in a new physical body), [67] and one seeks anywhere for such a place of entrance (into rebirth). Again and again one tries to to re-enter one's previous body, but because this link has been broken (and severed), one cannot obtain entrance on those occasions. Even though one now has the eye of gnosis (ye-shes kyi spyan), one cannot see anyone else, except those of the same race of Bardo beings. [68] At that time, like the bees cut off in late autumn and separated from warmth (and thus they become sluggish and inert), one wanders aimlessly from place to place, always without any physical support. Nevertheless, the individual is aware and can remember everything, but it comes forth that one is not able to do anything or obtain anything in terms of actions and causes.

According to the *Phyi rgyud*, "With regard to the visions (or appearances) of the Clear Light of Reality, because of a discriminating wisdom that understands is not produced (at this point), the previous gnosis remains concealed within the folds of the Kunzhi and so previous karma becomes visible as visions. [69] Apparently possessing the fleshly form of one's past rebirth that had originated previosuly, all of one's senses are complete and in tact and one can move about unimpeded (even through solid walls and objects). One possesses the power of karmic magical apparitions and one sees with pure divine eyes all of the deities in agreement with their Kulas or divine hierarchies. Nevertheless, one desperately searches for a physical body and dwelling place." [70] Because it was expounded so, one should now be aware of it.

C2. Cutting off the Experience of the Bardo of Rebirth

With regard to the second consideration, (the method for cutting off the experiences of the Bardo of Rebirth): At that time when there occurs the cremation of the dead physical body (or skandha), someone may call out the name (of the deceased person) or someone may weep (and lament his passing), whereupon (the dead person) may try to speak, but no one will answer him. (Then when he comes at meal time), there remains no portion of the food for him and no one provides a place for him at the table where he may sit. There exist for him no (physical supports) to be the opposite of these conditions.

At that time, the deceased individual) should become aware (and realize) that one is wandering in the Bardo of Rebirth. Having now remembered the instructions (of the Lama), one's mind becomes one-pointed without any hopes or fears or anxiety even for a moment, and because one practices in a concentrated, single-minded fashion, (the result) will become visibly manifest. The Mother and the Son having encountered each other, one will apprehend the rank of Buddhahold. [71]

However, if one is not able to do just that, everything, all thoughts and memories at that time, and all modes of arising (of objects) which are external, will be self-manifestations that self-arise, much like illusions and like dreams, and because one has practiced, one will not be deceived by them. And because one does not follow after them, they will proceed into self-annihilation. [72]

However, for the individual of inferior capacity, at that time, one should practice the Generation Process and the Perfection Process of one's Yidam or meditation deity (yi-dam bskyed rdzogs). And having practiced with fervent devotion to the Guru, because one strikes the essential point, one will shut the doors to an impure rebirth. And having awakened (and exhausted) all the karmic traces from a single rebirth, he will come to be liberated.

Therefore, for one who is at present familiar with the mode of the arising of the Essence. [73] and who has a little connection with faith and devotion, where (the instructions) were clearly elucidated during the process of dying and fixed in the ear (by the Lama whispering them there). Then having finally died, because of good karmic traces, one should be reminded (by the Lama while lying there dead) of what one has heard previously. Because one has purified one's obscurations, it is very important that they (his friends and relatives) practice virtue for seven weeks. The reason for this is to remind (the deceased person) of what one has heard (previously) in terms of recognizing and remember the Bardo (and what to do there). Then, having recollected the instructions, one practices and by way of forceful purification, it is not possible that it (the Bardo experience) will not be cut off. The essential point will not be reversed, the path will not be mistaken, and the result will be without effort. [74] This is similar to a pig digging along the road in the summer time (because he is easy to control).

According to the *gZer-bu*, "It is called the path of the thigleys that are not bent (or crooked), and having traversed the path into a good place, one will become liberated quickly." [75] So it is said.

C3. The Methods of Liberation

Third, in terms of the methods of liberation (grol tshul), there are three subdivisions (namely, the methods of liberation for the superior practitioner, for the intermediate practitioner, and for the inferior practitioner).

C3a. The Superior Practitioner

As for the first, this is the practitioner of superior capacity. For such a one, in the Bardo of the Base that abides, there will arise (spontaneously) an understanding that is like meeting again a man that one has known intimately in the past. Thereby one tears open (and rents asunder) the three nets (or veils) of the body, speech, and mind. This occurs just at the time of the separating of the body and the mind, where this individual is like the emerging of the lion cub (from the jungle) or the garuda chick (from the egg). The Trikaya will become visibly manifest and one comes to act always for the benefit of other living beings (having attained the Rainbow Body).

C3b. The Intermediate Practitioner

Second, as for the practitioner of intermediate capacity: Because one has become familiar with and knows intimately these instructions for the Bardo of the Clear Light of Reality, at that time, with regard to the base for the arising of the miniature-sized gnosis and the miniature-sized (coloured) lights, one's own body appears as a Body of Light one full fathom in extent, without either front or back, without cardinal or intermediate directions, without above or below. In the sky of the ten directions, there will arise incalculable numbers of thigleys, pavilions, and celestial palaces. And with regard to that also, in the middle where there arise these five-by-five pavilions, there will arise five-by-five divine forms and they will appear (as visions) both as masses and arrayed in rows. [76]

At that time, the six clairvoyant powers and the six recollections having arisen extensively, like (many) lamps illuminating a dark room, each of these (colored) lights arise for five-by-five days, whereupon Rigpa becomes intimately known to (the practitioner) as wheels and houses of lights and these divine form arise as primal awareness. [77] And just exactly, because these visions (or appearances) are cut off, one will come to attain Buddhahood.

C3c. The Inferior Practitioner

As for the method of liberation for the practitioner of inferior capacity (tha-ma'i grol tshul): One remembers that there exists the Bardo of secondary conditions known as the Bardo of Rebirth. With regard to that, because one recollects the instructions and practices them, one is like a beggar boy who knows that he is actually a prince. Therefore, one should simply remain in the inherent condition of Buddhahood and he will instantly apprehend the rank that is without rebirth. Even those individuals having little purification, because they know the real meaning (of the Natural State), and recognize it, they will not follow after these (Bardo visions). And, therefore, do not let them escape freely into their own condition. Rather, they can take rebirth while maintaining their independence and self-power. [78] Having arrived at the three aspects of discrimininating wisdom, namely, listening, reflecting, and meditating, they will come to realize extensive benefits for themselves and for others. And upon their previous good karma awakening, they will come to attain Buddhahood without (the necessity for undergoing) further Bardo experience.

C4. The Method of Delusion

With regard to the fourth consideration the method of delusion ('khrul tshul): For one whose mind-stream has not retained (in memory, or even received them in the first place) the instructions (of the Lama that are like that (above), or for one who has only entered into the gate of

Siddhanta (that is, mere intellectual philosophical knowledge), [79] or those who fail to shut down (and cut off) the Bardo experience by not remaining with the essential points of these instructions, at the time when the consciousness of such an individual always wanders about restlessly without any physical support, there will arise pure visions to the individual possessing virtues and impure visions to the individual who is a sinner. [80] There may come far visions of crazy behavior and visions of fighting and conflict.

Elsewhere, in one's mind-stream, there will be produced, whatever may be appropriate, the emotional defilements of anger, desire, and confusion, and one grasps at them (pursuing them), and thereby one will enter onto the pathways of the (dull) rays of light, which are yellow, red, and indigo respectively. In terms of visions, (these lights paths) come to self-occur at the crown of one's head. [81] And one becomes driven (and carried forward relentlessly) by snows and blizzards and red wind (storms). Because one comes to arrive at groves of thorn-trees, deep ravines, narrow valleys, holes in the earth, and so on, the inevitable result will be that one proceeds into one of the three evil destinies of rebirth (ngan-song gsum). Those who (at this time) take up an impure body will find that it to be similar (to their future rebirth). [82]

Moreover, there emotional defilements of pride and envy may also be produced in the mindstream (of the deceased individual wandering in the Bardo), whereupon one will grasp at and enter upon the pathways of the (dull) white light or the (dull) green light respectively. In terms of visions, one will go crawling about on one's belly, or else, creeping along (like an insect), and one will be carried along by fog, whirling thick mists, mirages, and other optical illusions, and so on. Having arrived at a rock cave, or a house, or a tent, or a hut, for those flung through the doors of rebirth among the Devas or Asuras, the result will be similar. But if there is produced in one's mind-stream the discipline of calmness, the Bodhichitta, and devotion (to the Lama and his instructions), one will not grasp at or even enter upon these pathways that are are rays of (dull coloured) lights (that is to say, dull white light or Devas rebirth and dull green light for Asura rebirth). Rather, in terms of one's visions, one will ascend upward or seem to be climbing up steps. One is carried along by rainbows, clouds, and sunbeams. Having arrived at an immeasurable celestial palace, the result is that one will go on to the fortunate realms of rebirth, with independence (and self-power). And in terms of the benefit of beings, it will be similar for those who come into the places of pure rebirth. [83]

In general, one should know (and be aware) that this Bardo (of Rebirth) is similar to a dream. Although it may be difficult, if one can remember this, it is like a royal barge for crossing the river, and it will be easy to change and transform the secondary conditions. If one changes (and transforms) them, it is similar to making gold out of copper (by way of alchemy). [84] That will be of very great benefit. Therefore, one should proceed to the essential point of these instructions with regard to the Bardo. If one practices with experiences and takes them in hand, it would be equal to engaging in virtuous conduct for many lifetimes.

Moreover, these instructions, which may be taught in whatever manner, are not even equal to all the precepts and scriptures. Futhermore, practicing them accordingly is not even equal to all the persons who are travellers on the road (to rebirth). [85]

This guiding explanation of the conduct for the forceful purification of the secondary conditions arising along the path (is hereby completed).

U-YA SMAR-RO! Virtue!

Chapter Seven

The Explanation
of the Fruit: *dMar-khrid*

Here is contained "The Guiding Explanation for coming to an
intensely Clear and Definitive Decision regarding the Trikaya, where
one remains in one's own Original Condition, which represents the
Fruit" ('bras-bu rang sa bzung-ba sku-gsum dmar thag-bcad-pa'i khrid
bzhugs-so).

Homage to Kuntu Zangpo, the all-pervading and all-encompassing
Guide of living beings, who is one's own Self-Awareness become
manifest! [1]

(As for the fourth supplementary text,) here, in terms of coming
to an intensely clear and definitive decision regarding the Trikaya,
where one remains in one's own original condition, there are three
principal divisions:

I.   The direct introduction where the example and the real meaning
     are linked together (dpe don 'brel-ba'i ngo-sprad),
II. The direct introduction to Energy as being self-manifestation
     (rang-snang rtsal gyi ngo-sprad), and
III. The direct introduction to the Trikaya that represents the Fruit
     ('bras-bu sku-gsum gyi ngo-sprad). [2]

I. Direct Introduction by Way of the Examples and their Meaning

Within the first topic (the direct introduction by way of examples), there are three further divisions:

A. The meaning of the example is illustrated by means of the lamp of illustrative examples (mtshon dpe'i sgron-mas dpe'i don mtshon-pa), and

B. One is directly introduced to the sign or indication by means of the lamp of the sign indicating primal awareness (ye-shes rtags kyi sgron-mas rtags thog tu ngo-sprad-pa),

C. Whereupon these two (the Natural State and primal awareness) should be linked together and unified (gnyis zung 'brel du bya).

I.ABC. Example, Meaning, and Indication

Furthermore, according to the *sGron-ma,* "As for this process of illustrating the real meaning by way of the (six) examples, the butter lamp (mar-me) illustrates the inherent clarity of primal awareness (and its primal cognitions), the lotus (padma) illustrates its immaculate and primordial purity, the sun (nyi-ma) illustrates the spontaneous perfection of the Clear Light, the mirror (me-long) illustrates that its inherent clarity is without obscurations, the crystal ball (shel sgong) illustrates that it is all-penetrating and naked, and the sky (nam-mkha') illustrates that primal awareness equally encompasses everything." [3]

At the beginning (of the instruction, the Lama) should actually display a butter lamp (to the disciple) and one should gaze at its image as it is reflected in a mirror and fixate one's awareness on it. Then, one should look back inside (one's mind) and gaze with wide open eyes at the essence of Awareness. [4] Thereby a firm belief (arises within one's mind-stream) and one is directly introduced (by the Lama saying:) "The essence of the butter lamp (that is, its light) frees everything (in the room) from obscuration and from the gloom of darkness. Just as (the lamp flame) is itself clear (and luminous in itself), so also (it makes everything in the dark room) clear (and illuminated) at the same time, so in the same way, Kunzhi and Rigpa, arising at the gateway of the lamp (of the eyes), dispel any gloom or obscuration (covering external objects). They are luminously clear at the same time in terms of their inherent clarity." So saying, one is directly introduced (to primal awareness or gnosis). [5]

Accordingly, (the disciple) should also practice meditation in terms of these other (examples) and the real meaning will thereby be well illustrated by way of these same examples. Consequently, inside of this (process), a definitive and certain knowledge (nges shes) will be clearly and definitively produced (within one's mind-stream, whereupon the Lama) should patiently continue to introduce directly (the disciple by saying as follows:) "Just as the lotus originally resides in the muck of the swamp, nevertheless, it abides there (as a blossom) nakedly and immaculately without being touched or attired in any way with the muck of the swamp, in the same way, even though Kunzhi and Rigpa exist in the hollow tube of the karmic traces, they do so nakedly and in their primordial purity, without being attired in any way with the taints that represent karmic traces. Just as the sun was not created by any one, but from the very beginning it arose effulgently as totally clear light, so the Kunzhi, at the gateway of the lamp (of the eyes), not being created by anything or anyone, is spontaneously perfected from the very beginning as totally self-originated clear light. [6] Just as the images are reflected in the mirror, in terms of its clarity, they arise clearly without obscurations and without any inherent existence, so in the same way, the Kunzhi, at the gateway of the lamp (of the eyes), in terms of its luminous clarity, arises in pure presence without grasping at anything. [7] Just as with the crystal ball, everything external and internal abides clearly, nakedly, directly penetratingly, and without obscurations, so in the same way, the Kunzhi, at the gateway of the lamp (of the eyes), is free from being attired in any obscurations or coverings (in terms of discursive thoughts or negative emotions), and arises nakedly (and open-eyed) in a directly penetrating manner. [8] Just as the sky (or space itself) pervades and encompasses everything equally, so in the same way, the Kunzhi, at the gateway of the lamp (of the eyes), pervades and encompasses everything equally as total primal awareness without any exterior or interior. [9]

II. Direct Introduction to Energy as Self-Manifestation

Second, in terms of the direct introduction (to the visions representing) the self-manifestations of the energy (of the Nature of Mind) (rang-snang rtsal gyi ngo-sprad), there are two considerations:

A. The direct introduction (to visions) as being self arising (rang shar du ngo-sprad-pa) and

B. The direct introduction (to visions) being self-manifestations (rang-snang dun go-sprad-pa).

A. Visions as being Self-Arising

With regard to the first consideration (the self-arising of visions), it is said according to the *gZer-bu*, "The examples that illustrate the unification of the object and Awareness, are water, the crystal, the sun, and the butter lamp, each of them representing the modes of light." [10]

As for the first of these four examples (water), because the sunlight strikes (the surface of) the water, the light fractures or separates and clearly visible rays (of light) arise in the atmosphere. Thereby one is directly introduced. Rigpa is similar (in this way) to the water and the manifestations of the three, that is, the sounds, the lights, and the rays, are similar to the light (reflected from) the water. This represents a direct introduction to (these visions) arising as self-originated. [11]

Similarly, when a crystal is placed in the sunlight, the (rainbow) lights come forth and thereby one is directly introduced. Rigpa is similar to the crystal and the three manifestations (of the sounds, the lights, and the rays) are similar to the lights coming from the crystal. In the same way, Rigpa is similar to the sun and the three manifestations are similar to the modes of its light. [12] Again, Rigpa is similar to the butter lamp and the three manifestations should be known to exist as its modes of light. [13]

B. The Visions as being Self-Manifestations

In terms of the second consideration (the visions being self-manifestations), there are three subsections:

(1) The direct introduction where the lights are like the inherent lights of the rainbow ('od rang 'od gzha'-tshon ltar ngo-sprad-pa),

(2) The direct introduction where the rays are like the inherent rays that are the reflected images (in the mirror) (zer rang zer gzugs-brnyan ltar ngo-sprad-pa), and

(3) The direct introduction where the sounds are like the inherent sounds of the echoes (sgra rang sgra brag-cha ltar ngo-sprad-pa'o).

B1–2. Inherent Lights and Rays

With regard to the first (and the second), one may be directly introduced to the lights and the rays at the same time. As for the methods (tshul) of doing this, (this is three fold:)

a. Externally, in terms of the Lamp of Existence one presses against (the neck) and presses down (on the eyeballs) (phyi srid-pa'i sgron-ma gtod la mnan-pa),

b. Internally, in terms of the Lamp of the Sense Faculties (that is, the eyes), one gazes fixedly into space (nang dbang-po'i sgron-ma ar la gtad-pa), and

c. Secretly, in terms of the Lamp of Awareness, one lets it abide and leaves alone everything (the visions that arise) and thereby one is directly introduced (rig-pa'i sgron-ma gnas la bor-ba ngo-sprad-pa'o).

B1–2a. The Lamp of Existence

With regard to the first, in terms of the purity of space, the assuming of the meditation position represents the essential point of the body (nam-mkha' dwangs-pa la bca'-ba lus kyi gnad) and by means of the gaze, which is the essential point of the sense faculties, the daytime visions are arrested and subdued at the margins in terms of the Lamp of Existence. This is in agreement with the practice of pressing down gently on the eyeballs. [14] Thereby everything arises into visible manifestation, such as the lights, the rays, and the thigleys. Thereby one is directly introduced (to these visions) as self-manifestations and one will become familiar with them.

B1–2b. The Lamp of the Sense Faculties

Second, internally, in terms of the Lamp of the Sense Faculties, one fixates (the gaze) into space and one suppresses the doorway of the lamp (of the senses) by way of the two immobilities. [15] At first one holds the breath and at the time when one is full (that is, one's lungs are full), because there will arise various different lights and rays, one is directly introduced to one's own inherent lights and inherent rays. At the time of twisting the torso (gzhil), one gulps more breath, and because one relaxes a little, there arise the five lights that are like rainbows. Thereby one will be directly introduced to one's own inherent light. Finally, at the time of relaxing (and exhaling the breath), one fixates on space. And because one gazes into that previous state and because the manifestations of the lights and the rays go into self-liberation, one is directly introduced to the inherent energy of Rigpa. [16]

B1–2c. The Lamp of Awareness

Third, secretly, in terms of the occurring and abiding of the Lamp of Awareness, one engages in meditation practice repeatedly many times, including the essential points of the body, the gaze, and the yoga of breathing, whereupon one fixates Awareness into the atmosphere that is without clouds or cold breezes. Because purity and impurity are separated, whereas clarity and translucency come forth, there arise the various different manifestations of the Clear Light (that is, the Thodgal visions). Thereby one will become directly introduced to these self-manifestations being like illusions. [17]

B3. Sounds as Inherent Sounds

Third, in terms of the direct introduction to sounds being one's own inherent sounds, (sgra rang sgrar ngo-sprad-pa), there are three considerations:

a. Externally, one is directly introduced to the self-returning of the empty sounds (phyi stong sgra rang log la ngo-sprad-pa),
b. Internally, one is directly introduced to the secondary conditions that are due to other (extrinsic causes) by way of symbolic methods (nang brda thabs gzhan rkyen la ngo-sprad-pa), and
c. Secretly, one is directly introduced to inherent sounds as self-awareness (gsang-ba rang-rig rang sgra la ngo-sprad-pa).

B3a. Inherent Sounds as Self-Arising

With regard to the first consideration, one shouts aloud among the rocks or in a deep ravine and the empty sounds, which are not made by anyone else, come forth in a self-arising manner. Thereby one is directly introduced. [18]

B3b. Inherent Sounds as Self-Manifestations

Second, in the condition of one's own place, one suddenly makes the sounds of music by playing cymbals and then dropping them, one presses again and again (one's fingers) into one's ears. Thereby one will be directly introduced to these sounds as being self-manifestations.

B3c. Inherent Sounds as Self-Awareness

With regard to the third, one suppresses at the secret gate with the two immobilities. The inherent sounds of Rigpa resound continuously and one fixates the functional mind on this. Thereby one is directly introduced to the self-arising (of these sounds). [19]

Furthermore, according to the *sGron-ma*, "At the navel of the coil of an ocean conch shell, there arises at the doorway (of the ear), the sounds of the wind which are empty. From the semi-circular hollow space of the secret of sound, there resounds the roar of self-originated sounds and the murmuring continues without interruption. Thereby the functional mind that moves is tamed (and subdued) in terms of the sound.('gyu-ba'i yid ni sgra la btul)." So it is said.

III. Direct Introduction to the Trikaya

Third, with regard to the Fruit (the direct introduction to the Trikaya that represents the Fruit), there are three principal sections:

A. The direct introduction to Buddhahood in its own form (sangs-rgyas rang chas su ngo-sprad-pa),
B. The mode of arising of the divine forms and primal awareness (lha sku ye-shes kyi 'char tshul), and
C. Showing in addition the methods for stopping and starting (btang bzhag gi tshul bstan-pa/ btang bzhag zur gyis bstan-pa).

A. Buddhahood in its Own Form

With regard to the first (Buddhahood in its own form), according to the *sGron-ma*, "This totally all-pervading and all-encompassing Nature of Mind, which is the Bodhichitta and the Kunzhi that abides, being without partiality or one-sidedness and without (hopes or) fears, in the Dharmadhatu, the Dimension of Reality. In its own place and location (gnas), self-awareness abides as total primordial purity. It is the

Dharmakaya. However, this realm (or dimension) of the Dharmakaya, even though in its own form, it always accompanies one, nevertheless, it is not recognized." [20]

"Moreover, in its own place or location (gnas), in the maroon-colored pavilion of cornelian, having projections of (white) crystal, which is the physical heart, there is an immeasurable celestial palace of light, which is clearly visible. In actuality, it is the realm of the transcendent and unrivalled Akanishtha. In that location, in terms of the primal cognitions of Rigpa, its energy manifests in spontaneous perfection as the sounds, the lights, and the rays, whereupon everything in Samsara and Nirvana is complete in its spontaneous perfection. This is the Sambhogakaya, the Body of Perfect Enjoyment. However, even though the realm of the Sambhogakaya exists in its own form (rang chas su), nevertheless, because one does not recognize it, (one perceives it) as delusion. [21]

"Moreover, there are six aspects pertaining to the chakras of the channels in the three places, in terms of the trunk, together with the limbs, the branches, and the twigs (that is, the nadis and the upanadis), which are all complete. This constitutes the perfect wheel of letters. In those places, with regard to the primal cognitions or Rigpa, there arise various different apparitions, such as the six energies and the six objects. Thereby the (various) realms of the Nirmanakaya, together with (their inhabitants), arise. Even though they abide as self-manifestations, because they are not (recognized and) understood, they arise as the visions of the six realms of rebirth." So saying represents the direct introduction. [22]

Within the physical heart, there is the interior arising of self-awareness. This is the Dharmakaya in its own form. Because the inherent energy of Rigpa is entirely complete on the pathway of the (kati) channel, the Sambhogakaya is self-arising. Because there arise at the doorway of the eyes all the magical apparitions of the mind, the Nirmanakaya is directly introduced as being self-arising. [23]

According to the *gZer-bu*, "Within the vast expanse of the physical heart, self-awareness abides as the Dharmakaya. In terms of the pathway of the (kati) channel (extending from the heart to the eyeballs), there is the Nature and this abides as the Sambhogakaya. The self-arising (of the visions) at the doorway of the lamp (of the eyes) represents the Nirmanakaya." [24]

Moreover, the primal awareness which is Rigpa has been primordially pure from the very beginning and has existed free from any root (or source). It is the Dharmakaya itself. However, due to the power of the linkage of the body and the mind, and because the powers of all the Kulas (or families) of divine forms come forth everywhere as primal cognitions (ye-shes), this is the Sambhogakaya. And this conduct as various different activities of the three gates (of body, speech, and mind) is the Nirmanakaya. [25]

Again, according to the *gZer-bu*, "The primal awareness of one's own Rigpa is the primordially pure Dharmakaya. The linkage of the body and mind is the Sambhogakaya. The various different activities occurring everywhere are the Nirmanakaya." [26] So it is said.

Moreover, in the middle of the physical heart, Rigpa (abides even at present) shining as Buddhahood and this is known as Primordial Buddhahood (ye sangs-rgyas-pa). In the hollow tube of the (kati) channel, the three energies are entwined without ever being separated. This is the Perfect Buddhahood (rdzogs snangs-rgyas-pa). And at the doorway of the lamp (of the eyes) it arises brilliantly and directly penetratingly everywhere without any obscurations. This is the Buddhahood becoming visibly manifest (mngon sangs-rgyas-pa). [27]

Moreover, the Nature of Mind, also known as the Essence and as emptiness, is the Dharmakaya in its own form. The aspect of luminous clarity is the Sambhogakaya in its own form. And the arising (of visions) as various different magical apparitions is the Nirmanakaya in its own form. Therefore, emptiness, clarity, and vision represent the Trikaya (in terms of one's own immediate experience). [28] So saying, one makes the direct introduction.

Furthermore, they are outer, inner, and secret in terms of their manner of arising. Because everything remains always as the Essence itself (that is, as emptiness), it is the Dharmakaya. Because it always abides naturally and unceasingly, it is the Sambhogakaya. And because the magical apparitions always arise in an uncertain manner, it is the Nirmanakaya. [29]

Again, because everything, whether subtle or coarse, even one's own discursive thoughts, all represent the side of emptiness, it is the Dharmakaya. As for the side of clarity, that represents the Sambhogakaya. And as for the side of magical apparitions, that represents the Nirmanakaya. [30]

Accordingly, (in the same way) seeing things as being external (to oneself) is the manner for the arising of visions, whereas experiences and understanding is the manner of producing things internally. Therefore, everything is mixed up together and this is introduced (to the disciple) in an extensive manner.

B. The Arising of Divine Forms and Primal Cognitions

Second, in terms of the manner of the arising of the divine forms and of primal cognitions (lha sku ye-shes 'char tshul), there are three sections:

(1) The manner in which the Bodies or divine forms arise (sku yi 'char tshul),
(2) The method for knowing them by means of primal cognitions (ye-shes kyi(s) mkhyen tshul), and
(3) The method of accomplishing deeds by means of enlightened activities (phrin-las kyi(s) mdzad tshul).

B1. The Arising of Divine Forms

As for the first, when the corpse and awareness are still linked together (and connected), the Base as the Trikaya abides in its own form and that is the Trikaya of the Base. On the occasion of the Path, when one is practicing (meditation) in whatever manner, there arise various visions and experiences in the mind-stream of the (individual) and that represents the Trikaya of the Path. [31]

And with regard to that, in terms of the originating and arriving (of these visions), the energy comes out (of the potentiality of space), perfectly and powerfully, and because it transforms in the vast expanse of space, it thereupon comes into visible manifestation as the Trikaya of the Fruit.

With regard to that, there are two further considerations, namely,

a. The base for their arising ('char gzhi) and
b. The manner in which they arise ('char tshul).

B1a. The Base for the Arising of the Divine Forms

With regard to the first (the base for their arising), "Having become liberated from the marks (and characteristics) of one's own (old) polluted physical body, which was both visible and material, thereafter in a supreme Body that is unpolluted, adorned with the (thirty-two) marks and (eighty) characteristics, seated on a throne, together with the (accompanying dimension or) realm, one becomes visibly manifest as the Sambhogakaya. From this profound state of Mind that is free of conceptual elaborations and which transcends the intellect, one abides without abandoning or freeing oneself from anything, and thereupon the Dharmakaya becomes visibly manifest. [32] One's speech becomes melodious and its tone and pitch are without any inherent existence. One expounds various different (scriptural discourses) such as the eighty-four thousand precepts transmissions (bka' brgyud) and thereupon one becomes visible (to sentient beings) as the Nirmanakaya.

"At the time when one's body, speech, and mind become visibly manifest as the Trikaya one's energy as the three, the sounds, the lights, and the rays, as well as the aggregates or skandhas, the sense organs and objects (dhatus), and the sense fields (ayatanas), together with one's states of consciousness and contents of consciousness, both root and branch arise (spontaneously) as the hosts of deities that are outer, inner, and secret. [33] Without even looking to any efforts for the attaining of Buddhahood, they come forth (spontaneously) from the power of the State (in order to accomplish) the benefit of living beings. Even without moving from (the state of) the Dharmakaya, emanations appear everywhere for the sake of benefiting living beings." So it is said.

B1b. The Manner of Their Arising

With regard to the second consideration (the manner in which they arise) ('char tshul), generally speaking, one's (inherent) energy consists of the sounds, the lights, and the rays, and these self-manifestations become liberated into the Essence of Rigpa.[34]

However, in particular, the clear white light becomes clearly visible as the heart of liberation, and this represents Kunnang Khyabpa (kun-snang khyab-pa), the Deity of the Mind without delusions. He signifies the primal awareness of emptiness becoming clearly visible in the (individual) mind-stream. His body colour is white and is located in the central direction, where he holds the Tathagata-kula, so that his hand-symbol is the chakra or wheel. [35] He abides in the state of the great bliss of the Dharmakaya, so that he comes forth with his hands in the Samadhi-mudra, the gesture of equipoise in meditation. Because he confers empowerment into the vast expanse of space, his consort is the space goddess, Namkhai Lhamo (nam-mkha'i lha-mo). Because he suppresses (and vanquishes) anger, he sits entroned on the seat of the lion. Because he possesses the power of total friendliness (byams-pa chen-po), he accomplishes the benefit of beings by way of vanquishing the suffering experienced in the hot and the cold hells.

Similarly, from the clear yellow light arises Salwa Rangjyung (gsal-ba rang-byung), the Deity of the Body that is unchanging, whereupon the mirror-like primal awareness becomes clearly visible in one's mind-stream. His body colour is yellow and is located in the eastern direction, where he holds the Swastika-kula, so that as a hand symbol, he has the golden sceptre with the (double) swastikas. As the sign of the Sambhogakaya, he unfolds before his heart center the gesture of marvel. And because he confers empowerment in the vast expanse of the earth element, his consort is the earth goddess, Sayi Lhamo (yum sa yi lha-mo). He is seated enthroned upon a great elephant (indicating that) he suppresses confusion. Because he possesses the power of total primal awareness, he accomplishes thereby the benefit of the animals who are unintelligent and inarticulate. [36]

Accordingly (in the same way), from the clear green light arises Gelha Garchyug (dge lha gar-phyug), from the clear red light arises Jyedrag Ngomed (bye-brag dngos-med), and from the clear blue light arises Gawa Dondrub (dga'-ba don-grub). Their symbols indicate the meaning for each among these five. One should be extensively introduced to all of them in terms of symbolic methods. [37]

Furthermore, in their outer aspect, they are the five (deities) Shenlha, Godse, Garse, Seje, and Namse, whereas in their inner aspect, they are the above five (deities) known as Kunnang, and the rest. Moreover, in their secret aspect, they are the five (deities) Tsochog, Trose, Ngamse, Walse, and Tumse [38] (Although five in number, nevertheless) in the presence of those to be subdued (and converted), they represent a single essence (ngo-bo gcig) and they are directly introduced (to the disciple) as displayed where they become located.

Accordingly (in the same way), from the eight aggregates of consciousness arise the eight Yeshen (ye-gshen brgyad, or male Bodhisattvas) and from the eight objects of consciousness arise the eight Yesang (ye-sangs brgyad, or female Bodhisattvas). [39] The discursive thoughts that grasp at the five poisons arise as the five immaculate deities. From the head, feet, eyes, and tongue arise the four flower maidens (me-tog bzhi). From the discursive thoughts that grasp at the six causes (for rebirth) arise the six Dulshen ('dul-gshen drug). From the grasping at the four seasons arise the four Queens (rgyal-mo bzhi). In this way, there arise the fourty-five (peaceful deities). Elsewhere, in their outer aspect, there arise the one hundred and eight hosts of Paushtika-devas, or Prosperity Deities, who increase wealth and prosperity (rgyas-pa'i lha tshogs), in the inner aspect there arise the fourty-five Shantika-devas, or Peaceful Deities, who bring about pacification and tranquillity (zhi-ba'i lha tshogs), and in their secret aspect the eighty-six host of Krodha-devas, or Wrathful Deities, both male and female (khro-bo khro-mo'i lha tshogs). [40]

As for the method of liberation in the mind-stream of the individual (rgyud la grol tshul), this method is in agreement with the above method of arising in terms of their being a single base for their origination, nevertheless, they reveal themselves individually for the subduing of anyone and one is thereby directly introduced to them. Their outer, inner, and secret aspects are similar to an interlaced network of illusions (sgyu-'phrul draw-ba). This has been expounded from the Tantra (Khro-bo dbang-chen). [41]

With regard to the hosts of deities who are like that, as for their originating in sexual union (as yab-yum images), the meaning here is that they abide as linked pairs representing Means and Wisdom, clarity and emptiness, and so on. As for their originating as the principal deities, together with their retinues, this represents the special power for the liberating the states of consciousness and the contents of consciousness (in the mind-stream of the individual). [42] As for their arising in the three aspects which are outer, inner, and secret, that is the symbol which teaches individually (to disciples) the gateways for entering (into the Dharma) which are prepared in the vessel (that is, teach them what they need according to their circumstances and capacities).

As for the arising (of their activities) as pacifying, increasing, enchanting, and fierce, they guide living beings by means of these four magical activities. As for their possessing of all the virtuous qualities of Body, Speech, and Mind, the meaning is that they abide from the very beginning as the Nature of the Trikaya. [43] Therefore, they are adorned with the (thirty-two) marks and the (eighty) characteristics and are seated upon thrones. As for their arising with such great virtuous qualities, and with lists of qualities that are certain, together with arrays of realms, it is a symbol (brda) that all faults to be renounced and all transgressions are indeed abandoned, and all good qualities are indeed (cultivated) and completely perfected. Moreover, due to that, there come forth millions of myriads of hosts of deities that are outer, inner, and secret, which are not all similar or in agreement. They surround them as their retinues. That is the symbol which reveals the antidotes for individually subduing those who should be subdued. [44]

B2. Knowing by way of Primal Awareness

Second (as for the method for knowing them by means of primal awareness), with regard to primal awareness (ye-shes), that primal awareness itself that represents self-originated awareness now becomes manifest. With regard to that, due to the manner of arising where the energy originates and proceeds (having been made and fixed), being sent forth perfectly and powerfully (from the Nature), there will arise the five primal cognitions, namely, the primal awareness of emptiness, the primal awareness of sameness, the primal awareness that accomplishes all actions, the primal awareness that discriminates, and the primal awareness that is like a mirror. If one condenses them, they may be condensed into two, namely, the knowledge of quality which represents the Ultimate Truth and the knowledge of quantity which represents the Relative Truth. Due to the activities of these primal cognitions, there are some eighty-four thousand such primal cognitions, which look in detail into the nature of what should be known. [45]

Furthermore, the masses of thoughts occurring in time for sentient beings arise and abide and liberate, and thereby infinite hundreds of thousands of gateways of samadhi will clearly illuminate the mind. The various different thoughts and memories occurring at the time of the cause merely arise into liberation. As for the arising of the entire universe as the emanation and reabsorption of the rays of light, [46] it is the symbol that everything which should be renounced in one's own mind-stream has been abandoned and that all the transgressions and obscurations (nyes sgrib) in the mind-stream of others have been purified.

B3. Enlightened Activities

Third, in terms of enlightened activities (phrin-las), there are two considerations, namely,

a. The actuality itself (dngos) and
b. The method for accomplishing it (mdzad tshul).

B3a. The Actuality of Compassion

With regard to the first, "Because of the three: great compassion, skill in means, and knowledge regarding everything, [47] from the very beginning, compassion will be immeasurable like the sky and equal everywhere like (the light of) the sun, uninterrupted like the flow of the river, and inexhaustible like the surface of the earth. Indeed, it will become manifest in this four-fold manner. As for the "I" (the sense of individuality), it will be impartial toward everything like the sun (shining equally on all objects) and it will flow continuously (and uninterruptedly) like the current of a river." [48] So it is said. (This represents the actuality of compassion.)

B3b. The Method of Accomplishment

As for the second consideration (the method of accomplishing it (mdzad tshul): Accordingly, one will be able to subdue (and discipline) everyone everywhere with such deeds of Body, Speech, and Mind that are pacifying, increasing, enchanting, and fierce, as well as displaying the twelve (great deeds of a Buddha). One will accomplish the benefit of incredible numbers of individuals who should be subdued by way of employing many different methods of subjugation, as well as exercising the path of skilful means (thabs lam dang gdul thabs), whereby one will guide living beings of uncertain diverse kinds. One will bring about a visible display with regard to subduing everyone everywhere." So it was said.

"In terms of the third, if one does not know the real condition of that which should be known, if it is not clear, then one will not accomplish (such enlightened actions) and one will not cause them to be manifest and they will not even exist. But by a single primal cognition of knowledge, the natural condition of what should be known will become clear." [49] So it is said.

With regard to the second, even though these enlightened activities can be made to pervade where there does not exist just a single benefit for sentient beings, or where at times they do not exist, nevertheless, they can be accomplished always. Where they do not exist on any side, they can be accomplished diversely. Without even looking at any effort, they can be accomplished in their spontaneous perfection. Where they do not exist in the mind-stream, they may be made to become manifest. Where they do not exist in one's own mind-stream, one can make them come to possess loving thoughts. As for the "I" or ego, having the nature of equanimity (nga ni snyoms-pa'i rang-bzhin), even those enlightened activities of the Buddha accomplished in order to benefit (others), such as actions possessing a nature which is peaceful, one strives for and exerts oneself in actions of the three gates (of the Body, Speech, and Mind) at the time of the cause. Thereby, all the marks of suffering (that characterize Samsaric existence), together with all efforts, are brought into liberation.

C. Granting Permission and Issuing the Command

Third, in terms of the successive stages of establishing a suitable arrangement for granting permission and sealing the commandments (btang-bzhag rjes-gnang bka' rgya'i rim-pa), there are two principal considerations:

(1) The granting of permission (rjes-gnang) and
(2) The issuing the command (bka' rgya gdab-pa).

C1. Granting the Permission

With regard to the first (the permission): A person who possesses good fortune and appropriate karma [50] should subsequently be kept as the principal (disciple). He is one who possesses diligence and is able to give generously, having heartfelt faith and devotion, who approaches (the Lama) with sincere humility, who can endure much suffering and hardship, who is suitable in all his actions according to plan, who possesses mindfulness and clear comprehension (dran-pa shes-bzhin), who can spread and abide in what is proper. In brief, he or she is one who is able to comprehend the Upadeshas, is able to practice them, and who knows how to teach them to others. To such a disciple, to one who has practiced in a single-hearted concentrated way, one should teach (the Dzogchen precepts) wholly and completely without keeping anything back, without concealing anything or keeping anything secret or reserved.

C2. Issuing the Command

With regard to the second (issuing the command regarding to whom the teachings should not be given): (The teachings should be kept) from those wrong persons who do not possess ripened karma or good fortune, who do not unite proper actions with their thoughts, who do not keep (and have a grasp on) mindfulness and clear comprehension who deviate into wrong views and conduct, whose four elements are waning, who are touched by the frivolous faults of youth, whose education is defective, and who does not pursue the real meaning, who has been struck with a bad reputation, and has carried on evilly (in society), who is not able to carry on with diligence in difficult circumstances, who does not perceive appearances with one's native intelligence, who know how to move about (in business and society) deceitfully, and who has not renounced pride and self-importance. In brief, he or she is one who is not a suitable vessel for receiving the teachings of the profound Upadeshas. (The Dzogchen precepts) should be kept very secret from those types of individuals who do not understand, who do not comprehend, who are not capable, and who do not practice. From them, it should be hidden and very well concealed. Not even the words should be spoken (in their presence).

Elsewhere, only to those who possess the karma should one give this manual of these intensely clear guiding explanations (dmar khrid lag-len), together with the written texts. They should be bestowed well upon those who have the samaya vows and the white (virtues). But if one should give this away for the sake of wealth or reputation to one who is not publicly revealed (that is, one whose qualifications have not been checked and examined), then this will dissolve the blessings adhering to the instructions. Whereupon, the Dakinis and the Protectors of the Precepts will cut one down with punishments for violating this commandment. [51] Therefore, one should keep the full measure of this suitable arrangement.

This guiding explanation for coming to an intensely clear and definitive decision regarding the Trikaya, where one remains in one's own original condition, which represents the Fruit, is hereby completed.

U-YA SMAR-RO!

Afterword

Likewise, these Upadeshas, which condense the essential points of the instructions of Dru (myself, Gyalwa Yungdrung) in this way, should overflow in one's heart. Moreover, this manual of the innermost disposition of his intention is condensed here in brief as the conclusion. In terms of this nectar of the intention of the Oral Transmission whose meaning is profound, even though it has been arranged with a pure intention, nevertheless, some errors and deviations, as well as some impetuosities and defects in composition wherever they may come, may indeed have appeared. Therefore, I confess without hesitation all my erroneous and confused thoughts. However, by this merit, may all living beings, myself as well as others, come to understand the supreme meaning of the Clear Light that is both aware and empty.

In the same way, here there have been condensed the essential points, which are outer, inner, and secret, as well as exceedingly secret, for the Dzogpa Chenpo Zhang-zhung Nyan-gyud, distilling the nectar of the various instructions of the core of the profound meaning. This is the ultimate one among the oral instructions of the previous Mahasiddhas. The monk of Dru, Gyalwa Yungdrung, because of the repeated entreaties of his good spiritual friend, Tashi Rinchen, who himself holds the saffron-coloured robe, composed this orderly arranged manual [52] at Yeru Wensakha monastery. It is now completed.

MU-TSUG SMAR-RO!

EMAHO!

One should not even show these written words to anyone, except to one who has met the Lama and received the instructions previously. May good fortune come! Virtue!

SARVA MANGALAM!

Notes to
the Transaltions

1. Notes to the Introduction

(1) See John Myrdhin Reynolds, *The Oral Tradition from Zhang-zhung: An Introduction to the Bonpo Dzogchen Teachings of the Oral Tradition from Zhang-zhung*, Vajra Publications, Kathmandu 2005, pp. 205–215

(2) *'Ja'-lus 'pho-ba chen-po*. Upon attaining of Buddha enlightenment by way of Thodgal practice during his life time, the physical body of the master dissolves into pure radiant energy and vanishes into space. He is thus able to reappear when required in any form he chooses, such as Tapihritsa appearing as a young boy to his disciple in the following century. This attaining of the Rainbow Body represents the Rupakaya, or Form Body of the Buddha, from the standpoint of the method of Thodgal, in contrast to the explanations in the Sutra and the Tantra systems.

(3) On the historical origins of Dzogchen, see Reynolds, *The Golden Letters*, Snow Lion Publications, Ithaca NY 1996, pp.215–286. Also see Samten G. Karmay, *The Great Perfection: A Philosophical and Meditative Teaching of Tibetan Buddhism*, Brill, Leiden 1988, and Per Kvaerne, "The Great Perfection in the Tradition of the Bonpos," in Whalen Lai and Lewis Lancaster (eds), *Early Ch'an in China and Tibet*, Asian Humanities Press,Berkeley CA 1983, pp.367–392.

(4) On the enlightened master Tapihritsa and his disciple Gyerpung Nangzher Lodpo, and the former's teachings to the latter, see Reynolds, *The Oral Tradition from Zhang-zhung*, ibid., pp.79–118. On the Zhang-zhung and Darok Lake, see John Bellezza, "Pre-history of Tibet," *Himal*, December 1999, Kathmandu, pp. 42–43, and John Bellezza, "High Country Culture: A Civilization Flourished in the Himalayas before Buddhism Reached Tibet," *Discovering Archaeology*, v.1, n.3, May-June 1999, pp.78–83.

(5) On the Dharmakaya (bon-sku), the Sambhogakaya (rdzogs-sku), and the Nirmanakaya (sprul-sku) in the Bonpo context, see Reynolds, *The Oral Tradition from Zhang-zhung*, ibid., pp.17–48. In both the Nyingmapa and the Bonpo traditions, the Primordial Buddha is named Kuntu Zangpo (kun tu bzang-po, Skt. Samantabhadra), "the all-good," and is depicted with the same iconography. The Sambhogakaya, Shenlha Odkar (gshen-lha od-dkar), "the Shen God of White Light," corresponds to the Buddhist Vajrasattva. The Nirmanakaya is here Tonpa Shenrab(stong-pa gshen-rab), rather than Garab Dorje (dga'-rab rdo-rje), as in the Nyingmapa lineage.

(6) *'Ja'-lus-pa.* The Rainbow Body represents the visible manifestation of a master attaining enlightenment by way of the practice of vision or Thodgal, where the material elements of his gross physical body are dissolved back into their pure form as radiant lights. It differs from the Great Transfer ('pho-ba chen-po) in that the process occurs at the time of dying.

(7) On Ponchen Tsanpo and his Tibetan disciples, see Reynolds, *The Oral Transmission from Zhang-zhung*, ibid., pp. 137–139, 141–150.

(8) See Reynolds, *The Oral Tradition from Zhang-zhung*, ibid.

(9) See Reynolds, *The Oral Tradition from Zhang-zhung*, ibid. pp.367–380. On the A-tri system of Dzogchen practice, see Per Kvaerne and Thubten Rikey. *The Stages of A-khrid Meditation, Dzogchen Practice of the Bon Tradition*, Library of Tibetan Works and Archives, Dharamsala 1996.

(10) *Bru-chen rgyal-ba g.yung-drung*, 1242–1290. He belonged to the famous Dru clan (gdung-rus bru), hence he was known as *Bru-chen*, "the great man of the Dru family." The Tibetan text of his *Phyag-khrid*, or practice manual, was published in *sNyan rgyud nam-mkha' 'phrul mdzod drang nges skor* and *Zhang-zhung*

snyan-rgyud skor, Tibetan Bonpo Monastic Centre, New Delhi 1972, ff. 539–726.

(11) *g.Yas-ru'i dben-sa-kha* monastery was founded in 1072 by *Bru-chen g.Yung-drung bla-ma*, b. 1040. It soon became the most famous Bonpo monastery in Tsang provence and was the ancestral foundation to the Lopon's own monastery of Tashi Menri (bKrashis sman-ri).

(12) *Bru-chen nam-mkha' g.yung-drung* was head of the Dru clan (gdung-rus bru) that was said to have come originally from the country of Drusha (Bru-sha) lying to the west of Tibet. It is now identified as Gilgit in modern day Pakistan where the native language is Burushaski.

(13) On *gShen-chen klu-dga'*, 996–1035, who discovered the largest single cache of old Bonpo texts, see Karmay, *The Treasury of Good Sayings*, ibid. pp.126–135.

(14) The 10th and 11th centuries was the axial period for the revival of both Bon and Buddhism in Central Tibet. On the revival of Buddhism and the inception of the New Translations (phyi 'gyur), see Snellgrove and Richardson, *A Cultural History of Tibet*, ibid., pp. 111–143.

(15) The *Srid-pa'i mdzod-phug*, in some ways, is considered to be a Bonpo Abhidharma, that is, a treatise on cosmology and cosmogony. There exist other Bonpo texts that may also be classified as Abhidharma, but the *mDzod-phug* is especially prominent. The root text exists in both the original Zhang-zhung language and in the Tibetan translation. There is a commentary in Tibetan attributed to Dranpa Namkha. A litho edition of the text has been published in India: *sNang srid mdzod-phug gi rtsa-ba dang spyi-don*, published as *mDzod-phug: Basic Verses and Commentary by Dran-pa Nam-mkha'*, Lopon Tenzin Namdak, Delhi 1966.

(16) On *Dran-pa nam-mkha'*, also called *bLa-chen* or *gShen* or *dMu-gshen*, see Note 84 in Chapter Five in John Myrdhin Reynolds, *The Oral Tradition from Zhang-zhung*, Vajra Publishing, Kathmandu 2005. See also Per Kvaerne, *The Bon Religion of Tibet*, ibid., p. 119, and S. Karmay, *Treasury*, ibid.

(17) *mTshan-nyid bru la bka' bab tshul*. The Tibetan term *mtshan-nyid* (Skt. lakshana), "essential characteristic," may be loosely translated as "philosophy," the emphasis here being on logic and

epistemology, rather than on metaphysics or ethics. When *Bru g.Yung-drung bla-ma* founded the monastery of *g.Yas-ru dben-sa-kha*, he made philosophy (mtshan-nyid) the principal course of study there. This was because the master Shenchen Luga (gShen-chen klu-dga') had commissioned his father and grandfather to recopy the philosophical texts he had discovered. Also the proximity of Yeru Wensakha to Sakya (sa-skya) monastery stimulated the development of logic and epistemology among the Bonpos, Sakya being at the forefront of the revival of Buddhist scholarship. According to the Lopon, Yeru Wensakha used to regularly send its Geshes (dge-bshes) to Sakya for their post-graduate studies.

(18) *Bru-chen nam-mkha' g.yung-drung* and his son *Khyung gi rgyal-mtshan* together established the philosophical and exegetical tradition of this lineage (mtshan-nyid kyi bshad-srol). However, there also exist other texts that the Bonpos consider to be Abhidharma, but the *Srid-pa'i mdzog-phug* is especially prominent.

(19) The Bonpo term for a fully ordained monk is Drangsong (drang-srong, Skt. rishi), corresponding to the Buddhist term Gelong (dge-slong, Skt. bhikshu). Upon his ordination, he received his monastic name of *rGyal-ba g.yung-drung*, meaning "the indestructible victorious one."

(20) *bLa-ma gdan-sa bzung.*

(21) *bLa-ma'i brgyud-pa'i rnam-thar*, ff. 98–104. *Bru-chen rgyal-ba g.yung-drung gi lo-rgyus la lnga/* (1) *gtsang-ma mi lus thob-pa yab dang yum gyi lo-rgyus ni/* (2) *bka'-drin-can gyi bla-ma dang ji-ltar mjal na/* (3) *sa gnas khyad-par-can gang du rten-pa tshe du bzhugs-pa ni/* (4) *thun-mong dang gnas-skabs kyi yon-tan dang grub rtags ni/* (5) *rtogs-pa mngon 'gyur thun-mong ma yin-pa ni.* Here we present the translation of that hagiography from the text.

(22) Among his most important masters was *gCig-chod dad-pa shes-rab* whom he follows in the lineage of transmission for the Zhang-zhung Nyan-gyud. See the later lineages for the Zhang-zhung Nyan-gyud summerized in Chapters Eight and Nine in Reynolds, *The Oral Tradition from Zhang-zhung*, ibid.

(23) *Yul ni g.yas- ru'i dben-sa-kha/ gdung-rus bru yin/ yab bru-zha bsod-nams rgyal-mtshan la/sras sku mched bzhi yod-pa'i tha-ltag yin.*

(24) *De nas 'dul-ba rin-po-che'i drung du dang-pa drang-srong gi sdom-pa blangs te/ tshul ming rgyal-ba g.yung-drung du mtshan gsol zhing/ bslab-pa tshul-khrims dan dang ldan-par mdzad.* His uncle *mTshan-ldan 'dul-ba*, as known as *mTshan-ldan-pa*, "the philosopher," is traditionally dated 1239–1293.

(25) *Phyi nang gsang gsum gyi bon-sde la dbang lung byin-rlabs dang bcas zhus shing thugs rgyud sbyangs........ rtse gcig yengs-med du thugs-dam mdzad de.*

(26) On *dByil-ston khyung-rgod-rtsal*, b. 1175, see Karmay, *Treasury*, ibid., pp. 173–174.

(27) On *Lung-ston lha-gnyan*, 11 cen., see Karmay, *Treasury*, pp. 113–115.

(28) On *rMa-ston srid-'dzin*, b. 1092, see Karmay, *Treasury*, pp. 167–168.

(29) *dBang lung khrid byin-rlabs bcas.*

(30) *La-stod gyi bLa-ma rtogs-ldan dad-pa shes-rab* had gone on pilgrimage (gnas bskor) to all the monasteries (grwa-sa), places of practice and realization (grub gnas), and great holy places (gnas chen) sacred to the Bonpos in Central Tibet (dbus gtsang) before he came to visit *dBen-sa-kha dgon-pa*. This master is also known as *bLa-ma rtogs-ldan*. The epithet *rtogs-ldan* means a yogin, literally "one who possesses understanding."

(31) From *mTshan-ldan 'dul-ba*, otherwise known as *Bru-sha 'Dul-ba rgyal-mtshan*, he requested the scriptural authorizations (lung) of the *rDzogs-pa chen-po A-khrid dmar byang* and the *Dri-med lhan-skyes dbang ye dbang chen-mo*. On the *A-khrid* system of Dzogchen, see Per Kvearne, "Bonpo Studies: The A-khrid System of Meditation, Part One: "The Transmission of the A-khrid System," in *Kailash* v. I, n. 1, pp. 19–50, Part Two: "The Essential Teachings of the A-khrid System, in Kailash v. I, n. 4, pp. 248–332, Kathmandu 1973. The second text is also known as the *sNyan-rgyud rig-pa gcer-mthong*. It has been republished as the *sNyan-rgyud rig-pa gcer-mthong gi skor* by the Tibetan Bonpo Monastic Centre, Dolanji, HP, India in 1972.

(32) *sNyan-rgyud kyi lung*. A *lung* or scriptural authorization takes the form of the Lama reading the text aloud to the student; this authorizes the student to read the text on one's own.

(33) *gDams-pa 'di'i bka'-babs kyi rgyud-pa ya-ngal-ba yin zer-ba thos nas..... bLa-ma ya-ngal-ba* was *Yang-ston rgyal-mtshan rin-chen*,

the master who transmitted the *Zhang-zhung snyan-rgyud* to *bLa-ma rtogs-ldan gcig-chod dad-pa shes-rab* and therefore preceded him in the lineage. See Chapter Nine above.

(34) *bLa-ma gdan-sa-pa* refers to *Yang-ston rgyal-mtshan rin-chen* whose monastic seat or place of residence (gdan-sa) was Samling (bsam-gling) in Dolpo.

(35) *Mi ma yin la bka'-bsgos*. These non-human spirits (mi ma yin) are presummably the guardian spirits of the Zhang-zhung tradition, *Nyi-pang-sad* and *sMan-mo*. See Appendix Three in Reynolds, *The Oral Tradition from Zhang-zhung*, ibid..

(36) As their dreams were auspicious and indicated that the non-human spirits would not cause disturbances, after requesting his two companions to leave the room, the Togdan conferred upon Lama Gyalwa the Single Transmission (gcig-brgyud), as recounted in section five below.

(37) *Grub-chen gong-ma rnams la mos-gus byas-pa'i thugs-rjes/ yid-ches thag-chod spros mtha' chod-pa 'byung gsungs-pas......* In this context, *yid-ches* is "belief," *thag-chod* is "definitive decision," *mtha'* is "extreme," and *spros-pa* is "conceptual elaboration." Here "belief" is not just an opinion or just something intellectual; it involves one's whole being.

(38) *De yang mi rtog ye-shes kyi bde-ba khong nas shar te/ bzung 'dzin mtshan-ma'i chu rgyun chad-pa dang*.

(39) That is to say, the Trikaya becomes visible as Thodgal visions (mthar thug 'bras-bu sku gsum mngon du gyur-pas).

(40) Thereby the Great Bliss remained in its own original condition of the Dharmakaya and he came to behold the face of his own Yidam Tsochok, whereupon the Generation Process (bskyed-rim) and the Perfection Process (rdzogs-rim), all emanating and reabsorbing, were liberated into their own original condition (bde-chen bon-sku'i rang sa zin-pa dang yi-dam gtso-mchog gi zhal gzigs/ bskyed rdzogs 'phro 'du rang sar grol). Thereafter immeasurable numbers of liberations of experience and understanding were born in his mind (myong rtogs kyi grol-ba dpag med-pa thugs la 'khrungs). Tsochok (gtso-mchog) is the central meditation deity (yi-dam lha) of the *Zhi-khro* cycle of the Bonpo Book of the Dead. Therefore, he is reminiscent of the Nyingmapa meditation deity *Che-mchog* who occupies much the same position. Tsochok is also one of the five principal Yidams of the the Bonpo system of the Father

Tantras (pha rgyud). Emanation and reabsoption ('phro 'du) is an important practice of the Generation Process (bskyed-rim), involving the emanating of rays of light from the seed syllable (sa-bon) that represents the essence of the meditation deity and the reabsorption of these same rays of light now bearing the blessings of the Buddhas into the seed syllable once again. Thereupon the transformation into the deity occurs.

(41) *'Khrungs nyid kyi mdzad-pa'i bka'-brten yang/ phyi nang gsang gsum bsdus nas.*

(42) The scripture (gzhung) referred to here is the *Thun-mtshams bco-lnga-pa.* And the back-up literature (rgyab) refers to the *rGyab skor rin-chen gsal-'debs,* var. *Ngo-sprod rin-po-che'i gsal-'debs rgyab skor gyi gdams-pa,* pp. 117–185 in *A Tri Thun Tsham cho-na dan,* ibid.

(43) *sPyang-'phags,* var. *rkyang-'phags,* otherwise unidentified.

(44) *bLa-ma'i brgyud-pa'i rnam-thar,* f. 103. *Bru-sha btsun* indicates *Bru-chen rgyal-ba g.yung-drung.* His previous incarnation, *sNang-ba mdog-can,* was a great Bonpo sage in early times.

(45) His younger brother was *Bru Nam-mkha' 'od-zer* and his nephew was *Bru-ston bSod-nams rgyal-mtshan.* The biography of this last master has also been translated by Kvaerne. See Per Kvearne, "Bonpo Studies: The A-khrid System of Meditation," Part One, ibid., pp. 41–46. As Kvaerne points out, there are some differences between the hagiographical text found in the collection that we have here and the one included in the *A-khrid* collection.

(46) This importanad *A-khrid* text has been translated in part by Per Kvaerne. See the translation of the *Thun-mtshams bco-lnga-pa man-ngag khrid kyi rim-pa lag-len thun-mtshams dang bcas-pa* in Per Kvaerne and Thubten Rikey, *The Stages of A-khrid Meditation: Dzogchen Practice of the Bon Tradition,* Library of Tibetan Works and Archives, Dharamsala 1996. Also see Per Kvearne, "Bonpo Studies: The A-khrid System of Meditation," Parts One and Two, ibid.

(47) For the translations of the hagiographies (rnam-thar) of the masters in the lineage of transmission (brgyud-pa'i bla-ma rnams), see Reynolds, *The Oral Tradition from Zhang-zhung,* ibid.

(48) The translation of the preliminary practice text (sngon-'gro), made in accordance with the oral commentaries by Lopon Tenzin

Namdak, is found in Appendix Two in Reynolds, *The Oral Tradition from Zhang-zhung*, ibid.

(49) According to the text of the principal practice (dngos-gzhi) composed by Druchen, "Second (that is, following after the first part consisting of the preliminary practices), in between (while one is on the spiritual path before attaining the goal), in terms of the stages of the principal practice that brings about the ripening and liberation of one's mind-stream, there are three parts:

1. At the beginning, without any grasping at thoughts, one fixates the mind (thog-mar sems ma zin-pa zin-par byed-pa),

2. In the middle, when mindfulness does not yet abide steadily, one employs (various methods) to bring about its abiding steadily (bar du dran-pa mi gnas-pa gnas-par byed-pa), and

3. And finally, when Self-Awareness is not yet clear, one employs (various methods) to make it clear (tha-mar rang-rig mi gsal-ba gsal-ba bya-ba)."

The first part outlines the practice of Trekchod by way of an explanation of how to fixate the mind (sems 'dzin gyi khrid), the second part explains the various methods of practice of the dark retreat, and the third part elucidates the various methods of the practice of Thodgal, that is, the practice of vision with sunlight. This text is translated below.

(50) Translations of the four supplementary texts dealing with the view, the meditation, the conduct, and the fruit (lta sgom spyod 'bras bzhi), respectively, will be found below.

(51) For a translation of this text, together with a commentary based on Lopon Tenzin Namdak's oral instructions for making a dark retreat, see Part Two below. It was originally privately published as Reynolds, *The Seven-fold Cycle of the Clear Light*, Bonpo Translation Project (privately printed), San Diego and Amsterdam 2001.

(52) See also Reynolds, *The Guru Yoga of Tapihritsa and the Preliminary Practices of the Zhang-zhung Nyan-gyud*, Bonpo Translation Project, Vidyadhara Publications, 1999. Also Reynolds, *The Oral Tradition from Zhang-zhung*, ibid., pp. 217–251.

2. Notes to the Outlines of the Contents

(1) *sNyan-rgyud rgyal-ba'i phyag-khrid* in the *sNyan-rgyud nam-mkha' 'phrul mdzod drang nges skor dang zhang-zhung snyan-rgyud skor*, Tibetan Bonpo Monastic Centre, Dolanji, HP India, 1972, ff. 539–726.

(2) *Zhang-zhung snyan-rgyud kyi lo-rgyus rnam-thar dang bcas-pa* (ff. 539–589).

(3) *sNgon-'gro rim-pa rnams*, "the stages of the preliminary practices," in the litho edition, whereas the text is entitled in the xylograph edition *Bon spyod dgu rim*, "the nine stages for the conduct of Bon," (ff. 591–607).

(4) *Tshig-bshad*, "the exposition of the words,"

(5) See Reynolds, *The Oral Traditon from Zhang-zhung*, ibid., pp. 260-279, 325–343.

(6) See the translation of *The Seven-fold Cycle of the Clear Light* below in Part Two.

(7) Oral communication LTN.

(8) See Reynolds, *Selections from the Bonpo Book of the Dead*, Bonpo Translation Project (privately printed), Copenhagen 1997.

(9) On dream yoga, see W. Evens-Wetz, *Tibetan Yoga and Secret Doctrines*, Oxford University Press, London 1935, and on a Bonpo system of dream yoga, see Tenzin Wangyal Rinpoche, *The Tibetan Yogas of Dream and Sleep*, Snow Lion, Ithaca NY 1998.

(10) This unfolding of the evolution of the visions of Samsara and of Nirvana are given in more detain in a number of texts in the collection, such as the *'Khor-lo bzhi sbrugs* and the *'Od-gsal sems kyi me-long*.

(11) On the dying process and the Bardo experience according to the Zhang-zhung tradition, see Reynolds, *Selections from the Bonpo Book of the Dead*, ibid. It is planned to reprint an expanded version of this work in the future under the title *Path of the Clear Light*, forthcoming. On Tibetan funeral customes in general, see Bryan J. Cuevas, *The Hidden History of the Tibetan Book of the Dead*, Oxford University Press, Oxford 2003, and on a Bonpo funeral rites in particular, see Per Kvaerne, *Bon Religion: A Death Ritual of the Tibetan Bonpos*, Brill, Leiden 1985.

(12) For discussion of the historical evelution of the Buddhist concept of the Bardo, see Cuevas, *The Hidden History of the Tibetan Book of the Dead*, ibid.

3. Notes to the Translation of the Principal Practices Text

(1) *Kun tu bzang-po khyab bdal 'gro 'dren/ rang-rig mngon du gyur la phyag 'tshal-lo.*

(2) *gNyis-pa bar du rgyud smin zhing grol-bar byed-pa dngos-gzhi'i rim-pa la gsum ste/ thog-mar sems ma zin-pa zin-par byed-pa/ bar du dran-pa mi gnas-pa gnas-par byed-pa/ tha-ma rang-rig mi gsal-ba gsal-bar bya-ba.*

(3) *Dang-po la sgron-ma las/ dran-pa'i sems ni 'od la bzhung.*

(4) *mThing-shog las/ 'od khyim 'khor-ba'i dmar-khrid.*

(5) *De la gsum ste/ lus kyi gnad dang/ lta-stangs kyi gnad dang/ bslab-bya'i gnad-do.*

(6) *Dang-po la/ lus kyi phyag-rgya lnga yis srog kyang bcing/ zhes-pa/ smad kyi rtsa rlung sdom phyir skyil-khrung bca'/ rus tshigs khrol bu sdom phyir tshigs-pa bsrang/ 'du-byed gnad du gcun phyir mnyam-bzhag bya/ smra brjod rtsol-ba gzhoms phyir mgrin-pa dgug/ gzung 'dzin gcud la bor phyir lta-stangs gzir.*

(7) *De yang g.yo na steng du 'don/ g.yas ni 'og tu mnan/ srin lag yid tsam bkug-pa ni khyad-par gyi gnad/ de'i dus su lus kyi nywa bzhi rtsa bzhi las sogs/ lus cha cha nas khrims kyis bsgrims la gcun-no/ lus ky nywa bzhi rtsa bzhi las sogs lus cha cha nas khrims kyis bsgrims la gcun-no.*

(8) *gNyis-pa la/ mdun phyogs mi nye mi ring-pa'i sar/ 'od 'khor ran-par bskor de/ rig-pa mig dang bstun la/ gyen thur g.yas g.yon du lta-ba ma yin-pa/ mdun tshugs dril la/ phur tshugs su 'bug-pa'i tshul lam/ khab mig tu khud-pa 'dzud-pa'am/ 'ben la mda' 'phen-pa ltar/ lus kyis rnam-'gyur/ ngag gis brjod rtsol/ sems kyis snga bsam phyi mno/ gang yang med-par hrig-ge-ba la/ rang-lugs rtse gcig tu tu-re bring-nge wal-le khyug-ge gzir-ro.*

(9) *De'i dus su kha chu sna chu ci byung yang rang babs su gtong/ lus sems gcun zhing gnad la bor-bar bya.*

(10) *Thun tshad ni snga thun la sa-le 'od nyis brgya la/ de nas phyi thun la sum-brgya las sogs bun thang du spar-ba'o.*

(11) *Yang snga dgos dus su sangs-rgyas sems-can bzang ngan/ yod med lta-mkhan/ kho la rgyu rkyen ngo-bo/ gzugs dbyibs kha-dog*

mtshan-nyid ngo-bzung ci 'dra-ba zhig 'dug/ yang yang lta ru bcug la dri.

(12) *Yang dang-po byung sa/ bar du gnas sa/ tha-ma 'gro sa tshol du bzhug.*

(13) *Yang phyi 'byung-ba/ nang rgyu lus/ mthe-ba spyi-bo nas dma'-ba rkang mthil yan-chad tshol du bzhug/skyon yon gyi zhu thug bya/ legs-par shes-pas rtsad bcad.*

(14) *De-ltar nyams su blangs-pas/ ci zhig la 'gyu byed kyi dran-pa rnal du phebs nas/ 'dzin-med chen-po rab ru-sbal 'khar gzheng du bcug-pa lta-bu gang la yang nyam mi nga pa dang/ 'bring lcags sbubs nas chu 'dren-pa lta-bu/ tha-ma bung-bas rtsi la 'jibs-pa lta-bu/ rnam-'gyur cung-zad ngang chas-par 'byung ste/ rnal du phebs shing zin rtags tshang-ba dang/ mtshan-med la pheb la bsgom du bzhug-go.*

(15) *Rig-pa mdun tshugs su mkha' la gtad-do/ de la yang zin rtags ma tshang na/ rig-pa tshugs su mkha' la gtad de/ HUM HRI las sogs ma ning sgra gang yang rung-ba la khrid-do.*

(16) *De nas kyang dka' nang la dub kyi las rtsol-pas/ dub-pa dang ngal-sos dang bstun te khrid.*

(17) *dMigs rten kyang me-long lha sku'i mdzod-spu las sogs su gtad-do/ lar me rlung shas che-ba la zin rtags snga-bar 'ong ste/ rjes nas gags su 'gro/ chu rlung shas che-ba la zin rtags 'phyi ste/ rjes nas grogs su 'ong/ sngar khrid ma phog na brda thabs rten 'brel la khrid-par sla/ dred-pa'i rigs la bya shor-bas gdab-pa dka'.*

(18) *bCud ldan gyi dpon-gsas yod ngang la yang mi thebs mi srid/ rang rig-pa'i rgyal-po btsan du zin-pas/ sems 'byung dran-pa'i dmag mi cham la phebs/ rtog tshogs 'khrul-pa'i khyi rgod rdong la thogs-pa yin te.*

(19) *sPyi rgyud las/ rgyal-po btson du bzung/ dmag mi cham la phab/ nyon-mongs-pa'i khyi rgod gtun la btags.*

(20) *Lung drug las/ mtshan dmag (mdag?) la sems gtad na/ je zhi je rnam-rtog zhi/ je gsal je gsal ye-shes skye.*

(21) *mTshan-ma sems-'dzin gyi khrid.*

(22) *gNyis-pa dran-pa mi gnas-pa gnas-par bya-ba la/ sgom-pa'i gnas rang-bzhin gyi mun bung-nga ldan-pa/ sa phug brag phug spyil-po khang-pa gang yin yang/ yang thog mtho zhing nang yangs-pa la/ zhal la legs-par byas la/ gsal khang phyi rub la nang yangs-pa sgo 'khyuog rim-pa gsum yod-pas bcad-pa'i nang du/ sang-ba'i gsal kung cung tsam yang med-par 'dugs bde-bar bcas te/ snang-ba'i gsal khung cung tsam yang med-par 'dugs bde-bar bcas te.*

(23) *Nyams su blang tshul la gsum ste/ ji ltar sgom-pa dang de'i bslab bya dang rgyud la 'char tshul-lo.*

(24) *Dang-po gzer-bu las/ bsdam-pa gsum gyis g.yeng-ba'i las spang/ glod-pa gsum gyis blo rnal du dbab ces-pa la gsum ste/ lus kyi bya-ba bsdam nas byar med du glod-pa/ ngag gi smra-ba bsdam nas brjod med du glod-pa/ sems kyi dran-pa bsam bsdam nas bsam 'das su glod-pas/ mi rtog-pa'i ting-'dzin skye-ba'o.*

(25) *De ni dmus shes-par byas te/ lus kyi bya-byed mi dge-ba gsum mam/ lung ma bstan son ma tshong khrom/ rgyug 'dur bza' bzo bya byed...... ngal-sos su gzhug/ de ltar ma byas na bya byed sna-tshogs kyis rtsa 'khrug des rlung 'khrug des sems 'khrug nas mi rtog-pa'i ting-nge-'dzin skye-ba'i gnas med-pa'i phyir/ de ltar glod-pas rtsa 'dul/ rlung 'jags/ shes-pa rang sa zin nas mi rtog-pa gnad du phebs-pas......*

(26) *De nas khyad-par gyi lus gnad la/ phyag-rgya lnga yis lus kyi srog kyang bcings/ zhes-pas zhabs skyil-krung/ phyag mnyam-bzhag sgal-tshigs drang-po/ mgrin-pa cung tsam dgug/ spyan thad-kar blta'o.*

(27) *De-ring nas ngag gi mi dge-ba bzhi las sogs-pa ma dag-pa dang/ lung ma bstan/ long gtam ku re bzhad-pa gad khad/ gleng long rnams dang/ dge-ba yin yang bzlas brjod/ klog 'don/ dbyangs gyer-ba thams-cad kyang spang la/ brjod med lkugs-pa'i tshul du glod la ngal-sos su gzhug.*

(28) *De-ltar bcug-pas/ brjod tshigs bskyed-pa'i rlung mi g.yo rtsa mi 'gul/ sems ni 'khrug-par mi rtog-pa'i ting-nge-'dzin skye-ba'i dgos-pa yod-do.*

(29) *Des na de-ring nas sems kyi ngan rtog mi dge-ba gsum dug lnga sogs dang/ lung ma bstan sngar byas zin dang/ dbye rgyu/ rang-bzhin gyi bsam mno rtog dpyod thams-cad/ bzang rtog yin yang lha sgom yig 'bru spro bsdu mtshan-ma'i ting-nge-'dzin las sogs thams-cad bshol la/ res shig 'dod 'dod re re dogs dungs dungs-pa gang yang med-par kun-gzhi'i klong du dran rig bsam 'das su glod la ngal sos su gzhug.*

(30) *De-ltar ma byas na rtsa'i lam la rlung gi rta zhon yid kyi mi 'gyus nas/ mi rtog-pa'i ting-nge-'dzin skye-ba gegs byed-pa'i phyir-ro/ des na rang sa rang thog tu bcas bcos dang nga sgre log med-par/ thol'byung rbad tshod gzhi med rtsa bral du khrol-le bzhag-go.*

(31) 'Das-pa'i rjes mi bcad/ ma 'ongs-pa'i sdun mi bsu/ kun-gzhi khyab-bdal chen-po'i klong du/ rig-pa rtsa bral so-ma rang sa rang thog tu bza' bzo bsgul bskyod med-par/ yin-lugs bzhin 'jog-pa'o.

(32) Bying rgod rmug-po gsum.

(33) Las dang-po'i dus su thun ches na/ bying rgod ldeng-po las sogs su 'gro/ chung na nyams rtogs mi skye-bas/ sa-le 'od 'phreng skor re nas/ zhag re la bun thang 'gyur bsring/ thun bar du snying-rje mos-gus gnad du bsnun/ sgsog gtsong sngo rngad las sogs 'byung-ba mi snyom-pa'i zas dang/ grib zas dang zas mi za/ zas gos kyi cha bsnyam/ me dang nyi-ma la mi bsdad/ phyi nang gi 'gul bcad/ ye-shes 'grib-pas gang gnyis kyi dus su ngal chun tsam gso/ bcud-ldan thabs la mkhas-pa'i dpon-gsas dang ma bral-ba bya/ le-lo dang btang-snyoms byung na bdag la mngan 'tshang bgrang/ brtson-'grus drag-pos yang dang yang du bskul 'phel-ba la dag 'brod/ 'grib-pa la zhum-pa mi bya'o.

(34) Dang-po blo byas kyi zhi-gnas skye/ bar du rang-bzhin gyi zhi-gnas 'char/ tha-mar mthat-thug gi zhi-gnas la brtan-pa thob-pa 'byung ste.

(35) sNyigs-ma klong du thim nas dwangs-ma 'od du gsal/ blo yi g.yang-lugs bud nas rig-pa gcer-bur 'char/ rtog-pa'i sprin tshogs sangs nas ye-shes sgrib g.yogs med.

(36) sNyigs-ma 'gyu byed rtog tshogs blo yi dran rig kun-gzhi la thim nas/ dwangs-ma rang-'byung ye-shes 'od du shar-ba ma rnyogs-pa'i chu dwangs-ma 'dra/ gzung 'dzin g.yang-lugs gos dang 'dra-ba bral nas/ rig-pa'i ye-shes rjen-par shar-ba bskyes-bu'i gos dang bral-ba 'dra/ bzang ngan dran rtog sprin dang 'dra-ba sangs nas/ kun-gzhi'i rang mdog rnyed-pas nam-mkha' dwangs-ma 'dra-ba rgyud la 'char.

(37) gZhan yang mun-khang skya 'od byed-pa'am/ de'i phyi nang thams-cad ma sgrib-par sa-le gsal-ba dang/ 'og gi 'byung lnga'i rtags rnams kyang cung-zad 'char la/ shes-pa la mi rtog-pa btang gis mi thong-ba'i ting-nge-'dzin rgyud la skye'o.

(38) mTshan-med zhi-gnas kyi khrid.

(39) gSum-pa mi gsal-ba gsal-bar byed-pa'i gdams-pa la gsum ste/ spyir nyams su blang-ba/ bye-brag tu nyams su blang-ba/ gnad kyi gdams-pas bogs 'don-pa'o.

(40) Dang-po la rgya-mtsho chen-po gyen du bskyod/ lcags ri mun-pa'i mtha' la gtad/ dran-pa'i sems ni 'od la bzung/ 'gyu-ba yid ni sgra la btul/ rig-pa'i rtsal ni zer la sbyang.

(41) *De la gsum ste/ gnad lnga'i sgo nas gcun-pa dang/ thabs lam gyi rkyen gyis btsa'-ba dang/ rgyud la bsten-pa'i 'char tshul-lo.*

(42) *sGom-pa'i gnas shin tu gnad che ste.*

(43) *De'i dus su snga bsam phyi mno dang/ glo-bur gyi dran-pa thams-cad thol-byung rtsad chod du btang la/ shes-pa la shar la ngar bskyed de/ gzhi med rtsa bral du hrig-ge-ba la bzhag-go.*

(44) *Srog gi rlung rig dril te.*

(45) *rGyu-mtshan g.yon phyogs la ye-shes kyi rtsa sgo yod cing/ nyon-mongs-pa'i rnam-rtog rgyun-chad-pa'o.*

(46) *gSum-pa la/ de ltar nyams su blangs-pas rig-pa'i dangs snyigs phyed/ rlung sems gnad du zin/ rtsa'i sgo phyed-pas rgyu rkyen tshang-ba'i me/ rlung gis spur-ba ltar rig-pa 'od gsal du gnas-pa'i rang mdangs/ phyi ru mi 'char-ba'i thabs med-do.*

(47) *gNas drug las/ gzhi tsi-ta'i dbus na gnas/ lam rtsa la phyung/ sgo chu'i sgron-ma la shar te/ dung-khang klad-pa'i dkyil dbus na/ dbu-ma la/ tsang-ri pur-lang gi rtsa zhes bya-ba/ rtsa-ba gcig la rtse-mo gnyis su gyes nas/ rtsa sgo zar-ma'i me-tog kha bye-ba lta-bu la rig-pa'i sgo dong de/ tsa de'i sbubs nas 'od lnga rma-bya'i mdongs lta-bu shar.*

(48) *sGron-ma las/ mun-pa zer-ldan smrag rum du gnang gsal 'od kyi gzhal-yas mthong.*

(49) *Lhag-mthong 'od-gsal gyi khrid-do.*

(50) *gNyis-pa bye-brag tu nyams su blang-ba la gnyis te/ snang gsal nam-mkha'i ting-nge 'dzin la sbyang-ba dang/ rang gsal sgron-ma'i ting-nge 'dzin la sbyang-ba'o.*

(51) *Dang-po la bzhi ste/ gnas gang du nyams su blang-ba dang/ dus nam gyi tshe nyams su blang-ba dang/ tshul ji-ltar nyams su blang-ba dang/ nyams snang 'od-gsal gyi 'cher tshul-lo.*

(52) *gNyis-pa dus ni gong gi mun-pa'i rnal-'byor gyi rtags rnams shar/ ting-nge 'dzin la brtan-pa cung-zad thob-pa......*

(53) *sNgo dro klu dbang phyogs su lta/ dgong kha dri-za'i phyogs su lta.*

(54) *gSum-pa sgom tshul la/ 'di nyid kyi sgrom-ma las/ kun gsal sems kyi me-long de/ snang gsal nam-mkha' mthongs su bstan.*

(55) *gNad lnga'i sgo nas nyams su blang-ba/ bca'-ba lus kyi gnad gong bzhin la.*

(56) *Lha khris las/ seng-ge 'gying-ba'am/ gsang-ba 'dus-pa lta-stangs kyis lta.* Sangwa Dupa (Skt. Guhyasamaja) was one of the principal

disciples of Tonpa Shenrab, being the source for both the Tantras and Dzogchen in the Bon tradition.

(57) *Nam-mkha' gsum sbyor gyi lag-len byas te/ bar-snang stong-pa/ phyi srid-pa'i nam-mkha' yin-pas de la gtad/ rtsa'i sbubs stong-pa/ nang dbang-po'i nam-mkha' yin-pas de la gcun/ dems-nyid stong-pa/ yang gsang don rtags kyi nam-mkha' yin-pas de la ngar bskyed.*

(58) *mThing-shog las/ bzung 'dzin gcud la bor la/ rlung rig gnad du bzung.*

(59) *Mi 'jug-pa gsum gyi lag-len bya/ srog rlung yang du mi 'jug ste/ rig-pa'i rta yin-pas/ rlung rig dril te bzung/ rtsol-bas dgag tu mi 'jug ste/ rtsol-bas dgag tu mi 'jug ste/ dbugs kyi cha bsnyam ste/ dal gyis phyi nang du/ rgyur gzhug gsang rlung rengs su mi gzhug ste/ khyad-par du rlung gi rlung rgyu dus su rab tu yang gcun-par bya ste.*

(60) *De nas mi 'bral dam-tshig gi gnad la/ gzer-bu'i rtsa 'grel las/ mig ma btsun-par/ yul la char-re bzhag-pas/ kun-gzhi rtog-med ngos zin.*

(61) *Mi 'gul-ba gsum gyi lag-len bya ste/ lus ma 'gul na rtsa mi 'gul-bas/ bya byed g.yo 'gul mi bya/ rtsa ma 'gul na mig mi 'gul-bas/ bca' bcu phrag phrig mi bya/ mig ma 'gul nas sems mi 'gul-bas/ zam-zim slab-sleb khral-khrel mi bya/ lar rig-pa'i gnad mig la 'char-bar shes-par bya'o.*

(62) *gZer-bu las/ bzhag thabs gsum gyis sems kyis bzung zhes-pas/ bzhag thabs kyi lag-len bya ste/ bzo mi bya-bar so-mar bzhag ces-pas/ ched 'dzin kyi dran blo dang bral-ba'o/ rang lugs chen-po gnyug-mar bzhag ces-pas/ kun-gzhi yin-lugs kyi glod thog tu 'jog-pa'o/ bcos bslad med-par rnal-mar bzhag ces-pas/ bcas bcos dang bsgre log mi byed-pa'o.*

(63) *sKya long long-ba/ breng-nge-ba.*

(64) *Ye-shes lnga'i rang mdangs las.*

(65) *Shel mdog rig-pa'i thig-le/ dngul-chu 'thor-ba lta-bu dang/ 'od lnga gur-khang gi thig-le/ 'od kyi mu-khyud lnga lnga yis bskor-ba dang/ zer gyi thugs-rje'i nyag-thag dngul dkar nyag-thag brkyang-ba'am lcags kyi lu-gu-rgyud dang gdugs kyiu rtsibbs ma gshigs-pa'am skra shad bar-snang la gtor-ba lta-bu....*

(66) *Thabs lam gnad kyi gdams-pas/ ye-shes bde rlung dbu-mar cun-zad 'dus/ rlung sems kyi sbyor-bas rtsa yi sgo cung tsam phyed/ nyams len gyi stobs kyis rig-pa'i dwangs snyig phyed nas/ phyi ru lhag-*

*mthong 'od-gsal kyi snang-ba 'char-ba'i mgo tshugs shing/ nang du
ka-dag gi rig-pa gcer-bur bud nas nyams rtogs ji gsal du 'byung-ba'i
dus yin te/ phyi nang yon-tan 'jug-pa dus gcig tu rgyud la sky-bas/
de'i dus su brtson-'grus bskyed-pa gal shin tu che'o.*

(67) *'Od-gsal nam-mkha'i ting-ng 'dzin gyi khrid.*

(68) *Rang gsal sgron-ma'i ting-nge 'dzin nyams su blang-ba la bzhi ste/
gnas gang du nyams su blang-ba dan/ dus nam gyi tshe nyans su
blang-ba dang/ tshul ji-ltar nyams su blang-ba dang/ de ltar nyams
su blangs-pas yon-tan 'char tshul-lo.*

(69) *Gang gyi spyi dang bye-brag gi nyams la brtan-pa cung tsam thob/
drod rtags rgyud la shar-ba dang/ gnas rang-bzhin gyis dben-pa
mtho-ba khang-pa'i phyed phubs sam/ mthongs chen-po nyi zer
'char-ba'am/ brag shing gad-pa'am/ sgrib yod-pa sogs kyi/ nyi grib
mtshams su nyams su blang-ngo.*

(70) *gSum-pa tshul ni/ 'di nyid kyisgron-ma las/ dran-pa sems kyi
mdung-ma de/ snang-ba 'od kyi phub la gtad.*

(71) *bLa-chen gyi gsungs las/ las dang skal-ldan skyes-bu yis/ nyi-ma'i
zer la 'khrul-pa bcad.*

(72) *Dang-po lus gnad la 'od-gsal glo-bur bskyed-pa'i/ lus gnad lnga
bca' ste/ seng-ge 'gying stabs dang/ glang-po-che'i brkyang thabs
dang/ dge-sbyor gi tsog-pu dang/ ngang-mo'i zur 'gros dang shel gyi
rwa-pho brag la 'dzeg-pa'i tshul-lo.*

(73) *'Og rlung cung-zad bsdam/ lag-pa dgye de bya te.*

(74) *Yid g.yo byed rlung non nas/ dbus-ma byang-chub kyi rtsa kha
phyed ste/ phyi ru snang-ba 'phral du 'char zhing/ nang du bon-sku
blo 'das kyi dgongs-pa 'char-ro.*

(75) *Lag- gnyis kyis 'gal bteg la pus brang sprad.*

(76) *Phyi ru zhing-khams rdzogs-par 'char zhing/ nang du nyams rtogs
la bogs skye'o.*

(77) *Phyi ru sprul-sku'i snang-ba 'char/ nang du gsal snang khyad-par-
can la skye'o.*

(78) *Yon-tan rlung dbus-mar tshud nas/ rdzu-'phrul ya am zung 'byung
mthong snang 'phral du 'char-ro.*

(79) *Pus brang sprad tsog-pur 'dug.*

(80) *Yon-tan ni dga'-ba'i bzung 'dzin 'gags nas/ g.yon ye-shes kyi rtsa
sgo bye ste/ phyi ru rtog tshogs ye-shes su 'char zhing/ nang du rang
rang gsal 'dzin-med kyi dgongs-pa 'char-ro.*

(81) *Seng-ge'i lus gnad dus su/ steng bon-sku lta-stangs/ smin-mtshams
su yar la/ hrig-ger gzer-ba'o.*

(82) *Thad du g.yo 'gul med-par char-re gtad-pa'o.*

(83) *gSum-pa la gcun-pa sems kyi gnad la/ lta-stangs de-dag gar byed kyang/ sgron-ma gsum sbyor gyi lag-len bya ste/ phyi srid-pa'i sgron-ma brtod la mnan/ nyi zla la sogs-pa gtad-pa'o/ nang dbang-po'i sgrom-ma ar la gtad de/ rig-pa mig dang btsun-pa'o/ gsang-ba rig-pa'i sgron-ma gnad la bor te/ bag yangs la mi 'jog-par ngar bskud-pa'o.*

(84) *gCes-pa rnam-pa gsum shes-par bya ste....... thams-cad kho la thug-pas le-lo mi bya-bar/ don du kho-rang la hril gyis gal-che'o.*

(85) *gSum-pa 'char tshul la/ nang na rig-pa 'od lnga'i bdag-nyid du 'dug-pas gnas-pa rtsa yi sbubs phyed de/ phyi nyi-ma'i dkyil-'khor gyi len-kha dang 'phrod-pas/ 'od dang zer dang thig-le'i snang-ba du-ma zhig mngon du 'char te/ de-dag la rtog dpyod kyis rtsol-ba mi 'jug-par/ gong ltar rang-'byung rang-shar rang-grol chen-par nyams su blangs te.*

(86) *Yon-tan ni lha khrid las/ khyab bdal nam-mkha'i lta-bu'i ting-nge 'dzin rgyud la skye.*

(87) *'Bum las 'od sal-sal breng-breng rab tu myur-ba'i ting-nge 'dzin zhes- bya-bas/ bzung nas thar-pa chen-po 'thob-par 'gyur.*

(88) *gZhan yang nyi khrid 'di nyid gong gi nyin snang/ mtshan snang gnyis-po'i bogs 'don thabs yin-pas/ gong gi dus su gang yin rnams skabs skabs su dar tsam nyams su len-pa las/ rgyun du bsten na khams dang dbang-po la gzan-pas/ de'i blang dor shes-par bya zhing/ lar nyams-len gsum-po 'di gcig gi steng du gcig bsnan-pa'i tshul gyis thams-cad zung 'brel du nyams su blang-ngo.*

(89) *Khams dang dbang-pos ma bzod na/ mthing-shog ltar rgya ras dwangs-pa'i dmar-khrid byas te/ ras sngon gyi yol-ba'i nang nas gong gi lag thabs byas la blta'o.*

(90) *Rang gsal sgron-ma'i nyi khrid-do.*

(91) *gSum-pa khyad-par gnad kyi gdams-pas bogs 'don-pa la gsum te/ thabs lam gnad gyis bogs 'don-pa dang/ rlung sems kyi sbyong-bas bogs 'don-pa dang/ mtshan snang gi gdams-pas bogs 'don-pa.*

(92) *sNang la 'od dang zer dang thig-le shar-ba dang kha-dog dkar shas-che shib/ dbyibs zla-gam mang-bar shar na nam-mkha'i rlung zin-pas/ steng bon-sku'i lha-stangs la gtsor bya'o.*

(93) *dByibs nar-mo dang kha-dog dmar shas-che-bar shar na me rlung zin-pas/ 'og sprul-sku'i lta-stangs la gtso-bor bya'o.*

(94) *Gru bzhi dang ser shas-che-bar shar na sqa rlung zin-pas/ thabs kyi lta-stangs la gtso-bar bya'o.*

(95) *Zlum-po dang ljang shas-che-ba ni/ rlung gi rlung zin-pas/ shes-rab kyi lta-stangs la gtso-bor bya'o.*

(96) *Gru gsum mthing shas-che-ba ni/chu rlung zin-pas/ dbus rdzogs-sku'i lta-stangs la gtso-bor bya'o.*

(97) *'Od zer thig-le thams-cad cha-mnyam zhing kha-dog kyang lnga-po tshang-ba dang/ dbyibs kyang lnga-po tshang gar byung na/ 'byung-ba lnga yi rlung lnga-po thams-cad gnad du 'chun-po yin-pas.*

(98) *Phyi'i 'char tshul dang bstan-pa'i thabs-lam gnad kyi lta-stangs 'di rnams ni/ nyin snang mtshan snang gi nyams-len thams-cad l spyir 'grims-pa yin-pas shes-par bya'o.*

(99) *gNyis-pa sems kyi sbyor-ba la gsum ste/ rtsa rlung thig-le'ignas tshul dang/ de la sbyang dgos-pa'i rgyu-mtshan dang/ ji ltar sbyong-ba'i tshul-lo.*

(100) *She-thun dbus-ma'i rtsa sbubs yar gyen 'dren gyi rlung gis phye ste/ tshangs-sgo kha la zhugs-pa ni myang 'das kyi lam/ mar la thur-sel gyis phye ste/ gsang-bar zug-pa ni 'khor-ba'i lam.*

(101) *g.Yas dkar tshigs-pa* (=the spine) *kha chen nas/ yar dbus-ma'i g.yas la 'grims.*

(102) *Lus sems kyi rten byed kyang bsdus na gsum du 'dus-so.*

(103) *Rig-pa'i rang rlung gi gnad.*

(104) *Thig-le mang yang dwangs-ma rig-pa'i thig-le/ snyigs-ma lus zungs kyi thig-le gnyis su 'dus la/ de yang snyigs-ma'i thig-le la brten nas/ dwangs-ma'i thig-le gnad du 'jug-pa yin-no.*

(105) *Kun-gzhi dang rig-pa gdod nas gnas-pa'i snying-po de gnas-pa tsi-ta'i dkyil na gnas/ lam rtsa la rang 'byung du shar-ba yin-pas......*

(106) *Kun-gzhi nam-mkha' bzhin du spyi blugs su khyab kyang/ 'khrul-pa'i sprin tshogs kyis bsgribs-pas gsal-ka med/ dbus-ma'i lam la sprin med nam-mkha' bzhin/ ye-shes zang-thal chen-por gnas-pa yin.*

(107) *gSum-pa sbyong-tshul la gsum ste/ 'jam rlung la sbyang-ba dang/ rtsub rlung la gcun-pa dang/ rang rlung la brtan-par bya'o.*

(108) *Dang-po la gsum ste/lus gnad dang/ yid gnad dang/ rlung gnad-do.*

(109) *bLa-chen dran-pa nam-mkha'.*

(110) *gNas ni mun-khang la rig-pa brtan zhing bogs che/ khams mi gzan.*

(111) *Tshul la gzer-bu las/ lus kyi gnad bsdam zhes-pa/ phyag-rgya lnga ni gong ltar bca' ste/ khrims kyis bsgrim zhing gcud la bor te/ gnad du 'gro-bar byed-pa'o.*

(112) *mThing-shog las/ rnam-rtog gi gnyen-po rlung lhyi nang du rgyu-ba rjes su dran-pa'i yig 'bru gsum gyi dmar-khrid byas te.*

(113) *De yang g.yon na OM g.yas na A dbus su HUM gi spro bsdu dbugs dang bstun la bya zhing/ de yang gnas-pa HUM/ 'jug-pa OM/ gtong-ba A ru bsam....*

(114) *gNyis-pa la gnyis te/ ci ltar bsgom-pa dang/ nyams-myong 'char tshul-lo.*

(115) *Dang-po la rtsa dang lus gnas gong ltar la/ rtsa gsum gyi sum mdor YAM ljang-khu/ de'i sor bzhi'i steng du RAM dmar nag/ snying-kha'i thad du rang-rig A'i rang-bzhin/ 'od lnga'i rgyas dril-ba bye'u co-ga'i sgo-nga tsam gsal la 'tsher-ba bkrag dang chas-par bsgom.*

(116) *rLung sems kyi thig-les gang-bar bsgom.*

(117) *De ltar rlung sbyor skor re la/ 'od-gsal dmigs bskor re bsgom/ de ltar bsgoms-pas/ phyi ru mtho snang gi 'char tshul gong bzhin la........*

(118) *rLung sems bogs 'don gyi khrid-do.*

(119) *gSum-pa mtshan snang gi gdams la gsum ste/ 'od-gsal gnyid dang bsre-ba dang/ de yi skyon yon 'char tshul dang/ gnad zung A la gtad-pa'o.* On dream yoga in general, see W.Y. Evens-Wentz, W. Y., *Tibetan Yoga and Secret Doctrines*, Oxford University Press, London 1935. And on dream and sleep yogas in the Bon tradition, also see Tenzin Wangyal Rinpoche, *The Tibetan Yogas of Dream and Sleep*, Snow Lion,, Ithaca NY 1998.

(120) *rMi-lam gyi bar-do la bag-chags kyi mtshams sbyar-ba chu-bo'i gzhung lta-bu'i gdams-pa.*

(121) *Seng-ge'i nyal stabs byas la/ gzhogs g.yas-pa 'og tu bcug/ mtheb mdzub gung srin rnams kyis bu-ga bkag-pas g.yas nyon-mongs kyi rtsa sgo rlung sgo khegs-pa'o.*

(122) *Nang rlung ngal-ba gsum gyis dug dbyung la/ rig-pa dbus-ma'i nang/ ag-sho 'khor-lo yi lte-bar 'od kyi dru-gu rma-bya'i sgong tsam lta-bur gsal-ba la/ snga bsam phyi mno'i rtog tshogs ma 'phros-par byas te/ mig zim bya.*

(123) *Rab la rmi-lam gyi 'khrul snang thams-cad 'od gsal du 'char te.*

(124) *sPyir rmi-lam mi zin-pa'i rgyu.*

(125) *mThar rmi-lam klong du gyur te/ shes-pa rang-dbang thob-pa dang/ 'gyu 'byed kyi dran-pa gar khrid du 'gro ste.*

(126) *rMi-lam gyi rig-pa.*

(127) *dMigs-pa bzung la......*

(128) *'Od-gsal gnyid dang bsre-ba'i khrid-do.*

(129) *De ltar snyan-rgyud yang snying man-ngag dgongs-pa'i bcud/ zab don gnad kyi gdams-ap mthar-thug-pa/ dngos-gzhi'i lag khrid go-rim bde-bar bkod/ snod-ldan kun gyi don du 'gyur-par shog/ rgyud smin zhing grol-bar byed-pa/ dngos-gzhi'i gdams-pa rdzogs-so/ rgya rgya U-YA AG-THAM!*

4. Notes to the Translation of the Explanation of the View

(1) *Kun tu bzang-po khyab-gdal 'gro-ba 'dren/ rang rig mngon du gyur la phyag 'tshal-lo.*

(2) Book Three, which follows Book One, the Preliminary Practices (sngon-'gro) and Book Two, the Principal Practices (dngos-gzhi), in the *Phyag-khrid* text of Druchen Gyalwa Yungdrung (Bru-chen rGyal-ba g.yung-drung), contains four supplementary texts of guiding explanation (khrid) concerning the Principal Practices. These are known in Tibetan as *the lTa-khrid*, the *sGom-khrid*, the *sPyod-khrid*, and the *dMar-khrid*. Given here is a translation of the *lTa-khrid* text which presents an explanation of the view (lta-ba) of Dzogchen.

(3) *gSum-pa rgyud rtogs cing mngon du gyur-bar byed-pa rjes 'jug gi yan-lag la.*

(4) *Ma kun-gzhi gshis kyi gnas-lugs*, that is to say, the Natural State (gnas-lugs), which is the real disposition of things (gshis), is the Kunzhi (kun-gzhi), "the basis of everything," which is the Mother (ma). It is the base and source of everything in both Samsara and Nirvana ('khor 'das thams-cad kyi gzhi rtsa); it is the first Great Ancestor of all the Buddhas, as well as of all sentient beings (sangs-rgyas sems-can kun gyi yang mes chen-po).

(5) *Ka-dag chen-po*, total primordial purity. This essence (ngo-bo), the state of Shunyata, is without obscurations (sgrib-med), inherently clear (rang-gsal), empty (stong-pa), without a source (rtsa bral), naked and denuded (gcer-bu rjen-pa) of discursive thoughts, and unattired in any delusions or obscurations or passions from the the very beginning (gdod nas 'khrul sgrib nyon-mongs gyid ma

gos-pa). Therefore, it is called the state of total primordial purity (ka-dag chen-po). According to LTN, here the text is speaking from the side of the Natural State only. Here also in the text a series of designations are applied to the the Kunzhi or the primordial Base, namely, 1. the state of total primordial purity (ka-dag chen-po), 2. total self-origination (rang-byung chen-po), 3. the state of total spontaneous self-perfection (lhun-grub chen-po), 4. the state that is totally beyond limitations (mtha' bral chen-po), 5. the state that is totally all-pervading (kun-khyab chen-po), 6. the total state of being (bdag-nyid chen-po), 7. the state that is totally universal or all-inclusive, and 8. the state that totally transcends the intellect and is inexpressible in words (blo 'das brjod med chen-po). Note that the Tibetan word *chen-po*, "great, large," may also be translated as total, that is, it includes everything and nothing is excluded.

(6) *Shes-bya 'khor 'das thams-cad kho'i ngang du rdzogs-pa*. According to LTN, *kho'i ngang du* refers to the Natural State (gnas-lugs).

(7) *rTogs de med-pas lhun-grub chen-po.*

(8) *Kho-nyid gang la*, according to LTN, this refers to the Natural State. *bDag-nyid chen-po*, the total state of being, the Great State or Nature, or 'the great owner" according to LTN.

(9) *Kun gzhi byung sems nyid/ 'od-gsal stong-pa bcos slad med.* (var. byang sems?- LTN)

(10) *Kun rdzogs yongs rdzogs thams-cad rdzogs.*

(11) *Nges-med sprul-sku lung ma bstan/ phyogs med cho-'phrul cir yang shar/ so-so tha-dad ma yin.*
It may arise anywhere as an apparitional display without any partialities (phyogs med cho-'phrul cir yand shar). But it does not exist distinctly and individually, as anything separate from the Natural State, according to LTN.

(12) *De la byang-chun sems zhes bya/ drang-pa'i don rtags gsum-mo.* This three-fold aspect of space is *mkha' klong dbyings*, that is, space, vast expanse, and dimension. In this case, the sky (mkha') is the example, the vast expanse of space (klong) is the real meaning (don), and dimension (dbyings) is the indication (rtags).

(13) *Don du dril rgyud la dbab/ go zhing shes-pa tsam du zad kyi.*

(14) *dMar thag-chad-pa*, "to clearly and definitive decide" with intensity upon something because it is directly experienced and, therefore, one has no doubts; here *dmar* is an intensifier.

(15) *Dus da-lta'i sems-nyid 'dzin-med rang-gsal nam-mkha' dangs-pa lta-bu sku gsum rang chas ye-shes lhun-grub rang-rig rang-gsal 'di yin.*

(16) This explanation is according to Thegchod. What follows is explained according to Thodgal.

(17) *De yin de la cher ste ltos.*

(18) *Da-lta gang na gnas lus spyir khyab kyang/ she-thun rtsa 'dzin gyi nang/ snying mchong gur smug-po shel gyi kha-ba-can gyi dkyil/ 'od lnga gur ltar phub-pa'I dbus su. She-thun* is the Zhang-zhung term for the heart.

(19) *Tsi-ta'i dbus na smag-bral nyi-ma bzhin/ rang-rig rang-shar chen-por gnas-pa yin.*

(20) *Bum-pa nang gi mar-me ltar gnas te/ lta mi mthong lus gyis sgrib/ bem rig bral nas 'ong-bar bshad.* These two quotations in the text explain the matter from the standpoint of Thodgal.

(21) When the master recites aloud the text on this occasion, the disciples are directly introduced to "the Cycle of the Base" (gzhi'i 'khor-lo'i ngo-sprod rnams). According to LTN, this direct introduction was taken from the first wheel or cycle of the *'Khor-lo bzhi sbrag* text. See the translation of this text in Reynolds, *The Path of the Clear Light*, forthcoming..

(22) *Bu rig-pa nyi-ma'i snying-po lta-bu bcud du shar......ma kun-gzhi nam-mkha' lta-bu la/ bu rig-pa nyi-ma'i snying-po lta-bu bcud du shar ste/ shar-ba de'i ngo-bo ni ma sgribs rjen-par sel gsal-ba la/ rang-bzhin stong-nyid rtsa-bral du sang-nge gnas-pa.* In this passage, luminous clarity (gsal-ba) is identified as the Essence (ngo-bo) of the Natural State and emptiness (stong-pa) as its Nature (rang-bzhin), which is the reverse of the usual distinction in Dzogchen. Rigpa is contained in the vessel (snod) of the Kunzhi, or space, like its nectar (bcud).

(23) *rNam-pa yul gyi don ji lta-ba shes-pa'i lba-le-ba rig-pa'i glo-bur rtog spyod g.yo rtsol gyis ma gos-pa'i gcer-bur ye-shes shar ste/ de'i tshe dran-med du had-de/ gtad-med phyad-de rtog-med rjen-ne/ 'dzin-med du hrig-ge-ba de la rang-byung rig-pa'i ye-shes zhes bya ste.*

Referring to this sense of presence (lba-be-ba) as a sudden awareness (rig-pa'i glo-bur), a startled or shocked awareness (had-de-ba), and a naked primal cognition (gcer-bur ye-shes), all points to the fact that there is a brief moment of immediate intuitive awareness arising before the onset of the operations of the functional mind (yid) in terms of memory, perception, thought, and conceptual elaboration. This brief instant of non-dual awareness is pure and naked, unconditioned by thoughts and memories. It exists only in the present instant and then is gone, clouded over by the subsequent operations of the mind. Hence it is called a primal cognition which is pure self-originated Awareness (rang-byung rig-pa'i ye-shes).

(24) *Rig-pa'i ye-shes bya-ba ni/ nam-mkha'i klong na nyi-ma bzhin/ kun-gzhi'i klong nas rig-pa shar/ ngo-bo gsal la rang-bzhin stong/ rnam-par shes-rig rtog-pa med.* Note that in the quotation, Essence (ngo-bo) is equated with clarity (gsal-ba) and Nature (rang-bzhin) with emptiness (stong-pa), the reverse of the usual correspondences. For the individual, there is only one Rigpa, or intrinsic Awareness, which is compared to the single sun that has risen in the sky, whereas there exist many primal cognitions (ye-shes), which may be compared to the rays of light of this single sun that illuminate the entire surface of the earth. These primary cognitions occur prior to and are free from the activities of perception and discursive thoughts.

(25) *Lus gnad gcun rlung sems gyi sbyor-ba bya ste/ rig-pa'i dangs snyegs phyed nas/ shes-pa gsal mdangs lags-po thon nas/ yid-ches-pa'i dus su/ kho'i ngo-bo la cer-re lta ru bcug la ngo-sprad.* In this context, *kho'i ngo-bo* means the Natural State. On this method, see the translation of the *Byang-chub sems kyi gnad drug,* "The Six Essential Points of the Bodhichitta," in a subsequent volume in this series. And according to LTN, also see the *A-khrid rig-pa'i dangs snyeg man-ngag.*

(26) *De rig-pa'i ye-shes gnas-lugs don gyi sangs-rgyas de/ dus da-lta'i rtog-med gyi shes-pa [=rig-pa] sel rjen-ne-ba/ sgrib-med zang-thal du shar-ba 'di yin te.* According to LTN, this *rig-pa'i ye-shes,* "the primal cognitions which are intrinsic awareness," arise in just this way.

(27) *Lhag-mthong spyan drug dpral du shar/ gcer mthong dgongs-pa yongs rdzogs yin.* The six eyes (spyan drug) are among the capacities that develop spontaneously upon the realization of enlightenement. For these six eyes, see the translation of the *'Khor-lo bzhi sbrag,* "The Setting Side by Side of the Four Cycles," in Reynolds, *The Path of the Clear Light,* op. cit., and also see the

sGron-ma drug text, "The Six Lamps," in the subsequent volume of this series. The passages quoted here are explaining matters from the standpoint of Thodgal.

(28) *Ye-shes tshon gang snang-med bon kyi sku/ gshen-lha dkar-po bdag-med kun gyi gzhi/ ngo-bo nyid gyi rig-pa zhes su grags..... rang la rang shar-ba.* Symbollically, the inner light of Awareness is depicted as the wisdom deity Shen-lha (gshen-lha), who is of a miniature size (tshon gang) and is white in colour (dkar-po). He is the embodiment of primordial awareness (ye-shes). He is the unmanifest or invisible Dharmakaya (snang-med bon kyi sku), but as the basis of everything he is insubstantial and without a self (bdag-med kun gyi gzhi).

(29) *rGyas-par ngo-sprad-do.* This direct introduction is called extensive because it not only involves oral explanations and examples, but meditation exercises that give rise to personal experiences that allow one to understand the Natural State.

(30) At the most primary and elementary level of experience, that is, when one awakens again into awareness in the Bardo after death, the inherent energy or potentiality (rtsal) of the nature of Mind suddenly reappears as the three great or total manifestations (snang gsum chen-po) of the sounds, the lights, and the rays (sgra 'od zer gsum). On how they arise to Awareness or Rigpa with the onset of the Bardo experience after resting in the state of Shunyata, see Reynolds, *The Path of the Clear Light*, ibid.

(31) *De ltar rig-pa'i ye-shes de'i mdangs dang rtsal las/ sgra 'od zer gsum rang-snang du ma 'gag-par shar/ byed-pa'i bdag rkyen med-par...*

(32) *Rig-pa'i gsal-cha sgrib g.yog med-pa'i mdangs las], ['od rig-pa'i rang 'od gzha' tshon lta-bu shar/ rig-pa'i stong-cha rtsa bral chen-po'i nus-pa las/ sgra rig-pa'i rang sgra brag-cha lta-bu shar.* Here translucency (mdangs) refers to a mode of the manifestation of energy (rtsal).

(33) *Rig-pa'i rang mdangs 'od lnga dang 'brel-ba'i 'char gzhi las/ sangs-rgyas kyi 'gyur-med sku'i rnam sprul thams-cad/ sems-can bzhi bsdus kyi rnam-sprul thams-cad 'char....*
rig-pa'i sgra dang 'brel-ba'i 'char gzh..... sems-can ngag gi sgra skad thams-cad 'char/ rig-pa zer dang 'brel-ba'i 'char gzhi la/ sangs-rgyas thugs kyi mkhyen ye-shes kyi rnam-sprul thams-cad dang/ sems-can gyi dran-pa yid kyi rtog tshogs thams-cad 'char-ba]......

[bu rig-pa'i ye-shes la sus kyang ma byung/ rang-snang du shar-ba'i snang-ba chen-po gsum gyi byas.

(34) *sNang-ba'i yul. Cho-'phrul,* apparitional display, magical apparition, hologram.

(35) *'Khor 'das skyon yon,* the defects of Samsara and the virtues of Nirvana. *Lus ngag yid* refer to the body, speech, and mind of ordinary deluded sentient beings, whereas *sku gsung thugs* refer to the Body, Speech, and Mind of enlightened beings

(36) *rLung sems kyi sbyor-bas rig-pa'i dwangs snyigs phyed-pa'i rjes la.* The blending or uniting of the vital winds (rlung) and the mind (sems) or consciousness refers to the practice in Tantra of creating the illusion body (sgyu-lus).

(37) *rGya-mtsho gyen bskyod la sogs kyi lus gnad gong ltar gcun de/ lta-ltangs smin 'tshams kyi gsal la 'byed ...... yid kyi rang sgra rgyun chags su grags gzungs la/ dran-pa rig-pa'i rang zer nyi zer lta-bu la thu-re gnad/ yid-ches des/ shes skyes-pa dang ngo-sprad de.*

(38) *Rig-pa'i ye-shes las rang mdangs su shar-ba'i sgra 'od zer gsum-po 'di/ sgros btags ma yin-par/ rig-pa'i ye-shes kyi ngang la ma 'gags-par rang snang du shar-ba yin.*

(39) *'Gyu-ba'i yid ni sgra las btul/ dran-pa'i zer la sbyangs/ rtsal gsum zer la sbyangs-pa.*

(40) *Rig-pa'i rang sgra..... rig-pa'i rang 'od...... rig-pa'i rang zer/ stong-pa'i rang zer nyi zer tshul/ gdod-ma gshis kyi gnas-lugs yin.*

(41) *Ngo-bo rgyud thog nas rang-bzhin zung-'brel/ mtshan-nyid tha-dad mi mnga'-bar gnas.*

(42) Kunzhi or the Base (gzhi) represents the Mother, whereas the heart or essence (snying-po) represents the Son, which is Rigpa, or intrinsic awareness, and the apparitional displays (cho-'phrul) represent the visible manifestations. These are known as the Mother, the Son, and the Potentiality of Energy in the mind-stream of the individual respectively. According to LTN, they are never separate, nor do they come together, but are unconditioned and naturally united from the very beginning ('du bral med-par gnas-tshul).

(43) That is to say, according to LTN, how one can practice.

(44) *Lhod-pa gsum byas-pa'i rjes la/ ngang la ngang gis ltas-pa'i dus su/ ma kun-gzhi stong-nyid rtsa-bral du sang-nge-ba 'di bon-nyid/ bu rig-pa rang-gsal rjen-pa ro ye-re-ba? rtsal cho-'phrul rang-byung*

rang-shar...... gdod nas sku gsum gyi bdag-nyid chen-por 'bral med rang chas su gnas.

(45) *sTong gsal kun-gzhi mkha' klong bon gyi dbyings/ ye-shes chen-po gang rang-byung bon gyi sku.*

(46) *Tsi-ta'i klong na rang rig bon gyi sku/ rtsa'i lam la rang-bzhin rdzogs-pa'i sku/ sgron-ma'i sgo la rang shar sprul-pa'i sku.*

(47) *bSam dran gyi shes-pa nyi zer ltar/ ma 'gags-pa ji snyed cig shar ste/ rang gi yul la sems-par byed-pas/ bsam-pa la yul de'i don ji ltar bar dran/ dran-pa'i don de nyams su myong-bar byed-pas.*

(48) *Shes rig rgyal-po rtog-med kyang/ bsam dran sna-tshogs 'char-ba'i gzhi... rig-pa'i rtsal las blo tu shar.*

(49) *gNad gsum gyis rig-pa gcun-pa'i rjes la/ lhod gyis lhod la bzhag/ de la cer-re lta ste/ gcun-mkhan dang lhod-mkhan 'jogs-mkhan gyi bsam-pa de la cer-re lta ste.*

(50) *Ma brtags na mi gsal-ba'i dran-pa thu-re 'bring-nge-ba de gnyis-ka bsam dran gyi shes rig ces bya ste.....snga bsam phyi mno'i rtog spyod thams-cad de yis byed-pa yin te. De nyid ka,* that state itself.

(51) *Rig-pa'i rtsal las blo tu shar/ bsam-pa'i blo/ dran zhing rig-pas dran zhes bya-ba/ yul la spyod-pas sems zhes bya.*

(52) *rTog-med gyi rig-pa nam-mkha' lta-bu'i ngang nas.* Here in this context, *ngang* indicates the Natural State.

(53) Because, in the beginning, one examines the secondary causes that originated and are produced (de dang-po byung-ba dang bskyed rkyen la brtags-pas), it is free of a base and a root, or source (gzhi rtsa dang bral). In the middle, because one examines their essence initially, they are without shape and colour, that is, one sees that they have neither shape nor colour. At the end, they are purified into self-purification as the state of the Nature of Mind (sems-nyid gyi ngang du rang sangs su sangs). According to LTN, one looks where they arise at the beginning, where they stay in the middle, and where they go in the end. Destroyed into self-destruction (rang rlog du rlog), lost into self-loss (rang stor du stor), and liberated into self- liberation (rang grol du grol). These empty movements ('gyu stong) become like gentle breezes in the atmosphere. And it arises as gnosis which is self-originated and without thoughts (rtog-med rang-byung gi ye-shes su shar-ba yin).

(54) *rTog-med ye-shes gzhi dran rtog sna-tshogs rtsal rjes su 'breng-ba 'khrul-lugs/ skyon tu lta-ba gol-sa/ rang sar glod-pa thabs]......* *gnyis su med rtogs-pa.* According to LTN, that is the method.

(55) *rTog-med dbyings su bsam dran sna-tshogs zad/ blo 'das dbyings su blo byas lam sna zad/ phyogs-med dbyings su phyogs 'dzin grub-mtha' zad.* What one does is let them liberate of themselves- that is the method, according to LTN.

(56) According to LTN, one should just leave them there without following after them and therefore there will remain no traces left behind, just a bird leaves no traces behind when flying through the sky.

(57) *rTog-med 'od-gsal chen-po'i ngang las.*

(58) *sKyon du lta-ba gol-sa/ rang sar lhod-pa thabs/ gnyis su med-pa rtogs-pa.*

(59) *Dug lnga dngos-por grub na/dug lnga spyod-pa spyod-pa'i mchog.* According to LTN, this is the supreme practice.

(60) *Zhe-sdang rtsal nyid na sdang-ba med-pa'i mthar phyin.*

(61) *Rang kha-ma la spyad-pa'i skabs su tshogs drug spyod-mkhan gyi shes-pa la hrig-ge lta ste.* According to LTN, at that time, when one is in the normal way, look back at the senses and just observe.'

(62) *rTsa bral gyi ngos nas/ stong la shar stong nam-mkha'i gzha'-tshon lta-bu shar gyis grol/ grol kyis shar-ba'i tshogs drug gi snang-ba sna-tshogs 'di.*

(63) If they are understood and recognized, they arise as the Nirmanakaya Buddhas, abiding in the realms of the Nirmanakaya. But if one does not understand this and fails to recognize them, then they arise variously as the six realms of rebirth (rigs drug).

(64) *Rig-pa dmar thag-bcad-pas 'khrul sgrib ka nas dag/ blo dmar thag-bcad-pas ye-shes rtsal du shar.*

(65) *gZhi rtsa med-pa'i bon 'di la/ gang ltar btang de ltar snang.* All of existence is rootless, baseless, and insubstantial; it is like this, according to LTN.

(66) *Seng-ge rang gzugs la 'khrul-pa ltar.* In the Gnostic myth, the demiurge (demiourgos) Ialdabaoth has a lion's head and gazes at his reflection in the waters of matter and chaos below.

(67) Rigpa is wrapped up and enveloped in a net of delusions.

(68) *Dran rig blo'i shes-pa yul rmongs/ rang-snang sgyu-mar ma shes gzhan snang bden-par mthong.* According to LTN, how does one not know their true nature? These three are like illusions.

(69) Because one does not recognize the Natural State and falls into duality due to the operations of the functional mind (yid), it is called the co-emergent ignorance or the spontaneously born ignorance (lhan-skyes ma rig-pa).

(70) *Rig-pa'i ye-shes mdog bsgyur/ 'gyu byed cher g.yos/ rang-snang sgra 'od zer gsum nges-pa-can rags-par bzung-pas.* The movements of energy become more and more powerful. Because the sounds, the lights, and the rays, which are self-manifestations, are apprehended and grasped at coarsely, whereupon they appear more and more gross and substantial, according to LTN. Thus, they arise in an uncertain manner (nges-pa-can) as subject and object.

(71) *'Gyu-ba'i yid 'phros/ yul shes ngos ma zin-par yod-pa las/ g.yo-ba'i rlung gis bskul-bas.* They become more and more powerful, more and more gross and coarse. The winds blow and the visions become like clouds disturbed by these winds. The visions become more and more like a network, becoming visible, even appearantly solid— according to LTN. The model for this process of evolution is the meteorological phenomena of the winds and the clouds obscuring the sky. At the beginning, the sky was clear and open and free of clouds, but then the winds arose and gradually the clouds appeared to fill the sky with clouds. The clouds are one's discursive thoughts.

(72) The five lights which are visible and manifest arise more densely as colours. They arise as five, namely, as subtle lights that are white and green and red and blue and yellow. In turn, they become visible as colours, and then subsequently as solid matter, that is, the elements space, air, fire, water, and earth respectively— according to LTN. And that is called the ignorance that conceptualizes everything (kun brtags gyi ma rig-pa).

(73) *Ma rig dbang gis shes-pa yul la 'gyus/ shes-pa yul la 'gyus-pas so ma zin/ so ma zin-pas snang-ba'i yul gsum 'khrugs.*

(74) *De la brten-pa'i don lnga chags.* The five internal organs (don lnga) are the heart, the spleen, the lungs, the liver, and the kidneys.

(75) *'Khrul tshul rgyas-par rten-'brel gyi 'khor-lo ngo-sprad-par bya.* This is found in the text entitled the *'Khor-lo bzhi brdag.* For the translation, see Reynolds, *The Path of the Clear Light,* ibid.

(76) They go down and circulate stage by stage from human to animal and upward again.

(77) *gZhan nyon-mongs-pa phra-ba nas je rags la 'khrul-pa ltar.* This is how things evolved in terms of delusion. But how can this process to be reversed? The karmic traces as visions become progressively more powerful. One's body and mind are like a dream and one experiences karmic visions as they are real. But when one reverses this process (ru log), one then becomes a body of light ('od lus). But when anger becomes increasingly powerful, it generates the intellect and the Rupadhatu. When sex desire becomes increasingly powerful, it generates the physical body and the dimensions of the Kamadhatu. Thus, with evolution, the kleshas or passions progressively become more and more coarse. But one can reverse this downward evolution and return back to the source. When one cuts the root of the passions, which is ignorance, then one will liberate – according to LTN.

(78) *Ma 'khrul-ba ltar yar grol-ba/ gnad cig 'khor-ba la byang-ba'i thog-ma yod-pas/ grol-ba'i tha-ma yod/ de dag kun kho-bos gnad cig tu 'dod-do.*

(79) *bLo'i 'dzin-pa ma zhugs-par.*

(80) *gZhi dang rig-pa bdag zhal mjal-bas.....sems-nyid kun tu bzang-po'i rgyal-sa tshur zin.* Thereupon all will be liberated naturally. By way of this method, one perceives the basic Awareness, whereupon the Son goes to the Mother. The sounds, the lights, and the rays represent the energy (rtsal) of the Nature of Mind, and this contrasts with limited consciousness in terms of the thought process (blo'i shes-pa).

(81) *Rig-pa gcer-bu rjen gyis shar...... sgrub-med shugs la 'char.*

(82) *gZhi'i ngo-bor grol-ba'i rang mdangs/ dag snang nus-pa'i rtsal las snang-ba'i rang 'od lnga shar/ de las bdag gi klong lnga shar/ de las bdag med-pa'i klong lnga shar.* Here in outline is presented the unfolding or evolution of the realms of pure vision on the side of Nirvana.

(83) *rGyas-par rtogs tshul rten-'brel 'khor-lo la ngo-sprad.* That is, it follows the *rTen-'brel 'khor-lo* section of the *'Khor-lo bzhi brdag.*

(84) *Yon-tan de dag kyang gdod nas ma bu rtsal gsum gyi don ji lta-bar rig cing rtogs-pa yi/ lam gyi byed-pa la ma ltos-par/ kun tu bzang-po sangs-rgyas-pa ste.*

(85) *gDod nas rtogs-pa'i shugs las byung.*

(86) *Da-lta yang de dang tshul mthun-par lam las sbyangs-pas/ mthar mngon du gyur/ sangs-rgyas-pa 'di ni lam grol snags-rgyas-pa'o.*

5. Notes to the Translation of the Explanation of the Meditation Practice

(1) *Kun tu bzang-po khyab-gdal 'gro-ba'i 'dren/ rang-rig mngon du gyur la phyag-'tshal-lo.*

(2) *Lam nyams su blangs-pa 'od-gsal bsgom-pa'i 'od-gsal,* that is to say, Thodgal practice.

(3) *Rig-pa rkyang 'ded nus-pa'i gang-zag gis/ gong du gdams-pa'i dmar-khrid phyag-len ngo-sprad las sogs rdzogs-par thob.*

(4) *Lar thabs-lam dang khrid tshul dang bogs 'don lam-khyer ngo-sprod las sogs mang du gsungs kyang/ gal-che shos kho-rang la thug-pas/ rig-pa sgrib-med 'od-gsal chen-po'i don la.*

(5) *Len tshul ni/ bla-ma bcud-ldan dang/ gdams-pa zab-mo'i dgongs-pa longs-pas bsgom shes-pa dang/ brtson-'grus drag-pos dar tsam yang btang-snyoms su mi lus-par brtson-par bsgom-pa dang/ lo zla zhag grangs ci song yang/ nyams-myong rgyud la ma shar bar la/ sran-nus-pa(s) yun ring du bsgom-pa dang/ dus dang rnam-pa kun tu/ gang gis kyang bar ma chod-pa/ 'di nyid la rkyang ded byed cing bar-chad med-par sgom-pa.*

(6) *Kun-gzhi ngos-bzung rig-pa dmar thag-bcad.*

(7) *sMos-pa'i phyogs su las byas nas/ ngal-ba med-par kun kyang 'grub.*

(8) *gNas-lugs theg-chen gyi don nyams su len-par byed-pa la.*

(9) *'Khrul-'khor rtsa-rlung dang dmigs.*

(10) *bsGom-pa nyams kyi gegs la mang yang.*

(11) *lTa-ba la.... lnga'i gol-sa tu ma shor-bar bya.*

(12) *gSungs rab,* "the supreme scripture," refers to the *Khams-chen,* the Bonpo version of the Prajnaparamita in sixteen volumes.

(13) *rTsal gyi(s) sbyangs thabs bstan-pa ni/ 'gyu-ba gser gyi nya-mo de/ mun-khang 'od kyi rgya la bzung/ kun gsal rig-pa'i me-long de/ snang gsal nam-mkha'i mthongs su bstan/ dran-pa sems kyi mdung-mo de/ snang-ba 'od kyi phab la gtad/ de'i tshe gzugs-sku'i sa-bon mthong/ mkha' la skar tshogs shar-ba 'dra.*

(14) *Dang-po dus su 'byung-ba lnga'i rtags gong ltar la.*

(15) *'Od dang zer dang/ za 'og gi snam-bu kha phye-ba'am/ gzha' tshon shar-ba'am/ dkyil-'khor 'bris-pa lta-bur grangs med-pa/ bsam gyis mi khyab-pa/ phyar-ba'am/ re-lde'am goms-pa dang yul 'gru'am/ nam-mkha' bar-snang gang-ba 'char te/ zhing-khams kyi gzhi yin-*

no/ de dag gi nang du gzugs-sku'i sa-bon/ thig-le skar tshogs bkram-pa ltar 'char te.

(16) *gZer-bu las/ snang-ba'i 'od lnga zhing-khams dkyil-'khor gzhi/ thig-le gur-khang rigs lnga'i gzhal-yas khang/ lhag-mthong sku las sna-tshogs gzugs-sku shar.*

(17) *'Od-gsal gyi snang-ba grangs med-par shar-ba rnams gyi nang du/ shel mdog rig-pa'i thig-le sran-ma tsam dang/ de bas che-ba dang/ rkyang-pa dang/ gnyis 'brel gsum 'brel dang mang-po sbrel-ba dang/ gyen la 'brel-ba/ 'phred la 'brel-ba la sogs dang/ rig-pa'i snying-po thugs-rje'i nyag-thag zhes bya na/ dar dkar nyag-thag lta-bu la/ lu-gu rgyud gyi thig-le/ 'phel-ba lta-bu rgyud-pa dang/ ma brgyus-pa rkyang-pa nyag-thag gis sbrel-ba dang/ thig-le dang ma 'brel nyag-thag rkyang-pa las sogs du mar snang-ba la.*

(18) *'Byung lnga thams-cad gnad du ma 'chun-pas.*

(19) *dNgul-chu 'thor dril bzhin du/ g.yo 'gul 'thor dril dang bcas-par snang.*

(20) *De la goms shing 'dris-pa yis/ goms-pa'i khyad-par rnam lnga 'byung/ dang-po sang-ba 'phel-bar 'gyur/ dngul-chu 'thor dril bzhin du mthong.*

(21) *Rig-pa'i zer dang thugs-rje'i nyag-thag ni/ dang-po ri gzar kha nas chu 'babs 'dra.*

(22) *Shes-pa gsal la mi 'phro-ba/ dangs seng-nge-ba gnas-pa'i nyams.*

(23) *sNang-ba mched-pa'i tshul la/ phyogs thams-cad 'od-gsal gyi snang-ba 'char/ de dag gi nang du shel mdog rig-pa'i thig-le yang kha-yar 'char/ 'byung-ba lnga-ka gnad du 'chun-pas/ shas-che 'od lnga gur-khang gi thig-le re re mu-khyud lnga lnga ldan-pa/ gsal la dwangs-pa/ bkra la gsal-ba.*

(24) *De nas snang-ba mched-par 'gyur/ mkha' la nyi zla lhag ltar mthong/ rig-pa 'od kyi gur-khang mthong.*

(25) *Phyi nang thams-cad rang grol chen-po khrol gyis song/ g.yo-med rang gsal chen-po'i ngang la mi 'da'-bar.*

(26) *De ni sems (nyid)-pa'i ngang sgom sleb-pa yin.*

(27) *Nang nas mchog gi 'od-gsal cung-zad mngon du 'char.*

(28) *Thig-le lngar gyes-pa dang de la 'od gyen 'greng rtsibs shar.*

(29) *Thams-cad che chung bsam gyis m khyab-pa mang nyung snang yul gang-ba 'byung.*

(30) *gSum-pa bya khra gzan tshul lta-bur 'gyur.*

(31) *De nas snang-ba rgyas-par 'gyur/ rigs lnga rdzogs-sku'i dkyil-'khor mthong.*

(32) *Gong gi spros-bral rang grol gnas-cha mthug-po dang bcas-pa de nyid/ ci zhig gcig la rig-pa gzhi med/ ye stong rtsa bral chen-po gcig tu har gyis song nas/ phyi nang yul shes 'khor 'das ci byung ci shar thams-cad/ kho'i du ro-gcig-pa zhig 'byung-bas/ de la du-ma ro-gcig bsgom zhes bya ste.*

(33) *Sangs-rgyas gyi dgongs-pa la phyed sleb tsam yin/ ngang bsgom zad sar skyol nas/ klong bsgom 'go tshugs-pa yin.*

(34) *mChog gi 'od-gsal du gyur te/snags-rgyas kyi sku dnag zhing-khams rang la lhun-grub du yod-pa.*

(35) *Dregs-pa lha klu dri-za gcan lnga las sogs-pa/ thul-ba rtags gyi gdan la.*

(36) *De nas snang-ba rdzogs-par 'gyur/ lhun-grub phyag-rgya'i dkyil-'khor mthong/ snang-ba 'od kyi zhing-khams mthong/ cho-'phrul g.yo 'gul med-par mthong.*

(37) *bZhi-pa ru-sbal 'khor gzhong du tshud-pa 'dra.*

(38) *De nyid ci zhig la bsgom bya bsgom byed kyi blo rtsol thams-cad sems su grol nas/ bsgom-med yengs-med kyi ngang la rig-pa rgyun chags su gnas/ de las mi ,da'-bar ,byung ste/ de'i dus su blos ched du bsgom mi dgos/ ngang gis cung tsam dran dgos-pa/ de la bsgom-med yengs-med kyi bsgom-pa.*

(39) *mThar thug rtogs-pa'i klong bsgom yang rgyud la nges-par shar/ mngon du legs-par ma gyur tsam gyi skabs-so.*

(40) *De ltar shar-ba'i zhing-khams thig-le 'od zer lha-sku las sogs/ rang-snang dag-pa'i 'char tshul la/ spros bcas dngos mtshan-can thams-cad kyang / stong-nyid rtsa-bral kun-gzhi spros-med kyi klong du mal gyis thim/ 'ubs gyis bsdus nas rtsol bcas spros-pa'i mtshams thams-cad khrol gyis grol ste/ sgra 'od zer gsum lha-sku ye-shes gyi snang-ba thams-cad sems su 'dus shing.*

(41) *Zer ni rig-pa'i rang zer te/ stong-pa'i gzugs brnyan chu zla'i tshul/ sgra ni rig-pa'i rang sgra ste/ stong-pa'i rang sgra brag-cha'i tshul/ 'od ni rig-pa'i rang 'od te/ stong-pa'i rang 'od ni 'ja'-tshon tshul.*

(42) *Bye-ma snyed kyi bder-gshegs mthong-ba ni/ rmi-lam sbrang-rtsi 'thung kyang/ sad-pa'i yul phyogs-med/ mi gnas mi mthong stong-pa phyogs dang bral/ bstan dka' lkug-pa'i rmi-lam 'dra.*

(43) *lNga'i 'byung-ba bzhi zad-pa'i nam-mkha' 'dra.*

(44) *Gong gi sanag-ba'i 'char tshul de dag thams-cad dang/ sgra 'od zer gsum las sogs-pa'i rang-snang la shar-ba thams-cad/ ma la bu thim gyi tshul du kun-gzhi klong du thim nas/ rang yal du yal/ rang grol du grol/ rang chod du chod/ rang shar du shar-bas/ zad-pa'i mthar*

thug ste/ 'khrul tshul dang gnod gcig tu go ste/ 'byung-ba'i phug dang grol-ba'i mtha' 'di la thug.

(45) *bsGom-med yens-med dran-pa yi thag-pa cung tsam dang bcas-pa de nyid.*

(46) *Ci zhig la dran-pa'i thag chod/ bsgom-pa'i brtod phur thon nas/ ci byas thams-cad rtsol-bral gyi ngang las mi 'da'/ ci 'char thams-cad ye-shes su 'char/ bsgom ma bsgoms la khyad-par med/ gnyid ma gnyid la khyad med/ bzhag na stod/ gtang na 'gro/ dgos dus slebs/ rang dbang rang gyis bsgyur/ dgra dang bu ru mnyam/ gser dang bong-ba ru mnyam/ yar la mi re/ mar la mi dogs-pa ni/ rtogs-pa'i klong bsgom mngon du gyur te/ bco lnga'i zla-ba ltar goms-pa mthar skyol/ kun tu bzang-po'i rang sa zin-pa yin-no.*

(47) *sNang-ba sgra 'od zer gsum gyi brdzun phugs legs-par bcar na/ sems su thug gis btugs nas/ 'khrul-pa'i phugs chod-pa dang 'bras-bu rdzogs-pa'i snags-rgyas bya-ba.*

(48) *gZhi thog tu 'khrul-ba'i phugs legs-par bcad-pas/ phyin chad mi 'khrul-pa dang/ rig-pa la dag dri-med ngo-bo nyid don la byung thebs rtsal rdzogs/ shugs thon lhag-ma ma lus thag chod/ mngon du gyur-pas de'i ngang las ma g.yos-pas bon-sku.*

(49) *De'i ngang las zag bcas kyi phung-po/ zag-med du grol-bas.*

(50) *De'i byung khungs khams dang skye-mched rtsa dang yan-lag/ tshogs brgyad sgo lnga las sogs kyi 'char tshul.*

(51) *De-dag gi 'gro-ba gang la gang 'dul du 'dren-pa'i thabs lam sna-tshogs su sprul nas 'gro-ba'i don la g.yel-ba med-par/ ngang ngam shugs las byung ni sprul-sku.*

(52) *De tsam na las sgrib sbyong-ba dang/ sa lam skye-ba dang/ bskal-pa du-mar 'bud mi dgos-par/ drang-don rgyu 'bras kyi rnam-bzhag thams-cad rdzun du btang nas/ lus phyag-rgya'i 'di steng du btsan-thabs kyi sangs-rgyas da-lta nyid du thob-pa ste.*

(53) *sNang-ba'i rdzun phugs sems su zad/ gzugs-sku'i dmar thag sems su bcad/ 'khrul-pa'i phugs chod 'khrul mi srid/ sku gsum da-lta mngon du gyur/ rgyu 'bras las dbang rdzun-po-che/ 'di ni sangs-rgyas btsan-thabs yin.*

(54) *sKyes-bu'i dbugs 'bring tshad skor brgya la/ 'od-gsal kyi thun tshad gcig tu byas-pa'i/ thun tshad khri phrag bco brgyad la/ dbang-po 'bring gcig gi rkyen gzhan gyis bar ma chod-par nyams su blangs na/ mthar thug-pai snang-ba yan-chad rdzogs-par 'char.* Note: That is, in 166 days or about five and a half months.

(55) *sNang-bai 'char tshul lnga'i thad sor dpe ris bzhin du ngo-sprod.*

(56) *De-dag lam gyi rim-pa dang sbyar-ba la shing-rta'i srol 'dra/ sngon gyi rgyal 'phags dam-pa rnams kyi tshul du la bgrod-par byas.*

(57) *Bon spyod dgu'i rim-pas sdig sgrib sbyangs.*

(58) *mTshan bcas dang bcas mtshan med kyi gdams-pa gnyis ni/ ngo-bo nyid kyi don la gsal snang bskyed cing/ gnas-lugs kyi don la sbyor-bas sbyor lam dang mthun.*

(59) *De nas spyi dang bye-brag gi 'od-gsal gdams-pa ni/ rig-pai ye-shes ji ltar mngon du ston-pas mthong lam dang mthun la/ de nas bogs 'don gyi gdams-pa ni/ ngo-bo nyid kyi don shar-ba la/ goms zhing 'dris-pa byed-pas/ bsgom lam dang mthun.* According to LTN, these instructions regarding the development (of the visions) refer to Tsalung (rtsa rlung) and visualization practices.

(60) *De yang skye-ba dang bskal-pa du-ma'i brtsol-ba lam ltos-par/ thabs lam gnad kyis skye-ba gcig gam skad-cig gis rang sa zin-par byed cing/ lam bgrod-med cig chod/ 'khrul-pa spang med rang grol/ 'bras-bu sku gsum lhun-grub du ston te/ lam na nye-lam der rdzogs-pas.*

(61) *rGyu 'bras las dbang rdzun-po-che/ 'di ni sangs-rgyas btsan thabs yin.*

(62) *Nyams rtogs dang sbyar na/ thun bsgom gyi dus su rig-pa'i ye-shes don gyi tshul du gom-pas/ tshogs lam dang mthun la/ sgom dus su gsal snang-can du 'byung-bas/ sbyor lam dnag mthun/ ngang bsgom gyi 'go shar-ba ni/ rang mtshan gsar du rtogs-pas/ mthong lam dang mthun/ de yang ngang gis goms shing mthar thon-par byed-pa ni/ bsgom lam dang mthun/ klong du gyur-pa ni mthar phyin-pa'i 'bras-bu'o.*

(63) *Phyi 'od-gsal mthong snang 'char tshul/ nang dge-sbyor gyi nyams-myong skye tshul/ bar du rdzu-'phrul gyi gsal snang/ phyi nang thams-cad zung-'brel 'jug-pa gcig tu sngar bzhin rim-par ltar 'char la.*

(64) *Thod-rgal-ba la thabs lam sna-tshogs nas sleb dgos/ de yang gdams-pa blo dang bstun nas 'debs-pa ni shin tu yang gnad che'o.*

6. Notes to the Explanation of the Conduct

(1) *Kun tu bzang-po khyab bdal 'gro-ba 'dren/ rang-rig mngon du gyur la phyag 'tshal-lo.*

(2) *mNyam rjes bsres.* One integrates (bsres-pa) the state of contemplation (mnyam-bzhag), being in the condition of Rigpa

or intrinsic awareness, with normal, everyday experience after the session of meditation practice, known as the subsequent realization (rjes thob).

(3) *bsKor-ba lha-phyag phyag-rgya 'khrul-'khor rnams.*

(4) *Rig stong 'od-gsal chen-po'i klong/ rang rig-pa'i ye-shes rjen-par gsal-ba'i ngang nas/ shugs 'byung du spyod-par bya.*

(5) *Lus kyi bya-ba sna-tshogs byar-med kyi rtsal du shar. Byar-med* means non-action.

(6) *Dran-pa'i rtsis bzung.*

(7) *Rig stong 'od-gsal chen-poi klong na/ rang-byung ye-shes rjen-par gsal-ba'i ngang nas/ 'gag-par spyod/ brjod-med kyi rtsal do shar.*

(8) *Rang rig ye-shes rjen-par gsal-Ba'i ngang nas/ ma 'gag med du spyod...... rtog med kyi rtsal du shar.*

(9) *Phyi nang med-par khyab bdal/ snang tshad skui rol-pa/ grags tshad gsung gi rol-pa/ dran tshad thugs kyi rol-pa/ byung tshad yon-tan gyi rol-pa/ byas tshad phrin-las kyi rol-pa.*

(10) *Shes-rab stong-pa nyid kyi ngang nas bya-bar ma bkag-pa thabs kyi rang-bzhin du 'char-ba zhig dgos te.*

(11) *sTong-nyid 'od-gsal chen-po'i nganag nas/ gzugs mthong stong rtsa bral chen-po nges med sgyu-ma lta-bur rtsal sbyangs te.*

(12) *Ci yang ma yin-pas cir yang bya ru med-pa/ kha-dog gsal-ba dbang-po'i yul/ kha-dog cir gsal sems kyi dbyings.*

(13) *Tshor stong rjes med chen-por rtsal sbyang.*

(14) *Myang stong rtsa bral chen-por rbad rbad bcud la nyams la nyams su blang.*

(15) *Reg stong rang-grol du rtsal sbyong nyams su blang ste.*

(16) *Rang rig-pa'i ye-shes las rtsal drug yul drug du shar nas/ bya byed sna-tshogs su byed-pa 'di ni/ sprul-sku rang la shar-ba yin-pas.*

(17) The scripture of Lachen Dranpa Namkha (bla-chen gyi gsung), the ancient prince of Zhang-zhung who was a famous master of Dzogchen.

(18) *sPyod cing lta-ba'i tshe/ lta-mkhan dang spyod-mkhan gyi shes-pa ched du ngos-bzung/ rang rig-pa'i ye-shes rjen-pargsal-ba'i ngang nas/ ma 'gag-par lta zhing rtog dpyod gyi rtsol-ba mi bya/ 'dres-pa tsam gyis mi chog ste/ shar-ba tsam gyis mi chog ste/ gnyis-med du ro snyoms-pa zhig dgos-so.*

(19) *rTog tshogs kyi ngo-bo la lta/ khungs bcar gzhi rtsa bcad/ 'gyed-pas zhe khrel gdab.*

(20) *Rang-'byung ye-shes gzhi/ nyon-mongs dug lnga rtsal/ rjes su 'breng-ba 'khrul lugs/ skyon du lta-ba gol-sa/ rang sar glod-pa thabs/ klong du grol-ba lam/ gnyis su med-pa rtogs-pa mngon du gyur-pa 'bras-bu.*

(21) *'Gal rkyen mi thun-pa thams-cad spang/ thabs phar-phyin bcu la sogs sems-dpa'i spyod tshul thams-cad dang du blangs te.*

(22) *Bogs 'don rtsal sbyong lam du khyer-ba/ brtul-shugs kyi spyod-pa gnad du bstun.*

(23) *'Dor len med-par spyod/ rtsis gdab med-pa spyod-pa.*

(24) *bSe rag g.yang du 'gug bar-chad dngos-grub tu len.*

(25) *Nyams rtogs mthar phyin-pa'i dus su.*

(26) *bDer-gshegs nyid du bdag rtogs na/ kun kyang bder-gshegs spyad-pa ste/ dpag gi(s) dpog-par mi 'gyur-ro.*

(27) *bDe sdug so-mtshams yin.*

(28) *Lus sems tha-ma bral-bai dus/ bde sdug gnyis kyi so-mtshams su.*

(29) *Nang du mtsher-pa sa'i khams nyams/ phyi ru lus kyi reg-bya mi 'tshor.*

(30) *'Byung-ba'i khams nyams-par go-bar byas.*

(31) *bLa-ma rjes su dran-par bya ste/ spyi-gtsug tu bsgon zhing mos-gus drag-po bya/ de nas yi-dam rjes su dran-par bya ste/ rang lus yi-dam du sgom la 'dzab bsnyen gsang-mtshan ma brjed-par bya/ de nas bar-do rjes su dran-par bya ste.*

(32) *De nas bar-do rjes su dran-par bya ste/ de ltar shar-ba'i yul snang 'di ni/ bar-do'i snang-ba nges-med sgyu-ma lta-bu yin snyom du bsam/ de nas gdams-ngag rjes su dran-par bya ste/ rtsa bral gyi don la rang-rig tsen-ne bzhag.*

(33) See John Myrdhin Reynolds, *Selections from the Bonpo Book of the Dead*, Bonpo Translation Project (privaely printed), San Diego and Copenhagen 1997.

(34) *Nang du lte-ba sa'i 'khor-lo zhig nas nus-pa chu la thim-pa'i rtags su/ phyi ru lus kyi stobs 'chor/ lus lji sa la byin-pa snyam byed/ rang snang la sa'i dwangs-ma ser-pa zhig shar te.*

(35) *sNang-ba thams-cad ser lam-lam 'byung.*

(36) *Sems ni kun-gzhir thim ste dbugs chod lus sems bral.*

(37) See Reynolds, *Selections from the Bonpo Book of the Dead*, ibid.

(38) *Rig-pa dri-med 'od-gsal chen-po'i ngang la zhog cig/ rang-snang la shar-ba'i 'od ser-po/ rang mdangs sgyu-ma lta-bur shes-par gyis shig/ 'od snang de 'dra-ba bon-nyid 'od-gsal gyi bar-dor 'byung-bas.*

(39) *'Dre gdon gyis mnan-pa lta-bu.*

(40) *De'i tshe bon-sku rig-pa'i dbu-ma'i lam la phyung/ sgron-ma'i sgo nas thon te.*

(41) *Rig-pa sprin-bral mkha' la nyi-ma shar-ba lta-bu/ de la khyad-par gnad kyi gdams-pa gdab.*

(42) *'Od kyi bag rgya bkral-ba'i bag rgya A la 'dus.*

(43) *Hrig gis tshangs-sgor 'phang.*

(44) *Rig-pa sems kyi mi-bo de/ dran-pa yid kyi rta zhon.*

(45) *Thogs-med rlung gis gshog-pas bskyod/ dbu-ma byang-chub lam la gshegs/ spyi-gtsug bde-ba'i gsang sgor byon/ rig-pa'i rgyal-po gcer-bu shar/ rnam-rtog blo yi g.yang lugs bud/ rang-byung ye-shes bdag zhal mthong/ ma rig 'khrul-pa'i mun-pa sangs.*

(46) *De dus kyi shes rig de/ sangs-rgyas rang chas sku gsum gsun lhun-grub/ rang-rig mngon gyur shar tshad ye-shes snang tshad sems-nyid mngon du gyur nas yod cing.*

(47) *De'i dus su rang-snang la shar tshad bden-med sgyu-ma lta-bu/ de dag thams-cad sems kyi rang-bzhin sems-nyid ni de'i dus kyi rig-pa rtsa-bral chen-po de/ bon-sku rang chas su/ gdod nas gnas-par ngo-sprad-pas/ yid-ches thag-chod de/ skye sgo chod-par the-tshom med.*

(48) *Rab rang shar rang grol/ 'bring lha-sku ye-shes/ tha-ma la yang bem rig bral-bai rang sgra rang 'od rang zer du ngo-sprad-do.*

(49) *gZung 'dzin rnam-rtog klong du thim/ de tshe rig-pa gcer-bu gnas/ rang-'byung ye-shes sgrib g.yogs med.*

(50) *Lus sems bral ma dag gi tshe.*

(51) *Len gcig sgrib-med rang gsal dag-pa zang-thal gcer-bu rjen-par gnas-so.*

(52) *De tshul ni kun-gzhi rig-pa'i rgyal-po pho mo'i míg g.yas g.yon nas bud de/ mdzod-spur dar-cig gnas/ rtags su de'i tshe ngo bzhin dang khyad-par du mdzad-spu'i bkrag mdangs nyams-pa'o.*

(53) *Ngo-shes tsam gyis skad-cig-ma la ma bu 'phrod/ lus ngag yid gsum gyi rgya gsum ral/ sku gsung thugs kyi rtsal gsum rdzogs.*

(54) *gNad gsum 'dzoms-pas grol te/ da-lta ngo-sprad-pai don la goms/ 'chi-khar yang yang gsal-gdab/ bag-chags legs-par 'dris su bcug-pa.*

(55) *De'i tshe sems ni drod dang 'grogs te/ 'chi-khai bsam stobs kyis gong ltar.*

(56) *Gal-te de las ma grol na/ ma kun-gzhi'i klong du bu rig-pa thim/ dran rig de'i bag la zha/ rtsal sgra 'od zer gsum gyi tshur-bcad/ rang-rig 'od kyi rgyar btums te/ kun-gzhi 'thug-po bsam dran snang*

gang yang med-pa'i ngang la/ zhag gsum dros bzhi'am lnga bdun la sogs su gnas-so/

(57) *Lus sems bral ma thag gi tshe gnas-pa gzhi'i dus su/ ma grol na/ de nas bon-nyid 'od-gsal kyi bar-do zhes bya myos-pa sangs-pa'am/ gnyid sad-pa lta-bu rig-pa sngar-bas gsal-ba/ rkyen gyis bsgyur sla-ba zhig 'byung/ de nas rang lus bag-chags rang gzugs kyi snang-ba 'od kyi tsi-ta'i ngang las/ ye-shes tshon-gang-ba shar te/ de'i byed-pas rig-pa sad/ bsam dran g.yos-pas/ snang-ba'i 'od rgya ral nas/ bum-pa'I mar-me byung-ba ltar/ shes-pa'i 'od-gsal mngon du 'char te.*

(58) *Rig-pa'i rang zer za-'og snan-bu kha phye-a'am nyi zer mtshon rtse lta-bu.*

(59) *sGra ni dngos-med klong na ldir/ rang-'byung rgyun med 'brug sgra'i tshul/ zer ni cho-'phrul nges-med ston/ za-'og snan-bu kha phye 'dra.*

(60) *Dwangs-ma rim gyis 'char.*

(61) Usually in Western publications, this term is translated as "the five wisdoms." But as explained previously, *ye-shes* means a non-dual primal awareness that is present before the functional mind (yid, manas) comes into operation, as well as the distinction of subject and object, whereas "wisdom" (shes-rab) is a dualistic, albeit higher intellectual function. *Ye-shes,* or *ye nas shes-pa,* prior awareness, translates Skt. jnana, cognate with the Greek gnosis. Here these five are correlated with the Five Deities or Five Dhyana Buddhas, which bare different names than they do in the Buddhist system, and with the five Bodies of the Buddha.

(62) *'Dir gdams-pa la sbyong stobs che-ba rnams ni/ snang-ba gsum shar-ba sngar dris kyi mi dang 'phrad-pa ltar/ slar rkyen bskul gsal gdab/ rang chod la song ste/ 'dir snang-ba zad sar ma skyol/ rgyas-pai nyams shar tsam rnams kyang/ der rdzogs-par shar ngo-shes nyams su blangs-pas mthar thug-par grol te/ goms zhing 'dris-pa gang-zag la/ sku dang dkyil-'khor rdzogs-par 'char.*

(63) *mNgon-shes rjes dran gyi(s) snang-ba rnam gsum sun-mar 'char.*

(64) *De dus kyi snang-ba gsum rang 'char mi 'chor te/ sgra 'od zer gsum rang snang sgyu-ma ltar shar-bas/ zhen chags sngangs mi skye-bar lha sku ye-shes sam rang snang sgyu-ma ltar du go-bas/ de dag mi bslu-bar grol-ba'o.*

(65) *Rang-mdangs su shes-pas nges-par grol.*

(66) *sNang-bas bdag zhal bdag gis mthong/ rang-rig bdag zhal bdag tu mjal/ ma rig 'khrul-pa rang shar sangs.*

(67) *Phyi-ma sum char 'char la skye sgo kun nyúl cing gang la yang 'jug sa 'tshol.*

(68) *Ye-shes kyi spyan dang bar-do nang rigs min-pa sus kyang mi mthong la.*

(69) *Bon-nyid 'od-gsal snang-ba la/ rtogs-pa'i shes-rab ma skyes-pas/ sngar gyi ye-shes bag la zha/ sngon gyi bag-chags snang-ba shar.*

(70) *sNgon 'byung srid-pai sha gzugs-can/ dbang-po kun tshang thogs-med rgyu/ las kyi rdzu-'phrul shugs dang ldan/ rigs mthun lha míg dag-pas mthong/ lus dang 'dug sa tshol-bar byed.*

(71) *Ma bu 'phrod nas sans-rgyas kyi dbyings-gral 'dzin.*

(72) *De-dag gi rjes su ma 'brengs-pas rang chod la 'gro.*

(72) *Des na da-lta ngo-bo 'char tshul la goms shing dad mos ser yod-pa.* The Essence (ngo-bo) means the Natural State of the Nature of Mind (sems-nyid gnas-lugs).

(74) *gDams-ngag dran nas nyams su blangs la rtsal sbyangs-pas/ gnad ldog-med lam 'chug-med 'bras-bu rtsol-med.*

(75) *Yo gal med-pa thig-le'i lam ces dang/ gnas bzang rgyud nas myur du thar.*

(76) *De'i tshe ye-shes tshon-gang dang 'od tshon-gang gi 'char gzhi la/ rang lus 'od sku 'dom gang mdun rgyab mtshams steng 'og med-par snang-ngo/ phyogs bcu'i nam-mkha' la/ gzhal-yas thig-le gur-khang grangs med-par 'char te/ de la yang gur-khang lnga lngar shar-ba'i dbus/ sku lnga lnga shar ste tshom-bu dang gral thabs kyi tshul du snang-ngo.*

(77) *De'i tshe mngon-shes drug dang rjes-dran drug shar nas/ rgyas-par sgron-ma ltar ram/ yang zhag lnga lnga la 'od re re shar te/ rig-pa 'od khyim 'khor-lo la 'dris sam/ de lha sku ye-shes su shar/ de-rang snang du chod-pas sangs-rgyas-so.*

(78) *Sangs-rgyas kyi rang sa zin te/ skye-med kyi dbyings-gral skad-cig la 'dzin/ sbyangs-pa chung-ba rnams kyang ngo-shes don don go-bas/ de-dag gi rjes su mi 'breng rang khar mi 'chor-bas/ rang dbang gyi skye-ba blangs te.* Do not let them escape freely into their own condition is literally, not escape into their own face (rang khar mi'chor).

(79) *Grub-mtha'i sgor zhugs.*

(80) *rNam-shes rten-med da-bur 'khyams-pa'i dus su/ dge-ba-can la dag-pa'i snang-ba 'char/ sdig-pa-can la ma dag-pa'i snang-ba 'char.*

(81) *sNang-ba la spyi-gtsug rang bab byed-pa.*

(82) *Ma dag-pa'i lus blang-ba.*

(83) *'Bras-bu rang dbang gyi bde 'gro'am/ 'gro don las dag-pa'i skye gnas su byon-pa rnams mtshungs ldan-no.*

(84) *Zangs la gser bzo dang 'dra.*

(85) *bKa' lung thams-cad kyi do ya min-no/ de yang gang-zag lam-pa thams-cad kyi do ya min-no.*

7. Notes to the Translation of the Explanation of the Fruit

(1) *Kun tu bzang-po khyab bdal 'gro-ba 'dren/ rang-rig mngon du gyur la phyag-'tshal-lo.*

(2) In the title of the text, "the Guiding Explanation for coming to an intensely Clear and Definitive Decision regarding the Trikaya, where one remains in one's own Original Condition, which represents the Fruit" ('bras-bu rang sa bzung-ba sku-gsum dmar thag-bcad-pa'i khrid). The term *dmar*, literally "red," i.e., "blood," acts as an intensifier for *thag-bcad-pa*, literally, "to cut the rope," but in this context, "to come to a definitive decision." The term *khrid* represents an explanation that gives guidance for proceeding along the path, from *'khrid-pa*, "to lead, conduct, guide." "To remain in one's own original condition, which represents the Fruit" ('bras-bu rang sa bzung-ba) indicates that the Dzogchen teachings belong to the Phalayana or Fruitional Vehicle, where one realizes the Fruit, or the ultimate goal of Buddhahood, by way of practicing the Fruit as the Path. The Fruit, that is to say, the Trikaya (sku gsum) has been present all along as the Base (gzhi), which is one's original condition (rang sa) to which one returns by way of the practice of vision or Thodgal.

(3) The crystal ball (shel sgong) illustrates that primal awareness is all-penetrating and naked (ye-shes zang-thal gcer-bur), that is, it can become aware of anything and is devoid of conceptual constructions of reality, and the sky (nam-mkha') illustrates that primal awareness equally encompasses everything (ye-shes spyi-blugs su mtshon).

(4) *De nas nang du kha gyu ste rig-pa'i ngo-bo gcer-re lta.* Gazing into empty space with wide-open eyes (cer-re lta) and with a mind freed from discursive thoughts, one comes to see the light of one's own naked awareness (rig-pa rjen-pa). Thus, in order to practice Thodgal, one must first realize Thekchod, or the state of contemplation. Otherwise, one will only come to see one's own conceptual constructions of reality that represent one's impure karmic vision.

(5) *Rang gsal du ye-re gsal-ba bzhin du/ kun-gzhi rig-pa ni sgron-me'i sgo la gang gis kyang smag sgrib dang bral nas/ rang gsal du ye-re gsal-ba yin.* Self-awareness (rang rig) is inherently clear and luminous (rang gsal). Like the flame of a lamp, it not only illuminates the space of the dark room and all the objects contained therein, but it equally illuminates itself.

(6) *gDod nas 'od gsal chen-por lhag gis 'char/ kun-gzhi ni sgron-me'i sgo la gang gis kyang ma byas/ gdod nas rang-'byung 'od-gsal chen-por lhun gyis grub.*

(7) *Kun-gzhi ni sgron-me'i sgo la/ gsal la 'dzin-med du hrig-ger shar.*

(8) *Shel sgong ni phyi nang thyams-cad sgrib-med zang-thal gcer-bu ru sang-nge gnas/ kun-gzhi ni sgron-me'i sgo la/ sgrib g.yogs kyi gos dang bral te/ zang-thal du gcer-re (ce-re) shar.*

(9) *Kun-gzhi ni sgron-me'i sgo la/ phyi nang med-par ye-shes chen-po spyi-blugs su khyab-pa'o.*

(10) *Yul dang rig-pa zung-'brel la mtshon-pa'i dpe/ chu shel nyi-ma mar-me 'od kyi tshul.*

(11) *Rig-pa chu dang 'dra/ sgra 'od zer gsum gyi snang-ba chu 'od dang 'dra ste/ rang-'byung du shar-bar ngo-sprod.*

(12) *Rig-pa nyi-ma dang 'dra la/ snang-ba gsum 'od kyi tshul-lo.*

(13) *Rig-pa mer-me dang 'dra la/ snang-ba gsum 'od kyi tshul du shes-par bya'o.*

(14) *Srid-pa'i sgron-ma nyin snang mtshams su gtad la gnon cing/ ka-ra 'khyor 'jug gi lag-len dang bstun la.*

(15) *Nang dbang-po'i sgron-ma ar la gtad-pa la/ mi bskyod-pagnyis kyis sgron-ma'i sgo mnan te.*

(16) *rLung zin dang-po dgang-ba'i dus su 'od zer sna-tshogs su 'char-bas/ rang 'od rang zer dungo-sprad/ dbugs thung gzhil-ba'i dus su cung-zad klod-pas/ 'od lnga gzha'-tshon ltar shar-bas rang 'od du ngo-sprad-do/ tha-ma glod-pa'i dus su ar la gtad-par/ sngar gyi ngang la bltas-pas/ 'od zer gyi snang-ba rang grol du 'gro-bas/ rig-pa'i rang rtsal du ngo-sprad-pa'o.*

(17) *gSang-ba rig-pa'i sgron-ma gnas la dbab-pa la/ lus gnad lta-stangs rlung sbyor las sogs-pa/ bskor ka yar zhig bsgom du bcugs te/ rig sprin dang ser-bu med-pa'i bar-snang la gtad-pas/ dwangs snyigs phyed gsal mdangs thon-pas/ 'od gsal gyi snang-ba du-ma 'char te/ rang snang sggyu-ma ltar ngo-sprad-par bya'o.*

(18) *Brag dang grog-po las sags-par khus gdab ste/ de'i stong sgra byed med rang shar du byung-ba la ngo-sprad-pa.*

(19) *Mi bskyod gnyis kyi gsang sgor mnan te/ rig-pa'i rang sgra rgyun chags su grags-pa la yid la yid gtad cing rang shar du ngo-sprad-do.*

(20) *gNas kun-gzhi byang-chub kyi sems-nyid khyab bdal chen-po/ phyogs ris med-pa (re) dogs-pa med-pa/ di ni bon-nyid kyi dbyings yin la/ gnas de na rang-rig ka-dag chen-por bzhugs-pa ni/ bon-sku yin te/ bon-sku'i zhing-khams rang chas dang/ gtan du 'grogs kyang zhal ma 'tsho.*

(21) *Yang gnas snying mchong gur smugt-po shel gyi kha-bad-can/ snang gsal 'od kyi gzhal-yas 'di ni/ 'og-min ('da-ba) 'gran-zla med-pa'i zhing-khams yin la/ gnas de la rig-pa'i ye-shes la rtsal sgra 'od zer gsum lhun gyis grub nas/ 'khor 'das thams-cad lhun-grub tu rdzogs-pa 'di ni/ longs-spyod rdzogs-pa'i sku yin-pas.*

(22) *Yang gnas gsum rtsa'i 'khor-lo rnam-pa drug/ yi-ge 'khor-lo rdzogs-pa'i zhing-khams yin/ gnas de na rig-pa'i ye-shes la rtsal drug yul drug las sogs kyi cho-'phrul sna-tshogs su shar-ba 'di ni/ sprul-pa'i sku yin-pas/ sprul-sku'i zhing-khams dang bcas-pa rang snang la gnas kyang ma rtogs-pas/ rigs drug gi snang-ba shar-ro.*

(23) *sNying la rang-rig khong shar deu yod-pa ni/ bon-sku rang chas/ rig-pa'i rang rtsal rtsa'i lam la ma lus-par rdzogs-pas/ rdzogs-sku rang shar/ mig gi sgo la sems kyi cho-'phrul ma lus-par shar-bas/ sprul-sku rang shar du ngo-sprad-pa.*

(24) *Tsi-ta'i klong na rang-rig bon kyi sku/ rtsa'i lam la rang-bzhin rdzogs-pa'I sku/ sgron-ma'i sgo la rang shar sprul-pa'i sku.*

(25) *Yang rig-pa'i ye-shes gdod nas ka-dag rtsa bral du yod ni bon-sku/ lus sems 'brel-ba'i stobs las/ lha sku rigs stobs ye-shes kun 'byung-bas rdzogs-sku/ sgo gsum gyi bya byed sna-tshogs su spyod/ sprul-sku ste.*

(26) *Rang rig-pa'i ye-shes ka-dag bon gyi sku/ lus sems 'brel-ba longs-spyod rdzogs-pa'i sku/ bya byed sdna-tshogs cir yang sprul-pa'i sku.*

(27) *Khong nas rang-'byung ye sangs-rgyas-par gnas/ sbubs nas lhun-grub rdzogs sangs-rgyas-par gnas/ mthong la sgrib-med mngon sangs-rgyas-par gnas.*

(28) *Yang sams-nyid ngo-bo stong-pa ni bon-sku rang chas/rnam-pa gsal-ba ni rdzogs-sku rang chas/ cho-'phrul sna-tshogs su 'char-ba ni sprul-sku rang chas yin te/ stong-pa snang gsal la sku gsum ngo-sprad gsungs.*

(29) *Yang phyi nang gsang-ba yin 'char tshul/ thams-cad ngo-bo nyid du 'dug-pas bon-sku/ rang-bzhin 'gag-med du gnas-pas rdzogs-sku/ cho-'phrul nges-med du 'char-bas sprul-sku.*

(30) *Yang rang gi rnam-rtog 'phra rags thams-cad stong-cha ni bon-sku/ gsal-cha ni rdzogs-sku/ cho-'hrul cha ni sprul-pa'i sku ste.*

(31) *gZhi bem rig 'brel-ba 'di sku gsum rang chas su gnas-pa de gzhi'i sku gsum la/ de ci ltar nyams su blangs-pa la lam gyi skabs su rgyud la shar-ba de lam gyi sku gsum/ de la byung thebs rtsal rdzogs shugs thon/ klong du gyur-pas 'bras-bu'i sku gsum mngon du byung-ba ste.*

(32) *bDag lus zag-pa'i mtshan-ma snang-yor gdos-bcas grol nas/ zag-med mchog gi sku la/ mtshan dang dpe-byad rgyan gdan khri/ zhing-khams dang bcas-pa rdzogs-pa'i sku mngon gyur la/ thugs-nyid spros-bral blo 'das zab-mo'i ngang las/ btang bral med-par bzhugs-pa ni/ bon-sku mngon gyur la.*

(33) *rTsal sgra 'od zer gsum phung-po khams dang skye-mched/ rtsa dang yan-lag sems dang sems 'byung thams-cad/ phyi nang gsang gsum lha tshogs su shar cing.*

(34) *sPyri rtsal sgra 'od zer gsum/ rang-snang rig-pa'i ngo-bor grol zhing.*

(35) *Khyad-par 'od dkar-po grol-ba'i snying-po ltar gsal-ba ni/ 'khrul-med thugs kyi lha kun-snang khyab-pa/ stong-nyid ye-shes rgyud la gsal-ba/ sku-mdog dkar-po/ dbus phyogs de-bzhin nyid kyi rigs 'dzin-pa/ phyag-mtshan 'khor-lo/ bon-sku bder chen ngang la gnas-pa'i phyag mnyan-bzhag 'byung-ba nam-mkha'i klong la dbang bskur-bas/ yum nam-mkha'i lha-mo/ zhe-sdang zil gyis gnon las seng-ge'i gdan/ byams-pa chen-po'i stobs dang ldan-pas/ tsha grang dmyal-ba'i sdub-bsngal 'joms shing don mtshad-pa'o.*

(36) *De bzhin 'od ser-po las 'gyur-med sku yi lha gsal-ba rang-'byung/ me-long ye-shes rgyud la gsal-ba/ sku-mdog ser-po/ shar phyogs g.yung-drung gi rigs 'dzin/ phyag-mtshan gser gyi chags-shing ngam g.yung-drung/ longs-spyod rdzogs-pa'i sku'i brda ru ngo-mtshar*

gyi phyag-rgya thugs-kar bkrol-bas/ 'byung-ba sa'i klong la dbang bskur-ba/ yum sa yi lha-mo/ gti-mug zil gyis gnon-pa'i glang-chen gyi gdan/ ye-shes chen-po'i stobs dang ldan-pas/ gten lkugs byol-song gi don mdzad-pa'o.

(37) *brDa thabs thams-cad rgyas-par ngo-sprad.*

(38) *Phyi ltar gshen-lha rgod-gsas gar-gsas gsas-rje gnam-gsas lnga'am/ nang ltar kun-snang las sogs lnga'o/ gsang-ba ltar gtso-mchog khro-gsas rngam-gsas dbal-gsas gtum-gsas.* These represent the outer, inner, and secret aspects of the same deities.

(39) These eight male Bodhisattvas (ye-gshen brgyad) and eight female Bodhisttvas (ye-sangs brgyad) correspond to the eight aggregates of consciousness (tshogs brgyad) and the eight objects of these consciousnesses.

(40) *rGyu drug gi 'dzin rtog las 'dul-ba'i gshen drug.* Thus, altogether this makes a total of fourty-five peaceful deities. In addition, there are further hosts of deities, performing the functions of increasing prosperity in the outer aspect, causing pacification in the inner aspect, and performing wrathful activites of subjugation in the secret aspect: *Phyi ltar na rgyas-pa'i lha tshogs brgya rtsa brgyad/ nang ltar na zhi-ba'i lha tshogs zhe lnga/ gsang-ba ltar na khro-bo khro-mo'i lha tshogs brgyad cu rtsa drug las sogs kyang.*

(41) The interlaced network of illusions (sgyu-'phrul draw-ba) refers to the cycle of Peaceful and Wrathful Deities (zhi khro lha tshogs) as found, for example, in the Tibetan Book of the Dead (bar-grol thos-grol). The principal Bonpo source for this cycle is the Tantra known as the *Khro-bo dbang-chen.* The chief deity in the cycle is Tsochok Khagying (gtso-mchog mkha'-'gying), corresponding to Chemchok Heruka in the Nyingmapa tradition.

(42) *De ltar-ba'i lha tshogs la/ yab yum du 'byung-ba/ thabs shes gsal stong las sogs zung 'brel du gnas-pa'i don/ gTso 'khor du byung-ba ni/ sems dang sems 'byung gi grol stobs kyi khyad-par dang/ phyi nang gsang gsum du shar-ba ni.*

(43) *Las bzhi'i thabs kyis 'gro-ba 'dren-pa/ sku gsung thugs kyi yon-tan dang ldan-pa ni/ sku gsum gyi bdag-nyid du ye nas bzhugs-pa'i don dang.* The four magical activites are pacifying (zhi-ba'i phrin-las), increasing or enriching (rgyas-pa'i phrin-las), enchanting or magnetizing (dbang gi phrin-las), and fierce or wrathful actions (drag-po'i phrin-las).

(44) See Reynolds, *Selections from the Bonpo Book of the Dead*, ibid. See Shardza Rinpoche, *mTshan snang ar-gtad gdams-pa 'od-gsal 'khor-yug*, "The Horizon of the Clear Light, being the Instructions for Fixation on the Visions that appear in the Darkess (of the Dark Retreat)," pp. 371–415, in *rDzogs-pa chen-po sku gsum rang shar gyi khrid gdams skor*, New Delhi 1974. See the transcript of Lopon Tenzin Namdak's commentary in Reynolds, *The Instructions of Shardza Rinpoche for the Practice of Vision and the Dark Retreat*, Bonpo Translation Project, Amsterdam 1992.

(45) *Ye-shes kyis mkhyen tshul ni/ ye-shes la rang-'byung rig-pa'i ye-shes de nyid mngon du gyur/ de la byung thebs rtsal rdzogs shugs thon-pa'i 'char tshul las/ stong-nyid mnyam-nyid bya-ba nan-tan sor-rtog me-long ye-shes dang lnga ste/ don-dam ci lta-ba mkhyen-pa dang kun-rdzob ci snyed-pa mkhyen-pa/ ye-shes de yi byed-pas shes bya'i gnas-lugs sil-bur gzigs-pa'i ye-shes brgyal khri bzhi stong ste.*

(46) *De yang sems-can gyi dus kyi rtog tshogs gnas grol-ba la shar dang/ ting-nge 'dzin gyi sgo 'bum phrag mtha'-yas-pa thugs la gsal-ba ni/ rgyu'i dus kyi bsam dran sna-tshogs grol-ba la shar/ 'od zer gyi 'phro 'du.*

(47) *Thugs-rje che-ba/ thabs la mkhas-pa/ thams-cad mkhyen-pa gsum gyis.*

(48) *Nga ni nyi bzhin kun la snyoms-pa la/ chu bzhin rgyun mi 'chad.*

(49) *Shes-bya'i gnas-lugs mi mkhyen-pa..... mkhyen-pa'i ye-shes gcig gis ni/ shes-bya'i gnas-lugs gsal-bar ston.*

(50) *Gang-zag las dang skal-pa dang ldan-pa.*

(51) *mKha'-'gro bka' skyong rnams kyis bka' chad-pas gcod-par byed-do.*

(52) *Lag-len go-rim.*

Part TWO

Translation of the Seven-fold Cycle of the Clear Light

Preface

I translated the present text on the dark retreat practice according to the Zhang-zhung Nyan-gyud shortly before meeting Lopon Tenzin Namdak in person for the first time at Tsegyalgar in Conway, Massachusetts, in the spring of 1989. Over the course of two afternoons, the Lopon was kind enough to answer my questions regarding the translation of this text and to give certain instruction in terms of the practice. Subsequently, at Bischofshofen in Austria, the Lopon gave further instructions pertaining to the dark retreat, this time those according to Shardza Rinpoche. However, the dark retreat described by Shardza Rinpoche was according to the cycle of the *bsGrags-pa skor gsum*, rather than the Zhang-zhung Nyan-gyud. I also transcribed the Lopon's oral commentary on that text and published it separately in the Bonpo Translation Project as *The Instructions of Shardza Rinpoche for the Practice of Vision and the Dark Retreat* (Amsterdam 1992). Futhermore, the Shardza text relies much more heavily on the Tantric practices of visualization than the text we have here, where matters are kept much more simple and direct, as suits Dzogchen generally. For this reason, the practitioner will find the dark retreat from the Zhang-zhung Nyan-gyud a bit easier and simpler.

My thanks are extended first of all to the Lopon for transmitting and explaining these dark retreat texts. And secondly I would like to thank all those involved in organizing the retreats at Conway and Bischofshoven. It is the hope of the translator that all who may enter into this retreat shall find the light in the darkness.

San Diego
July 1997

Second Preface

Due to the vicissitudes of Samsara, it has taken me sometime to bring into print this translation of the Seven-fold Cycle of the Clear light. In the meantime, a number of Western practitioners have made a dark retreat for various lengths of time, and even the full forty-nine days, at Triten Norbutse Monastery in Nepal and also elsewhere, following the methods outlined in this text. It continues to be the translator's hope that the work presented here will provide both inspiration and practical help to practitioners of the Dharma who in the future choose to embark upon the dark retreat.

MU-TSUG SMAR-RO!

John Mydhin Reynolds
San Diego
September 2000

Chapter One

Introduction

The text presented in translation here outlines the practice of the forty-nine day dark retreat according the Bonpo system of Dzogchen known as the Zhang-zhung Nyan-gyud, the Oral Transmission from the country of Zhang-zhung (zhang-zhung snyan-rgyud). The text used for the translation is found in the *sNyan-rgyud nam-mkha' 'phrul mdzog drang nges skor dang Zhang-zhung snyan-rgyud skor*, Tibetan Bonpo Monastic Centre, New Delhi 1972 (ff. 714–722). Here the title in Tibetan reads *rDzogs-pa chen-po zhang-zhung snyan-brgyud las gcig brgyud 'od-gsal bdun skor zhes bya-ba bzhugs-so*. The meaning of this title will be discussed below in the Commentary to the translation. The text belongs to the cycle of Dzogchen teachings from Zhang-zhung in Northern Tibet, which, as the title *snyan-rgyud* suggests, was originally an oral teaching transmitted in private from master to disciple. However, according to the Zhang-zhung tradition, the Dzogchen precepts were first written down in the eighth century by Gyerpung Nangzher Lodpo in the Zhang-zhung language, but mainly in the tenth century by Kundul Orgom (Kun-'dul 'or-sgom) and Yangton Chenpo Sherab Gyaltsan (Yang-ston chen-po Shes-rab rgyal-mtshan). A practice manual for these practices, which included the dark retreat (mun-mtshams), was composed sometime in the twelth century by Druchen Gyalwa Yungdrung (Bru-chen rgyal-ba g.yung-drung) and entitled the *sNyan-rgyud rgyal-ba phyag-khrid*. At a later time, the present text was included with that collection as a kind of appendix, although, according to Lopon Tenzin Namdak, it was not composed by Druchen himself, but by some other author.

As is also the case with the vision practice of the Clear Light ('od-gsal), elsewhere known in the Buddhist tradition of the Nyingmapa school of Tibet as Thodgal (thod-rgal), the principle in dark retreat practice is not visualization (dmigs-pa), the transforming of impure karmic vision into pure vision as is done in Tantric sadhana, but simply the practice of vision as such. This is because visualization is something created by the mind. With visualization, the discursive mind is still operating, still thinking, whereas although in terms of vision (snang-ba), the senses continue to be open and operating, in the condition known as clarity (gsal-ba), but the usual mental processes of thinking, perceiving, and conceiving have all been suspended or transcended because one has entered into the state of contemplation. With the practice of Dzogchen, one finds oneself beyond the mind in the state of contemplation (mnyam-bzhag, ting-nge 'dzin), where the practitioner has entered into and remains in the Natural State of the Nature of Mind (sems-nyid gnas-lugs). The condition of the Nature of Mind is called Rigpa or intrinsic awareness and may be compared to the innate capacity of the mirror to reflect whatever may be set before it. In this case, metaphorically speaking, the practitioner, while in the state of contemplation, abides in the condition of the mirror rather than that of the reflections. This state of contemplation is elsewhere in the Nyingmapa tradition called Trekchod (khregs-chod), the releasing (chod) of all tensions and rigidities (khregs-pa), for which reason Dzogchen is also known as *lhod-pa chen-po*, the state of total relaxation. Indeed, during the course of the dark retreat one comes to relax totally. However, the terms Trekchod and Thodgal do not actually occur in the texts belonging to the Zhang-zhung Nyan-gyud cycle, even though this cycle of Dzogchen teachings from Zhang-zhung is classified as Upadesha (man-ngag gi sde) among the three classes of Dzogchen teachings.

In general, among all the spiritual paths to enlightenment, Dzogchen represents the Path of Self-Liberation (grol lam) in contrast to the methods of Sutra and Tantra. Therefore, the principal practice (dngos-gzhi) in Dzogchen is always that of contemplation, or simply remaining in the Natural State. As said above, contemplation is a state that transcends and lies beyond the mind (sems) and its manifold operations and reality-creating processes. In Dzogchen, a clear distinction is made between, on the one hand, mind (sems) and the thought process (blo), which are conditioned by karma and circumstances, and which exist in time and, on the other hand, the Nature of Mind which is timeless and unconditioned. The latter is the source and matrix of the former, like a mother and her many children, and both are present in one's everyday experience, although the Nature of Mind and its capacity for Rigpa, or illumination or awareness, normally goes unnoticed, just as when the presence of the sun in the sky is concealed by a thick layer of clouds. Nevertheless, the sun is present there all of time in the sky for, otherwise, the world would be in total darkness.

The practice of contemplation contrasts with the methodology of the Tantras that represents the Path of Transformation (sgyur lam) where, by way of visualization practice during long retreats, the impure karmic vision of Samsara is purified and transformed into the pure vision of Nirvana with its mandalas (dkyil-'khor) and meditation deities (yi-dam lha). But according to the view of Dzogchen, there is no need to transform anything because everything that manifests, or appears to vision, or arises into consciousness, is complete and perfect just as it is. It represents spontaneous self-perfection just as it is because it is a manifestation of the inherent energy of the Nature of Mind. On the one hand, the Nature of Mind represents Shunyata, the state of emptiness, what is called primordial purity (ka-dag), but on the other hand, at the same time, it is pregnant with an inexhaustible supply of creative energy (rtsal). This represents a pure potentiality for the visible manifestation of all possible forms, all possible universes and all possible lifetimes. This principle is called spontaneous perfection (lhun-grub). It seems paradoxical that the void, an apparent nothing, is, at the same time, a source of inexhaustible energy that is inherent in it. But such is the case. Shunyata (stong-pa nyid), in terms of the Dzogchen teachings, is not mere nothing or absence.

Whatever comes into manifestation within consciousness, whether impure or pure, whether the visions of Samsara or of Nirvana, is in fact a manifestation of the innate inexhaustible energy of the Nature of Mind (sems kyi snang-ba). When one speaks of the Nature of Mind, this does not refer to some substance such as a mind-stuff, or an isolated atomic entity called a self (bdag). When one looks into oneself and observes the arising, the abiding, and the dissolving of thoughts, one does not discover any such entity. What is found there within oneself is an unceasing flow and flux like that of a river, a veritable stream of consciousness. And all of the contents of consciousness, whatever phenomena may occur or arise in this stream of consciousness, are conditioned, impermanent, insubstantial, that is, lacking in any inherent existence. Their nature is empty. So one may characterize the Nature of Mind as the state of Shunyata, or emptiness. But as said, this "emptiness" is not a mere absence or nothingness because the manifestations of phenomena are constantly and continuously arising out of it, just as waves continuously arise out of the sea. They represent the continuous and unobstructed manifestations of the inherent energy (rang rtsal) of the Nature of Mind. But this does not mean that the Nature of Mind in its Natural State merely remains blank and devoid of thoughts. The goal of Dzogchen is not just a condition of being without thoughts (mi rtog-pa). That is simply an experience (nyams) and it is not what is meant by Rigpa, or intrinsic awareness. The Nature of Mind is not only emptiness, which is primordial purity (ka-dag), but it is equally characterized by a luminous clarity (gsal-ba) and intrinsic awareness (rig-pa). In terms of this Primordial State that is the Base, these two, emptiness and clarity, have been inseparable from the very beginning (ye nas gsal stong dbyer-med) and never otherwise. These two sides or aspects of a single non-dual reality are only distinguished for purposes of discourse and human understanding. Moreover, the Nature of Mind of the individual is not inert or passive like a lump of clay, but dynamic and creative; it is natural for thoughts and appearances to arise continuously and incessantly from out of the infinite pure potentiality of the Nature of the Mind. Furthermore, this process of continuous manifestation is unobstructed and unceasing (ma 'gag-pa).

And by entering into a prolonged dark retreat, entering into a sensory deprivation experience and temporarily suspending the normal operations of the mind, one comes to experience this in a very direct way and, furthermore, one comes to understand this in an experiential rather than a theoretical way. For this reason, in the *Phyag-khrid* of Druchen, the practice of the dark retreat is presented before the practices of the sky and the sunlight. However, one must first become proficient and somewhat stable in the practice of contemplation through fixation on the white letter "A" and by other appropriate means known as Semdzin (sems-'dzin), or fixating the mind. If one is not stable in contemplation first, the dark retreat will be of little use, of little more use than watching television in a dark room, or engaging in daydream fantasies.

When one enters into the dark retreat, a condition of nearly total sensory deprivation, at least in terms of vision, and when there is no interference from the functional mind or Manas (yid) that creates thoughts and conceptions, and when the obscurations due to karma have been sufficiently purified, like clearing away the clouds in the sky, then the visions that spontaneously arise will be expressions of purity. That is to say, they are pure visions rather than impure karmic visions. But in order for this to occur, one must enter into a condition of total relaxation of body, energy, and mind and find oneself in a alert state of contemplation that is beyond the mind.

How do these visions arise in the total darkness that is the medium for their manifestation? Dzogchen texts speak of four or six lamps (sgron-ma drug) that describe this process. Generally, lamps represent sources of light, but here "lamp" is a metaphor. The light spoken of here is not so much ordinary physical light, such as may come an electric bulb, but a metaphysical light – the light of awareness that illuminates our world. The source for this light of awareness known as Rigpa is, metaphorically speaking, the physical heart (tsi-ta) of the individual. This inner light (nang 'od), the light of awareness, resides in the hollow space inside the heart, which is said to resemble a maroon-colored carnelian stone decorated with white crystals of fat. Then connecting the physical heart to the eyeballs is a hollow translucent channel called kati, or the smooth white nerve ('jam dkar rtsa), that rises up from the heart and proceeding into the brain it divides into two and enters into the eyeballs. This inner light of awareness proceeds from the hollow space in the heart, moving upward through the kati channel, to the two eyes which are like lenses to focus this light. The two eyes are the gateways for the emergence into outer space of this inner light of awareness. Thus, this light and the images that appear in this light, are actually something internal, residing in the interior space of the heart, but here they manifest in the empty space in front of oneself. The light from the lamp of the heart is projected upward through the hollow translucent kati channel and out through the lenses of the two eyes into the space in front, much like one is watching a cinema show. This process may be compared to a magic lantern or a cinema projector. However, here the medium for the manifestation of the images is not a flat two-dimension screen on a wall in the cinema theatre, but they are projected into empty space as three-dimensional images. In other words, these visions experienced in the dark retreat are holographic images. And for this reason, even in a retreat in total darkness, the visions arise in the empty space in front of the eyes of the practitioner.

But this is not like a torch or flashlight suddenly illuminating the objects in a dark room. The objects that appear are not really outside oneself. They are holographic projections, structures of light, projections of what exist inside oneself, within one's own unconsciousness psyche. In the dark retreat one is totally alone, alone in a dark room with one's own mind. Therefore, sufficient preparation before hand is required, particularly the practice of contemplation. The prolonged dark retreat is not something to be jumped into prematurely.

Entering into a dark retreat is entering into an intense sensory deprivation experience for more than a month. So, it is only natural that visions will arise in the darkness. This may not occur at first because the mind is still tense and active, functioning discursively in its usual mode of operation. When visions do arise they are more likely to be worldly and of a karmic nature. But with the regular practice of contemplation, both previously as preparation, and then in the dark retreat itself as the principal practice, gradually the mind will relax its tensions until its usual and habitual functions fall into abeyance. This allows material from below the surface of consciousness, normally suppressed or forgotten, to emerge and be projected out into the space of the dark retreat room as visions. At first these visions will be most definitely the products of the individual's impure karmic vision. Therefore, it is of crucial importance that one remain firmly settled in contemplation, or the Natural State. When visions do come, they should not be judged as good or bad, beautiful or ugly, high or low; one must remain without any attachment (zhen-pa med-pa) with regard to them and not elaborate them in terms of thoughts. They are just what they are and one lets them be.

Furthermore, the dark retreat in terms of Dzogchen is not an exercise in dream interpretation, nor even vision interpretation. Interpretation entails elaboration by means of thoughts. The discursive mind is functioning and one is no longer in the Natural State, or contemplation. As soon as one starts thinking, one has lost the Natural State, which is simply a matter of being present and aware without deliberate thought or judgment. When the intellect intervenes and one begins to analyze and interpret and evaluate the visions, one will become distracted and fall out of the Natural State. The point is not to assign this or that meaning or interpretation to a vision, but just to it be in a state of awareness and presence, like a mirror reflecting images. Interpretation is a secondary process, occurring at the level of the operations of the mind. But here in the dark retreat one simply lets the visions present themselves and nothing more. The visions arise and dissolve again spontaneously without interference from the mind or thought processes. Like the nature of the mirror remaining unaffected by whatever reflections may appear in it, so, in the same way, the practitioner in the dark retreat is unaffected by whatever visions arise in the darkness and simply remains in the Natural State.

But if one pursues and follows after these visions, one is no longer remaining in the Natural State and one will come to spoil one's dark retreat. The process of realization is like pressing sesame seeds. The oil comes naturally. If one remains in contemplation in total darkness, without thinking about or judging the visions that arise, they will continue to come naturally and spontaneously without effort. These visions arise out of the Natural State of the Nature of Mind and they will dissolve again into it. It does not matter whether these visions are beautiful or ugly, they are just visions, visible expressions of energy. They arise out of the Natural State; they are illusions like mirages seen on the horizon; they are just visible manifestations of the energy of the Nature of Mind (sems kyi snang-ba).

One discovers that this is true of the visions that occur in the dark retreat. And it is not difficult to understand that the same is true of the visions that one experiences every night in the dream state. Dreams are equally illusions and manifestations of energy. But then one needs to go further and discover that this is true as well of one's normal visions of reality experienced in everyday life. These visions of our everyday concrete reality, experienced in our waking state of consciousness, equally arise out of the Nature of Mind and dissolve again into the Nature of Mind. Just as one wakes up in the morning and realizes that one has been dreaming, so when one dies, one wakes up from the extended dream we call our everyday reality. Reality consists of vision; it appears to be stable, firm, real, solid, opaque, and substantial. It appears to be really out there, but it is only vision. It is only space and light. This is what the mind actually senses, actually knows, not abstractions like things and substances that we think are real and enduring. But the dark retreat, indeed, vision practice in general, as well as dream practice, can dissolve this habit of thought. This is the point of vision practice – to breakdown our conventional notions of what constitutes reality and to take us beyond our limitations.

Even though they are seemingly real and solid and opaque, these visions in everyday life are empty appearances lacking any inherent existence. They are like rainbows in the sky. The methods of philosophical analysis of Madhyamaka found in the Sutra system reveals that their nature is Shunyata. But here matters are only considered on the emptiness side (stong-cha). Madhyamaka philosophy of the Sutra system does not take into consideration spontaneous perfection (lhun-grub) on the clarity or manifestation side (gsal-cha). Indeed, in the perspective of Dzogchen, the Nature of Mind is empty and lacking any inherent existence, yet this Shunyata is not a mere nothingness. Shunyata is pregnant with all possibilities; there is the potentiality for all possible visions to manifest out of it spontaneously. Therefore, Dzogchen goes beyond the discourse of Madhyamaka, asserting that the Natural State of the Nature of Mind is both Shunyata or primordial purity (ka-dag), and energy continuously manifesting in spontaneous perfection (lhun-grub). In the dark retreat one comes to understand that inseparability experientially.

What is the source of this inexhaustible energy? These visions arise spontaneously just as oil comes forth when one presses mustard seeds. But if one squeezes sand, no oil will come forth. Although initially no oil is visible, when the mustard seeds are pressed, this oil manifests as spontaneously perfected. So when one practices contemplation, all possible visions, even all possible universes and all possible lifetimes, may arise as visions out of the Natural State. These visions are spontaneously produced and effortlessly perfected because the Nature of Mind, in and of itself, is outside the temporal and the causal sequence, even though it represents the matrix and context of time and causality. All events and all lifetimes, from the infinite past and equally of the infinite future, exist simultaneously in the Nature of Mind. Because it is the Primordial Base (ye gzhi), all events or visions of Samsara and Nirvana unfold out of this single Nature of Mind of the individual. Just as the mirror has the capacity to reflect the image of whatever is set before it, so the Nature of the Mind has the capacity to be aware of whatever manifestation may arise. But the Nature of Mind is not simply a mirror that reflects; equally it is the source of the energy that comes into visible manifestation. So it is also like a crystal placed in the sunlight, refracting this light and producing the rainbows seen on the wall. But the Nature of Mind is more than a crystal. Its light does not come from some outside source like the sun; its light is internal. But in saying it is like a mirror or like a crystal, or again like the sky or like the sun, we are employing examples (dpe) and none of them are perfect. However, they can contribute to understanding the real meaning of the Nature of Mind.

Generally speaking, the visions may be classified as of two kinds, the pure and the impure. Impure visions arise from the individual's past karma and give rise to the karmic visions of the various destinies of rebirth in Samsara. It is within this labyrinth of Samsaric vision that we habitually find ourselves. These visions are called impure because they are engendered by ignorance or a lack of understanding and awareness and because they are mixed up with the kleshas, or negative emotions, tied up with the notion of an ego. Pure visions, on the contrary, arise out of understanding and awareness and are free of the pollutions and distortions of the kleshas. They are the archetypal images of the Buddhas and the Buddha realms arising in the recognition of the Clear Light. These pure visions (dag snang), which are spontaneous manifestations of enlightened awareness also called Thodgal visions, must be distinguished from impure karmic visions (ma dag las snang) that cloud consciousness and which arise from memories and karmic traces. These latter are Samsaric and conditioned in nature.

Practicing in the dark retreat with total darkness, or with the empty open spaces of the sky free of clouds, or with the light of the rays of the sun in the early morning shortly after sun rise, only represent the secondary causes for the development of these Thodgal visions, or visions of the Clear Light. The actual cause of the Natural State is the practice of contemplation. In addition to total darkness, the practitioner may use other supports, which are secondary causes such as sunlight, moonlight, lamp light and so on. But this should only be done in a safe and comfortable fashion, never looking directly into the source of the light, especially in the case of the sun. Rather, one should look one cubit below or to the side of the orb of the sun and never when the sun becomes bright later in the morning. One should also look a little below the moon or to the side. And, in the same way, look to the side of a candle or the flame of a butter lamp.

Why does one spend seven weeks or forty-nine days in a retreat in total darkness? Just as does dream practice, vision practice in the dark retreat serves as a preparation for the Bardo experience after death. Just as one experiences sensory deprivation in the dark retreat and during sleep, even though one remains encased within the physical body, when the senses are withdrawn from their external objects and the Manas, or discursive mind (yid), ceases temporarily to function in its normal fashion, the contents of the unconscious psyche rise to consciousness as visions. This occurs in dreams and it occurs also after death in the Bardo of Existence. But these visions are karmic and do not represent enlightened awareness. During the process of dying, known as the Chikhai Bardo, when the external breathing has ceased and one is pronounced dead, one's Namshe or consciousness (rnam-shes), finds itself deprived of the physical body. Nevertheless, consciousness continues and this consciousness finds itself in a subtle or mind-made body, where the mind and the senses are still operative. For some days the deceased consciousness sees and knows what is going on around it and what is being done to its corpse. But after three or four days when the internal breathing ceases, that is to say, the circulation of psychic energy, then the subtle body that is the vehicle for consciousness, as well as the personality begin to disintegrate. Then the second death approaches, the moment of true psychic death or dissolution of consciousness. One experiences the white dawn and the red dawn and finally the moment of eclipse or total black-out when dualistic consciousness is dissolved and extinguished. Then there subsists only the state of Shunyata. This is called the Bardo of Emptiness and it represents the culmination of the process of dying.

At this moment, one experiences a total sensory deprivation because neither the senses nor the mind are functioning. One finds oneself in a condition of total and complete nakedness with neither a mind nor a body. One is simply suspended in space. One is simply Shunyata itself. All the clouds have vanished from the sky. This allows the space and the clarity for the manifestation of one's own Buddha nature, one's Nature of Mind. What manifests in this state of Shunyata is the Clear Light. This is like seeing one's face in the mirror. This Clear Light is one's own intrinsic awareness, or Rigpa, which represents the inherent quality of the Natural State of the Nature of Mind. Just at this moment, the border or Boundary (so-mtshams) between dying and the onset of the Bardo experience, the moment when the Clear Light manifests in emptiness, one has the maximal opportunity to attain enlightenment and liberation from Samsara. If one recognizes the Clear Light and understands that it is the manifestation of one's own Nature of Mind, one becomes liberated. If not, then a spontaneously born ignorance arises that is dualistic in its operation, giving rise to the dichotomy of subject and object. One does not intuitively understand that this Clear Light is oneself, but one comes to feel it is something out there in space separate from oneself. Then the mind comes once more into operation at a subtle level and the archetypal images of the Peaceful and Wrathful Deities spontaneously manifest within the chaos of colors forming in this Clear Light. Still, if one has done meditation practice as preparation during one's previous lifetime, one will have the opportunity to recognize these pure visions as manifestations of one's Nature of Mind and one may liberate at this point. If not, these images become more active and energetic and appear as the Wrathful Deities. Still, even at this time, one may recognize their nature and liberate. But if the individual has not been prepared by previous meditation practice, these visions in the Clear Light flash by in less than an instant, like a flash of lightening seen on the distant horizon in the middle of the night. The Clear Light having faded, the gross discursive mind comes back into operation and memories re-awaken. One finds oneself again inhabiting a mind-made body in which the subtle senses are fully operational. But instead of finding oneself in the material conditions that once surrounded one's corpse, one discovers oneself wandering in a visionary symbolic landscape where one's own past karma rises up before one in visual manifestations much as in dreams. Having departed from the Bardo of the Clear Light of Reality, one finds oneself in the Bardo of Existence, the process leading to rebirth. Lacking understanding and the presence of awareness, one becomes distracted by these visions, thinking them to be real, and one wanders lost in this expanding holographic landscape. This landscape develops, proliferates, and transforms as one's memories and karmic traces germinate and re-awaken. Literally, one becomes lost in a labyrinth of the visions of one's own karma. Then propelled by the winds of karma, like a dried leaf blown about in the empty streets by the autumn winds, one is driven relentlessly toward a new rebirth within Samsara.

However, time in the Bardo is not the same as time experienced in the waking state of consciousness; it is more similar to time experienced in dream. But the duration of the Bardo experience is symbolically forty-nine days. For a particular individual, the Bardo may last for only a moment, or it may last for centuries, or even millennia, before that stream of consciousness again takes up embodiment. It all depends on one's individual karma. But seven and forty-nine are ultimately related to the Old Babylonian and to the Hermetic and Gnostic systems of symbolism, not only to the seven days of creation, but to the septenary phases of the ascent of the soul into the heavens and the descent of the soul into reincarnation on earth. In the Gnostic perspective, the soul must journey in its descent through the seven planetary spheres, acquiring as a vestment within each sphere a specific passion, or vice, or klesha. In the case of the Tibetan Books of the Dead, this acquiring of vestments and the encounter with the seven Archons or deities embodying these passions and, who rule the seven planetary spheres above the earth, are presented as the sequential manifestations of the Wrathful Deities. For this reason, a practitioner often receives an initiation into the mysteries or practices of the *Zhi-khro*, or the Peaceful and Wrathful Deities, before engaging in the forty-nine day dark retreat. However, in the case of this dark retreat from the Zhang-zhung tradition, matters are expounded much more simply from the Dzogchen point of view without recourse to the complexities of Tantric practice.

Outline of the Text

"The Seven-fold Cycle of the Clear Light", from the Single Transmission Oral Tradition of Zhang-zhung for the Great Perfection Teachings [rDzogs-pa chen-po zhang-zhung snyan-brgyud gcig rgyud 'od-gsal bdun bskor].

PART ONE: The Yoga of the Psychic Channels and the Vital Winds

The instructions (in general) concerning the essential points for the yoga of the psychic channels and vital winds [rtsa-rlung], according to the Oral Transmission Lineage from Zhang-zhung for the Great Perfection Teachings which belongs to the Secret Mantra system [gsang-sngags zab-mo rdzogs-chen snyan rgyud kyi rtsa rlung gnad kyi gdams-pa 'di rnams] are presented below:

I. The Basic Body Posture for Training the Psychic Channels

The essential points for the basic body position and the yantra exercises for training the psychic channels [rtsa 'dul gyi bca' gzhi 'khrul-'khor gyi gnad] are as follows:

A. Balancing the Body and the Mind in Equipoise

First, there is the balancing of the body and the mind in equipoise [lus sems mnyam-par bzhag-pa]:

A1. The Body Posture possessing Five Aspects

Putting the body in the mudra or posture possessing the five aspects [lus cha-lugs lnga ldan gyi phyag-rgya bca'], which are as follows:

(1) The legs are held in a cross-legged position [zhabs skyil-krung bca'],
(2) The hands are kept in the samadhi mudra, the gesture of equipoise [phyag mnyam-gzhag],
(3) The spinal column is held straight like an arrow [sgal-tshigs mda' ltar bsrang],
(4) The neck is pulled back like an iron hook [mgrin-pa lcags-kyu ltar bkugs], and
(5) The shoulders are hunched like the wings of a vulture that soars in the sky [dpung-pa rgod (bya) gshogs lding-ba].

Furthermore, the tongue floats and does not touch the palate [ljags ya-rkang la ma reg rtsam]. Moreover, there is a space between the teeth of the mouth like one is subtly sounding the letter "A" [kha so bar-du yi-ge A phra-mo mthar tsam bya].

A2. Visualizing the Psychic Channels

The essential point of the channels that are visualized [bskyed-pa rtsa'i gnad], namely, one clearly visualizes the three psychic channels:

(1) The right channel is white,
(2) The left channel is red, and
(3) The central channel is azure colored.

B. Expelling the Stale Air

Second, there is the training the breath and the mind so that they function properly [rlung sems gcun la bor-ba].

II. Securing the Boundaries

Then there are the essential points of the bodily position and the yantra exercises that secure the boundaries, thereby dispelling disturbances [mtshams-bcad bca' gzhi 'khrul-'khor gyi gnad]. Herein there is

(1) The balancing of the body and the mind in equipoise [lus sems mnyam-par bzhag-pa],
(2) The training the breath and the mind so that they function properly [rlung dang sems gcun la bor-ba], and
(3) The training of the psychic channals and integrating this with the breathing [rtsa 'dul rlung sbrugs], and so on – these are all accomplished as described above [gong ltar].

A. The Posture of the Wrathful Deity

First, there is the essential point of the body that represents the posture [bca'-ba lus kyi gnad], namely, one assumes the essential point of the body which represents the haughty posture of a wrathful deity [khro-bo'i 'gying stabs gyi lus gnad bca'].

B. The Visualizing of the Three Psychic Channels

Second, there is the essential point of the psychic channels that are to be visualized [bskyed-pa rtsa yi gnad], namely, one clearly visualizes the three channels as described previously [rtsa gsum gong ltar gsal-gdab].

C. The Breathing

Third, there is the essential point of the breath that is to be held [bzung-ba rlung gi gnad], namely, one expels the stale air nine times by way of a cleansing [rlung-ro sangs kyis 'bud].

D. The Visualization of the Bindus and Syllables

Fourth, there is the essential point of the bindus (droplets of light) that are to be meditated upon [bsgom-pa thig-le'i gnad], in terms of the visualization described.

III. The Perfection Process [rdzogs-rim]
Colophon

This little text, which is concerned with securing the boundaries against disturbances in terms of the Clear Light practice, was explained by the author [bdag khrid 'od-gsal gyi mtshams-bcad yig chung].

PART TWO: The Practices for the Seven Weeks

Here is contained "(The Practices in particular for) the Psychic Channals, the Vital Winds, and the Yantra Exercises for the Clear Light," according to the Oral Transmission from Zhang-zhung [zhang-zhung snyan-rgyud rtsa rlung 'khrul-'khor 'od-gsal bzhugs-so].

Introduction

Here are the essential points concerning the psychic channels, the vital winds, and the yantra exercises (or the positions and the movements of the body) [rtsa rlung 'khrul-'khor gnad 'di] for developing the visualizations in accordance with the root text of the Oral Transmission [snyan-rgyud rtsa-ba'i dmigs-pa], connected with the visualizations from the Seven-fold Cycle of the Clear Light ['od-gsal bdun skor dmigs-pa], (that is to say, there is one particular visualization for the beginning of each meditation session during each of the seven weeks spent inside the dark retreat).

I. The First Week

As for the first week, with respect to the essential points of the basic posture and the yantra exercises known as "the dust specks in the sun light" [nyi rdul-ma'i bca' gzhi 'khrul-'khor gyi gnad], these are as follows:

(1) The balancing of the body and mind in equipoise [lus sems mnyam-par bzhag-pa],

(2) The training of the breath so that it functions properly [rlung gcun la bor-ba], and

(3) The training of the channals by way of the nine breathings [rlung rtsa 'dul dgu phrug]. These are in agreement with what was described above [gong ltar mthun].

(4) The essential point of the body that is the position assumed [bca'-ba lus kyi gnad].

(5) The essential point of the channels to be visualized [bskyed-pa rtsa'i gnad].

(6) The essential point of the breath that is to be held [gzung-ba rlung gi gnad].

(7) The essential point of the bindus on which one meditates [bsgom-pa thig-le'i gnad].

II. The Second Week

As for the second week, the basic posture is known as "the rays of the sun" [bdun gnyis-pa nyi zer-ma'i bca' gzhi]. There are the following considerations:

(1) The essential point of the body that is the position assumed [bca'-ba lus kyi gnad],

(2) The essential point of the channels that are to be visualized [bskyed-pa rtsa'i gnad], and

(3) The essential point of the breath that is to be held [gzung-ba rlung gi gnad].
These three are the same as above.

(4) The essential point of the bindus on which one meditates [bsgom-pa thig-le'i gnad]. This visualization is different from the above.

III. The Third Week

As for the third week, the essential points for the basic position and the yantra exercises of the right white channel and the left red channel [bdun gsum-pa rtsa g.yas dkar g.yon dmar gyi 'khrul-'khor bca' gzhi'i gnad] are as follows:

(1) The essential point of the body that is the position assumed [bca'-ba lus kyi gnad],

(2) The essential point of the channels that are to be visualized [bskyed-pa rtsa'i gnad], and

(3) The essential point of the breath that is to be held [gzung-ba rlung gi gnad].
These three are the same as above.

(4) The essential point of the bindus on which one meditates [bsgom-pa thig-le'i gnad]. This visualization is different from the above.

IV. The Fourth Week

As for the fourth week, the essential points concerning the yantra exercises of the basic position of one's own azure-colored central channel [bdun bzhi-pa la dbus mthing rang gi bca' gzhi 'khrul-'khor gyi gnad] are as follows:

(1) The essential point of the body that is the position assumed [bca'-ba lus kyi gnad],

(2) The essential point of the channels that are to be visualized [bskyed-pa rtsa'i gnad], and

(3) The essential point of the breath that is to be held [gzung-ba rlung gi gnad].
These three are the same as above.

(4) The essential point of the bindus on which one meditates [bsgom-pa thig-le'i gnad]. This visualization is different from the above.

V. The Fifth Week

As for the fifth week, the essential points for the basic position and the yantra exercises that are like the rainbow [bdun lnga-pa la gzha'-tshon-ma'i bca' gzhi 'khrul-'khor gyi gnad] are as follows:

(1) The essential point of the body that is the position assumed [bca'-ba lus kyi gnad],

(2) The essential point of the channels that are to be visualized [bskyed-pa rtsa'i gnad]., and

(3) The essential point of the breath that is to be held [gzung-ba rlung gi gnad].
These three are the same as above.

(4) The essential point of the bindus on which one meditates [bsgom-pa thig-le'i gnad]. This visualization is different from the above.

VI. The Sixth Week

As for the sixth week, the essential points for the basic position and the yantra exercises where the HUM abides, the A emanates, and the OM integrates [bdun drug-pa la gnas-pa HUM spros-pa A bsdu-ba OM 'khrul-'khor gyi bca' gzhi'i gnad] are as follows:

(1) The essential point of the body that is the position assumed [bca'-ba lus kyi gnad]. This is the same as above.
(2) The essential point of the channals that are to be visualized [bskyed-pa rtsa'i gnad]. This visualization is different from the above.
(3) The essential point of the breath that is to be held [gzung-ba rlung gi gnad].
This is the same as above.
(4) The essential point of the bindus on which one meditates [bsgom-pa thig-le'i gnad]. This visualization is different from the above.

VII. The Seventh and Final Week

As for the final week, the essential points for the basic position and the yantra exercise where the HUM abides, the OM emanates, and the A integrates [bdun tha-ma la gnas-pa HUM spros-pa OM bsdu-ba A yi bca' gzhi 'khrul-'khor gyi gnad] are as follows:

(1) The essential point of the body that is the position assumed [bca'-ba lus kyi gnad]. This is the same as above.
(2) The essential point of the channels that are to be visualized [bskyed-pa rtsa'i gnad]. The visualization is the same as the sixth week.
(3) The essential point of the breath that is to be held [gzung-ba rlung gi gnad].
This is the same as above.
(4) The essential point of the bindus on which one meditates [bsgom-pa thig-le'i gnad]. This visualization is different from the above.

Conclusion

Here there are three further methods:
1. The general method [spyi khyab] where one keeps the same position,
2. The equal parts in harmony [cha mthun], and
3. The reverse order [go ldog] where the positions are performed in the reverse order.

Colophon

Chapter Two

Translation of the Text

Here is contained "The Seven-fold Cycle of the Clear Light", from the Single Transmission Oral Tradition of Zhang-zhung for the Great Perfection Teachings (rDzogs-pa chen-po zhang-zhung snyan-brgyud gcig rgyud 'od-gsal bdun bskor).

Emaho!
Homage to the Body of the Primordial Teacher! [1]

PART ONE: The Yoga of the Psychic Channels and the Vital Winds

Here are presented the instructions concerning the essential points of the yoga of the psychic channels and vital winds according to the Oral Transmission Lineage from Zhang-zhung for the Great Perfection Teachings that belong to the Secret Mantra system: [2] (From the beginning) the Sugatas, the Siddhas, and the Gurus transmitted them successively from master to disciple like a necklace of pearls; and having practiced them themselves, they all obtained the realization (of the Rainbow Body of Light). However, for the benefit of those individuals belonging to future generations, I (the author) have set these instructions down in writing. The preliminaries have already been elucidated previously. [3]

I. The Basic Body Posture for Training the Psychic Channels

Now, according to the clear exposition of the yoga of the psychic channels and the vital winds (known as Tsa-lung), one should practice as follows: In terms of the essential points of the yantra exercise that represents the basic body position for training the channels, first there is the balancing of the body and the mind in equipoise, and second there is the training of the body and the mind so that they function properly. [4]

A. Balancing the Body and the Mind in Equipoise

As for the balancing of the body and the mind in equipoise, one proceeds as follows: [5]

The Body Posture possessing Five Aspects

One places the body in the mudra (or posture) possessing five aspects, namely,

1. The legs are held in a cross-legged position,
2. The hands are kept in the samadhi-mudra, the gesture of equipoise,
3. The spinal column is held straight like an arrow,
4. The neck is pulled back like an iron hook, and
5. The shoulders are hunched like the wings of a vulture that soars (in the sky).

Furthermore, the tongue (floats and) does not touch the palate. Moreover, there is a space between the teeth in the mouth like one is subtly sounding the letter "A". [6]

Visualizing the Psychic Channels

In terms of the essential point of the psychic channels that are to be visualized: One clearly visualizes the three principal channels (in the center of the body). The right channel is white, the left channel is red, and the central channel is azure-colored. As for this large channel (in the middle), at the lower extremity of the spinal column it is penetrated (by the two side channels) like the feet (or lower parts) of the Tibetan letter CHA. At the upper extremity, having already opened into the three folds of fat (on the surface of) the heart, at the crown of the head this central channel opens its mouth like the *spang-rgyan* flower. [7] (Above the heart) the right and the left channels go back to the spine and then they are thrust upward from inside the junction of the spine and the skull; and they pass inside the skull casing over the top of the brain membrane (of the cerebrum) until they come to clearly extrude at the two nostrils of the nose. [8]

Furthermore, these two channels remain just like very fine silk threads, whereas the central channel is visualized to open wide at its upper end just like a bamboo walking cane. The right and the left channels are (visualized to be) very straight in the manner of reed arrows. The right channel is crystal (white) like the color of a kangkari crystal and the left channel is vermilion like the color of powdered coral. The central channel, or *Nye-lo u-dpal* , [9] is a clear azure like the color of the bright sky. Thus, one should visualize these three in this way.

B. Expelling the Stale Air

As for the training the breath and the mind so that they function properly: (First, at the beginning of a session of practice), the stale air should be expelled nine times in order to remove it (from the lungs). In addition, within a single session of practice, at the beginning one remains for a short time in awareness and then in order to train the psychic channels, one proceeds to purify nine times the three channels on the right, on the left, and in the center respectively. [10]

II. Securing the Boundaries

As for the essential points of the yantra exercise represents the body position that secures the boundaries (thereby dispelling disturbances):

(1) There is the balancing of the body and mind in equipoise,
(2) The training the breathing and the mind so that they function properly, and
(3) The training of the psychic channels and their integration with the breathing, and so on –

These are all accomplished as described above. [11]

A. The Posture of the Wrathful Deity

Then, in terms of the essential point of the body that is the posture assumed, one assumes the essential point of the body that is the haughty posture of a wrathful deity. [12]

B. The Visualizing of the Three Psychic Channels

In terms of the essential point of the channels that are to be visualized, one clearly visualizes the three channels as described previously. [12]

C. The Breathing

Again, in terms of the essential point of the breath that is to be held, one expels the stale air nine times by way of a cleansing. [14]

D. The Visualization of the Bindus and Syllables

And finally, in terms of the essential point of the bindus (droplets of light) that are to be meditated upon, because on utters aloud the syllable BSWO, from unmanifest space there is emanated a sparkling effulgence of primal awareness consisting of (a multitude of) dark red BSWO syllables. They enter into the crown of one's head and are transmitted downward inside the azure-colored central channel. Then, in the middle of the heart center, they merge into a oneness without any duality with the essence of one's own intrinsic awareness, or Rigpa. Whereupon one's own being is transformed into an active wrathful deity, whose body color is dark red and who possesses a single face and two arms. He has an appearance that is heroic, enraged, and brilliant. Because one utters aloud the syllable BSWO, from the BSWO syllable that abides as the Base (in the heart center), there is emanated a sparkling effulgence of dark red BSWO syllables that come to fill to overflowing the interior of the azure-colored central channel. [15]

Again, because one utters BSWO aloud, and because one holds the breath just a little for the right channel, from the BSWO syllables in the azure-colored central channel, countless numbers of BSWO syllables are emanated which come to fill to overflowing the interior of the white right channel. Then, when the breath is exhaled from the right channel, a sparkling effulgence of primal awareness consisting of dark red BSWO syllables come to fill to overflowing the entire dark retreat house, as well as the entire sky, the atmosphere, and the earth's surface.

Again, because one utters aloud the syllable BSWO, and because one holds the breath a little bit for the left channel, there having been emanated countless numbers (of BSWO syllables) from the BSWO syllables in the white right channel, they come to fill to overflowing the interior of the red left channel And when one exhales the breath from the left channel, there is emanated a sparkling effulgence of primal awareness consisting of dark red BSWO syllables that come to fill to overflowing everywhere in the front and back of the trunk of one's body, in one's skandhas (aggregates), dhatus (elements), and ayatanas (sense fields), in the psychic channels that abide therein, and even in the hair pores of the body. And because of that, no Bhutas, or restless spirits, that are obstructers, and no wrong guides can cause any disturbances. One fixates one's awareness upon that, and one meditates (on the visualization) while adding seven times a little breath on top of that already held. Then one exhales and the process is complete. [16]

III. Dissolving the Visualization

As for the Perfection Process: Those external BSWO syllables, having melted into light, are then re-absorbed into the BSWO syllables in the white right channel and into the red left channel. Then these BSWO syllables in the right and left channels, having melted into light, are absorbed into the BSWO syllables in the azure-colored central channel. Then these BSWO syllables in the azure-colored central channel, having themselves melted into light, are absorbed into the BSWO syllable that abides as the Base (in the heart center). Thereupon the wrathful deity itself and the BSWO syllable that abides as the Base (in the heart center) become affixed with the seal of non-conceptuality, like the rainbow dissolving into the sky. [17]

This little text concerning securing the boundaries against disturbances in terms of the Clear Light practice (in the dark retreat) that has been explained by me is hereby completed. [18]

PART TWO: The Practices for the Seven Weeks

Here is contained "(The Practices of) the Psychic Channels, the Vital Winds, and the Body Positions for the Clear Light," according to the Oral Transmission from Zhang-zhung (Zhang-zhung snyan-rgyud rtsa rlung 'khrul-'khor 'od-gsal bzhugs-so).

Emaho!

Homage to the divine form of the Primordial Teacher!

Homage to the Gurus of the Lineage! [19]

Introduction

As for the essential points concerning the psychic channels, the vital winds, and the body positions for developing the visualizations in accordance with the root text of the Oral Tradition, these instructions, which are similar to the moist blood found inside the heart, consist of the visualizations for the seven-fold cycle of the Clear Light, (that is, one particular visualization for each of the seven weeks spent inside the dark retreat). These instructions were transmitted only from one individual to another individual by the Siddhas of the past, and these precepts, which were not subsequently taught to a second individual, were kept sealed. However, for the benefit of future generations, I (the author) have arranged them in writing the clear explanations, together with an index (or outline). [20]

Now, with respect to the sevenfold cycle of visualizations relating to the Clear Light practice (in the forty-nine day dark retreat), (there is one particular visualization to be performed at the beginning of each session for each of the seven weeks). [21]

The First Week

As for the first week, there are seven essential points connected with the basic body posture and the movements known as "the dust specks in the sun light". [22] These are as follows:

(1) The balancing of the body and the mind in equipoise,
(2) The training of the breath so that it functions properly, and
(3) The training of the channels by way of the nine breathings. These are in agreement with (what has been described) above.
(4) Then, in terms of the essential point of the body that is the position to be assumed, the body assumes the mudra or posture which displays the five natural aspects (as described above). The breath is retained by means of a large (kumbhaka) and the ocean (the stomach) is pulled back against the Meru mountain (the spine). The tongue is held imprisoned by the palate (without touching it) and the eyes are rolled upward (as high as possible).

(5) In terms of the essential point of the channels that are to be visualized, the three psychic channels are clearly visualized as described above.

(6) The essential point of the breath is holding it and one purifies it by expelling the stale air nine times as a cleansing (as described previously).

(7) The essential point of the bindus (or tiny spheres of light) upon which one is to meditate is that the essence which is a bindu (tiny luminous sphere of energy) comprised of subtle vital energy (vayu) and mind (chitta) at the nostrils of the nose is clear and bright like a beam of sun light, that is similar to an arrow, coming through a small hole (in a totally dark room). One meditates on these two bindus (at the nostrils) as being a clear blue and green. [23]

One fixates the awareness upon them, and the breath, which is held a little bit, is transmitted inside the right and left channels. These (bindus) merge into a very bright and clear maroon (bindu) at the lower extremity of the azure-colored central channel where the three channels unite and thereafter it goes straight upward through the azure-colored central channel and is expelled outside by way of being ejected about one full digit above the crown of the head. Then it descends gently downward and comes to reside in the middle of the heart center, filling it to overflowing. One fixates the awareness on that (while holding the breath) and continues to meditate while exhaling and inhaling the breath seven times. Thus the cycle is completed.

Then again, the bindus are integrated into immateriality by way of thinking that they dissolve into the empty space of the sky. One expels the stale air for purification and affixes the seal of non-conceptuality (thereby remaining in the Natural State and one proceeds with the principal practice of the dark retreat). [24]

The Second Week

In terms of the second week, (there is the yantra exercise of) the basic posture known as "the rays of the sun". Everything else, the essential point of the body that is the yantra, the visualizations of the channels, and the breathing are similar to the above. [25]

But with respect to the essential points of the bindus upon which one is to meditate, (there is a different visualization). In the right nostril there is a yellowish white bindu and in the left nostril an orange-colored bindu. Both of them are just the size of grains that are Chinese peas and they emanate rays of light of five kinds like the rainbow. When one inhales, they traverse down inside the right and left channels, and from the lower extremity of the azure-colored central channel, the bindus ascend upward, like ping-pong balls being juggled, until they are expelled at the crown of the head for a distance of about one full finger width or digit. They descend gently and come to reside in the middle of the heart side by side or one on top of the other. One fixates awareness upon them and does so while holding the breath and adding (a little air on top of this holding) for seven times.

When (this seven-fold cycle of inhaling, holding, adding more breath, and exhaling) is completed, if there should occur any dullness or fogginess, the bindus should be dissolved into the brain at the skull casing. But if the proliferating (of thoughts) or agitation should occur, they (the bindus) should be dissolved into the middle of the heart. If there exist no (problems with) proliferation, agitation, dullness, or fogginess, one should think that they are dissolved into their own place at the two nostrils. One then expels the stale air by way of purification and affixes the seal of non-conceptuality (thereby remaining in the Natural State). [26]

The Third Week

With respect to the third week, the essential point is the yantra exercise of the basic body position for the right white channel and the left red channel. The essential point of the body position that is assumed is in agreement with the foregoing. [27]

Then, with reference to the essential points of the channels that are to be visualized (this visualization being different from the preceding two weeks), at the lower extremity, like the feet of the Tibetan letter CHA, the three channels penetrate into each other at the great column of the spine. At the upper extremity, having opened into the three folds of fat around the heart, then the three channels (go back to the spinal column, up through the neck), and come to extrude through the hole at the crown of the head like wheat stubble cut at harvest time.

In terms of the essential points of the breath that is to be held, one expels the stale air nine times by way of a purification (as described previously).

Then, with respect to the essential points of the bindus upon which one is to meditate: One meditates that on top of the right white channel (above the crown of the head) is seated the Lord who is the king of the sky, Khayi Gyalpo Kuntu Zangpo, who embodies the essence of the moon, and on top of the left red channel is his Consort, Nangma Kokyi Gyalmo, who is the essence of the sun. (They both are the size of grains) and are like the rainbow. Furthermore, the Lord gazes at his Lady to the left out of the corner of his eye and the Lady gazes at her Lord to the right out of the corner of her eye. These two are visualized as bodies of light and they express (in visible manifestation) love and wisdom. Rays of light emanate upward from them (into the heavens) where they invoke a multitude of deities who dwell in the dimension of space, who are similar to this Lord and Lady; (whereupon these deities descend like rain) and are absorbed into non-duality (with the deities visualized on the crown of the head). One fixates awareness upon that, and because one holds the breath a little after inhaling, the heat of the breath comes to strike the Lord and Lady deities. Instantly they melt into light and become white and red bindus having the size of grains that are like Chinese peas. These two emanate rays of light of five kinds like the rainbow. They then descend inside the right and left channels and thereafter they ascend up the central channel, going upward like ping-pong balls being juggled until they are expelled outside at the crown of the head for about one finger width. Then they descend gently and one meditates on them residing in the middle of the heart, either side by side, or one on top of the other. One fixates the awareness on them and one holds the breath and adds (a little air on top) for some seven times.

When this cycle is completed, on those occasions when either dullness or fogginess arises, (the bindus) should be dissolved at the mouth (the upper end) of the azure-colored central channel. On the occasion of proliferation or agitation, one should meditate on the middle of the heart. If neither of these (problems) arise, one should think that (the bindus) are dissolved into their own places at the mouths of the right and left channels. [28]

The Fourth Week

With reference to the fourth week, the essential point is the yantra exercise of the basic position of one's own central channel. The essential point of the body, the channels, and the breathing are as before. [29]

Then, in terms of the essential points of the bindus upon which one is to meditate: One meditates that on a petal at the right side of (the mouth of) the azure-colored central channel (above the crown of the head) is seated the Lord Khayi Gyalpo and on the left is the Lady Nangma Kokyi Gyalmo as before. One fixates the awareness upon them, and when one inhales and holds the breath a little, the heat and vapor of the breath come to strike the Lord and Lady deities. Instantly they melt into light and become white and red bindus having the size of grains that are like Chinese peas. These two emanate rays of light of five kinds like the rainbow. They then descend inside the azure-colored central channel and from the juncture of the three channels, they ascend up the right and left channels until they are expelled outward at the crown of the head for about one finger width. Then they descend gently and one meditates on them staying in the middle of the heart, either side by side or one on top of the other. One fixates the awareness on that and one holds the breath and adds (air on top) for some seven times.

When the cycle is completed, on the occasions when either dullness or fogginess arise, (the bindus) should be dissolved at the mouths of the right and left channels. On the occasions of proliferation or agitation, they are dissolved into the middle of the heart. If neither of these problems come forth, one should think that (the bindus) are dissolved into their own places at the mouth of the azure-colored central channel. One then expels the stale air by way of purification and affixes the seal of non-conceptuality (remaining thereafter in the Natural State). [30]

The Fifth Week

With respect to the fifth week, the essential point is the yantra exercise of the basic position that is like the rainbow. The essential point of the body posture, the channels, and the breathing are like that of the rays of the sun (of the second week above). [31]

Then, with reference to the essential point of the bindus upon which one is to meditate: At the two nostrils there are two bindus having the essence of subtle energy and mind. They are vibrant and sparkling like the sun surrounded by rainbows and they are the size of grains that are like Chinese peas. These two emanate rays of light of five kinds like the rainbow. They then transit inside the right and left channels and (after reaching the bottom) these two bindus move upward inside the azure-colored central channel, like ping-pong balls being juggled, ascending until they are expelled outside at the crown of the head for about one finger width. Then they descend gently and the remain in the middle of the heart, either side by side or one on top of the other in the manner of a *gau* amulet. One fixates the awareness on that and one holds the breath and (adds a little air on top) for some seven times .

When the cycle is completed, on the occasions when proliferation or agitation arise, one meditates on the middle of the heart. On the occasions when either dullness or fogginess arise, one should meditate on the mouths of the right and left channels If neither of these problems come forth, one should think that (the bindus) dissolve in a self-occurring fashion at the top of the azure-colored central channel. One then expels the stale air by way of a purification and affixes the seal of non-conceptuality (thus remaining in the Natural State). [32]

The Sixth Week

In terms of the sixth week, the essential point is the yantra exercise of the basic position where the HUM abides, the A emanates, and the OM integrates. The essential point of the body posture that is to be assumed is the same as above. The essential point of the channels that are to be visualized is that (the two side channels) are clearly visualized as being curved like a noose (so that they terminate at the nostrils of the nose). The essential point of breathing is the same as above. [33]

Then as for the essential point of the bindus upon which one is to meditate: In the middle of the heart there is an azure-colored HUM syllable, which represents the essence of one's own intrinsic awareness (or Rigpa). It is the size of a thumb joint and it emanates rays of light of five kinds like the rainbow.

Because one holds the breath a little bit, that HUM syllable, in the manner of being blown by the wind, flies upward inside the azure-colored central channel and is expelled outward above the crown of the head about one finger width. Thereafter it gently descends and at the juncture of the three channels (at the bottom), one thinks that it is transformed into two white A syllables that emanate rays of light of five kinds like the rainbow. Thereupon they transit inside the two side channels on the right and left and arrive at the two gateways of the nose. One expels the stale air (forcefully) by way of a purification and one meditates that the interior of the entire dark retreat house, as well as the sky, the atmosphere, and the earth's surface, becomes filled with sparkling A syllables that are like rainbows. One fixates awareness on that.

One holds the breath a little, whereupon these A syllables are absorbed one into the other and then are transformed into the two white A syllables at the two nostrils. These A syllables melt into light and one meditates that they transform into two orange-colored OM syllables that emanate rays of light of five kinds like the rainbow. These transit inside the right and left channels and one meditates that they become (a blue) HUM syllable at the lower extremity of the azure-colored central channel. This (syllable) proceeds upward and is expelled at the crown of the head for about one finger width. Then it descends gently where it comes to rest aligned in the middle of the heart and abides there brilliantly (radiating light). One fixates awareness upon that. Then for seven times one holds the breath and adds a little air on top of that. When that (cycle) is completed, the HUM syllable is absorbed into the middle of the heart. One expels the stale air by way of a purification and affixes the seal of non-conceptuality (thereby remaining in the Natural State). [34]

The Seventh and Final Week

With respect to the final week, the essential point is the yantra exercise of the basic position where the HUM abides, the OM emanates, and the A integrates. The essential points of the body posture, the channels, and the breathing are the same as above. [35]

As for the essential point of the bindus upon which one is to meditate: In the middle of the heart there is an azure-colored HUM syllable, which represents the essence of (one's own) intrinsic awareness (or Rigpa). It is the size of a thumb joint and it emanates rays of light of five kinds like rainbows. One fixates awareness upon that.

Because one holds the breath a little bit (after inhaling), that HUM syllable, in the manner of being blown by the wind, flies upward inside the azure-colored central channel and is expelled outward above the crown of the head about one finger width. Thereafter it gently descends and at the juncture of the three channels (at the bottom), one thinks that it is transformed into two red OM syllables that emanate rays of light of five kinds like the rainbow. Thereupon they transit inside the two side channels on the right and left and arrive at the two gateways of the nose. One expels the stale air (forcefully) by way of purification and one meditates that the interior of the entire dark retreat house, as well as the sky, the atmosphere, and the earth's surface, becomes filled with sparkling OM syllables that are like rainbows. One fixates awareness on that.

One holds the breath a little, whereupon these OM syllables are absorbed one into the other and then are transformed into two white A syllables, which emanate rays of light like rainbows at the two nostrils. (These A syllables) transit inside the right and left channels and they become (single a blue) HUM syllable at the juncture of the three channels. This (HUM syllable) proceeds upward and is expelled at the crown of the head for about one finger width. Then it descends gently where it comes to rest, abiding in the middle of the heart as brilliantly (radiating light). One fixates awareness upon that. Then for seven times one holds the breath and adds a little air on top (of each holding). When that cycle is completed, the HUM syllable is absorbed into the middle of the heart. One expels the stale air by way of a purification and affixes the seal of non-conceptuality (thereby remaining in the Natural State). [36]

Conclusion

Here there exist three methods to be considered:

1. The general method (where one keeps the same position used for each week at the conclusion),
2. The equal parts in agreement (where the retreat has been broken in the middle), and
3. The reverse order (where the positions and exercises for each week are done in the reverse order).

These are the Upadeshas and one should request the oral instructions (from the master at the appropriate time). [37]

1. The General Method for each Session

The five-fold posture and the clear visualization of the three channels are in agreement with the above. One has (previously) expelled the stale air nine times by way of a purification.

As for the essential point of the bindus upon which one is to meditate: (one visualizes that) on top of an orange-colored solar disc seat, which is in the brain, is an orange-colored HRI syllable. And on top of a yellowish white moon disc seat, which is the membrane above the brain, is a yellowish white HRI syllable. Both of them emanate rays of light of five kinds like rainbows. These two HRI syllables that signify Means and Wisdom (respectively), are stacked high (one above the other). They abide there as sheer presence. One fixates one's awareness upon them while holding the breath and adding (a little air on top of this) for seven times.

When this cycle is completed, these two HRI syllables are absorbed into their respective seats of the sun and moon and they in turn are dissolved into oneself. One expels the stale air by way of a purification and affixes the seal of non-conceptuality (thereby remaining in the Natural State). That is the general method (for any session) during the Seven-fold Cycle of the Clear Light. [38]

Now, with regard to the principal practice of the seven-fold cycle of the Clear Light, this has been elucidated elsewhere, where it is said that the visualization (of the white letter A in the heart) is expelled into the sky (and dissolves into space, whereupon one rests in the Natural State). [39]

And in terms of purifying oneself in general, one fixates on the visualization (of the white letter A) in the heart center. One meditates, holding the breath and adding (a little air on top of that) for seven times (during the principal practice). [40]

According to the oral explanation (concerning the principal practice in general), each of these visualizations for the Clear Light practice are presented here as visualizations that are indeed beyond conception (that is, not a matter of discursive thought). And with respect to each of these visualizations that are beyond conception, the body remains in equipoise and the three channels are clearly visualized. Then one expels the stale air. [41]

As for the meditation (during each session): In the middle of the heart, one meditates on a white A syllable of light, possessing five colors. Furthermore, inside the right and left channels, there are two green YAM syllables. And moreover, one meditates that at the crown of the head there is a (white) wheel of light (like a moon disc). Because one (inhales and) holds the breath a little bit, it transits inside the right and left channels and because the breath strikes the two YAM syllables there, instantly these syllables become green lights, two green bindus just about the size of grains that are like Chinese peas. They descend and at the juncture of the three channels, they coalesce into one. (The green light or bindu) ascends upward inside the central channel and is absorbed into the A syllable in the middle of the heart. At that, one proceeds (repeatedly) holding the breath and expelling the stale air for a single session. One fixates awareness on that (white syllable A) and meditates while holding the breath and adding air on top seven times. [42]

As for the Perfection Process (at the conclusion of a single session or a week of practice): The A syllable goes upward from inside the central channel, and having been expelled from the crown of the head, it is absorbed into the wheel of light. The wheel of light is dissolved into space, and one settles into the clarity and emptiness of intrinsic awareness without grasping at anything whatsoever. In these terms, the above represents the stages of the general practice. [43]

2. The Equal Parts in Agreement

As for the equal parts (where the retreat has been interrupted in the middle for some reason and then resumed), one proceeds with the same mudras from the top to the bottom (that is, with the positions and the exercises in the same order as given above). Having held the breath during the four sessions, one follows these in succession during the day and the evening. [44]

3. The Reverse Order

As for the reverse order [45] (where one doubles the time one spends in the dark retreat), one proceeds upward (from the last exercise of the final day to the first exercise) "the dust specks in the sunlight," following in succession the days and nights.

These represent the cycle of visualizations according to the scripture.

SAMAYA gya gya gya! Virtue! ITI. [46]

Chapter Three

Commentary One: Beginning the Dark Retreat

The Practice of the Dark Retreat

According to Lopon Tenzin Namdak, there exist two principal reasons for making a dark retreat (mun-mtshams). The first is to stabilize being in the Natural State and the second is to develop visions. That is to say, there is one kind of dark retreat that is meant for Trekchod (khregs-chod) alone, the practice of contemplation, and the second for Thodgal practice (thod-rgal) that entails the development of vision. A retreat for this first purpose may be of any length of time, but, in terms of the second purpose, the shortest retreat is traditionally forty-nine days. The dark retreat may also serve as a preparation for the Bardo, or after-death experience, and the Bardo is said to endure similarly for forty-nine days. The Dzogchen cycle of the *bsGrags-pa skor gsum* also has a forty-nine day dark retreat, and in addition, one for seven years. The dark retreat described by Shardza Rinpoche in his *sKu-gsum rang-shar* is elaborated according to the system of the *bsGrags-pa skor gsum*. However, here we are exclusively concerned with the dark retreat connected with the Zhang-zhung Nyan-gyud cycle of practice.

Again, according to the Lopon, the present text is anonymous and was added as an appendix to the basic text of the *rGyal-ba phyag-khrid* of Druchen Gyalwa Yungdrung (Bru-chen rGyal-ba g.yung-drung, 12th cen.), probably sometime afterwards. Nevertheless, it represents his oral teaching on the matter, even though it was written down later. One may note that the term *phyag-khrid* itself means an explanation that derives from the personal experience of an accomplished master. The dark retreat we have here is compared to a limb growing out from the trunk of the *Zhang-zhung snyan-rgyud* and the author furthermore informs us that it is especially connected with the *gZer-bu nyi-shu rtsa gcig*, or "Twenty-one Little Nails," the root text of the fourth section of this cycle, the teachings that are exceedingly secret (yang gsang). This cycle pertains to the fruits of the practice of Thodgal. Although this term Thodgal is not found in the texts of this cycle, the practice is described in some detail where it is called *'od-gsal* or the practice of the Clear Light. In terms of vision practice, there are three systems or methodologies where the practitioner gazes either into sunlight, or into empty space, or into total darkness. The sunlight, the empty space, or the total darkness are merely secondary causes serving as supports (rten) for the manifesting of the Thodgal visions. The visions themselves arise from out of the pure potentiality of the Natural State of the Nature of Mind of the individual.

Traditionally, these teachings regarding Thodgal practice in both the Bonpo and the Nyingmapa schools have been kept strictly secret. However, the guardian deity Sidpai Gyalmo (Srid-pa'i rgyal-mo) appeared in a vision to the former abbot, Yongdzin Sangye Tenzin, of the Bonpo monastery at Dolanji in India and prophesied that if the Dzogchen teachings were not given out to those who are sincerely interested, they would be entirely lost within a generation. It is, therefore, with the specific permission of the Goddess and under her patronage that the Dzogchen teachings from Zhang-zhung are now disseminated to a wider audience than was the case in the past.

The Title of the Text

In the title, *rDzogs-pa chen-po zhang-zhung snyan-rgyud* refers to the cycle of teachings, namely, "the Dzogchen teachings from the Oral Transmission of Zhang-zhung." Single transmission (gcig rgyud) indicates that originally a master transmitted the Dzogchen precepts to a single disciple only, although this procedure is no longer the case. *'Od-gsal bdun bskor* is the actual title of the text. Clear Light ('od-gsal) refers to Thodgal, or vision practice, in this case within a dark retreat, and the seven-fold cycle (bdun bskor) refers to the cycle of seven weeks spent in total darkness, each week having its own special preliminary purification practice. The principal practice, however is that of the Clear Light or Thodgal vision practice while remaining in the state of contemplation or Trekchod.

The Rushan Exercises

In the commentary to the principal practices in the *rGyal-ba phyag-khrid*, it is explained how to build a dark retreat house (mun-khang). Then, in terms of the preparations as the Lopon informs us, one should consult the appropriate section of the Zhang-zhung Nyan-gyud for the Rushan exercises ('khor 'das ru-shan dbye-ba). There are six of these exercises, with the addition of the Bardo practice. One engages in these exercises during a retreat of forty-nine days. In order to realize the conditions of the hells, and so on, one employs mantras and visualizations in the Tantric style of practice, as well as visualizing the emanations of the six Dulshen ('dul gshen drug). They were originally emanations of Tonpa Shenrab projected into the six destinies of rebirth. There exist outer, inner, and secret Rushan exercises. The practice described here in the text represents an inner Rushan. These exercises serve as preparation for Thodgal and for the dark retreat, both of which are principal practices of Dzogchen. It is said that is necessary to perform these Rushan exercises before one can engage in Thodgal practice in order to release the pent up energies of one's negative accumulations of karma.

Practicing Fixation

But crucial to the practice of the dark retreat is developing beforehand the ability to relax and enter into the state of Rigpa or contemplation. Therefore, one must first practice fixation on the white Tibetan letter A as the means to develop this capacity. This practice is described in the commentary on the principal practices (dngos-gzhi) in the *rGyal-ba phyag-khrid*. [1] A white letter A is painted on the dark background of a card that is affixed to the end of a stick. This stick is then thrust into the ground at a comfortable distance in front of oneself. Preparing a comfortable seat, one stares fixedly with half closed eyes at this white letter A, focusing on it as a skilled archer would fixate on his target while holding his bow and arrow. This focused attention leaves no space for distracting thoughts to arise. Then one relaxes one's attention a bit. If distracting thoughts then arise, one does not pursue them or try to suppress them, but merely fixates more acutely on the target, the white letter A.

Through practicing fixation regularly in meditation sessions, one discovers a calm state that opens up between thoughts, like the clouds parting in the sky so that the clear blue heavens beyond might be seen. Gradually one becomes able to remain in this calm state undisturbed by thoughts for longer and longer periods. Nevertheless, thoughts continue to arise occasionally and this is only natural because thoughts represent manifestations of the inherent energy (rang rtsal) of the Nature of Mind. Thus one becomes aware of not only the calm state (gnas-pa), but also of the movements of thoughts ('gyu-ba). However, these two are only experiences (nyams). The principle to be discovered here is the presence of awareness (rig-pa), whether there is a state of calm or the movement of thoughts. Remaining in this pure presence without distraction is what is meant by contemplation (ting-nge 'dzin).

One must first know how to rest and remain in Rigpa, or contemplatio, before one can gain any value from the dark retreat. Otherwise the dark retreat, as a sensory depravation experience, will only give rise to hallucinations or impure karmic visions. Such visions do not represent Thodgal.

Posture and Breathing

Although the text speaks here of *rtsa rlung gnad kyi gdams-pa.*, that is, the instructions regarding the essential points of the psychic channels (rtsa) and vital winds, or psychic energies (rlung), the reference is not to the Tantric yoga practices (rtsa rlung thig-le'i rnal-'byor) belonging to the Perfection Process (rdzogs-rim), but only to the postures and breathing related to Thodgal practice. This dark retreat practice pertains to Dzogchen, the path of self-liberation (grol lam), rather than to the methods of Tantra, the path of transformation (sgyur lam). Consequently, the visualizations here are much simpler and related to the preliminary purification of the psychic channels, not to the principal practice of contemplation. There is no visualization (dmigs-pa) done here in the state of contemplation; there is only vision (snang-ba), that is to say, whatever may spontaneously arise to awareness in the space before one while sitting in the total darkness of the retreat. Contemplation is a state beyond the mind, whereas visualization represents a deliberate activity of the mind.

According to the clear exposition regarding the channels and the vital winds (rtsa rlung zhal-shes) presented in the text, the essential points of the yantra exercises ('khrul-'khor) that represent the basic body position for training the psychic channels [2] are two-fold:

(1) The balancing of the body and the mind in equipoise (lus sems mnyam-par bzhag-pa) and

(2) The training of the breath and the mind so that they function properly (rlung sems gcun la bor-ba). The first point refers to the five-fold body position or mudra [3] described in the text. The second point refers to the breathing exercises for purification. By harmonizing the physical body, one harmonizes and balances the psychic energies, and by harmonizing these energies, one calms and harmonizes the mind or flow of thoughts.

When one has completed the preliminaries (sngon-'gro) as represented by the Rushan exercises, then one begins the training in Tsa-lung (rtsa-rlung), the yoga of the channels and energies. In order to harmonize and balance the body, one must first assume the proper sitting position. One sits down in the usual way upon a comfortable seat in the five-fold posture, with the spine straight, the neck bent, the shoulders up, the tongue floating, but not touching the palate, and so on. The mouth is not closed, but neither is it wide open. Rather, it is like sounding "Ah......"

In terms of the mudra, or gesture of the hands, the left hand is placed over the right hand resting on the lap. The thumbs press down at the base of the ring fingers. This action seals the klesha-nadi, or psychic channel for the impure energies, that runs from the tip of the ring finger to the heart. Sealing this channel prevents access to one's consciousness by evil spirits and their negative provocations (gdon). By sitting in the five-fold posture as described, one balances the body and harmonizes the flow of one's energies. Thus, distracting thoughts tend not to arise. One may also use a meditation belt (sgom thag) for additional support. And as preparation for the sessions of practice, one recites the preliminary prayers every morning, such as the Guru Yoga and Invocation for Tapihritsa. [4]

Visualization of the Psychic Channels

The essential points of the psychic channels that are to be visualized (bskyed-pa rtsa'i gnad) refer to how and where one visualizes these psychic channels. In the Buddhist system, the three principal channels are known as Rasana (ro-ma) on the right, Lalana (rkyang-ma) on the left, and Avadhuti (dbu-ma) in the center. In the Hindu system, they are called Pingala, Ida, and Sushumna respectively. The Avadhuti is visualized in the precise center of the body, not in the spinal column, but in front of it. The psychic channels (rtsa, Skt. nadi) represent potential pathways for the movements of psychic energy; they are subtle structures, not gross physical anatomy. Therefore, by visualizing or imagining them (dmigs-pa) one makes them actual and moves one's vital winds (rlung, Skt. vayu) through them. Thus, there exist in the Tantras, both Buddhist and Bonpo, a number of different systems for visualizing the three principal psychic channels. What visualization system the practitioner employs depends on how and where one is moving these psychic energies or vital winds.

One visualizes the central channel as dark azure in color [5] in the middle of the body, beginning at the secret center, some four fingers widths below the navel, and extending to the aperture or opening at the crown of the head. This channel is the size of a hollow bamboo cane. Parallel to it on both sides are two smaller channels. The right-hand channel is white in color, and the left channel is red in color. They symbolize the white lunar masculine energy and the red solar feminine energy respectively, as in the Tantra system. These channels and colors are the reverse in women. These two side channels enter into the central channel at the Kunda, or juncture of the three channels (rtsa gsum 'dus mdor), below the navel. This junction resembles the Tibetan letter CHA. These three channels extend upward to the physical heart and then curve behind it and go to the spine and up through the neck. They join again at the *Ag-tse*, or joint of the spine and skull. Previously running in parallel to the central channel, they now go inside the skull case (klad phor) and arch over the membrane of the brain (klad sprin). These two side channels, which are very thin like fine silk threads, then turn down to the nostrils of the nose where they terminate. Inside the skull, the central channel widens a bit as its approaches the aperture so that it comes to resemble a horn or a flower. Thus, it has been compared to the blue flower called *spangs-*

rgyan (Gentiana stipitala Edjew.) which blooms in autumn. The mouth or upper extremity of the central channel extends out through the aperture at the crown of the skull. This is known as the aperture of Brahma (tshangs-pa'i bu-ga, Skt. brahmarandhra).

Expelling the Stale Air

The training of the breathing and the mind so that they function properly [6] refers to the breathing exercises done at the beginning of each session of practice (thun), commencing with the nine breathings for purification. [7] In general, purification by way of breathing is known as Tsa-dul (rtsa 'dul), the taming or training of the breath.

For men, using the left hand, one closes the right nostril with one's ring finger and inhales the fresh clean air through the left nostril and the left channel while visualizing that one is absorbing into oneself luminous light blue wisdom air (ye-shes kyi rlung). And one holds the breath a little. Then closing the left nostril with the thumb and opening the right nostril, one blows the stale polluted air (rlung-ro) out the right nostril and the right hand channel. One visualizes this stale air that is being expelled as light bluish-gray smoke, which represents the polluted residues of the negative emotion of anger. Thereupon one changes nostrils and does just the opposite. Closing the left nostril with the thumb of the left hand, one inhales the wisdom air through the right nostril and holds the breath a little. Then opening the left nostril and closing the right nostril with the ring finger, one exhales the stale air while visualizing it to be light red in color representing the polluted residues of the negative emotion of desire. Thereby each side is purified in this way alternatively three times. Women should proceed in exactly the opposite fashion, first purifying desire and then anger.

Then one inhales the clean luminous wisdom air through both nostrils simultaneously and, in the same way, proceeds to expel the stale polluted air, visualizing it as smoke of a dirty brown color representing the polluted residues of the negative emotion of confusion. This negative emotion, or klesha, is actually a mixture of the two principal passions, anger and desire, and is characterized by ignorance, confusion, indecision, and bewilderment.

In each case, the inhalation is done slowly and gently, whereas the blowing out of the disturbances is done a bit more forcefully.

Men begin by cleansing the right channel, whereas women begin by cleansing the left channel, because these two side channels are the reverse in men and women due to tantric polarity. The white lunar channel, where the residues of anger accumulate, is on the right side in men and on the left side in women, whereas the red solar channel, where the residues of desire accumulate, is on the left side in men and on the right side in women.

One does this three times: closing the right nostril, inhaling through the left nostril, then exhaling through the right nostril. Thus one expels the negative energy of anger that has four characteristics:

1. Anger (zhe-sdang, Skt. dvesha),
2. Wind diseases, that is, diseases due to lack of vitality or imbalance in the Vayu, or wind humor (rlung gi nad),
3. The color of light blue, and
4. Disturbances coming from male spirits (pho gdon).

Next one closes the left nostril, inhales through the right nostril, then expels the stale air, exhaling through the left nostril. One does this three times. Thereby one expels the negative energy of desire, which also has four characteristics:

1. Desire ('dod-chags, Skt. raga),
2. Diseases due to imbalance in Pitha, or the bile humor (mkhris-pa'i nad),
3. The color of light red, and
4. Disturbances coming from female spirits (mo gdon).

Finally one inhales and exhales three times through both nostrils. Here the fresh wisdom air goes into the central channel and the stale air is forcefully expelled. The negative energy of confusion also has four characteristics:

1. Confusion or bewilderment (gti-mug, Skt. moha),
2. Diseases due to an imbalance in Kapha, or the phlegm humor (bad-kan gyi nad),
3. The smoky color, and
4. Disturbances due to the Nagas (klu gdon).

Securing the Boundaries

Generally, when beginning the dark retreat, one enters into the dark retreat house in the afternoon or in the evening. Then it is sealed so that no light can enter and all the proper precautions should have been taken beforehand to insure proper circulation of air within the room. One prepares a comfortable seat and assumes the five-fold position of the body. This represents the balancing of the body and mind in equipoise (lus sems mnyam-par bzhag-pa). Then one performs the nine breathings for purification, which represent the training of the breathing and the mind, so that they function properly (rlung sems gcun la bor-ba) and the training of the channels integrated with the breathing (rtsa 'dul rlung sbrugs). These are accomplished as described above. In this way one's body, energy, and mind become balanced and harmonized.

However, at the beginning of the retreat, one performs the practice known as securing the boundaries (mtshams bcad-pa). The essential points of this yantra exercise is the body position that secures the boundaries [8] thereby preventing disturbances and negative provocations (gdon) from outside, such as those caused by Bhutas, or restless spirits ('byung-po). Then, in terms of the essential point of the body that is the posture to be assumed (bca'-ba lus kyi gnad), one assumes the confident and haughty position of a Krodha, or wrathful deity (khro-bo), inclining the head to the left side a little, while visualizing oneself as this. [9] The wrathful deity, whether male or female, is dark red in color, having one face and two arms. In terms of the essential point of the channels that are to be visualized (bskyed-pa rtsa yi gnad), as described above one clearly visualizes the three channels inside the body of the wrathful deity. And in terms of the essential point of the breathing that is to be held (bzung-ba rlung gi gnad), one expels the stale air nine times as the means for cleansing oneself. [10] This is done as described previously.

Finally, in terms of the essential point of the bindus (or tiny spheres of light) that are to be meditated upon (bsgom-pa thig-le'i gnad), that is to say, the actual meditation practice, one proceeds as follows. Before visualizing oneself as the wrathful deity, first one focuses on the luminous dark red BSWO syllable in one's heart center that abides as the Base (gzhi gnas BSWO). Then one utters aloud the syllable BSWO! very forcefully (pronounced SWO.....!). This sound goes out into unmanifest space, becoming millions of luminous dark red BSWO syllables that appear in space and fill the entire dark retreat room. These mantric syllables terrify and frighten away all disturbances and negativities in the immediate environment about oneself. Then, like a magnet attracting iron filings, these millions of tiny luminous syllables, which are like spheres of light (thig-le), come together and enter the crown of one's head. Descending through the central channel, they enter into one's heart center where they are absorbed into one's own Rigpa, or intrinsic awareness, that has the aspect of the original dark red BSWO syllable. They merge into oneness without duality with the essence of one's own intrinsic awareness in the center of one's heart. Thus, they are integrated into one's Natural State, whereupon the practitioner instantly transforms and manifests one's being as a dark red luminous wrathful deity. This deity's appearence is heroic, enraged, and brilliant. [11]

While visualizing oneself in that divine form as the wrathful deity, again one sounds BSWO! aloud. From the BSWO syllable in one's heart center emanate countless numbers of dark red BSWO syllables, like bindus, or tiny spheres of light (thig-le), that come to fill one's central channel to overflowing. They are all luminous and shining. Again one sounds aloud BSWO! Inhaling a little breath in though the right nostril, having closed the left nostril with one's thumb using the left hand, one sees the breath go down to the bottom and hitting the BSWO syllables, the numbers of syllables increase so that the right white channel becomes filled to overflowing with luminous dark red BSWO syllables. Holding the breath for a little bit, then one exhales through the right nostril. Having kept the left nostril closed, the BSWO syllables increase in numbers and going out the right nostril, they come to fill the room with dark red BSWO syllables, so that the entire dark retreat house is aglow and filled with them.

Again one sounds BSWO! Inhaling a little air through the left nostril, having closed the right one with the ring finger of one's left hand, one sees the breath go down to the bottom, to the junction with the central channel where it strikes the BSWO syllables, whereupon these syllables increase in numbers and come to fill the left red channel to overflowing while holding the breath for a little bit. When one exhales though the left nostril while keeping the right nostril closed, the glowing syllables come to fill everywhere the exterior of one's body. Indeed, one's whole body, both front and back, becomes covered with luminous dark red BSWO syllables. Thus, one is filled everywhere with these BSWO syllables, both the inside and the outside of one's body. They even fill all of one's hair pores. Because everywhere is filled with dark red glowing BSWO syllables, there is no space left in the retreat house for disturbances to arise due to the activities of Bhutas or elemental spirits who are wrong guides and obstructers. [12]

As was described above, men begin the exercise by inhaling through the right nostril while closing the left nostril with the thumb of the left hand, whereas women do the opposite: first inhaling through the left nostril while closing the right nostril with the ring finger. In both cases, the breath is seen to descend inside the respective side channel until it reaches the bottom where the three channels converge. As one begins to exhale, the respective side channel fills from the bottom upward with luminous and sparkling dark red BSWO syllables, which are then expelled from the corresponding nostril and come to fill the entire room. The second time they come to cover the entire exterior of one's body like donning a suit of armor.

Then sounding BSWO! once again, one begins inhaling through both nostrils. One inhales as much air as one can and holds it (gnon) as long as one can. Then one breathes in a bit more to add more air on top of that (rlung bzhur). In that way, one can hold even the breath even longer. When doing this, one fixates on one's body being filled to overflowing with these luminous BSWO syllables. When one cannot hold the breath any longer, one exhales, expelling the stale air. Again one inhales, holds, adds more air, and exhales. This focuses and increases protective energy within one's body. The cycle is repeated seven times. [13] One continues to visualize and focus on the BSWO syllables. Filling the entire space of the dark retreat room, as well as covering the entire exterior of one's body, with these luminous dark red syllables, allows no space for obstructions or disturbances to manifest. This exercise represents a kind of protection.

In terms of the symbolism of the BSWO syllable, according to the Lopon, in ancient times it was used to summon the gods and spirits, where one shouted BSWO BSWO LO! meaning "Glorious! Victorious!" Furthermore, this symbol mystically represents the Trikaya, that is to say, the letter "B" symbolizes the Dharmakaya, the letter "S" the Sambhogakaya, and the letter "O" the Nirmanakaya. Because in the old language the word *bso* meant "goat,", one needs to add the wazur or "W" to make the distinction here. The letters "BSO" also signify the three transcendental functions of the Body, the Speech, and the Mind, that is to say, the consonants "BS" are the Body, the vowel indication or naro "O" is Speech, and the wazur "W" is Mind. This mantric syllable visualized in the heart center is known as "the BSWO that abides as the Base" (gzhi gnas kyi BSWO). It arises from the Natural State of the Nature of Mind (sems-nyid gnas-lugs) and the vast multitude of dark red miniature BSWO syllables emanate, multiply, and increase from the larger principal syllable held in the heart center.

Dissolving the Visualization

Then, at the conclusion, there comes the Dzogrim, or Perfection Process, for the visualization of securing the boundaries (mtshams-bcad gyi rdzogs-rim). All of the BSWO syllables that fill external space coagulate into one another and melt into light. [14] The syllables covering one's body re-enter through the left channel, while the external syllables in the room re-enter through the right channel. All of them congregate in the central channel where they merge into the principal BSWO syllable in the heart center that represents one's Natural State or Base. [15] Finally, one then visualizes the wrathful deity dissolving into space like a rainbow slowly fading into the sky, so that the entire deity is absorbed into the Natural State. Thereafter, only the principal BSWO syllable in the heart center remains and then the syllable itself dissolves slowly into the space of the Natural State, so that no visualization at all remains. One breathes normally as everything dissolves. And for a moment one remains in this state of contemplation (mnyam-bzhag); this is known as affixing the seal of non-conceptuality. [16] Everything has dissolved and one remains in the Natural State as long as one can. This is the practice of securing the boundaries.

This process of securing the boundaries represents a preliminary practice and one does it only once when one first goes into the dark retreat. On the contrary, one does the nine breathings for purification at the beginning of each session of practice (thun). Generally, one does four sessions of practice a day while in retreat, namely, early morning, mid morning, mid afternoon, and evening before retiring to sleep.

Chapter Four

Commentary Two: The Practices for the Seven Weeks

Title and Homage

Part Two is actually a separate text concerned with the particular visualization practices for each of the seven weeks of the forty-nine day dark retreat according to the *Zhang-zhung snyan-rgyud*. This text is entitled, "(The Practices of) the Channels, the Vital Winds, and the Positions for the Clear Light practice, according to the Oral Tradition from Zhang-zhung" (Zhang-zhung snyan-rgyud rtsa rlung 'khrul-'khor 'od-gsal bzhugs-so). *E-ma-ho* means "how wonderful!" There are two homages that open the text: "Homage to the divine form of the Primordial Teacher" (ye-nyid ston-pa'i sku la phyag 'tshal-lo), who is none other than the Primordial Buddha Kuntu Zangpo, the ultimate source for all of the Dzogchen teachings, and "Homage to the Gurus of the Lineage" (brgyud-pa'i bla-ma rnams la phyag 'tshal-lo), meaning the Mahasiddhas who attained realization of the Rainbow Body and liberation from Samsara through the practicing of Dzogchen in the past.

Introduction

The subject matter found in this second text represents the essential points (gnad) concerning the psychic channels, the vital winds, and the yantra exercise movements [1] linked to the visualizations done in accordance with the root text of the Oral Tradition. [2] These instructions are said to be very rare and precious and so they are compared to the moist blood found inside the heart itself. [3] Here are presented descriptions of the visualizations done at the beginning of each session of practice according to the Seven-fold Cycle of the Clear Light practice ('od-gsal bdun skor dmigs-pa), that is to say, there is one particular visualization for each of the seven weeks spent inside the dark retreat. These visualizations represent a kind of preliminary performed initially in order to purify the stale air (rlung-ro) lodged in one's lungs, as well as in one's psychic energies. This stale air in the channels contains pollutants or the residues and traces left behind by the various negative emotions experienced during the day. The breathings for purification are performed nine times. Then the practice session proper (thun) begins with the exercises described below and the principal practice that follows the completion of these exercises is simply to remain relaxed in the state of contemplation (mnyam-bzhag).

As said before, in the *Zhang-zhung snyan-rgyud* the term *thod-rgal*, referring to the practice of vision, does not actually occur in the text, but instead the word *'od-gsal*, literally "clear light," is used, and this may be translated as "the Practice of the Clear Light". In this context, the Clear Light refers to the visions that spontaneously emerge from the Natural State when practicing with sunlight, or empty space, or total darkness as the support while in the state of contemplation. However, in this case, the text is only concerned with the dark retreat (mun mtshams). As explained in the commentary on the Principal Practices (dngos-gzhi) found in the *Phyag-khrid*, after having been directly introduced to the Natural State and gaining some stability in contemplation through practicing fixation, one enters into the dark retreat in order to facilitate the developing of visions. The word *bdun skor* means the seven-fold cycle or the cycle (skor) of seven weeks (bdun) into which the forty-nine day dark retreat is divided. Thus, the dark retreat symbolically endures for the same period of time as the Bardo experience after death and so the practice may also serve as a preparation for death and what occurs afterwards in the continuum of consciousness.

These instructions were originally transmitted only from one individual to another individual by the Siddhas of the past, that is, from a realized master to just a single disciple, and the oral precepts (bka') were not subsequently taught to a second individual. Rather, they were sealed and kept secret. [4] However, now that historical circumstances have changed, these teachings have become more public. Consequently, the anonymous author has arranged in writing these clear explanations drawn from oral tradition, together with an index or outline, for the benefit of future generations of practitioners. [5]

I. The First Week

Generally the practitioner does four sessions (thun bzhi) each day while in the dark retreat house. First one assumes the five-fold position of the body described previously and performs the nine breathings for purification. Then one proceeds to balance and harmonize one's psychic energies or vital winds by way of a different visualization process for each of the seven weeks.

With reference to the first week, there are seven essential points (gnad) that are concerned with the basic posture (bca' gzhi) and the yantra movement exercises ('khrul-'khor). The visualization exercise that accompanies them is known as "the dust specks in the sunlight" (nyi rdul-ma' bca' gzhi). [6] These considerations are as follows:

(1) The balancing of the body and mind in equipoise (lus sems mnyam-par bzhag-pa),

(2) The training of the breath so that it functions properly (rlung gcun la bor-ba),

(3) The training of the channels by way of the nine breathings (rlung rtsa 'dul dgu phrug),

(4) The essential point of the body which is the position assumed (bca'-ba lus kyi gnad),

(5) The essential point of the channels that are visualized (bskyed-pa rtsa'i gnad),

(6) The essential point of the breath which is held (gzung-ba rlung gi gnad), and

(7) The essential point of the bindus on which one meditates (bsgom-pa thig-le'i gnad).

The first three are in agreement with what was described above in Part One. The remaining five points are considered below.

In terms of the essential point of the body that is the position assumed, one assumes the mudra (phyag-rgya) or posture of the body, that displays the five natural aspects described above. [7] But here the breath is fixated by way of a large holding of the breath. [8] The retention of the breath is known as kumbhaka or vase-shaped breathing (bum-can), because of the shape of the belly when filled with air. Special esoteric terms and phrases associated with yoga are employed in order to conceal the real meaning from the uninitiated. For example, "the ocean" (rgya-mtsho) indicates the stomach, which is pulled back against "the Meru mountain" (ri-rab), the latter indicating the spinal column (rgya-mtsho ri-rab la bcar). The tongue floats in the mouth, but does not touch the palate. [9] "The great planets", indicating the eyeballs, are averted upward as high as possible. [10] The essential point of the three channels are clearly visualized as described above. [11] The essential point of the breath is the retaining of it in kumbhaka, or vase-shaped breathing. One purifies the breath by way of expelling the stale air (rlung-ro) nine times in order to cleanse it, [12] but only at the beginning of each practice session.

The essential point of the bindus on which one meditates (bsgom-pa thig-le'i gnad) is the actual visualization done at the beginning of each session after assuming the meditation position and purifying oneself by way of the nine breathings. As said, this visualization changes with each week in the dark retreat. At the beginning of each week, the Lama returns to the dark retreat house and presents the new visualization exercise to the practitioner.

One visualizes at the nostrils two bindus (thig-le), or tiny spheres of radiant light, about the size of Chinese peas, being blue-green in color and very clear. They are composed of vital wind, or psychic energy (rlung), and subtle mind (sems). They are clear and bright like a beam of sunlight, that is similar in shape to an arrow, coming through a small hole in the wall into a totally dark room. [13]

The text says that one side channel is clear like sunlight and the other one is like turquoise, but it does not say which one. When one breathes in, one visualizes these bindus that are located in each of the two nostrils and one fixates awareness on them. [14] As one inhales, they go down the two side channels to the juncture at the bottom where they enter into the central channel and merge into a single, very bright maroon bindu. Then this bindu goes up gradually like juggling ping-pong balls (yar ta-la-la) to the top of the head in one breath, where it is expelled one digit or finger span above the head. Then it descends gently into the middle of the heart where it stays, filling it to overflowing. [15] One fixates awareness on this bindu and rests in its presence. Then for seven times, one inhales, holds the breath, adds a little air on top of that, and exhales. During these seven cycles, the bindu in the heart does not move and one simply fixates awareness on it while inhaling and exhaling. After the seven cycles are completed, the bindu goes up the central channel and out into space where dissolves. One exhales strongly and remains thereafter in the Natural State. One does this exercise only four times a day, at the beginning of each session, in order to help the development of visions.

Then again, the bindu is integrated into immateriality by way of thinking that it dissolves into the sky. [16] One expels the stale air for purification and affixes the seal of non-conceptuality (mi dmigs-pa'i rgyas gdab). Non-conceptuality means remaining in the Natural State in a condition of contemplation without grasping at thoughts or concepts. It is said that it is necessary to perform these visualization exercises first, because otherwise, even though the visions will surely come in the total darkness of sensory depravation, they will be only ordinary visions like those experienced in dreams as the products of karma and memory. One does this for four sessions a day for one week.

In terms of Thekchod, this is the way in which one is introduced to the Natural State. One allows one's thoughts to dissolve into space and then one keeps everything just as it is (co-bzhag). This represents the practice for the Dzogchen view.

II. The Second Week

As for the second week, the visualization is known as "the fundamental position of the rays of the sun" (nyi zer-ma'i bca' gzhi). Everything else, the posture, the visualization of the channels, and the breathing is as before. [17] In the right nostril one visualizes a yellowish white bindu or tiny luminous sphere and in the left nostril an orange-colored bindu. Having the size of Chinese peas (rgya sran), they are luminous, emanating the five colors of the rainbow. [18] When one inhales, they go down to the bottom of the two channels, then they go up the central channel like two pebbles being juggled or tossed upward. They proceed to the crown of the head and exit outside the body for a height of one finger span. Then they come down again to the heart center where they sit side by side or one on top of the other. [19] One fixates one's attention on them strongly while breathing and holding the breath, as well as adding air on top of the holding of the breath for seven times. [20] When everything has gone well, then the two bindus go downward to the bottom and separate, going up once more the two side channels to the nostrils and disappear there when one exhales forcefully. Then one remains in the Natural State for as long as possible. This being in the state of contemplation is called affixing the seal of non-conceptuality. [21]

Therefore, after breathing seven times as described above, one enters into the Natural State. Nevertheless, one may be disturbed by either drowsiness or agitation. Even during regular meditation it is possible that drowsiness ('bying-ba) may be experienced and the object may become dull and unclear (rmug 'thibs). With drowsiness alone, the object is still sharp, but with dullness one feels tired and the object is not sharp and may be out of focus. One's energy level is very low. The opposite is finding oneself diffused and agitated ('phro rgod). If one feels drowsy or the mind becomes dull, one should visualize that the bindus go up to the crown of the head and dissolve into the brain, [22] energizing it, and one remains thereafter in the Natural State. But if agitation is the problem and too many discursive thoughts come, one should just keep the bindus in the heart and absorb them there, [23] dissolving any discursive thoughts at the same time. If one does not have either problem, one see them descend through the central channel again to the bottom and then separate, whereupon they go up the two side channels to the nostrils. One should think that they dissolve into their own place at the two nostrils. [24] One exhales the breath forcefully and remains in the Natural State. This exercise is repeated for the four sessions per day for one week.

III. The Third Week

As for the third week, the essential point is the basic position of the yantra exercise of the right white channel and the left red channel. [25] The posture is the same as before, but the visualization is different.

Four fingers below the navel is the juncture of the three channels in the form of the Tibetan letter CHA. [26] Here the Avadhuti or central channel originates. At the heart level it goes into the folds of fat attached to the surface of the heart (snying sul-ba gsum) and then it goes back to the spinal column, up through the neck, and up to the crown of the head by way of curving over the brain membrane (klad sprin). The sizes are the same as before: the central channel like a bamboo and the side channels are like thin arrows. In this visualization, the two side channels do not bend down to meet the nostrils, but all three channels come out of the crown of the head like a cut stalk of wheat or a cut bamboo. [27] They all have the same height above the crown, extruding beyond the top of the head just a little. They are like the stubble of wheat cut at harvest and one can see inside them. The channel on the right side is white and the one on the left side is red, the reverse for women. The breathing for purification is the same as before.

Then one visualizes that on top of the right-hand white channel is seated the Dharmakaya in the guise of the King of the Sky, Khayi Gyalpo (bon-sku mkha' yi rgyal-po), that is to say, Kuntu Zangpo, who has the essence of the moon. He is naked and luminous white, being the size of a single grain. On the top of the left-hand red channel is seated his divine Consort, Nangwa Gunggi Gyalmo (yum snang-ba gung gi rgyal-mo), that is to say, Kuntu Zangmo, who has the essence of the sun. She is naked and red (or orange), also having the size of a single grain. They look at each other out of the corners of their eyes. Both of them are transparent bodies of light and they express visibly both bliss and wisdom. One should recall that this visualization is the reverse in women. Rays of light come out of them and these go upward into the heavens to all the Deities and invoke a multitude of Jnanasattvas, or wisdom beings (ye-shes-pa), having the same appearance as themselves, who descend and are absorbed into them. The wisdom beings and the symbolic beings thereby become united. One focuses one's full attention on this blissful divine couple on the crown of one's head. [28]

Then one inhales a little and this breath goes down to the bottom where the three channels meet, then it ascends upward to touch the two blissful deities, whereupon they melt into light and become two luminous bindus, a white bindu on the right and red bindu on the left. These bindus are very bright and luminous, emanating with the five rainbow colors. The white bindu comes down the right channel and the red bindu comes down the left red channel. Then they go up the central channel again in ping-pong fashion, go out of the crown, and then go back down into the heart center. There they sit side by side, or one on top of the other as one desires. One focuses attention on them strongly while breathing and holding for seven times. The full cycle is inhaling, holding, adding a little air, continue holding, and then exhaling. This cycle is performed seven times.

If one feels drowsy or dull, one visualizes that they go up the central channel to the crown and disappear, and one remains in the Natural State. If one feels agitated and too many discursive thoughts arise, one sees them dissolve into the central channel at the level of the heart. But if one is not disturbed by either problem, they go down to the bottom, separate, come up again by way of the two side channels to the crown. There they dissolve and one remains in the Natural State. [29] One does this for four sessions a day for one week.

IV. The Fourth Week

As for the fourth week, the essential point is the yantra exercise of the basic position of one's own central channel. [30] The body posture, the channels, and the breathing are all as before.

However, the visualization is different, that is to say, the essential point of the bindus upon which one meditates (bsgom-pa'i thig-le'i gnad). Again one visualizes that the three channels come out the crown of the head like wheat stubble. But this time, the Lord (yab) is sitting on the right-hand side and the Lady (yum) on the left-hand side of the central channel. [31] They have the same size, colors, and positions as described previously. Their gnosis, or primal awareness of bliss, is the same as before. They are not facing one another, but look at each other out of the corners of their eyes.

One inhales a little and when the breath ascending through the two side channels touches the two deities, they melt into light and become two luminous bindus, white and red, as before, emanating rainbow colored lights. They descend through the central channel to the juncture at the bottom and then go separately, ascending inside each of the channels, the white bindu into the white channel on the right and the red bindu into the red channel on the left. They come out the top of the head a little, about one digit. And then go down to the bottom once more, and come up the central channel like juggled ping-pong balls (yar ta-la-la), going up and out. Then they descend into the heart center. Here they stay side by side and one focuses one's attention on them, while breathing and holding the breath seven times as before. [32]

If one feels drowsy or dull, one sees them go down, separate, go up to the doorways of the side channels at the crown and dissolve. If one feels agitated, one sees them absorbed into the central channel at the heart center. If one experiences neither problem, they go up to the door of the central channel and dissolve into their respective sides. Thereafter one expels the stale air and affixes the seal of non-conceptuality, remaining in the Natural State. One does this for four sessions a day for one week.

V. The Fifth Week

As for the fifth week, the essential point is the yantra exercise of the basic position that is like the rainbow. Again the body posture, channels. and breathing are like "the rays of the sun" exercise of the second week above. [33] At the nostrils, one visualizes that there are two bindus the size of Chinese peas, which are comprised of vital wind and subtle mind. [34] They are radiant like sunlight and are luminous with five colors like rainbows around the sun. When one breathes in a little, they go down the side channels to the bottom, and then come up the central channel one after the other again like juggling pebbles. They come out above the crown about one finger width. Then they descend into the heart and come to stay side by side, or one on top of the other, in the heart center as one desires. They remain there face to face like a gau amulet. One fixates one's awareness on them and breathes seven times as before, that is, the cycle of inhaling, holding, adding air, and exhaling. [35]

If one finds that one is agitated, one dissolves the bindus inside the heart center. However, if one is drowsy or dull, one sees them go down to the bottom and separate into the right and left channels and come up to the nostril openings and outside into space where they dissolve. If one has neither problem, one sees them go to the top of the central channel and out into space where they dissolve. One expels the breath and remains in the Natural State. One does this for four sessions a day for one week.

VI. The Sixth Week

As for the sixth week, the essential point is the yantra exercise of the basic position of the HUM abiding, the A emanating, and the OM integrating. The essential point of the body posture that is assumed is the same as above, that is, in the rays of the sun exercise (nyi zer-ma). One performs the nine breathings as usual for purification. But the visualization is different. Here the two side channels curve like a noose or two umbrella handles. [36] In the central channel at the level of the heart, one visualizes an azure-colored HUM syllable the size of a thumb joint. This syllable represents the essence of our own Rigpa, or intrinsic awareness. It is brilliant and emanates rays of light. One fixates one's attention on this HUM syllable in the heart center. [37]

One breathes in a little and the breath goes down the two side channels and comes up the central channel and touches the HUM syllable. Thereupon the HUM flies upward and is expelled above the crown of the head about one finger width. Then it descends through the central channel to the juncture of the three channels at the bottom. Here the azure blue HUM syllable becomes two white A syllables, each radiating rainbow lights, which then enter into the two side channels and transiting them, they go out the nostrils and transform into a multitude of A syllables, sparkling and emanating rainbow lights. Exhaling strongly, they come to fill the entire dark retreat house. One fixates awareness on this. [38]

Then one draws in a little breath. All of these white A letters come together and dissolve one into the other, and then into the two white A syllables at the nostrils. These A syllables dissolve and become two orange OM syllables which are brilliant and emanate rainbow lights. With the inhalation, they go down the two side channels to the juncture at the bottom where they transform into a single blue HUM syllable. This syllable comes up the central channel to the crown of the head and is expelled outside for about one finger width. Then it descends down to the heart center again. Here one fixates attention on this HUM syllable. One breathes seven times maintaining the usual cycle as before. When this cycle is completed, the HUM syllable dissolves into its own place in the heart and one affixes the seal of non-conceptuality, thus remaining in the Natural State. Indeed, the Natural State is the actual point of all this practice, but it takes time to stabilize the Natural State when making a dark retreat. One does this for four sessions a day for one week.

VII. The Seventh and Final Week

As for the final week, the essential point is the yantra exercise of the basic position where the HUM abides, the OM emanates, and the A integrates. The essential points of body posture, the channels, and the breathing are the same as above. [39]

As for the visualization that is the essential point of the bindus upon which one meditates (bsgom-pa thig-le'i gnad): The blue syllable HUM is visualized inside the central channel at the level of the heart, about the size of the thumb joint. It has the nature of Rigpa, that is, one's intrinsic awareness. Rainbows of five colors emanate from it. One fixates one's full attention on it. [40] When one breathes in a little, the breath goes down to the juncture of the three channels at the bottom and entering the central channel, it ascends and comes up to touch the HUM syllable in the heart. It flies upward, exiting at the crown of the head about one finger width. Then it descends to the juncture at the bottom where the HUM transforms into two orange colored OM syllables, emanating rainbow lights. These enter the right and left channels and go up to the nostrils. When one exhales strongly, these OM syllables are expelled into space and become a multitude of luminous OM syllables, sparkling with five colors, which fill the entire dark retreat house. One fixates awareness on this. [41]

Then one begins to inhale. All of these OM syllables dissolve one into the other and entering the nostrils, they become two white A syllables, emanating rainbow lights. These go down through the two side channels to the juncture at the bottom and transform into a single blue HUM. This ascends to the top of the head and is expelled outside into space for about a finger width. Then it descends into the heart. One fixates one's awareness on this HUM syllable in the heart center and breathes seven times as before. When the cycle is complete, the HUM dissolves into the central channel at the heart level. One exhales strongly and then affixes the seal of non-conceptuality, remaining in the Natural State. [42]

Conclusion

The above seven exercises are performed over the course of forty-nine days, one week for each. Then, in terms of the conclusion, there are three systems to be considered:

1. The general method (spyi khyab),
2. The equal parts in agreement (cha mthun), and
3. The reverse order (go ldog).

One may choose to do the full forty-nine days and then conclude the retreat at that point. The general method (spyi khyab) for this is given below and it is not restricted to any particular week. If for whatever reason, one must break the retreat in the middle, for example, because of severe illness, or some other serious circumstance, then it may be resumed at the point where it was broken. Therefore, there are two equal parts (cha mthun) to the retreat. If one chooses to make a one hundred day retreat, thereby doubling the time spent in the dark retreat, then the purification exercises for the second half of the retreat are done in the reverse order (go ldog).

However, with regard to all this, one must ask the Lama supervising the retreat for the instructions at the conclusion of each week. This is because not all practitioners possess the same capacity and may have individual special problems. The final Dzogrim instructions are given on the forty-ninth or last day. On the final day there are four sessions (thun) as usual, and the Dzogrim is practiced after the conclusion of the final session. It is done only one time.

1. The General Method for Each Session

The Visualization in General

The following exercise represents a general method for the Dzogrim employed throughout the cycle of seven weeks. Having visualized the channels as before, one proceeds with the essential point of the bindus upon which one meditates (bsgom-pa thig-le'i gnad). One visualizes the entire brain to be a reddish-yellow or orange-colored sun disc, on top of which there is an orange syllable HRI. Above this, one visualizes the membrane at the top of the brain to be a white moon disc and above this is a second HRI syllable, a yellowish-white in color. Both HRI syllables emanate rays of five colors resembling rainbows. The syllables are one above the other and signify Means and Wisdom respectively. One visualizes them very clearly and focuses one's attention on them. [43]

Then one inhales, holds, and exhales the breath seven times as usual. One holds the breath for as long as possible, adding air on top while focusing awareness on the two HRI syllables. When the cycle is completed, the HRI syllables dissolve into their respective sun and moon disc seats and then these seats dissolve into their own places. With the last breath, the moon disc dissolves into space. One exhales forcefully and remains in the Natural State. One expels the stale air by way of purification and affixes the seal of non-conceptuality, thus remaining in the Natural State thereafter. That represents a general method for concluding each session of practice within the Seven-fold Cycle of the Clear Light. [44]

The Principal Practice

In general, in terms of each of the seven week cycles, there is a particular teaching on the visualization where one fixates on the bindu in the heart and inhales and exhales seven times. This visualization changes with each of the seven cycles. These visualization exercises for purification represent preliminary practices (sngon-'gro)

Then one comes to the principal practice (dngos-gzhi) in relation to the Seven-fold Cycle of the Clear Light. This is contemplation (mnyam-bzhag), or being in the state of intrinsic awareness (rig-pa) that lies beyond thought and visualization. These preliminaries are processes that pertain to mind rather than the Nature of Mind. The state of contemplation, or Trekchod, is elucidated elsewhere in the literature of the Zhang-zhung Nyan-gyud cycle. However, the practitioner may enter into the state of contemplation by way of the visualization of expelling the white letter A, the symbol of Rigpa, out from the central channel into the space above the crown of the head. Thereupon the white A dissolves into the sky and one rests in the Natural State.

In general, one purifies oneself by way of fixating awareness on the visualization of the white luminous letter A inside a bindu of rainbow light within the heart center, while inhaling and holding and adding a little air on top of that for seven times. The oral explanation (zhal-shes) asserts that this visualization of the white A in the heart, or its being expelled from the central channel into space above the crown of the head, is something beyond conceptions (la zla'i dmigs-pa), that is to say, it is not a matter of discursive thought. [45] While engaging in the principal practice of contemplation, one sits in the meditation position of equipoise, observing the five aspects previously described, and clearly visualizes the three channels while inhaling, holding, and expelling the stale air. When one inhales and holds the breath, it comes to touch the luminous letter A in the central channel, whereupon it leaps out into space and dissolves there. However, one does not loose consciousness, for one remains in a condition that is clear, alert, and aware. This is a Trekchod practice that represents a kind of method for forceful purification (rtsal sbyong). But actual Trekchod lies beyond any fixation of mind.

As for the meditation practice involved here, it may begin with a visualization that is beyond concepts (la zla'i dmigs-pa). In the middle of the central channel at the level of the heart, one visualizes a brilliant white letter A, a syllable of light, inside a bindu or tiny sphere radiating five colors like the rainbow. Furthermore, inside the right and left channels, there are two green YAM syllables more or less inside the two nostrils. And moreover, one meditates that at the crown of the head there is a brilliant white wheel of light like the disc of the full moon. When one inhales and holds the breath a little bit, it strikes the two YAM syllables which melt and instantly become green bindus of light, like Chinese peas, that go downward inside the right and left channels to the bottom at the juncture of the three channels where they coalesce into a single bindu. This bindu of green light ascends upward inside the central channel and is absorbed into the A syllable in the middle of the heart. [46] At that, one fixates awareness on the white syllable A and meditates while repeatedly holding the breath, adding air on top, and expelling the stale air for a single session in cycles of seven. One exhales forcefully. When the cycle is completed, the A goes up the central channel and out the top of the head. It goes out and dissolves to the wheel of white light. This wheel dissolves into space and one remains in the Natural State.

This exercise is meant to induce the state of contemplation and may need to be repeated at the discretion of the practitioner during the retreat.

The Perfection Process in General

At the end of each session (thun), one may perform the following Dzogrim exercise, or one may perform it simply at the end of the entire seven day cycle. This is according to the choice of the individual practitioner.

The instructions for the final Perfection Process, or Dzogrim (rdzogs-rim), which concludes the entire dark retreat, are only given on the forty-ninth or last day of the retreat. On this final day, there are four sessions (thun) as usual and the Dzogrim is performed only after the conclusion of the last session. It is done, therefore, only one time. Here one assumes the same posture with the five aspects. The visualization of the three channels is the same as before and one does the nine breathings for purification as usual.

Then visualizing the three channels as before, one also sees the A syllable in the middle of the central channel at the level of the heart and a white wheel of light, or moon disc, above one's head. When one inhales, the breath descends through the two side channels to the point where they converge and then rises up in the central channel. When the breath touches this white A syllable, it goes upward inside the central channel and having been expelled from the crown of the head, it is absorbed into the wheel of light above. Thereupon this wheel of light or moon disc dissolves into space, and one settles into the clarity and the emptiness of an intrinsic awareness that is without grasping at anything whatsoever . [47]

It is not exactly clear in the text how one is to proceed with the Dzogrim, or Perfection Process, at the end of the dark retreat because different aspects of the practice are described in different places. However, on a number of occasions the Lopon has clarified this Dzogrim exercise in his oral instructions. He said that this exercise could be added at the end of each session or just done once at the conclusion of the fourth session on the seventh day. As described above, one visualizes a reddish-yellow (dmar gser) solar disc in the brain with a reddish-yellow HRI syllable above it. Above the brain membrane, there is a while moon disc and above this a yellowish-white HRI syllable. Both syllables are radiant with five colored rainbow lights.

Elsewhere the text provides a further elaboration. Visualizing the three channels as usual, one sees a luminous white syllable A inside the central channel at the level of the heart. One inhales as described, visualizing the breath becoming two luminous green bindus that merge into one in the central channel. Striking the white A syllable in the heart, this syllable flies up through the central channel and merges into the moon disc. One inhales and exhales for seven times, holding for as long as possible, while fixating awareness on the two HRI syllables.

When the cycle is completed with the last exhalation, one sees the two HRI syllables dissolve into their respective seats and the sun and moon discs dissolve into their respective locations in space. Thereafter one remains in the Natural State.

After finishing this concluding exercise, one recites the dedication of merit and shares the good karma accumulated from doing the retreat with all other sentient beings. One also makes the aspiration that they may be relieved of their suffering and become liberated from rebirth in Samsara. [48]

The above exercises represent the stages of the practice in general (spyi khyab rim-pa).

2. The Equal Parts

Having broken the dark retreat for whatever reason, one resumes it where one had left off, thereby harmonizing the two parts (cha mthun) of the retreat. Having repeatedly held the breath as a practice over the course of four sessions in the darkness, one resumes the purification exercises in the same order as given above. One sits in the same meditation position, but now the hands are reversed, the right hand being above the left hand.

3. The Reverse Order

Following the reverse order (go ldog) means that one doubles the time spent in the dark retreat, from forty-nine days to one hundred days in total darkness. Having completed the first forty-nine day cycle of seven purification exercises, one repeats the seven weeks doing all the exercises in the reverse order, proceeding to complete the first week as described before engaging in the Perfection Process.

Leaving the Dark Retreat House

One should come out of the dark retreat before midnight. At first one makes a hole in the dark retreat house wall in order to let in a little light. But one should not come out too suddenly into the light because that is very dangerous for the eyes. One should remain inside the room for two days, with the curtains drawn during the day, but with the window open during the night.

The Practice of Contemplation: Trekchod and Thodgal

According to the Lopon, as the result of the dark retreat, one will come to realize that all of one's waking state visions of the every day world are like the visions which have appeared in the dark retreat. They are only illusions, projections of the mind. What one sees before one is only created by one's thoughts.

Practicing in the dark retreat represents the secondary condition for the development of the Thodgal visions, or the visions of the Clear Light. The actual cause of the visions is the Natural State of the Nature of Mind. In addition to total darkness, one can use as supports, or secondary conditions, the sunlight, the moonlight, or the lamp light. But this must be done in a comfortable fashion, and one should never look directly into the source of the light, especially the sun. One looks one cubit below the sun and one looks a little below the moon or to the side. One also looks to the side of the candle or the flame of the butter lamp.

In the Zhang-zhung tradition, the practice of vision known as Thodgal, whether practicing with the dark retreat or with gazing into the empty sky, is thought to help reinforce and stabilize the practice of contemplation. The principal practice in Dzogchen is Trekchod, or just being in the state of contemplation (mnyam-bzhag). This state is characterized not by any particular thought, but by an intrinsic awareness (rig-pa). The practitioner is globally alert and aware, with all the senses fully operational. But if one becomes distracted and strays from the practice of contemplation, then even if one remains for a hundred years in a comfortable and luxurious dark retreat, it will mean nothing in the end. One might just as well be a prisoner in an underground dungeon in solitary confinement. If one's Trekchod practice has not attained a certain degree of stability and firmness, there will be no value in the practice of Thodgal. It will mean little more than watching television. But once one has become familiar with the state of contemplation by way of doing fixation practice (sems-'dzin), one may find a dark retreat useful for stabilizing contemplation. For such a retreat there is no specific time limit, but when contemplation is linked with the development of vision, we have the forty-nine day dark retreat described above. Once one knows how to relax and settle into the Natural State, it will no longer be necessary to continue practicing fixation as one did at the beginning of a retreat. No specific qualities or capacities need to be artificially cultivated. Everything that one needs, all the ten perfections, are already present, indeed, primordially present, in the Natural State. Emptiness and clarity are already inseparable in the Natural State of the Nature of Mind. One does not need to coerce anything nor make strenuous efforts. The Thodgal visions will arise naturally and spontaneously of themselves, totally without effort.

But the practitioner must realize that Dzogchen practice and genuine understanding have nothing to do with discursive thoughts or the conceptual constructions that we conventionally call "reality". These thoughts and concepts do no apply to the immediate intuition of our experience. They cannot grasp nor apprehend the Nature of Reality (bon-nyid) – for this can only be seen or reflected by Rigpa, or intrinsic awareness. And it is just this Rigpa that characterizes the Natural State of the Nature of Mind. However, even though it is empty and lacks any inherent existence, the Natural State is not a mere absence or nothingness. The practitioner can be in the Natural State and still sense things. This is what is meant by clarity (gsal-ba). The Natural State is like a mirror reflecting whatever is set before it. The individual continuously sees, hears, smells, tastes, and touches, but without elaborating anything into conceptual constructions (spros-med). One is clear like a mirror, without being distracted or distorted. This is clarity; the senses are fully operational. But one does not judge nor think about nor conceptualize what is sensed. When one is thoroughly familiar with this condition of pure intrinsic awareness and has the capacity to remain in it for a time continuously, then sensations will not disturb it. There ceases to be any distinction between sensing and what is sensed, that is to say, what is called subject and object on the level of perception. One becomes deconditioned and moves beyond the conventional processes of perception which are the products of social and cultural conditioning.

In terms of the state of contemplation, it does not matter whether one finds oneself in a condition of calm with no thoughts or in the movements of energy we call thoughts and experiences, for one's circumstance is totally that of intrinsic awareness. Everything that arises is just like an illusion, just a manifestation of space and energy (or light), with nothing substantial in or behind it. And although these appearances are like illusions, nevertheless they are spontaneously self-perfected just as they are. They do not need to be evaluated, modified, nor corrected. The vision is just as it is. The visions that arise are the self-manifestations of the inherent energy of the Nature of Mind and nothing else. Nothing stands beyond them. And when one becomes stable in the Natural State, nothing will come to disturb it. Visible phenomena may indeed manifest to the senses, but they will not lead one anywhere else. They are just phenomena, manifestations of energy. Thoughts may arise in the mind-stream, but they equally do not distract from intrinsic awareness. The processes of delusion that we call Samsara will no longer hold sway over the mind and one discovers the possibility of freedom and liberation.

MU-TSUG SMAR-RO!

Notes to Part Two

Notes to the Translation

(1) *Emaho/ ye-nyid ston-pa'i sku la phyag 'tshal-lo.* E-ma-ho means
"How wonderful!" The Primordial Teacher, or the Teacher
in Eternity (ye-nyid ston-pa), is the Primordial Buddha Kuntu
Zangpo. The reference is to Rigpa as the Primordial Teacher or
Awareness (rig-pa) being embodied in the stream of consciousness
of the individual sentient being.

(2) *gSang-sngags zab-mo rdzogs-chen snyan rgyud kyi rtsa rlung gnad
kyi gdams-pa 'di rnams/ bder-gshegs grub-thob bla-ma yis/ mu-
tig phreng-ba bzhin du rim-par brgyud nas.......* Here the author
classifies Dzogchen as belonging to the Secret Mantra system of
the Tantras. This transmission is compared to a string of pearls
(mu-tig phreng-ba).

(3) The preliminary practices for the Zhang-zhung Nyan-gyud are
found in the *rGyal-ba phyag-khrid* of Bru-chen rGyal-ba g.yung-
drung. See the transaltion in the Appendix of Reynolds, *The Oral
Tradition from Zhang-zhung,* ibid.

(4) *Da ni rtsa rlung zhal-shes 'di ltar bsgom/ rtsa 'dul gyi bca' gzhi
'khrul-'khor gyi gnad/ lus sems mnyam-par bzhag-pa/ rlung sems
gcun la bor-ba.* According to the Lopon, *zhal-shes* means a clear
explanation. *rTsa-lung,* more fully, *rtsa rlung thig-le'i rnal-'byor* is
the internal yoga discipline that works with the psychic channels
(rtsa), the vital winds or psychic energies (rlung), and the droplets
or quanta of psychic energy (thig-le). By way of the control and

the harmonization of these energies, the body and the mind are brought into a condition of balance and harmony (lus sems mnyam-par bzhag-pa).

(5) *Lus sems mnyam-par bzhag-pa.*

(6) *Lus cha-lugs lnga ldan gyi phyag-rgya bca'/ zhabs skyil-krung bca'/ phyag mnyam-gzhag/ sgal-tshigs mda' ltar bsrang/ mgrin-pa lcags-kyu ltar bkugs/ dpung-pa rgod (bya) gshogs lding-ba/ ljags ya-rkang la ma reg rtsam/ kha so bar-du yi-ge A phra-mo mthar tsam bya.*

(7) *sPang-rgyan*, "ornament (rgyan) of the alpine meadows (spang)"; flowers that bloom in the high meadows in autumn. There exist several varieties, but here the reference is to the blue flowers of Gentiana Stipitata Edgew, *spang-rgyan sngon-po.*

(8) *bsKyed-pa rtsa'i gnad..... yar sne snying sul bar gsum du phye nas/ ag-rtse'i nang nas thon-pa.... klad phor..... klad sprin..... klad phor gyi nang klad sprin phyir 'grims nas/ sna sgo gnyis thal-ler zugs-pa.* In the Buddhist system, these three principle channels are known as Rasana (ro-ma), Lalana (rkyang-ma), and Avadhuti (dbu-ma). They represent potential pathways for the movement of psychic energies and by visualizing or imagining them (dmigs-pa), one makes them actual and thereby moves the energy through them.

(9) *Nye-lo u-dpal* is the name for the Avadhuti-nadi, or the central channel, in the Zhang-zhung language. The word *u-dpal* is from the Sanskrit utpala, the blue lotus, referring to the color of the channel.

(10) *rLung sems gcun la bor-ba ni/ rlung-ro dgu phrag gcig sangs kyis 'bud/ nyams-len thun gcig gi steng du shes-pa dar tsam bzhag/ rtsa 'dul/ rtsa 'dul g.yas g.yon dbus gsum dgu phrag sbyangs.*

(11) *mTshams-bcad bca' gzhi 'khrul-'khor gyi gnad ni/ lus sems mnyam-par bzhag-pa/ rtsa 'dul rlung sbrugs la sogs/ gong ltar.*

(12) *bCa'-ba lus kyi gnad la/ khro-bo'i 'gying stabs gyi lus gnad bca'.*

(13) *bsKyed-pa rtsa yi gnad la/ rtsa gsum gong ltar gsal-gdab.*

(14) *bZung-ba rlung gi gnad/ rlung-ro sangs kyis 'bud.*

(15) *bsGom-pa thig-le'i gnad la/ bsgom-pa thig-le'i gnad la/ ngag tu BSWO zhes brjod-pas/ mi mngon-pa'i dbyings nas BSWO dmar nag ye-shes kyi tshwa-tshwa si-li-li 'phro-ba zhig/ spyi-tshug nas dbus mthing gi nang du brgyud/ snying gi dkyil du rang gi rig-pa'i ngo-bo dang gnyis su med-pa gcig tu 'dres-pa la/ bdag-nyid las kyi khro-bo sku mdog dmar nag/ dpa' rngam brjid-pa'i chas dang ldan-pa/ gzhi gnas BSWO.* Gnosis, or primal awareness (ye-shes, Skt.

jnana), is that immediate intuition of awareness that is present before the mind and the perception process comes into operation. This is an awareness that is present prior to the operations of the thought process and the making of the distinction into subject and object. It represents, therefore, a non-dual awareness.

(16) *Ngag tu BSWO zhes brjod-pas/ g.yas nas rlung nyams tsam zhig bzug-bas/ dbus mthing gi BSWO las BSWO grangs med-par 'phros nas, g.yas dkar gyi nang ltem gyis gang/ g.yas nas rlung phar zhugs dus mun-khang nam-mkha' bar-snang sa-gzhi dang bcas-pa BSWO dmar nag las ye-shes kyi tsha-tsha si-li-li 'phros-bas ltem gyis gang/ BSWO zhes brjod-pas g,yon nas rlung nyams tsam zhig bzung-bas/ g.yas dkar gyi BSWO las grangs med-par 'phros nas. g.yon dmar gyi nang ltem gyis gang/ bgegs dang log-'dren 'byung-po gang gis/ de la shes-pa gtad la/ rlung bzhur gnon bdun gyi bar du bsgom/ de tshangs-pa.* The skandhas, the dhatus, and the ayatanas refer to the factors and the processes in conscious experience. Sensation, feeling, perception, impulses, and consciousness itself are the five skandhas. The dhatus (elements or dimensions) are the six sense organs and the six sense objects, including mental consciousness and mental objects. The ayatanas are the six sense fields, that is, the spheres of activity of the six senses.

(17) *rDzogs-rim ni.... phyi'i BSWO rnams 'od du zhu nas/ g.yas dkar g.yon dmar gyi BSWO la thim/ dbus mthing gi BSWO rnams 'od du zhu nas/ gzhi gnas kyi BSWO la thim/ gzhi gnas kyi BSWO dang khro-bo rnams mkha' la gzha' yal-ba ltar mi dmigs-pa'i rgyas gdab-bo.* Affixing the seal of non-conceptuality (mi dmigs-pa'i rgyas gdab) means dissolving the visualization into the state of Shunyata and thereupon remaining for a time in contemplation (mnyam-bzhag).

(18) *bDag khrid 'od-gsal gyi mtshams-bcad yig chung.*

(19) *E-ma-ho/ ye-nyid ston-pa'i sku la phyag 'tshal-lo...... brgyud-pa'i bla-ma rnams la phyag 'tshal-lo.*

(20) *rTsa rlung 'khrul-'khor gnad 'di ni/ snyan-rgyud rtsa-ba'i dmigs-pa/ snying nang khrag rlon dang 'dra-ba'i gdams-pa/ 'od-gsal bdun skor dmigs-pa/ gcig brgyud/ sngon gyi grub-thob rnams kyis gcig nas gcig tu brgyud-pa'i gdams-pa/ gnyis phyin-chad la mi bstan-pa'i bka' rgya gdab/ zhal-shes dkar-chags yi-ger bkod.* Possibly the author speaking here is Yangton Chenpo Sherab Gyaltsan who is largely responsible for the present form of the Zhang-zhung

collection. See Reynolds, *The Oral Tradition from Zhang-zhung*, ibid.

(21) *'Od-gsal dmigs-pa bdun skor la.....*

(22) *Nyi rdul-ma'i bca' gzhi 'khrul-'khor gyi gnad.*

(23) *Lus sems mnyam-par bzhag-pa/ rlung gcun la bor-ba/ rlung rtsa 'dul dgu phrug/ gong ltar mthun/ bca'-ba lus kyi gnad/ lus rang-bzhin cha-lugs lnga ston gyi phyag-rgya bca']/ rlung chen ar la gtad/ rgya-mtsho ri-rab la bcar/ ro-'dzin btson du bzung/ gza' chen gyen du ldog/ bskyed-pa rtsa'i gnad la rtsa gsum gong ltar gsal-gdab/ gzung-ba rlung gi gnad/ rlung-ro dgu phrug gcig sangs kyis 'bud/.... bsgom-pa thig-le'i gnad ni/ sna sgor rlung sems thig-le'i ngo-bo nyi-ma'i srab mda' lta-bu khra lam-me gcig dang sngo ljang khyug-ge-ba gnyis (thig-le) gnyis bsgom.*

(24) *De la shes-pa gtad/ rlung nyams tsam zhig bzung-ba'i rtsa g.yas g.yon nang du brgyud/ rtsa gsum dbus mthing gi mar sner smug (-po) bring-nge-ba 'dres nas/ rtsa dbus mthing gi nang yar ta-la-la song nas/ spyi-tshug sor gang tsam 'bor gyis thon/ mar dal kyis babs/ snying gi dkyil du ltem gyis gnas-pa/ rlung phar thsur lan bdun bsgom/ de tshangs-pa...... thig-le yang nam-mkha' la dngos-med yal-bar bsam bsres/ rlung-ro sangs kyis 'bud/ mi dmigs-pa'i rgyas gdab.*

(25) *bDun gnyis-pa nyi zer-ma'i bca' gzhi la/ 'khrul-'khor lus gnad rtsa rlung gong dang 'dra.*

(26) *bsGom-pa thig-le'i gnad la/ sna sgo g.yas su thig-le dkar-ser/ g.yon du dmar-ser tgya sran gyi 'bru-ma tsam las/ gzhah'-tshon sna lnga'i 'od zer 'phro-ba cig/ rtsa g.yas g.yon gyi nang brgyud/ rtsa dbus mthing gi mar sne nas/ thig-le sgong spor-ba bzhin du yar ta-la-la spyi-tshug (tu) sor gang tsam 'bor gyis thon/ mar dal gyis babs/ snying gi dkyil du gral thabs sam/ ga'u kha-sbyor gyi tshul du gnas-pa/ de la shes-pa gtad la rlung bzhur gnon bdun gyi bar du bya/ de tshangs-ba/ rmugs 'thibs dus su klad-pa'i dung-khang bstim/ 'phro rgod gyi dus su snying gi dkyil du bstim/ 'phro rgod rmugs 'thibs gang yang med na/ sna sgo gnyis su rang mal du yal-bar bsam/ rlung-ro sangs kyis 'bud/ mi dmigs-pa'i rgyas gdab.*

(27) *bDun gsum-pa rtsa g.yas dkar g.yon dmar gyi 'khrul-'khor bca' gzhi'i gnad/ bca'-ba lus gnad gong dang mthun.*

(28) *bsKyed-pa rtsa yi gnad la/ rtsa gsum mar sne sgal-tshigs kha-bo-che la yi-ge CHA'i zhabs ltar zugs-pa/ yar sne snying sul-bar gsum du phye nas/ rtsa gsum spyi-gtsug tu gro sog bcad-pa ltar sbu-gu*

rog-ge-ba/ bzung-ba rlung gi gnad la/ rlung-ro dgu phrug gcig sangs kyi 'bud/ bsgom-pa thig-le'i gnad la/ g.yas dkar gyi steng la yab mkha' yi rgyal-po kun tu bzang-po zla-ba'i snying-po nas 'du tsam bsgom/ g.yon dmar gyi steng la yum snang-ma skos kyi rgyal-mo nyi-ma snying-po/ de yang yab kyis yum la g.yon zur du gzigs-pa/ yum gyis yab la g.yas zur du gzigs-pa/ 'od kyi sku mkhyen brtse dang ldan-pa gnyis bskyed/ 'od zer yar 'phros dbyings na bzhugs-pa'i lha yab yum de 'dra-ba spyan-drasngs gnyis-med bstim/ de la shes-pa gtad la rlung nyams tsam du bzubg-bas/ dbugs drod lha yab yum la phog/ lha yab yum 'od du zhu nas thig-le dkar dmar rgya-sran 'bru-ma tsam la/ gzha'-tshon sna lnga'i 'od zer 'phro-ba gnyis/ rtsa g.yas g.yon gyi nang mar babs/ dbus mthing gi nang du yar sgong spor-ba bzhin yar ta-la-la spyi-gtsug tu sor gang tsam 'bor gyis thon/ mar dal gyis babs/ snying gi dkyil du gral thabs sam/ ga'u kha-sbyor tshul du bsgom/ de la shes-pa gtad la/ rlung bzhur gnon bdun bya/ de tshangs-pa dang rmugs 'thibs dus su dbus mthing kha la bstim/ 'phro rgod dus su snying gi dkyil du bsgom/ gang yang ma byung na/ g.yas g.yon kha la rang mal du yal-bar bsam.

(29) *bDun bzhi-pa la dbus mthing rang gi bca' gzhi 'khrul-'khor gyi gnad la/ lus gnad rtsa rlung gong ltar-ro.*

(30) *bsGom-pa thig-le'i gnad la/ rtsa dbus mthing gi rtsa 'dab g.yas su yab mkha'i rgyal-po/ g.yon du yum snang-ma skos kyi rgyal-mo gong ltar bskyed/ de la shes-pa gtad la rlung nyams tsam zhig bzung-bas/ dbugs dang drod rlangs tsam zhig lha yab yum la phog/ lha yab yum 'od du zhu nas thig-le dkar dmar rgya-sran 'bru-ma tsam la/ gzha'-tshon sna lnga'i 'od zer 'phro-ba gnyis/ rtsa dbus mthing gi nang du mar babs/ rtsa g.yas g.yon nang du yar ta-la-la spyi-gtsug tu sor gang tsam du 'bor gyis thon/ mar dal gyis babs/ snying gi dkyil du gral thabs sam/ ga'u kha-sbyor tshul du bsgom/ de la shes-pa gtad la/ rlung bzhur gnon bdun bya/ de tshangs-pa dang rmugs 'thibs dus su g.yas g.yon kha la bstim/ 'phro rgod dus su snying gi dkyil du bstim/ gang yang ma byung na rtsa dbus mthing gi kha la rang mal du yal-bar bsam/ rlung-ro sangs kyis 'bud/ mi dmigs-pa'i rgyas gdab.*

(31) *bDun lnga-pa la gzha'-tshon-ma'i bca' gzhi 'khrul-'khor gyi gnad/ lus gnad rtsa rlung nyi zer-ma ltar-ro.*

(32) *bsGom-pa thig-le'i gnad la/ sna sgo gnyis rlung sems thig-le'i ngo-bo nyi-ma gzha' 'khrigs-pa ltar rgya-sran 'bru-ma tsam las/ gzha'-*

tshon sna lnga'i 'od zer 'phro-ba gnyis/ rtsa g.yas g.yon nang du brgyud/ dbus mthing gi nang du yar thig-le gnyis sgong spor-ba ltar/ yar ta-la-la spyi-gtsug tu sor gang tsam du 'bor gyis thon/ mar dal gyis babs/ snying gi dkyil du gral thabs sam/ ga'u kha-sbyor tshul du gnas/ de la shes-pa gtad la/ rlung bzhur gnon bdun bya/ de tshangs-pa dang 'phro rgod dus su snying gi dkyil du bstim/ rmugs 'thibs dus su rtsa g.yas g.yon kha la bstim/ gang yang ma byung na dbus mthing gi steng du rang babs su yal-bar bsam/ rlung-ro sangs kyis 'bud/ mi dmigs-pa'i rgyas gdab.

(33) *bDun drug-pa la gnas-pa HUM spros-pa A bsdu-ba OM 'khrul-'khor gyi bca' gzhi'i gnad/ bca'-ba lus kyi gnad gong dang 'dra/ bskyed-pa rtsa'i gnad zhags-pa ma ltar gsal-gdab.*

(34) *bsGom-pa thig-le'i gnad ni/ snying gi dkyil du rang gi rig-pa'i ngo-bo HUM mthing-kha tshon gang-ba las/ gzha'-tshon sna lnga'i 'od zer 'phros-ba/ de la shes-pa gtad/ rlung nyams tsam zhig bzung-bas/ HUM de rlung gis 'ded-pa'i tshul du/ dbus mthing gi nang yar ta-la-la spyi-tshug tu sor gang tsam 'bor gyis thon/ mar dal gyis babs/ rtsa gsum 'dus mdor A dkar-po gzha'-tshon sna lnga'i 'od zer 'phro-ba gnyis su bsam/ rtsa g.yas g.yon nang du brgyud/ sna sgo gnyis su phyin-pa/ rlung-ro sangs kyis 'bud/ mun-khang nang dang nam-mkha' bar-snang sa-gzhi dang bcas-pa gzha'-tshon A yis khrig-ger gang-bar bsgom/ de la shes-pa gtad la rlung nyams tsam zhig bzung la/ A rnams gcig la gcig thim/ sna sgo gnyis la A dkar-po zhig tu gyur/ A de 'od du zhu-ba las/ OM dmar ser la gzha'-tshon sna lnga'i 'od zer 'phro-ba gnyis su bsgom/ rtsa dbus mthing gi mar sner HUM du bsgom/ yar ta-la-la spyi-tshug tu sor gang tsam 'bor gyis thon/ rlung bzhur gnon bdun bya/ de tshangs-pa dang HUM de snying gi dkyil du bstim/ rlung-ro sangs kyis 'bud/ mi dmigs-pa'i rgyas gdab-bo.*

(35) *bDun tha-ma la gnas-pa HUM spros-pa OM bsdu-ba A yi bca' gzhi 'krul-'khor gyi gnad/ lus gnad rtsa rlung gong ltar-ro.*

(36) *bsGom-pa thig-le'i gnad ni/ snying gi dkyil du rig-pa'i ngo-bo HUM mthing-kha tshon gang-ba las/ gzha'-tshon sna lnga'i 'od zer 'phros-ba/ de la shes-pa gtad/ rlung nyams tsam zhig bzung-bas/ HUM de rlung gis 'ded-pa'i tshul du/ dbus mthing gi nang na/ yar ta-la-la spyi-tshug tu sor gang tsam 'bor gyis thon/ mar dal gyis babs/ rtsa gsum 'dus mdor OM dmar-po las gzha'-tshon sna lnga'i 'od zer 'phro-ba gnyis su gyur/ rtsa g.yas g.yon nang nas brgyud/ sna sgo gnyis su phyin-pa/ rlung-ro sangs kyis 'bud/*

*mun-khang nang dang nam-mkha' bar-snang sa-gzhi dang bcas-pa
gzha'-tshon OM yis khrig-ger gang-bar bsgom/ de la shes-pa gtad
la/ rlung nyams tsam zhig bzung la/ OM rnams gcig la gcig thim/
sna sgo gnyis su A dkar-po la gzha'-tshon sna lnga'i 'od zer 'phro-
ba gnyis su gyur/ rtsa g.yas g.yon gi nang brgyud/ rtsa gsum 'dus
mdor HUM du gyur/ yar ta-la-la spyi-tshug tu sor gang tsam 'bor
gyis thon/ mar dal gyis babs/ snying gi dkyil du 'bol-le lam-mer
gnas-pa]/ rlung bzhur gnon bdun bya/ de tshangs-pa dang HUM de
snying gi dkyil du bstim/ rlung-ro sangs kyis 'bud/ mi dmigs-pa'i
rgyas gdab-bo.*

(37) *sPyi khyab/ cha mthun/ go ldog.... man-ngag yin zhal las shes rjes
bya la.*

(38) *bsgGm-pa thig-le'i gnad la/ klad-pa nyi gdan dmar-ser gyi steng du
HRI dmar-ser/ klad sprin zla gdan dkar-ser gyi steng du HRI dkar-
ser/ thabs shes kyi HRI gnyis mtho brtsegs su hrig-ger gnas-pa/.....
'od-gsal bdun skor spyi mnan yod.*

(39) *dNgos-gzhi 'od-gsal bdun skor la.....*

(40) *sPyi mnan du sbyang-ba ni/ dmigs-pa snying-khar gtad ching rlung
bzhur gnon bdun bsgom.*

(41) *Zhal shes/ la zla'i dmigs-pa re re sprad/ la zla'i dmigs-pa la lus
mnyam-bzhag tsa gsum gsal-gdab.* A visualization beyond
conception (la zla'i dmigs-pa) means that the normal thought
processes of the mind are operating at a bare minimum or entirely
suspended.

(42) *bsGom-pa ni/ snying dkyil du 'od kyi A dkar-po kha-dog lnga-ldan
zhig bsgom/ spyi-gtsug tu 'od kyi 'khor-lo bsgom/ YAM gnyis la
phog-pas/ 'od ljang-khu dar skud tsam mar song/ rtsa gsum 'dus
mdor dbu-ma'i nang nas yar tal gyis song/ snying dkyil gyi A la
thim/..... rtsa gsum 'dus mdor gcig tu 'dril.*

(43) *rDzogs-rim ni/ A de dbu-ma'i nang nas yar la song/ spyi-gtsug nas
thon nas/ 'od kyi 'khor-lo la thim/ 'od kyi 'khor-lo yang nam-mkha'
la yal/ rig-pa gsal stong 'dzin-med du bzhag/ de ni spyi khyab rim-
pa.*

(44) *Cha mthun.*

(45) *Go ldog.*

(46) *De rnams gzhung gi dmigs bskor yin/* SAMAYA *rgya rgya rgya/
dge'o* ITI. Samaya means "I promise" or "this is my promise";
rgya rgya rgya meanes "thrice sealed"; *dge'o* means "virtue!"; and
ITI is Sanskrit for "thus".

Notes to the Commentary One: Beginning the Dark Retreat

(1) This practice is described in the commentary on the principal practices (dngos-gzhi) found in the *rGyal-ba phyag-khrid* which is entitled *Zhang-zhung snyan-rgyud kyi khrid rim lag-len*. See the translation above.

(2) *rTsa 'dul gyi bca' gzhi 'khrul-'khor gyi gnad.*

(3) *Lus cha-lugs lnga-ldan gyi phyag-rgya bca'.*

(4) See the translation of the Guru Yoga for Tapihritsa in Appendix One of Reynolds, *The Oral Tradition from Zhang-zhung*, ibid.

(5) *rTsa dbu-ma mthing-kha.*

(6) *rLung sems gcun la bor-ba.*

(7) *rTsa 'dul dgu phrag sbyangs-pa.*

(8) *mTshams-bcad bca' gzhi 'khrul-'khor gyi gnad.*

(9) *Khro-bo'i 'gying stabs gyi lus gnad bca'.*

(10) *rLung-ro sangs kyis 'bud.*

(11) *sNying gi dkyil du rang gi rig-pa'i ngo-bo dang gnyis su med-pa gcig tu 'dres-pa..... bdag-nyid las kyi khro-bo sku mdog dmar nag dpa' rngam brjid-pa'i chas ldan-pa.*

(12) *bGegs dang log-'dren 'byung-po.... de la shes-pa gtad.*

(13) *rLung bzhur gnon bdun gyi bar du bsgom.*

(14) *Phyi'i BSWO rnams 'od du zhu nas/ g.yas dkar g.yon dmar gyi BSWO la thim.*

(15) *dBus mthing gi BSWO rnams 'od du zhu nas/ gzhi gnas kyi BSWO la thim.*

(16) *gZhi gnas kyi BSWO dang khro-bo rnams mkha' la gzha' yal-ba ltar mi dmigs-pa'i rgyas gdab-bo.*

Notes to the Commentary Two: The Practices for the Seven Weeks

(1) *rTsa rlung 'khrul-'khor gnad 'di.*

(2) *sNyan-rgyud rtsa-ba'i dmigs-pa.*

(3) *sNying nang khrag rlon dang 'dra-ba'i gdams-pa.*

(4) *sNgon gyi grub-thob rnams kyis gcig nas gcig tu brgyud-pa'i gdams-pa/ gnyis phyin-chad la mi bstan-pa'i bka' rgya gdab.*

(5) *Phyi-rabs don du zhal-shes dkar-chags yi-ger bkod.*

(6) *bDun dang-po ni nyi rdul-ma'i bca' gzhi 'khrul-'khor gyi gnad.*

(7) *bCa'-ba lus kyi gnad..... lus rang-bzhin cha-lugs lnga ston gyi phyag-rgya bca'.*

(8) *Lung chen ar la gtad.*

(9) *Ro-'dzin btson du bzung.*

(10) *gZa' chen gyen du ldog.*

(11) *bsKyed-pa rtsa'i gnad la rtsa gsum gong ltar gsal-gdab.*

(12) *gZung-ba rlung gi gnad/ rlung-ro dgu phrug gcig sangs kyis 'bud.*

(13) *sNa sgor rlung sems thig-le'i ngo-bo nyi-ma'i srab mda' lta-bu khra lam-me gcig dang sngo ljang khyug-ge-ba gnyis [thig-le] gnyis bsgom.*

(14) *De la shes-pa gtad.*

(15) *rLung nyams tsam zhig bzung-ba'i rtsa g.yas g.yon nang du brgyud/ rtsa gsum dbus mthing gi mar sner smug [-po] bring-nge-ba 'dres nas/ rtsa dbus mthing gi nang yar ta-la-la song nas/ spyi-tshug sor gang tsam 'bor gyis thon/ mar dal kyis babs/ snying gi dkyil du ltem gyis gnas-pa.*

(16) *Thig-le yang nam-mkha' la dngos-med yal-bar bsam bsres.*

(17) *bDun gnyis-pa nyi zer-ma'i bca' gzhi/ 'khrul-'khor lus gnad rtsa rlung gong dang 'dra.*

(18) *sNa sgo g.yas su thig-le dkar-ser/ g.yon du dmar-ser rgya sran gyi 'bru-ma tsam las/ gzha'-tshon sna lnga'i 'od zer 'phro-ba cig.*

(19) *rTsa g.yas g.yon gyi nang brgyud/ rtsa dbus mthing gi mar sne nas/ thig-le sgong spor-ba bzhin du yar ta-la-la spyi-tshug [tu] sor gang tsam 'bor gyis thon/ mar dal gyis babs/ snying gi dkyil du gral thabs sam/ ga'u kha-sbyor gyi tshul du gnas-pa.*

(20) *De la shes-pa gtad la rlung bzhur gnon bdun gyi bar du bya.*

(21) *rLung-ro sangs kyis 'bud/ mi dmigs-pa'i rgyas gdab.*

(22) *rMugs 'thibs dus su klad-pa'i dung-khang bstim.*

(23) *'Phro rgod gyi dus su snying gi dkyil du bstim.*

(24) *'Phro rgod rmugs 'thibs gang yang med na/ sna sgo gnyis su rang mal du yal-bar bsam.*

(25) *bDun gsum-pa rtsa g.yas dkar g.yon dmar gyi 'khrul-'khor bca' gzhi'i gnad.*

(26) *rTsa gsum mar sne sgal-tshigs kha-bo-che la yi-ge CHA'i zhabs ltar zugs-pa.*

(27) *Yar sne snying sul-bar gsum du phye nas/ rtsa gsum spyi-gtsug tu gro sog bcad-pa ltar sbu-gu rog-ge-ba.*

(28) *bsGom-pa thig-le'i gnad la/ g.yas dkar gyi steng la yab mkha' yi rgyal-po kun tu bzang-po zla-ba'i snying-po nas 'du tsam bsgom/*

g.yon dmar gyi steng la yum snang-ma skos kyi rgyal-mo nyi-ma snying-po/ de yang yab kyis yum la g.yon zur du gzigs-pa/ yum gyis yab la g.yas zur du gzigs-pa/ 'od kyi sku mkhyen brtse dang ldan-pa gnyis bskyed/ 'od zer yar 'phros dbyings na bzhugs-pa'i lha yab yum de 'dra-ba spyan-drangs gnyis-med bstim.

(29) *De tshangs-pa dang rmugs 'thibs dus su dbus mthing kha la bstim/ 'phro rgod dus su snying gi dkyil du bsgom/ gang yang ma byung na/ g.yas g.yon kha la rang mal du yal-bar bsam/ rlung-ro sangs kyis 'bud/ mi dmigs-pa'i rgyas gdab.*

(30) *bDun bzhi-pa la dbus mthing rang gi bca' gzhi 'khrul-'khor gyi gnad.*

(31) *rTsa dbus mthing gi rtsa 'dab g.yas su yab mkha'i rgyal-po/ g.yon du yum snang-ma skos kyi rgyal-mo gong ltar bskyed.*

(32) *De la shes-pa gtad la/ rlung bzhur gnon bdun bya.*

(33) *bDun lnga-pa la gzha'-tshon-ma'i bca' gzhi 'khrul-'khor gyi gnad/ lus gnad rtsa rLung nyi zer-ma ltar.*

(34) *rLung sems thig'i ngo-bo.*

(35) *bsGom-pa thig-le'i gnad la/ sna sgo gnyis rlung sems thig-le'i ngo-bo nyi-ma gzha' 'khrigs-pa ltar rgya-sran 'bru-ma tsam las/ gzha'-tshon sna lnga'i 'od zer 'phro-ba gnyis/ rtsa g.yas g.yon nang du brgyud/ dbus mthing gi nang du yar thig-le gnyis sgong spor-ba ltar/ yar ta-la-la spyi-gtsug tu sor gang tsam du 'bor gyis thon/ mar dal gyis babs/ snying gi dkyil du gral thabs sam/ ga'u kha-sbyor tshul du gnas/ de la shes-pa gtad la/ rlung bzhur gnon bdun bya.*

(36) *bDun drug-pa la gnas-pa HUM spros-pa A bsdu-ba OM 'khrul-'khor gyi bca' gzhi'i gnad/ bca'ba lus kyi gnad gong dang 'dra/ bskyed-pa rtsa'i gnad zhags-pa ma ltar gsal-gdab.*

(37) *bsGom-pa thig-le'i gnad ni/ snying gi dkyil du rang gi rig-pa'i ngo-bo HUM mthing-kha tshon gang-ba las/ gzha'-tshon sna lnga'i 'od zer 'phros-ba/ de la shes-pa gtad.*

(38) *rLung nyams tsam zhig bzung-bas/ HUM de rlung gis 'ded-pa'i tshul du/ dbus mthing gi nang yar ta-la-la spyi-tshug tu sor gang tsam 'bor gyis thon/ mar dal gyis babs/ rtsa gsum 'dus mdor A dkar-po gzha'-tshon sna lnga'i 'od zer 'phro-ba gnyis su bsam/ rtsa g.yas g.yon nang du brgyud/ sna sgo gnyis su phyin-pa/ rlung-ro kyis 'bud/ mun-khang nang dang nam-mkha' bar-snang sa-gzhi dang bcas-pa gzha'-tshon A yis khrig-ger gang-bar bsgom.*

(39) *bDun tha-ma la gnas-pa HUM spros-pa OM bsdu-ba A yi bca' gzhi 'krul-'khor gyi gnad/ lus gnad rtsa rlung gong ltar-ro.*

(40) *bsGom-pa thig-le'i gnad/ snying gi dkyil du rig-pa'i ngo-bo HUM mthing-kha tshon gang-ba las/ gzha'-tshon sna lnga'i 'od zer 'phros-ba/ de la shes-pa gtad.*

(41) *rLung nyams tsam zhig bzung-bas/ HUM de rlung gis 'ded-pa'i tshul du/ dbus mthing gi nang na/ yar ta-la-la spyi-tshug tu sor gang tsam 'bor gyis thon/ mar dal gyis babs/ rtsa gsum 'dus mdor OM dmar-po las gzha'-tshon sna lnga'i 'od zer 'phro-ba gnyis su gyur/ rtsa g.yas g.yon nang nas brgyud/ sna sgo gnyis su phyin-pa/ rlung-ro sangs kyis 'bud/ mun-khang nang dang nam-mkha' bar-snang sa-gzhi dang bcas-pa gzha'-tshon OM yis khrig-ger gang-bar bsgom/ de la shes-pa gtad la.*

(42) *rLung nyams tsam zhig bzung la/ OM rnams gcig la gcig thim/ sna sgo gnyis su A dkar-po la gzha'-tshon sna lnga'i 'od zer 'phro-ba gnyis su gyur/ rtsa g.yas g.yon gi nang brgyud/ rtsa gsum 'dus mdor HUM du gyur/ yar ta-la-la spyi-tshug tu sor gang tsam 'bor gyis thon/ mar dal gyis babs/ snying gi dkyil du 'bol-le lam-mer gnas-pa/ rlung bzhur gnon bdun bya/ de tshangs-pa dang HUM de snying gi dkyil du bstim/ rlung-ro sangs kyis 'bud/ mi dmigs-pa'i rgyas gdab-bo.*

(43) *bsGom-pa thig-le'i gnad ni/ klad-pa nyi gdan dmar-ser gyi steng du HRI dmar-ser/ klad sprin zla gdan dkar-ser gyi steng du HRI dkar-ser/ thabs shes kyi HRI gnyis mtho brtsegs su hrig-ger gnas-pa.*

(44) *'Od-gsal bdun skor spyi mnan yod.*

(45) This exercise is described in the text of the *Byang-chub sems kyi gnad drug*, "The Six Essential Points of the Bodhichitta", which has been translated and published elsewhere in this series.

(46) *sNying dkyil du 'od kyi A dkar-po kha-dog lnga-ldan zhig bsgom.... spyi-gtsug tu 'od kyi 'khor-lo bsgom..... rtsa gsum 'dus mdor gcig tu 'dril/ YAM gnyis la phog-pas/ 'od ljang-khu dar skud tsam mar song/ rtsa gsum 'dus mdor dbu-ma'i nang nas yar tal gyis song/ snying dkyil gyi A la thim.*

(47) *A de dbu-ma'i nang nas yar la song/ spyi-gtsug nas thon nas/ 'od kyi 'khor-lo la thim/ 'od kyi 'khor-lo yang nam-mkha' la yal/ rig-pa gsal stong 'dzin-med du bzhag.*

(48) *bsNgo-ba dang smon-lam.*

Bibliography

Books in English

Bellezza, John Vincent, "High Country Culture: A Civilization Flourished in the Himalayas before Buddhism Reached Tibet," *Discovering Archaeology*, v.1, n.3, May-June 1999, pp.78–83.

Bellezza, John Vincent, "Pre-history of Tibet," *Himal*, December 1999, Kathmandu, pp. 42–43.

Cuevas, Bryan J., *The Hidden History of the Tibetan Book of the Dead*, Oxford University Press, Oxford 2003.

Evens-Wentz, W.Y., *Tibetan Yoga and Secret Doctrines*, Oxford University Press, London 1935.

Karmay, Samten G., *The Great Perfection: A Philosophical and Meditative Teaching of Tibetan Buddhism*, Brill, Leiden 1988.

Karmay, Samten G., *The Treasury of Good Sayings*: A Tibetan History of Bon, Oxford University Press, London 1972.

Kvaerne, Per, *Bon Religion: A Death Ritual of the Tibetan Bonpos*, Brill, Leiden 1985.

Kvearne, Per, "Bonpo Studies: The A-khrid System of Meditation," Part One: "The Transmission of the A-khrid System," in *Kailash* v. I, n. 1, pp. 19–50, Part Two: "The Essential Teachings of the A-khrid System, in Kailash v. I, n. 4, pp. 248–332, Kathmandu 1973.

Kvaerne, Per, "The Great Perfection in the Tradition of the Bonpos," in Whalen Lai and Lewis Lancaster (eds), *Early Ch'an in*

China and Tibet, Asian Humanities Press,Berkeley CA 1983, pp.367–392.

Kvaerne, Per, and Thubten Rikey, *The Stages of A-khrid Meditation: Dzogchen Practice of the Bon Tradition*, Library of Tibetan Works and Archives, Dharamsala 1996.

Kvaerne, Per, and Thubten Rikey. *The Stages of A-khrid Meditation, Dzogchen Practice of the Bon Tradition*, Library of Tibetan Works and Archives, Dharamsala 1996.

Reynolds, John Myrdhin, *The Golden Letters*, Snow Lion Publications, Ithaca NY 1996.

Reynolds, John Myrdhin, *The Guru Yoga of Tapihritsa and the Preliminary Practices of the Zhang-zhung Nyan-gyud*, Bonpo Translation Project, Vidyadhara Publications, 1999. Also Reynolds, *The Oral Tradition from Zhang-zhung*, ibid., pp. 217–251.

Reynolds, John Myrdhin, *The History and the Lineages of the Zhang-zhung Nyan-gyud*, Bonpo Translation Project, Vidyadhara Publications, San Diego 2000.

Reynolds, John Myrdhin, *The Instructions of Shardza Rinpoche for the Practice of Vision and the Dark Retreat*, Bonpo Translation Project, Amsterdam 1992.

Reynolds, John Myrdhin, *The Oral Tradition from Zhang-zhung: An Introduction to the Bonpo Dzogchen Teachings of the Oral Tradition from Zhang-zhung*, Vajra Publications, Kathmandu 2005.

Reynolds, John Myrdhin, *Selections from the Bonpo Book of the Dead*, Bonpo Translation Project (privaely printed), San Diego and Copenhagen 1997.

Reynolds, John Myrdhin, *The Seven-fold Cycle of the Clear Light*, Bonpo Translation Project, San Diego and Amsterdam 2001.

Snellgrove, David, and Hugh Richardson, *A Cultural History of Tibet*, Geo Weidenfeld & Nicolson, London, 1968.

Snellgrove, David, *The Nine Ways of Bon*, Oxford University Press, London 1967.

Tenzin Wangyal Rinpoche, *The Tibetan Yogas of Dream and Sleep*, Snow Lion,, Ithaca NY 1998.

Tibetan Texts

rDzogs-pa chen-po sku gsum rang shar gyi khrid gdams skor, New Delhi 1974.

sNang srid mdzod-phug gi rtsa-ba dang spyi-don, published as *mDzod-phug: Basic Verses and Commentary by Dran-pa Nam-mkha'*, Lopon Tenzin Namdak, Delhi 1966.

sNyan-rgyud rig-pa gcer-mthong gi skor, Tibetan Bonpo Monastic Centre, Dolanji, HP, India in 1972.

sNyan-rgyud rgyal-ba'i phyag-khrid in the *sNyan-rgyud nam-mkha' 'phrul mdzod drang nges skor dang zhang-zhung snyan-rgyud skor*, Tibetan Bonpo Monastic Centre, Dolanji, HP India, 1972, (ff. 539–726).

sNgon-'gro rim-pa rnams, in the litho edition, New Delhi, n.d.

Zhang-zhung snyan-rgyud kyi lo-rgyus rnam-thar dang bcas-pa in the *sNyan-rgyud nam-mkha' 'phrul mdzod drang nges skor dang zhang-zhung snyan-rgyud skor*, Tibetan Bonpo Monastic Centre, Dolanji, HP India, 1972, (ff. 539–589).

Glossary of Tibetan Terms

K

ka-ti rtsa –the Kati channel
ka-dag –primordially pure, primordial purity
ka-dag chen-poa –the state of total primordial purity
kun-khyab chen-po –the state that is totally all-pervading
kun tu bzang-po –the Primordial Buddha
kun tu bzang-mo –the Primordial Wisdom
kun brtags ma rig-pa –the ignorance that conceptualizes everything
kun-snang khyab-pa –the Dhyanai Buddha of the clear white light in
    the center
kun-gzhi –the basis of everything, i.e., the state of shunyata
klad spring –membrane covering the brain
klad phor –skull casing
klu gdon –disturbances due to Nagas
klong –vast expanse
klong bsgom –meditation in the vast expanse of understanding
klong-sde –the Space Section of Dzogchen teachings
dkyil-'khor –mandala
bka'-skyong –protector of the precepts
bka' rgya gdab-pa –issuing the seal of the command
rkyang-ma –Lalana, the left channel
rkyen –secondary condition
sku gsum –Trikaya, the Three Bodies of the Buddha
bskyed-pa –producing, generating, visualizing
bskyed-rim –the generation process,the visualization process

KH

khams-chen —the Bonpo version of the Prajnaparamita Sutra
khrid —guiding instruction, explanation
khro-bo'i lha tshogs —the hosts of Wrathful Deities
khregs-chod —Trekchod, cutting through tensions and rigidities, the
        principal practice in Dzogchen
"khrul-'khor —Yantra exercises, the yoga of movements
'khrul-pa —delusion
'khrul-tshul —the method of delusion
'khrul-lugs —the delusion system
'khor 'das ru-shan dbye-ba —Rushan exercises, discriminating
        between Samsara and Nirvana
'khor-lo bsgyur-ba'i lta-stangs —the gaze of a Chakravartin, a
        universal monarch

G

go-ldog —reverse order
grol-tshul —method of liberation
grol-lam —the path of liberation
dga'-ba don-grub —the Dhyani Buddha o0f the clear blue light
        in the south
dge-sbyor —pious religious practices
'gyu-ba —the movement of thoughts
rgod-pa —agitation, wildness
rgyu —primary cause
sgom-khrid —explanation of the meditation
sgom-thag —meditation belt
sgom-lam —the path of meditation development
sgyu-'phrul drwa-ba —the interlaced network of illusion
sgyur-lam —the path of transformation
sgra 'od zer gsum —sounds, lights, and rays
sgron-ma —lamp, source of light

NG

ngang-sgom —meditation in the state of the Nature of Mind
ngo-sprod-pa —direct introduction
ngo-bo —essence

ngo-bo nyid –essential state
ngo-bzung-ba –recognition
dngos-gzhi –the principal practice, the principal section
mngon sangs-rgyas –visibly manifest Buddhahood

C

cer-re lta-ba –staring with wide-open eyes
co-bzhag –leaving just as it is
gcig-brgyud –single transmission
gcig-car-ba –an individual who understands instantly
gcer-mthong –seeing nakedly
gcer-bur ye-shes –naked primal awareness
bca'-ba –posture
bca' gzhi –the basic posture

CH

cha mthun –equal parts, harmonizing the two parts
chu yi lha-mo –the goddess of the water element
cho-'phrul –apparitional display, magical apparition
'char tshul –the mode of arising (of visions)
'char gzhi –the base of arising
'chi-kha –the process of dying
'chi-kha'i bar-do –the Bardo of the Dying Process

J

'jam rlung –gentle breathing
'jam dkar rtsa –the smooth white nerve, i.e., the Kati channel
'ja'-lus –rainbow body
'ja'-lus-pa –one who has realized the rainbow body
rjes-thob –subsequent realization, post-meditation experience
rjes-dran drug –the six recollections
rjes-gnang –permission

NY

nyams –experience
nyams-rgyud –experiential transmission

nyams rtags —experiences and signs

nyi rdul-ma – dust specks in the sunlight

nyi 'od —sunlight practice

mnyam rjes bsres —integrating even contemplation and subsequent realization

mnyam-bzhag —the state of even contemplation

snying-po —heart, heart-essence, heart mantra

snying sul-ba gsum —the three fatty folds around the heart

T

ting-nge 'dzin —samadhi, contemplation

gti-mug —confusion

lta-khrid —explanation of the view

lta-stangs —gaze

lta-ba —view

rtags —sign, indication

rten —support

rtog-pa —a thought, thinking

rtogs-pa —understanding

brtul-shugs kyi spyod-pa —ascetic conduct

stong-cha —on the side of emptiness

stong-pa nyid —Shunyata, the state of emptiness

TH

thag-bcad-pa —definitive decision

thabs-lam —path of methiod

thig-le —bindu, essence drop, droplet of light

thim-rim —dissolution process

thun —meditation session

thun-sgom —meditating indiscrete sessions

thun tshad —full measure of the meditation session

thod-rgal —the practice of vision, especially with sunlight

thod-rgal du —immediately

thod-rgal-ba —a Thodgal practitioner of intermediate capacity

mtha' bral chen-po —the state that is totally beyond limitations

mthong-lam —the path of vision

D

dag-snang –pure vision
dam-tshig –samaya vow, connection
dam-tshig-pa –samaya being, symbolic being
dran-pa –memory
dran-pa lnga –the five recollections
dran-pa shes-bzhin –mindfulness and clear comprehension
don –meaning, real meaning, topic
gdams-ngag –oral instruction
gdon –an evil spirit, a negative provocation of energy
bdag –self
bdag-nyid chen-po –the total state of being
bdag-med –without a self, insubstantial
bdun skor –seven cycles
bde gsal mi rtog-pa'i nyams –experiences of pleasurable sensation, clarity, and non-discursiveness
'dul-gshen drug –the Six Delshen, or manifestations of the Buddha in the six realms of rebirth
'dod-chags –desire

N

nang 'od –inner light
nam-mkha' –space, sky, sky practice
gnad –essential point
gnas-pa –calm state
gnas-pa gzhi'i bar-do –the Bardo of the Base that Abides
gnas-lugs –the Natural State
rnam-shes –consciousness
snang-ba –vision, manifestation, appearance
snang-ba mthar thug-pa –final visions
snang-ba'i yul –visible object

P

pu-she-li –the three chakras along the central channel above the juncture
dpa'-bo'i gseb lam –the pathway of the hero
dpe –example

spyi-khyab –general practice
spyi-blugs chen-po –a state that is totally universal
spyod-khrid –explanation of the conduct
spyod-pa –conduct, action
sprul-sku"i lta-stangs –the gaze of the Nirmanakaya
spros-med –without conceptual elaborations

PH

pho gdon –disturbances due to male spirits
phyag-khrid –practice manual, handbook
phyag-rgya –body, form, gesture, position, seal
'par rtsa –the two channels on the sides of the neck
'pho-ba –transference of consciousness
'phro rgod –diffused and agitated

B

bu-ga dgu –the nine orifices of the human body
bu rig-pa –the Son who is awareness
bum-can –kumbaka, vase-shaped breathing
bogs 'don –development
bon-sku –Dharmakaya
bon-sku'i lta-stang –the gaze of the Dharmakaya
bon-nyid –the Nature of Reality
non-nyid 'od-gsal gyi bar-do –the Bardo of the Clear Light of Reality
dbang bskur –conferring an empowerment
dbang-po lnga –the five sense faculties
dbang-po tha-ma –an individual of inferior capacity
dbang-po 'bring-po –an individual of intermediate capacity
dbang-po rab –an individual of superior capacity
dbu-ma rtsa –Avadhuti, the centarl channel
'bying-ba –drowsiness
'byung-po –Bhuta, restless spirit
'bras-bu –fruit, result, fruitional
sbyor-lam –the path of unification

M

ma 'gag-pa –unceasing, unobstructed

ma dag las snang –impure karmic vision
man-ngag –Upadesha, secret oral instruction
man-ngag gi sde –Dzogchen Upadesha, secret instruction section of
    the Dzogchen teachings
mi rtog-pa –non-discursive, without thoughts
mi rtog-pa'i nyams –the experience of non-discursiveness
mi dmigs-pa'i rgyas-gdab –affiing the seal of non-conceptuality
me yi lha-mo –the goddess of the fire element
mun-khang –the dark retreat house
mun-pa'i rnal-'byor –the yoga of the dark retreat
mun-mtshams –the dark retreat
mo gdon –disturbances due to female spirits
dmigs-pa –visualization, imagination, conception
rmug-po –dullness, dull
rmug 'thibs –dull and unclear

TS

tshang-ri pur-lang –the channel in the middle of the brain
tsi-ta –the physical heart
rtsa –channel, nerve
rtsa gsum 'dus mdor –the juncture of the three channels below the
    navel
rtsa 'dul –taming the channels
rtsa-rlung –breathing practice
rtsa rlung thig-le'i rnal-'byor –the yoga of the channels, the winds,
    and the essence drops
rtsal –energy, potential energy
rtsal-sbyong –forceful purification
bstan thabs –forceful method

TSH

tshogs-lam –the path of accumulation
tshor stong –empty perceptions
tshangs-pa'i bu-ga –the aperture of Brahma at the crown of the head
mtshan-nyid –philosophy, philosophy text, essential characteristic
mtshams-bcad –securing the boundaries

DZ

mdzad tshul —method of accomplishing
rdzogs-sku —Sambhogakaya
rdzogs-sku'i lta-stangs —the gaze of the sambhogakaya
rdzogs-pa chen-po —the Great Perfection
rdzogs-rim —the perfection process
rdzogs snags-rgyas —Perfect Buddhahhod

ZHI

zhal-shes —a clear oral explanation
zhi-khro —the Peaceful and Wrathful Deities
zhi-gnas —Shamatha meditation, attaining the calm state
zhi-ba'i lha tshogs —the hosts of Peaceful Deities
zhe-sdang —anger
gzhan-snang —manifestation due to another
gzhi —the Base
gzhi gnas —the Base which abides
gzhil-ba —twisting the belly to swallow more air
bzhag thabs gsum —the three methods for lettings things be as
     they are

Z

zin rtags —signs of success in fixation practice
zung 'jug —unified, unification
zung 'brel —linked together, unified
gzer-bu —a little nail, an essential point
"A
'od-gsal —the Clear Light, clear light vision practice, i.e., Thodgal
'od-lus —body of light

Y

yang-gsang —exceedingly secret
yan-lag —branch, limb, auxiliary
yab yum —the Lord and the Lady, the father and the mother
yar ta-la-la ltar —gradually, like juggling ping-pong balls
yi-dwags —Preta, hungry ghost

yi-dam lha –meditation deity
yid –the functional mind
yin-lugs –system of existence
ye-gzhi –primordial base
ye-shes –gnosis, primal awareness, primal cognition, wisdom
ye-shes kyi spyan –eye of gnosis, wisdom eye
ye-shes kyi rlung –wisdom winds
ye-shes lnga –the five gnoses, the five primal cognitions,
    the five wisdoms
ye-shes-pa –wisdom being,
ye-shes zang-thal –all-penetrating primal awareness
ye sangs-rgyas –Primordial Buddhahood
yon-tan –virtuous quality

R

rang sgra –inherent sounds
rang-grol –self-liberation
rang-snang –self-manifestation
rang-byung chen-po –the state of total self-origination
rang-byung ye-shes –self-originated primal awareness
rang-bzhin –nature, natural
rang zer –inherent rays
rang 'od –inherent lights
rang rtsal –inherent energy
rang-rig –self-awareness
rang sa zin-pa –remain in its original condition
rang-gsal –inherent clear luminosity
rig-pa –awareness, intrinsic awareness
rig-pa rjen-pa –naked awareness
rig-pa'i ye-shes –primal cognitions of awareness
rigs lnga –the five families
rim-gyis-pa –gradualist in terms of practice
rim-pa –process, stage
ro-snyoms –equal taste, the same even taste
ro-ma –Rasana, the right channel
rol-pa –visible manifestation of energy
rlung –breath, wind, vital wind

L

la zla'i dmigs-pa —beyond conception
lag-len —practice manual, handbook, practice
lam mthar phyin-pa —the path of ultimate attainment
lam dau khyer-ba —carrying on along the path
lus gnad —the essential point of the body
lus sbyin —offering one's own body
glod-pa gsum —the three relaxations
blo —mind, thought process, intellect
blo 'das brjod med chen-po —the state totally transcending the
        intellect and expression in words
blo'i shes-pa —consciousness associated with the thought process
rlung gi lha-mo —the goddess of the air element
rlung gcun —training the breath, training the vital winds
rlung gnad —the essential point of the breath
rlung-ro —stale air in the lungs

SH

she-thun —the heart
shel sgong —crystal ball
shes-rab —discriminating wisdom
shes-rab kyi lta-stangs —the gaze of discriminating wisdom
shes rig gi rgyal-po —the King who is knowing Awareness, i.e., Rigpa
gshen lha 'od dkar —"the white light Shen god," the Sambhogakaya

S

sa yi lha-mo —the goddess of the earth element
seng-ge" 'gying-pa'i lta-stangs —gaze of the dignified lion
sems —mind
sems kyi snang-ba —manifestation of mind
sems-bskyed —Bodhichitta, generating the thought of enlightenment,
        semen
sems-nyid —the Nature of the Mind
sems-nyid gnas-lugs —the Natural State of the Nature of Mind
sems-sde —the Mind Section of the Dzogchen teachings
sems 'dzin —fixating the mind
srid-pa'i bar-do —the Bardo of Existence, i.e., the rebirth process

srog rtsa –the principal channel in the heart

gsang-sngags –the Secret Mantras, the Tantra system

gsang-spyod –secret conduct, private conduct, sexual activities

gsang-ba 'dus-pa'i lta-stangs –the gaze of Sangwa Dupa

gsal-ba –clear, clarity, luminous clarity

gsal-ba rang-byung –the Dhyani Buddha of the clear yellow light in the east

H

had-de-ba –startled awareness

lhag-mthon –Vipashyana meditation, higher insight

lhan-skyes ma rig-pa –spontaneously born ignorance co-emergent ignorance

lha sku –divine forms

lhun-grub –spontaneously perfected, spontaneous perfection

lhun-grub chen-po –the state of total spontaneous perfection

lho gter lugs –the system of the southern treasures

lhod-pa chen-po –total relaxation

A

ag-tse –the joint of the spine and the skull

ag-sho 'khor-lo –the throat center

e-ma-ho –how wonderful!

INDEX